英语语言与英语文化研究文库　　主编：戴卫平

美国社会与文化研究

杨卫东　戴卫平◎著

STUDIES ON AMERICAN SOCIETY AND CULTURE

中国出版集团

世界图书出版公司

广州·上海·西安·北京

图书在版编目（CIP）数据

美国社会与文化研究 / 杨卫东 , 戴卫平著 . —广州：
世界图书出版广东有限公司，2014.11
　ISBN 978-7-5100-8899-5

　Ⅰ .①美⋯　Ⅱ .①杨⋯ ②戴⋯　Ⅲ .①美国—概况
Ⅳ .① K971.2

中国版本图书馆 CIP 数据核字（2014）第 259441 号

美国社会与文化研究

责任编辑　宋　焱
出版发行　世界图书出版广东有限公司
地　　址　广州市新港西路大江冲 25 号
http：// www.gdst.com.cn
印　　刷　虎彩印艺股份有限公司
规　　格　710mm×1000mm　1/16
印　　张　20
字　　数　380 千
版　　次　2014 年 11 月第 1 版　2015 年 6 月第 2 次印刷
ISBN　978-7-5100-8899-5/H・0882
定　　价　60.00 元

版权所有，翻版必究

前　言

一、美国英语与美国历史

美国的历史，一般都是从英国在北美建立殖民地开始。殖民地时期，则是指1607—1776年宣布独立时为止。1607年，英国殖民者在北美东海岸建立了第一个城市 Jamestown（以新登基的英王命名），后来由此发展为殖民地 Virginia。Virginia 的意思是"圣洁的女王伊丽莎白一世的土地"，美国独立后，又沿用它为州名。1620年，一批英国移民乘"五月花"号来到麻州南端的 Plymouth（因纪念从英国起航的港市Plymouth 而得名），开始了 New England 一带的殖民。在东起大西洋沿岸西迄阿巴拉契亚山脉的整个狭长地带，英国殖民统治者先后建立起13个殖民地，按照殖民地的行政管理形成分为三种类型：Royal Colony（皇家殖民地），Proprietary Colony（作业主殖民地），Charter Colony（特许殖民地）。这些殖民地多是以英王、总督、殖民者本人或殖民者的故土的名字命名的。

Plantation 是与早期殖民地有关的一个词语。英殖民者统治期间，plantation 并不是现在所称之为的"种植园"。英国殖民者1607年在北美建立的第一块殖民地 Jamestown，当时被称为 plantation。Plantation 一词旧时的英文意思是：a newly established settlement or colony（殖民地）。只是到后来真正的种植园纷纷建立起来之后，plantation 才具有了"种植园"的意思。

从历史的渊源来说，如今的美国是从不列颠美洲殖民帝国的一部分衍生、发展而来的。Planter（英殖民主义者），colonist（移民），settlement（殖民），proprietor（英王特许独占某块殖民地的"领主"），dominion（领地），burgess（殖民地时期弗吉尼亚或马里兰的"下议院议员"），redcoat（英军），Yankee（英格兰移民），Royal Colony（皇家殖民地），General Assembly（大议会），Charter colony（特许殖民地）等美语就是美国曾作为英殖民地的历史见证。

"边疆是美国历史的特产。美国之所以成其为美国，离开边疆的推进或领土的扩展，是无从谈起的。众所周知，当今的美国幅员辽阔，地大物博，但这恰恰是经历了近 1 个世纪边疆不断自东向西、移民与拓殖的综合成果。"（杨玉圣）西进运动是美国人民在建国后百余年内从东向西、横跨北美大陆的拓殖运动。1784—1785 年和 1787 年，联邦政府连续制定了三个土地法令，在西部设立领地制度，实行 Homestead Act（宅地法）。依照这个法令，分得的土地便被称为 homestead，得到土地的定居移民是 homesteader。但实际上，许多 squatter 早已捷足先登，擅自占有大量土地。还有许多所谓的 Mountain Men（山人），即首批开拓边疆的人。西进运动构成了美国历史上最为扣人心弦的一章。多少年来，"边疆精神"或"开拓精神"，一直是美国人引以为豪的民族文化特征的一个重要成分。当年的美国边疆是向西部定居地推进文明和荒野间的边界地带。边疆的生活极为艰苦，而且时常还有生命的危险。但早期的开拓者忍受住了荒山野林和沙漠中极其恶劣的生存条件，冒着各种各样的风险，开垦荒地或寻找宝藏，从而开始了一种新的生活。美国英语中的 blaze the trail（在树皮上刻痕标示林中路径；开辟道路）这一词语形象、生动地描绘了当年边疆开拓者艰苦拼搏的经历。Pioneer（拓荒者）敢于与饥饿、严寒、疾病做斗争的奋斗精神作为整个民族的文化精髓被传承下来。

每个词大都反映创造使用者的背景，某一历史时期产生的词汇犹如一幅再现社会生活的画卷。与他们跨洋过海到北美洲开拓殖民地的前辈一样，西部开拓者们向西部进发的时候，也是怀着获得大片土地和财富的金色美梦。在西部边疆开发的漫长历史中，Gold Rush（淘金热）可以说是一件异乎寻常的事。1848 年，人们在加利福尼亚亚美利加河边一锯木厂发现黄金，第二年便出现了大规模的 Gold Fever，大批淘金者蜂拥而入，仅在 1849 年这一年，就有 10 万人前往西部加利福尼亚加入淘金。直到今天，加州仍被称为 The Golden State。当年的淘金人史称 Forty-Niners（1849 年的淘金者，亦称 49-ers）。他们还被称为 Argonauts（阿尔戈英雄）。阿尔戈原指希腊神话中随伊阿宋（Jason）乘阿尔戈快船到海外觅取金羊毛的英雄，在美国则喻指 1848—1849 年涌入加利福尼亚的淘金者。淘金人到 pay dirt（淘金场），pan for gold（用淘盘法淘金），提供给探矿者的贷款为 grubstake。为数极少的淘金者发了一笔做梦也想不到的大财，一夜之间成了富翁。在美国西部由于淘金而变成的巨富，被称为 Bonanza King。美语中有不少烙上"淘金"印记的词语，diggings（淘金者采金的地方），gold digger（淘金者），pan out（用淘盘选淘金子），prospect（一个有希望能开出金矿的地区），stake a claim（立标界以表明对采矿地区拥有所有权的过程），make a stake（赚钱；发财），claim jumper（强夺他人采矿权者）等只是其中几例。

寥寥几个词语把美国历史上淘金时代的年月、淘金的手段以及淘金工场的艰苦环境再现出来。

西部开发过程中还产生出不少"专利术语"，而且至今有许多在美语中仍被沿用，如 saloon（酒馆），firewater（烈酒），bootleg（私酿的酒），tanglefoot（蹩脚的酒），roll one's own（卷自己抽的烟），coffin nails（香烟），deuce（纸牌的二点），trey（三点的纸牌），cold deck（洗牌时作弊的一副牌），sweep the deck（把赌桌上所有的赌注全部赢来）等。这些西部开发时期产生的"专门词语"反映出西部开发者的业余消遣活动在当时大多是抽烟、喝酒、玩纸牌赌钱，他们可以不必像东部的清教徒那样极度检点，不受宗教伦理的严格制约。西部的 Cowboy（牛仔）是美国所特有的社会、文化和历史的产物，他们是拓荒者的化身，因此成为美语中带有浓厚西部色彩的一个词语。当时与 Cowboy 具有同一含义的词语还有 waddy, cowpoke, cowpuncher, vaquero, broncobuster, buckaroo；Cowboy 还可以用于引申：tenderfoot（西部荒凉艰苦地区的"新来者"），horse sense（粗浅但实用的知识），bite the dust（受伤倒下；失败；完蛋）。

二、美利坚族裔称谓与族裔来源

美国是一个十足的、典型的世界各国移民的汇集之所，它的民族形成是人类历史上颇具特色的一章。美国的国民来自世界上不同的民族，操持着不同的语言，有着迥异的文化背景，代表不同的肤色和宗教信仰。美国国玺正面的拉丁文 E Pluribus Unum（万众一体）是美利坚合众国的箴言。美国英语是"合族国"人们用于社会交往、思想沟通和信息传递的工具。为了表达美利坚民族独具一格的特征，美国英语独创和发展了大量极富美民族文化内容的词语。它们是人们了解美利坚的族裔构成、族裔渊源和族裔文化不可缺少的史料。

在中国，提起"中华民族"，人们自然就会想到"炎黄子孙"，共同的祖先将中国人联系在一起。美国与中国截然不同，美利坚民族是由来自世界各地的移民及其后裔组成的。他们没有共同血统、共同宗教、共同语言、共同文字、共同习俗、共同经济生活、共同历史遗产、共同地域以及表现在共同文化上的共同心理素质。美利坚民族素有 The Nation of Nations 之称。

美利坚民族包括白人、黑人、亚裔人、印第安人和拉美裔人这五个种族。由于美利坚的民族是"天下会聚、四方杂处"，因此产生各种各样奇异的族群称谓。Hispanic/Hispano（西班牙语裔美国人）是最复杂的群体，他们是来自母语为西班牙语的移民及其后代。他们中有 Mestizo（西班牙人与印第安人的混血种后代），

Mulatto（西班牙人与黑人的混血种后代），Latino（拉丁裔美国人）等。Chicano 系 Mexicano 的简称，原是对美国的墨西哥人的一种贬称，但经过 20 世纪 60 年代的民权运动，就如 Black（黑人）不再是贬称一样，Chicano 已作为种族自主和自豪的象征而为墨西哥裔美国人所接受，成为"墨西哥裔美国人"的同义词。Chamorro 是具有西班牙人、菲律宾人和密克罗西亚人的混合血统的美国人，亦称 Guanmanian（关岛人）。路易斯安那州因居住着众多 Creole（克里奥尔人），即欧洲人（尤其是西班牙和法国人）的后裔，因此被冠上 The Creole State 的别称。第二次世界大战后大批波多黎各人移居纽约市，其中大部分居住在 Harlem，现该社区被称为 Spanish Harlem（西班牙语哈莱姆）。这些原籍为波多黎各的纽约人被称为 Neorican，Nuyorican 和 Newyorican 是 Neoricand 的变体。来自欧洲的西班牙移民则被称为 Spanish-American（西班牙裔美国人，或美籍西班牙裔）。

美国的犹太人不是来自某一特定的国家，而是来自许多国家，如 Sephadi 是来自于西班牙和葡萄牙的塞法迪犹太人，Ashkenazi 是来自于中欧和西欧的阿什肯纳齐犹太人。Gullah 指那些居住在北卡罗来纳、佐治亚、北佛罗里达沿海岛屿和海岸地区的非裔美国犹太人。

Cajun 这一称谓是指 18 世纪末期由加拿大阿卡地亚地区（Acadia）迁至美国路易斯安那州和缅因州的法裔移民及其后代，Cajun 系 Acadian 的变体。Issei 一词源于日语，是出生在日本的第一代日裔美国人的称谓，而 Nisei（日文"二世"的意思）则是称呼那些父母出生在日本、自己生长于美国的日裔美国人。Hapa Haole 指有部分白人血统的人，尤指夏威夷土人与白人混血的人。黑人中有 Black Jew（黑人犹太人）、Black Muslim（黑人穆斯林）和信奉 African Orthodox Church（黑人正教）的黑人。Bohemian 是居住在威斯康星州和大平原地区的捷克裔美国人，他们主要来自捷克西部的波西米亚省（Bohemia），因此被称为"波西米亚人"。波西米亚是捷克民族文化的核心之一，在捷克语里，波西米亚人常常是捷克人的同义词。Pennsylvania Dutch 德裔宾夕法尼亚人，是 17—18 世纪在宾夕法尼亚东部定居下来的德国移民的后代。他们是 Deutsch（德意志人），而非 Dutch（荷兰人）。美国人称之为 Dutch，是出于对 Deutsch 一词的误解。

从人口的民族属性角度来看，美国人的"族性"是世界上最为复杂的。到目前为止，美国的民族已达 200 多种。可以说，不管你从世界哪个角落来到美国，你都可以找到你的同胞。从美国英语中对外来民族的称呼（包括贬称），我们就可知道浩浩荡荡流入美国的族裔根源。在美国这样一个人种庞杂、族裔繁多的社会里，不同种族之间通婚的现象非常普遍。因此，年轻一代中，有两个或两个以上种族血统的人越来越多。今天的美国有相当一部分人的血统成分显得异常复杂而无法用传统的方法来界定他们的种族属性。这不仅因为他们自己是混血儿，他们的父母可能也是混血儿，或许他们的祖父也是如此。他们中有一些人可能既有白人血统，又有黑人血统、亚裔血统和印第安人血统。这部分人就是今天美语中称之为 Hapa（混种）或 Multiracial Category（多种族人）的那部分美国人。

三、美语用法与马赛克民族

美利坚多元族群构成了现今的美利坚民族。20 世纪以来，美国新移民的族裔成分有了显著的变化。他们大部分来自欧洲以外的地区。这些移民的到来扩展了美民族的多源性，丰富了美国文化，使美国社会呈现出更纷繁芜杂的面貌。今天的美国正越来越变成一个多源种族、族群沙拉碗，而越来越不像一个过去广为人知的 melting pot（大熔炉）或 crucible（坩埚），将各种族、族群在这里冶炼和重铸。耶鲁大学教授 Robert Thompson 称现代美国为 a cultural bouillabaisse（文化大杂烩），bouillabaisse 是一类用多种鱼和蔬菜，加佐料炖成的美味佳肴。纽约前黑人市长 Mayar Dinkins 称之为 a diverse society（多元社会）。美国黑人民权领袖杰西·杰克逊把美国比作是 a fraying quilt（一床由各种民族美丽图案拼缝成的花被子）。除此之外，美语中还有许多生动、丰富多彩的词汇来形容美利坚杂交民族，如 a salad bowl（色拉钵），kaleidoscope（万花筒），rainbow（七彩虹），a set of tributaries（支流群），a tapestry（挂毯），a fruit cake（各种水果制成的水果蛋糕），gorgeous mosaic（多姿多彩的马赛克），pot of stew（杂烩锅），pizza（比萨饼），tossed salad（拼盘）等。在一些美国人口学家看来，美国正在变成一个 universal nation（世界性的民族）。

美国多元种族、族群带来了大学学科设计和教学内容的改革。自 20 世纪 60 年代起，美国的许多大学相继建立了专门研究不同民族社会文化的专业，如 Asian Studies，Russian Studies，Black Studies，Indian Studies，Hispanic Studies 等。社会史学在研究领域比传统史学更为宽广，分类更为精细，出现了许多专门领域，如 Black History，American Indian History，Hispanic American History，Asian-American History 等。African American Studies，Native American Studies，Latino American Studies，Asian American Studies 等，在美国学术界此起彼伏。

在美国，不同的种族和民族仍然保持着她们自己的文化和传统。物以类聚，人以群分。人根据血缘、语言、习俗、宗教等产生群体认同感。出于文化习俗上认同的原因，各国各地区的移民，尤其是亚裔美国人，喜欢与同民族的人聚居在某些城市或城市中的某一区域，由此形成了众多的国中之"国"，诸如 Little Italy（小意大利），Little Poland（小波兰），Little Bohemia（小波西米亚），Germantown（德国城），

Chinatown（唐人街），Japantown（日本街），Little Seoul（小首尔），Tokyo City（东京城），Little Saigon（小西贡），Little Havana（小哈瓦那），Capital of Latin America（拉丁美洲移民文化的影响把迈阿密拉美化了，使其成了他们在美的"首府"）等。他们在自己的民族聚居区中保持着母族的生活方式、信仰、习俗和语言。同样，希腊人、爱尔兰人、犹太人的后裔也努力地维持着各自先祖的古老传统和习俗。

移民的多源性构成了美利坚民族的多元性，而美国社会的多元性又构成了美国文化的多样性。正是因为美利坚是一个由多人种、多宗教、多文化、多族群的移民及其后代共同组成的国家，因此，美国传媒和日常生活中出现频率很高的词语，如co-culture（并存文化），cultural pluralism（文化多元论），cultural equity（文化平等），intercultural community（跨文化社团），biculturalism（双文化），multicultural society（多元文化社会），pluralistic society（多元社会），multi/plural culturalism（多元文化主义），multiculturalists（多元文化主义者），American pluralism（美国多元主义），trans-racial culture（超种族文化），mixed-race culture（种族混合文化），multicultural America（多元文化美国），cultural diversity（文化多样性），acculturation（文化适应），ambivalent American（两性人），multiethnic（多民族的）等也就不足为怪了。美利坚文明经历了由"合众为一"到"由一为众"的轨迹。美国人创造了一个看似矛盾的奇迹：不同种族/族群，统一民族（美利坚民族）；单一语言（美国英语），多元文化。

四、美国移民与美国英语

语言是与时共进的，美语中的部分新词语显然与美国多族裔文化有关。在美国，大量来自西班牙语国家的移民在使用英语时将许多西班牙语的词汇掺杂到英语中来，美国英语和西班牙语杂交，例如：faxear（发传真），la jacket（夹克），taipear（打字）等，这种现象在美国英语中叫作Spanglish（Spanglish为Spanish与English的混合词）。

19世纪40年代以前，现在美国南部的大片领土，例如，得克萨斯州、加利福尼亚州、新墨西哥州；重要城市，如洛杉矶、旧金山等，都属于墨西哥。1848年美墨战争，墨西哥战败，墨西哥政府被迫将上述土地割让给美国，大批原来的居民成了"美国公民"。但是，他们仍然保持原来墨西哥的风俗习惯，而且100多年来世世代代相传。美国英语中的Mexicanization（墨西哥化）一词就是这一事实的写照。

Thanksgiving（感恩节）是美国最大的一个传统节日。从感恩节的名称来看，它似乎是一个宗教的节日，其实并非如此。感恩节起源于当时北美的英国殖民地普利茅斯，移居该地的外来移民于1621年获得丰收后，在这一天举行欢庆，以感谢上帝赐予丰收之"恩"。美国独立后感恩节逐渐成为美全国性节日。过感恩节美国人在习俗上一定要大嚼的 turkey(火鸡)也与美国早期移民有关。当美国人的祖先移居到新大陆,初登陆就遇到农业歉收。正值寒冬来临,移民以为在劫难逃,就听天由命,不料在这绝望之际,从远处飞来了一大群火鸡,这才使他们绝处逢生。人们一直以为是上帝给他们恩施火鸡渡过难关,因而为"感"此"恩",形成吃火鸡以纪念的习俗。

19 世纪末美国"淘金热"期间大批中国劳工在美国爱达荷州的山区做苦工。一个深受疾病折磨的中国劳工预感到自己将不久于人世,于是爬上了一处山顶,等待着死亡的降临。后来,人们只发现了他尸体的一些碎片,其余已落入野兽之口。在附近干活的矿工为了纪念他,将这座山命名为 Chink。

产生于美国英语的 immigrant(从外国移入的移民)一词于 1789 年问世。美国英语中 nativism 也与移民有关。Nativism 意思是美国的本土主义,其实质是美国历史上的一场以排外思想为理论根基,以反对天主教、犹太教、亚洲和拉丁美洲移民为主要任务,以维护美国白人主流文化为主要目标的运动。U.S. English(美国英语)就是 1983 年建立的一个全国性的本土主义者的组织。Americanization 特指美国历史上 20 世纪上半叶掀起的同化外来移民的"美国化"运动,其目的是要使移民不但在思想上认同美国的自由、平等和民主观念,而且要在生活方式上与美国白人社会相适应。美国英语中没有"英国方式"、"中国方式"、"日本方式"、"阿拉伯方式"等专门术语,但却有 Americanism(美国方式)一词,Americanism 一词的产生也与美国的移民息息相关。

美语中 nigger 这个词来自拉丁语 niger,最早的文字记载可追溯到 1786 年,当时的奴隶主用这个词来称呼他们的非洲裔奴隶。Wigger 是由 white(白人)和 nigger(黑人)结合而成,意指"采纳黑人文化的白人"。Negro 一词源自 Negroid,意思是"黑人人种"。美国的黑人可能是来自海地、牙买加、塞内加尔、尼日尔、佛得角、埃塞俄比亚或索马里。当今美国黑人的"根"千差万别。因此在美国英语中,在更多的情况下,African-American/Afro American(或 Aframerican)与 black/black American 同时被使用。

在美国,除了最常用的称呼 white 表示白人外,另一个称呼白人的词是 Caucasian。Caucasian 一词源自 Caucasoid(白人种)。Caucasian 一般是指北欧、东欧和西欧人的后裔。美国白人被统称为白人种族,后来用 Caucasoid race(高加索种族)代表白人种族。

拉丁美洲(简称拉美)通常用来指称美国以南的美洲大片以罗曼语族语言作为官方语言或者主要语言的地区。因为罗曼语族衍生于拉丁语,拉丁美洲由此而得名。拉丁美洲由墨西哥、大部分的中美洲、南美洲以及西印度群岛组成。20 世纪 60 年代之前，美国的拉丁后裔缺乏一个单一的称呼，不管他们是否出生在美国，一般是把他们分别称呼。1978 年，Hispanic 这一称呼创立了出来，于是所有西班牙语裔的美国人都归纳到了这个称呼之下。Latino 这个称呼比 Hispanic 的范围要狭窄，其仅仅表示西半球的拉丁国家在美国居住的后裔。Hispanic 这个称呼如今在美国包含得越来越广，不仅包括讲西班牙语的民族，还包括不讲西班牙语的巴西人、海地人等。

族群关系紧张和种族歧视，一直是造成美国最大内伤的社会痼疾。美国主流社会同伊斯兰教徒、少数族裔的相互猜疑，族群矛盾同宗教矛盾、文化矛盾、移民问题、外国人的法律地位问题等纠缠在一起，日趋复杂。美语新词 Islamophobia（伊斯兰恐惧症）一词的出现则是由于很多美国人把 Islamism（伊斯兰教）等同于恐怖主义的结果。

亚裔美国人不被当作真正的美国人在美国社会是一种普遍存在的现象。Oriental（东方人）一词含有贬义，是一个带有侮辱性的名称。Oriental 这个词贬低了亚洲人，它是在 17 世纪英国向东方扩张势力时出现的。生活在欧洲东部的人一概被称为 Oriental，意思是看起来充满神秘和异国气息的，有着塌鼻梁和黑头发的人。Asian Americans，Easterners，Asians 这样的称呼不受亚裔美国人的待见，因为这样的范畴掩盖了日裔、韩裔、华裔等亚裔人之间的重要文化差别。他们有自己独特的文化传统和风俗习惯，有自己的"母国根"。因此，很多亚裔美国人更愿意被称为 Chinese-American，Japanese-American，Filipino-American 等。

英语 indigenous 一词虽然有本土的意思，但印第安人却被称为土著民，因此不被当作美洲的主人来看待。印第安文化也就当然地被视为土著文化而没有被称为本土文化。20 世纪 60 年代开始使用的 American Indian，Native American 称呼纠正了哥伦布把美国原著民称呼成 Indian（印第安人）的错误。如同美利坚其他民族都在保留自己的风俗与传统，并努力表现各自的文化特色、各自的身份个性一样，同样的情况也发生在美国印第安人的称谓上。虽然一些美国印第安人认为 American Indian 和 Native American 这两个称呼可以互用，单独的 Indian 这个称呼也仍然沿用，但大多数的印第安人更愿意被叫能代表各自部落和文化的称谓，如 Shone，Kiowa，Apache，Seminale，Navajo，Cherokee 等。Inuit（因纽特人）也不愿意被称为 Eskimo（爱斯基摩人）。

为了使广大英语学习者丰富美国英语词汇知识，提高美国文化的修养，在跨文化交际中提高语言理解能力和使用能力，作者特潜心编写此书。本书适合学习英语的学生、从事英语教学的教师、语言研究者、翻译工作者、外事工作者和其他爱好英语学习的人士使用。

杨卫东撰写本专著中的 18 篇（约 25 万字）。彭运佳（翻译"美国'总统'"，"美国文学名著"篇目，共计 2 万字）、李言（翻译"美国的财经大亨"、"美国的艺术奇才"、"美国的国务卿"，共计2万字）、袁野（翻译"美国人的健康观"、"美国人的嗜好"，共计2万字）、刘晓濛（翻译"美国的名胜"、"美国的科学之星"，共计2万字）收集并翻译了相关文献。全书由戴卫平统稿。感谢世界图书出版广东有限公司武汉学术出版中心宋焱编辑的帮助和支持，感谢宋焱编辑为本著作的出版所付出的辛勤工作。

杨卫东　戴卫平
2014年9月

目录

第一篇 美国的个体主义

美国历来是一个创业者的国度，广阔的地域，丰富的资源使美国人认为美国是个充满机遇的社会。从 17 世纪初开始移民北美的欧洲人要么是逃避宗教迫害，要么是摆脱政治专制，要么是寻求经济解放，无论如何都是在追求个性自由，正是这种追求使个体主义成为美国文化的核心。

在美国这样一个年轻的国家，来自世界各国的移民没有共同的祖先和传统，拓荒、冒险和个体主义至上的精神深入人心。另外，美国没有像英国等欧洲国家那样根深蒂固、泾渭分明的社会等级制度。所有这一切使得沿着社会阶梯向上升迁成为可能。无论是土生土长的美国人，还是漂洋过海迁徙到美国的移民，都怀有一个梦，即通过自己的努力，改变自己的社会地位，实现自己的人生之梦，这就是人们常津津乐道的 American Dream（美国梦）。美国人相信他们的国家是上帝特意恩赐的人间乐园，相信美国的自然环境和美国民主使美国人超越任何限制，使每个人的潜力得以充分发挥。美国人的成功价值就是美国梦的体现。

价值是个人、阶级、社会所崇拜的、值得为之而追求的社会原则、目标或标准。美国人所追求的价值纷繁杂陈，但"个体主义"则是重中之重。在英语中，individualism 被定义为"主张个人正直与经济上的独立，强调个人主动性、行为与兴趣的理论，以及由这种理论指导的实践活动"。

一、个体主义的定义

所谓个体主义，用霍勒斯·M·卡伦（董小川，2006：158）的话来讲就是，当个人意识到自己是什么和如何存在的时候的一种感觉、一种情感、一种动力和限制、一种习惯和行为。个体主义是个性的本质，因而个体主义的存在和发展是不可避免的；只有当具有个体主义特点的个性死亡之后，个体主义才会消失；当个体主义侵犯其他个人利益的时候，个体主义是维护个人利益的工具；当个体主义用以自责并不涉及其他个人利益的时候，个体主义是公平的原则；当个人自愿与其他人合作、与其他人联系在一起并形成一种自由关系的时候，个体主义被描绘成为以社会为先的法则。但不论如何，只有在个人拥有了清楚的、有区别能力的思想以后，因此而具有了为自己的生存和发展而斗争的时候，个体主义才会存在。

二、个体主义的本质

上面引用的著名思想家对个体主义的论述充分阐述了美国个体主义的本质：

（1）个体主义是人文主义的代名词，这种个体主义追求的是人的尊严、人的地位和人的不可剥夺的权利。

（2）个体主义是自由主义的温床。自古以来，人们就一直在追求自由，就是因为个人受到了太多的束缚，在各种形式的专制制度下，从思想到行动，各种规范和清规戒律使人们感到自己已经失去了自由。这正是欧美政治革命把自由和平等作为头等目标的原因。因此，个体主义成为人们追求自由的一个结果。

（3）个体主义是民主主义的产物。西方人把个体主义理解为民主主义的产物是良知的结果。

（4）个体主义是利己主义的体现。自文艺复兴以来，个体主义追求中的利己主义因素是无可否认的。文艺复兴时期的个体主义在某个角度来看是一种极端个体主义，因而缺乏对整个社会负责的理性思维。所以，个体主义既是美国文化的核心，也是美国文化的毒瘤。

（5）个体主义是非理性主义的思维。众所周知，任何个人离开了集体或社区都无法生存，集体或社区的形成需要每个人相互负责和支持，而个人意志的充分自由却常常要损害或涉及其他人的利益和自由。例如，自 19 世纪末 20 世纪初现代主义思潮产生以后，个体主义在西方恶性膨胀，非理性主义思维给社会带来了严重后果，从嬉皮士到摇滚乐、从吸毒到卖淫、从同性恋到婚前性行为、从精神污染到自然污染，都使人们对这种非理性主义的现代思潮从反感到反对。（董小川，2006：159-160）

三、美国的个体主义

《简明不列颠百科全书》关于"个人主义"的解释是这样的：一种政治和社会哲学，高度重视个人自由，广泛强调自我支配、自我控制、不受外来约束的个人或自我。作为一种哲学，个人主义包含一种价值体系，一种人性理论，一种对于某些政治、经济、社会和宗教行为的总的态度。依据这种理解，个人主义作为个性参与社会生活的态度、倾向和信念，有其历史表现的必然性。在西方社会的文明进程中，个人主义作为一种生活方式、人生观和世界观，具有整体性和普遍性意义，它构成了西方人赖以把握人和世界关系的基本方式和存在状态。具体而言，个人主义在西方社会生活各方面的渗透可以粗线条地归纳为表现在哲学上的人本主义、政治上的民主主义、经济上的自由主义以及文化上的要求个性独立的自我意识等层面的内容。（百度百科）

美国的个体主义文化源于欧洲，这毋庸置疑。在西方，个体主义既是一种价值观念和思想体系，也是一种人生哲学。自文艺复兴以来，它强调的就是个人在社会中的地位和价值，要求的就是个人意志和行为的自由。个体主义的核心理念是一切都要以人为中心：社会要体现个人的意愿，政府要保护个人的利益，个人有权决定自己的一切。个体主义是美国文化的核心、个体主义是深深根植于美国社会历史之中的等观点已成为美国学者的共识。（董小川，2006：156）

美国人把自我看作是与其他人、与整个世界分离的独立整体。个人权利至上的自由平等观念是自清教徒移民新大陆200多年来，美利坚民族所生生不息追求的目标，也是吸引四面八方的移民不断涌入美国的重要原因。早期的美国移民大多是为了摆脱欧洲封建统治和各种权势的压迫来到北美大陆寻求新生活的，这就决定了他们性格中具有反抗束缚、追求自由的因素。其次，美国的缔造者们的建国思想也与个体主义传统有关。美国的开国元勋从一开始就拒绝建立古典共和国，即要求每个人自制、守纪律，能为某种社会公益而牺牲个人的权利。美国西部的扩张对个体主义的发展起到了推动作用。西部广阔富饶的土地使人们真正体会到了个人的自由，也由此带来了影响到生活各个领域的个体主义。作为一个多数人信仰上帝的国度，美国个体主义是建立在神的意志基础之上的。从《圣经·旧约》的《出埃及记》到《圣经·新约》的《哥林多前书》，都描述了犹太——基督教共有的部落、民族、社区和教会思想，包括强烈的成员含义和所属的确认问题，但同时也强调了个人的信仰、忠诚和对社区整体的自觉的效忠行为。

四、自我奋斗

为数众多的美国人都想成为 self-made man 或 self-made woman（靠自己奋斗成功的人）。从殖民地时期到19世纪末期以前，美国是一个以农业经济为主体的社会，边疆开拓者仅仅是农民冒险者，他们的经济生活集体仅仅是农业家庭，而不是个人工厂，所以，典型的美国人就是一些靠个人奋斗、勇敢和具有冒险精神的人。

美国人心中的英雄是 a self-made man。美国公众注重成就，仰慕英雄，有深厚的成就崇拜和英雄崇拜心理积淀。个人成就是所有美国人价值观中评价最高的价值之一。实际上，美国前总统林肯之所以成为美国人崇拜的偶像就是因为他是一位靠自己奋斗成功的人，即所谓的 a self-made man。富兰克林是美国人中最受欢迎的科学家、哲学家，他被公认为美利坚民族和美国精神的化身。他刻苦勤奋、自力更生、求实进取，他把"自我奋斗、取得成功"在其著作中具体化：God helps those who help themselves.（天助自助者。）美国英语中的 upward mobility（向上流动倾向）正是众多的美国人梦寐以求的发迹机会。美国社会的特殊环境也使得许多美国人深信并接受这样的生活信条：

Everybody for himself, the devil takes the hindmost.（人不为己，天诛地灭。）

Near is my shirt, but nearer is my skin.（自己的利益最切身。）

Every man for himself, and God for us all.（个人为自己，上帝为大家。）

Every man is the architect of his own fortune.（每个人都是自己命运的建筑师。）

这些谚语告诫人们：只有依靠自己，靠个人奋斗，才能得到和保持个性的自由，才能实现个人的价值。

五、隐私权与私域

美国的革命、历史上的开疆拓土、发展中的投机竞争等导致了个体主义的生长，而个体主义同时又意味着注重和追求个人隐私权和对私域的保护。美国是一个极为重视和保护个人隐私的社会。"私域"在追求自我的美国社会中被当作是合法、合理的，是人们的最高需求。得到它，就得到了最大满足，它受到侵犯，个人就如同受到侮辱。Private affairs, private business, private concerns, private thoughts, private zone, private autonomy, private life 等私域对个人来说是神圣不可侵犯的。美国英语中有些词语被经常用来形容令人讨厌的打听别人私事的家伙，例如：meddle in other people's affairs（干涉别人的事）；nosy（爱打听他人的事的）；poke（push）one's nose into other people's business（探听或干预别人的事）；inquisitive（爱打听别人隐私的）等。

英语中有句谚语：A man's home is his castle. 在美国人看来，privacy 就是个人的"城堡"。美国人对私域的强烈要求，使美国宪法把它列为公民的不可侵犯的权利。美国宪法中的人权法案共十条，其中第四条讲到的就是保障 privacy。

参考文献

[1] 戴卫平，张志勇 . 美语词汇的文化意蕴 [J]. 天津外国语学院学报，2002（4）.

[2] [美] 丹尼尔·布尔斯延 . 美国人建国的历程 [M]. 上海：上海译文出版社，1997.

[3] 董小川 . 美国文化概论 [M]. 北京：人民出版社，2006.

[4] 顾嘉祖 . 语言与文化 [M]. 上海：上海外语教育出版社，1990.

[5] 汪榕培，卢晓娟 . 英语词汇学教程 [M]. 上海：上海外语教育出版社，1997.

[6] 郑立信，顾嘉祖 . 美国英语与美国文化 [M]. 长沙：湖南教育出版社，1993.

第二篇　美国地名文化

地名是语言词汇中文化载荷量较重的成分。作为历史文化的产物,地名深深地烙上了社会变迁的痕迹,以及一个民族所特有的文化特征。美国地名作为美国历史文化的"化石",从一个具体的侧面再现出美国的自然景观,揭示出美国历史上重大的政治变革、经济发展、社会变迁,反映出美利坚民族的文化传统、历史背景、思维方式、宗教信仰,以及美国社会独有的多元文化特色。

一、美国地名与英殖民统治

美国的历史,一般都是从英国在北美建立殖民地开始。殖民地时期,则是指1607—1776年宣布独立时为止。追溯美国地名的根源,我们便会发现美国许许多多的地方曾被英殖民主义者占领统治过。詹姆斯敦(Jamestown)是英国殖民者1607年在北美东海岸建立的第一个以新登基英王命名的城市,后来由此发展为殖民地弗吉尼亚(Virginia),意思是"圣洁的女王伊丽莎白一世的土地"。1620年,一批英国移民乘"五月花"号船来到马萨诸塞南端的普利茅斯(Plymouth),此名是为纪念从英国起航的港市普利茅斯而命的名,由此开始了英国在北美最早的殖民地区新英格兰(New England)一带的殖民。在东起大西洋沿岸西迄阿巴拉契亚山脉的整个狭长地带,英国殖民统治者先后建立起13个殖民地,其中很多是以英王、王后、总督、殖民者本人、殖民者的故土的名字命名的。

为了奉迎统治者,英殖民主义者还将许多殖民地的首府和主要城市冠以英王或王室成员的名字。例如:位于马里兰州的安纳波利斯市(Annapolis)是由当时的英国女王Anne的名字和希腊文Polis(市镇)构成,意为"安妮之城"。普林斯敦(Princeton)始建于17世纪末,为纪念英王威廉三世而得名,意为"王子城"。夏洛特(Charlotte)是北卡罗来纳州最大城市,它始建于1750年,1768年设市。为了奉迎英国王室,于是以英王乔治三世的王后夏洛特命名此城。

在美国，一些原装的英国地名，如丹比（Danby），安多弗（Andover），诺威奇（Norwich），布伦特里（Braintree），剑桥（Cambridge），亚茅斯（Yarmouth），爱克塞特（Exeter），诺福克（Norfolk），哈特福得（Hartford），伊普斯威奇（Ipswich），巴斯（Bath），索尔兹伯里（Salisbury）等显然带有浓厚的英殖民主义色彩。

此外，还有很多地方被命名为新伦敦（New London），新里士满（New Richmond），新巴尔的摩（New Baltimore），新贝德福德（New Bedford），新波士敦（New Boston），新黑文（New Haven）等。这些殖民地时期新拓居地名字的由来都可追溯到殖民地的宗主国——英国。

二、美国地名与美国自然景观

美国的许多城镇沿河（湖泊）而建，其形成的原因也是显而易见的。历史上理想的建城地点一般来说应是那些乘舟沿河（湖泊）上下，便捷可达的地方，或是河流较浅（窄），既可涉水而过，又便于建桥之处。例如：罗克福德（Rockford）是伊利诺斯州北部的城市，位于罗克河畔，其名称是由英语 rock（石头）和 ford（涉水处）构成，意为多岩石的可以徒步涉水而过的地方。印第安纳州北部城市南本德（South Bend）位于圣约瑟夫河南端（south）的河湾（bend）处，故名。苏福尔斯（Sioux Falls）是南达科他州最大的城市。该市临大苏河，因河上的瀑布而得名。此外，爱达荷州首府博伊西（Boise）、依阿华州首府得梅因（Des Moines）、加利福尼亚州首府萨克拉门托（Sacramento）、犹他州首府盐湖城（Salt Lake City）、亚拉巴马州西南部港市莫比尔（Mobile）、康涅狄格州南部城市沃特伯里（Waterbury）、华盛顿州东南重镇沃拉沃拉（Walla Walla）、得克萨斯州中南部城市圣安多尼奥（San Antonio）等也都是因水而得名。

美国还有相当多的城镇名称是人们根据当地的地理特点而命名的。例如：小石城（Little Rock）是阿肯色州的首府和州内唯一重要城市，因建在小岩石附近而得此名。科罗拉多州的一座城市叫科罗拉多斯普林斯（Colorado Springs），因为城西有一大温泉（Spring）而得名。汽车之都底特律（Detroit）的字面意义是"峡地"，得此名是因其位于两个大湖之间的狭长地带之间。Flint 一词在英语中意为打火石或坚硬物，密执安州东部城市弗林特（Flint）地区的石头特别坚硬，故名。加利福尼亚州的森尼韦尔城（Sunnyvale）坐落在一条山谷（vale）间，冬季阳光和煦（sunny），是冬季的避寒胜地。阿克伦（Akron）是俄亥俄州东北部的一座城市，名称来源于希腊文，意为顶端，因为该市位于两条河分流处最高的地方。其所属的一个县也因相同的地理位置而被定名为萨米特（Summit）。

三、美国地名与美利坚民族大熔炉

众所周知，美国是一个移民国。在过去的几百年里，数千万移民越海跨洋，从世界各个角落涌入美国。他们操持不同的语言，携带不同的文化风俗，代表着世界上不同的民族、不同的肤色和宗教信仰。身居异国他乡的海外移民无时无刻不缅怀故乡。出于感情上的需要和受到思乡情绪的影响，美国有不少移民聚居区在兴城建镇时采用了其故乡的地名。挪威人把他们在明尼苏达州的拓居地命名为奥斯陆（Oslo），瑞典人在威斯康星、缅因和南达科他等州建立了许多叫斯德哥尔摩（Stockholm）的地方。苏格兰人则命名了许多格拉斯哥（Glasgow）、爱丁堡（Edinburgh）和邓迪（Dundee）。圣彼得堡（Saint Petersburg）位于佛罗里达州西部，是由当地铁路公司的俄方经理以其在俄国的故乡圣彼得堡命名的。旅居美国的海外华侨多来自于中国的广东，省会广州旧英译名为 Canton，美国现有 18 处以坎顿（Canton）命名的地方。爱尔兰是欧洲最早向美国移民的国家，故土的首都成了移民建城镇时首选的名称，美国现有 8 处以爱尔兰首都都柏林（Dublin）命名的城市。其他来自不同国家的移民也都喜爱用他们国家首都命名其所在地，例如：美国全境有 5 个马德里（Madrid）、8 个里斯本（Lisbon）、6 个哈瓦那（Havana）、12 个雅典（Athens）、9 个罗马（Rome）、10 个巴黎（Paris）。

四、美国地名与美国历史重大事件、杰出人物

如果说 1630 年一批来自英国林肯郡波士顿（Boston）镇的清教徒在马萨诸塞州建立的波士顿是为了缅怀故乡、纪念祖先，那么，美国其他州以波士顿命名的地方则是让世人铭记"波士顿倾茶案"，因为这一行动点燃了自由的火炬，成为美国革命的先声。列克星敦（Lexington）则记载了美国青史的另一大事件。独立战争期间，美国民兵在此狙击了前往镇压的英军，打响了独立战争的第一枪，从此，以列克星敦命名的地方有 20 处之多。

19 世纪之后，用美国总统的名字来命名地方成为时尚。美国首都华盛顿（Washington）是为了纪念美国开国元勋华盛顿总统而命名的。美国各地有 43 处以林肯（Lincoln）命名的城镇。其实，有很多以林肯命名的地方林肯总统本人从未到过。这些地方的人民，有感于这位总统维护联邦统一、坚持解放黑奴、不惜以身殉职的伟大人格，自愿将他们的城镇以林肯总统的名字命名。以美国宪法重要起草人之一，后又任两届美国总统的麦迪逊（Madison）名字命名的地方有 40 多处。密西西比州

府杰克逊（Jackson）是为了纪念第七任总统杰克逊而命的名，另外还有30多个以杰克逊名字命名的县市。

历史上曾为美国的独立解放、联邦统一、侵略扩张立过汗马功劳的军事将领们也是美国地名的来源之一。例如，独立战争期间美军将领蒙哥马利（Montgomery）、迪尔泊恩（Dearborn）、纳什（Nash），南北战争期间北方军的将军丹佛（Denver）、谢尔曼（Sherman）、埃文斯（Evans），美墨战争中的美军指挥官斯托克顿（Stockton）、休斯敦（Houston）等的姓氏或姓氏加 ville（ville 源于法语，意为"城市"）成为了当时美国兴城建镇首选的名字。

美国地名的由来有着丰富而广泛的文化背景，它与美国的民族传统、自然景观、社会变革、意识形态等诸多因素密切相关。深入细致地研究与探讨美国地名的始源会有助于我们详尽领悟美国自身所特有的民族风味、文化风貌以及美国文化发展史。

参考文献

[1] 戴卫平 . 美国地名与美国文化 [J]. 中山大学学报论丛，2002（6）.

[2] 戴卫平 . 美国城名渊源和文化涵义 [J]. 大学外语教学研究，2004.

[3] 高关中 . 美国州市大观 [M]. 北京：当代世界出版社，1999.

[4] 邵献图 . 外国地名语源词典 [M]. 上海：上海辞书出版社，1983.

[5] 苏晓玉 . 浅谈美国地名的文化含义 [J]. 解放军外语学院学报，1997（6）.

[6] 俞希 . 从地名看美国文化 [J]. 外语教学，1999（4）.

[7] 中国地名委员会 . 美国地名译名手册 [J]. 北京：商务印书馆，1994.

第三篇　美国体育习语文化

　　人类的生产力发展到一定程度，不再需要把全部时间和精力都放到维持温饱的生产劳动中去的时候，各种娱乐活动应运而生。人类的体育娱乐活动历史非常悠久，与人类的文明是同步发生发展的。今天举世瞩目的国际奥林匹克运动会就起源于前776年古希腊人为了纪念希腊神话中的主神宙斯而每四年举行一次的运动、诗歌和音乐竞赛会。

　　体育娱乐是民族文化的一部分。目前流行的国际性体育竞赛项目很多都是从原始的民族体育活动形式中发展起来的。不同的原始部落有各自不同的原始体育娱乐形式。各种体育娱乐形式相互交流、相互补充，形成了规模更大的体育活动项目。有些项目从一个部落传入另一个部落，从一个民族传入另一个民族，竞技难度不断提高，竞赛规则不断完善，最后成为世界性的体育竞赛项目。时至今日，世界各民族仍然保持着不少本民族的体育活动项目。虽然这些民族体育项目多没有进入国际赛坛，但仍然是该民族人民的文化盛事。

　　既然体育娱乐活动与民族文化紧密相关，那么作为社会文化生活的一面镜子的习语就必然会反映出这方面的内容。

一、拳击词语文化喻义

　　拳击（boxing）是戴拳击手套进行格斗的运动项目。它既有业余的（也称奥运拳击），也有职业的商业比赛。比赛的目标是要比对方获得更多的分以战胜对方或者将对方打倒而结束比赛。与此同时，比赛者要力图避开对方的打击。拳击被称为"勇敢者的运动"。在古代奥运中，拳击运动就已经是比赛项目之一。

　　拳击是一种古老的比赛项目，起源于古希腊的奥林匹克运动会和古罗马的格斗，后来随着罗马帝国的衰亡而走入低谷。到了18世纪初，拳击又在英国兴起。1719年，英国人詹姆斯菲格（James Figg）在伦敦开办了第一个拳击场（Boxing Arena）。1865 年，英国的昆斯伯里侯爵（Marquess of Queensbery）制定了一套完整的拳击比赛规则，并首次规定在业余拳击比赛中要戴上特制的专用手套（padded gloves），从此，开始了比较文明的现代拳击比赛的历史。1904 年，拳击成为国际奥林匹克运动会的正式比赛项目。

现在的拳击来自旧时的角斗。当时的规则很简单：先在地上划上（scratch）两条线。角斗即将开始时，双方分别站在各自的线（scratch）上，只要听到比赛开始的口令，他们就冲上场打斗起来。所以一个人 come (up) to scratch（站 [使某人] 到起始线上）则意味着他准备"挺身迎敌"。该习语现在转义为"立即行动"、"达到（参赛的）标准"、"合格，令人满意"等意思。该习语亦可以写作 bring sb. to scratch（使某人站到起跑线上）。

当比赛的铃声响起，两名拳手就会 come out swinging（挥动着双臂冲出来），都企图在对方还没有时间出击的时候先发制人，给予对方致命一击。Swing 意为"摇摆、摆动"，come out swinging 用在竞选的时候，就成了"相互攻击"之意。如：After a day off, President Bush and Governor Clinton this morning again launched another hard week of campaigning, and they both came out swinging. 这句话的意思是"休息了一天之后，布什总统和克林顿州长在今天早上又开始了一个星期的艰苦竞选旅程，他们两人一开始就相互攻击"。

拳击比赛（bout）是在一个用绳子拦隔的拳击台（boxing ring）上进行的。当拳击比赛的一方被对方打得惨败，到了几乎毫无防御能力的时候，他往往会靠在四周的绳子上（be on the ropes），以免摔倒。现在，习语 be on the ropes 已经不仅仅局限于拳击方面了，它可以用在生活中的各个方面。这个习语被用来形容一个人面临难题，几乎快要垮台或崩溃的局面。如果一个拳击手被对手打倒在地，裁判马上开始数秒。数完 10 下（或过了 10 秒钟）他还不能重新站起来，就被判失败，不能再打了。Down and out（倒下出局），现用来比喻"击败；筋疲力尽；无能为力；穷困潦倒"的意思。另外，out for the count（数完出局）这条习语的来源与上一条一样，本义是"数完 10 下还不省人事"，现在比喻"（某人）失去知觉"。

现在正规的拳击比赛中拳击手都要戴上专用手套（gloves）和头盔作为保护。如果我们脱掉手套去打，就意味着"毫不留情"地打起来了。Take off gloves 这条习语用来比喻"（对某人）不客气，（在争辩中）言词激烈"。

在拳击规则中最引人注意的一条是不得攻击对方的下身，即腰带以下部位（below the belt），否则被判为犯规。Below the belt 一语后来就转义为"卑劣的（地）"、"不公正的（地）"，在使用时常常与动词 hit, strike 及 be 连用。Hit/strike below the belt 是"玩弄卑鄙手段"的意思，相当于汉语中的"暗箭伤人"。例如：You were hitting Tom below the belt when you said that.（你那样说对汤姆是不公正的。）To refer in public to his father being in prison was below the belt.（在公开的场合提及他在狱中的父亲是卑劣的。）In business Bill is difficult to deal with. He hits below the belt.（在生意上比尔很难打交道，他爱玩弄不正当手段。）In the run-up to the election,politicians won't hesitate to aim below the belt.（在选举前的竞选时期，政客们在玩弄卑鄙的手法时是不会迟疑的。）

在拳击比赛中有经验的拳击手会耸起肩，缩着头以缩小自己身体的体积使自己不那么容易受到对手的攻击。如果哪位拳击手在比赛时把脖子伸得老长 stick one's neck out（把脖子伸出来），就会"惹祸殃；招麻烦"，容易挨打了。所以习语 stick one's neck out（把脖子伸出来）就转义为"做有风险的事情"。在比赛中，如果一个拳手能在对手的周围不停地移动的话，他的拳头就可以从各个角度如雨点般地打击对手。这说明他技高一筹，占上风。习语 make/run rings round /around someone（围着某人转圈），现在用来比喻"做事比某人好得多；大大胜过某人"。

Straight from the shoulder（直接从肩膀上来）流行于 19 世纪中叶。拳击手出拳要狠才能打击对手，在猛击时不仅用臂力而且用肩部的力量。A punch straight from the shoulder（直接从肩部出拳）被认为是既快捷又有力，而且往往打得准。后来，straight from the shoulder 这一个拳击用语又转喻为"毫不留情；开诚布公；直截了当"。Throw in the sponge/towel（扔进海绵 / 毛巾）中的 throw 就是扔的意思，towel 和 sponge 就是擦身用的毛巾和海绵。按照字面来理解，就是把毛巾或海绵扔进去。但是，作为习语，它的意思是：放弃你想达到的目的。在进行拳击比赛的时候，要是把毛巾或海面扔到拳击的场地里去给一名拳击手擦脸，就意味着这个拳击手失败了。在拳击比赛中，有这样一种习俗：当拳击运动员的副手把擦身用的海绵或毛巾抛向空中时，就表示这个拳击手认输，不参加下一轮比赛了。后来这条习语泛指"认输；投降"的意思。I think it's time to throw in the towel.（我想该认输了。）Don't give up now! It's too soon to throw in the sponge.（不要现在就放弃！承认失败还为时过早。）After losing the election, he threw in the towel on his political career.（选举失败之后，他便放弃了自己的政治生涯。）I hate my work. Sometimes I feel like throwing in the sponge.（我不喜欢我的工作，有时真想撒手不干了。）Three of the original five candidates for the Democratic presidential nomination have now thrown in the towel.（获民主党总统提名的原先五位候选人中的三位已经承认失败。）

在拳击比赛时拳击手每打一拳都应该使出全部力气，才能把对手击倒。如果一个拳击手有意不使尽全力去打，而是手下留情，有所保留，那么他就是在 pull his punches 了。因此，pull one's punches 一语的含义是否定的，就是"故意不用全力打"。语中 punch 指用拳猛击，即"一拳"、"一击"，而 pull 的字面义是"抽回（拳头）"，含有"故意不使力"，即"空（拳）"之意。在口语中，这个成语一般多用于喻义，表示"不全力攻击（某人）"、"故意不猛烈批评"、"谨慎地行动"或"婉转地讲话"等，常用于否定式，亦作 pull punches，而且常以 pull no punches/not pull any punches 的形式出现。The boxer has been barred from the boxing-ring for pulling his punches.（这位拳击手因不卖力打而被禁止参加拳击赛。）The new manager pulls no punches when he finds anyone negligent in work.（新来的经理一发现哪一位工作马虎，批评起来是丝毫不客气的。）I didn't pull any punches. I told him just what I thought of him.（我毫无保留地和毫不客气地把我对他的看法告诉他。）He never pulls any punches. He always talks straight.（他从不留情面，说话总是直来直去。）The teacher doesn't pull any punches when it comes to discipline.（关于课堂纪律，老师是不留情面的。）We generally pull our punches when talking to her.（我们在和她说话时措辞通常都较婉转。）

二、球类运动词语文化喻义

球类运动在人们的日常体育娱乐中占有举足轻重的地位。它们既可以作为观赏性的体育项目为人们所享受，又是人们可以直接参与的全民性健身活动。尤其是在当今欧洲和美国，在电台和电视台等媒体的介入下，球类运动更成为了人们的"消费热点"。球类运动种类很多。美国人热衷的球类有橄榄球、垒球、篮球、网球、高尔夫球、棒球，因此不少习语与球类有关。

（一）篮　球

男子篮球在 1904 年被列入奥运会的比赛项目，到 1936 年柏林奥运会成为正式项目。而女子篮球则到 1976 年蒙特利尔奥运会才成为正式比赛项目。篮球队员以位置来划分分为前锋、中锋、后卫。篮球比赛是在长 28 米，宽 15 米的场地上进行的。

篮球是诞生于美国的重要体育比赛，是美国目前最普及的运动之一，1891 年由马萨诸塞州斯普林菲尔德基督教青年会的体育教练 James Naismith 发明。斯普林菲尔德现为美国全国篮球名人堂所在地。1949 年，美国成立全国篮球协会（NBA）后职业篮球运动开展更加活跃。

在美国，有些出色的篮球运动员有一种才能，那就是在球场上不管球在谁的手上，也不管那只球在场地上的哪个角落，他们总是在离球不远的地方，一有机会就会把球抢到手里。(be)on the ball 这条习语在日常对话中用来形容一个人很机灵，在工作方面做得很出色，总是名列前茅。该习语也意为"对新的思路、动向等敏感而熟悉"。篮球得分是把球投进赛场一端对方篮里，然后队员通常迅速跑回自己一侧的球场进行防守，防止对方得分。而在 full court press（全场紧逼盯人战术）中，得分的一方不是撤回，相反，而是进攻，或者用有力的进攻性防守压制对方。所以，当某人决定加倍努力，完成某件事情时，他就是在实行"full court press"。

（二）棒　球

棒球（baseball）运动是一种以棒子打球为主要特点，集体性、对抗性很强的球类运动项目。棒球在国际上开展较为广泛，影响较大，被誉为"竞技与智慧的结合"。在美国棒球尤为盛行，被称为"国球"。棒球比赛法定比赛人数最少为 9 人，与其近似的运动项目为垒球。棒球球员分为攻、守两方，利用球棒和手套，在一个扇形的棒球场里进行比赛。比赛中，两队交替进攻：当进攻球员成功跑回本垒，就可得 1 分。9 局中得分最高的一队就胜出。

美国的全国棒球联合会（The National League）成立于 1876 年，美国棒球联合会（The American League）成立于 1900 年。这两个联合会组成了美国职业棒球联合总会（The Major League），共有 26 个球队。每年十月举行"世界锦标赛"（The World Series），由两个联合会的冠军队争夺最后冠军。

100 多年前，在棒球队比赛前，裁判员就会叫："Play ball, play ball." 这是给两个球队发出信号，意思是球赛马上就要开始了。随着时间的推移，play ball 逐渐变成日常用语，意思是"跟别人共同合作"。美国人在打棒球时经常喜欢发曲线（curve）球，使球的方向发生变化，这样给对方造成错觉，不能回击那球。逐渐的，这种让对方产生错觉，因而无法应付的球艺——发曲线球（to throw a curve）变成了日常用语，意思是"给别人造成错觉，让他难以应付"。棒球场成直角扇形，设有四个垒位（bases）：一垒（first base）、二垒、三垒和本垒（home base）。攻队队员在本垒依次用棒击守队投球手投来的球，并乘机跑垒，能跑完一、二、三垒后回到本垒者得一分。击球员若能安全跑到第一垒，就有得分的可能即取得初步成功。Get to first base 现在成为了日常用语，表示"获得初步成功"，"跨出第一步"。此语又作 reach /make first base。Touch all bases 本义为"触遍各垒"，即依次跑完一、二、三垒回至本垒，用脚触及就算跑过。人们将此语用于商业、法律、学校和政治等各个方面，比喻"探讨某个问题的各个方面"，意指考虑事情全面周到，做事彻底而不留尾巴，尤指在与人商议、交流意见方面。Home run（本垒打）指在棒球比赛中能使击球员跑及所有垒并返回本垒而得分的安全打。美国人现在常用 hit a home run/make a home run 比喻成功。

例如：The way you do, you'll not even reach first base.（照你这样做，你连第一步都跨不出来。）I wish I could get to first base with this business deal.（如果这笔商业交易能取得初步成功，那就好了。）He couldn't get to first base with that girl. She wouldn't even speak to him.（他对那女孩的追求第一步都没能跨出。她连话都不跟他讲。）Plan hasn't been properly prepared. I'll be surprised if it even reaches first base.（计划尚未拟好。哪怕有个良好的开端，我就惊喜不已了。）He has some good ideas but none of his projects ever gets to first base.（他有一些很好的想法，但他所有方案始终未能开始实行。）The reporter has touched all bases in his story.（记者在报道中谈到了问题的各个方面。）

（三）网　球

网球是一项优美而激烈的体育运动。网球运动的由来和发展可以用四句话来概括：孕育在法国，诞生在英国，开始普及和形成高潮在美国，现在盛行全世界，被称为世界第二大球类运动。网球通常在两个单打球员或两对双打组合之间进行。球员在网球场上隔着球网用网球拍击打空心橡胶球。现代网球运动诞生于19世纪的英国伯明翰。20世纪，网球在世界各地得到广泛发展，并成为一项世界性的体育运动。

习语 from pillar to post（从桩子到柱子）原作 from post to pillar，这个习语源自14世纪或更早的庭院网球（court/royal tennis），即室内网球。这种网球打法有别于现在流行的草地网球（lawn tennis）。网的一端系在网柱（post）上，另一端则系在建筑物的柱子（pillar）上。当时运动员常使用的一种战术是相互截击网柱和房柱之间的长距离空中球（long volley from post to pillar），使对手来回奔跑，穷于应付，由此产生了 from post to pillar tossed，一个世纪之后演变为 from pillar to post，仍用以表示"来回地"，"东奔西跑"。人们用球来比喻某些被迫"东奔西跑"的人。而（go）from pillar to post 指"处于到处奔走、四处碰壁的窘境"。习语"Now the ball is in your court."的字面意思是：现在这只球在你的场地上了。实际上，这是打网球时用的一句话，即你已经把球打过了网，到了对方的场地，现在是对方采取行动的时候了。美国的生意人和律师经常用这个俗语来告诉对方，他们已经提出了建议和要求，现在是对方采取行动的时候了。

（四）橄榄球

橄榄球，球类运动的一种，盛行于英国、美国、澳大利亚、日本等国家。橄榄球 1823 年起源于英国拉格比（Rugby），原名拉格比足球，简称拉格比。因其球形似橄榄，在中国称为橄榄球。拉格比（Rugby）是英国中部的一座城市，那里有一所拉格比学校，它是橄榄球运动的诞生地。

美式橄榄球（American football），或称美式足球，是橄榄球运动的一种，为北美四大职业体育之首。美式橄榄球源自英式橄榄球，传入美国后规则改变，改为采取攻防线进行回合制争球、没有跑位限制，并且可以向前抛掷传球。美式橄榄球是一种对抗性很强的接触性体育运动，由于球赛中往往会与对方球员有强烈的身体冲撞，因此球员需穿戴头盔和护具出场。

在美国，橄榄球（American football）实际上要比足球（soccer）的人气旺得多。每到周末，电视上常常播放精彩的橄榄球赛事，以至于好多男人都与朋友周末观看比赛，他们的妻子则被冷落在一旁成了 football widow。Football widow 指一个妻子由于丈夫只顾看球赛而感到好像没有丈夫一样。习语 go for it（豁出去）是催促人大胆尝试，不要担心失败，也不要过分小心，应该勇敢坚定，敢于冒险。这种球的玩法是一个队必须持续不断地将球向对方球门线运传，否则就要将球交给对方。其中一条规则是得球的队可以连续进行四次进攻，若四次进攻能将球向前运传 10 码（1 码 = 0.9144 米），则有权再组织四次进攻，否则丧失进攻权，由对方在第四次攻成死球的地点组织进攻。在橄榄球比赛中最激动人心的时刻莫过于得球队在三次传球后仍未能传出 10 码远。这时该球队面临两种选择：①保守的选择，那就是把球踢开，表示放弃进攻；②做第四次即最后一次进攻，力争把球传到规定的距离。看球赛的人有的会声嘶力竭地喊"Go for it!"（拼一次），鼓动队员铤而走险。Game plan（竞赛规则）开始用于橄榄球运动，20 世纪 50 年代以来在美国英语中常用于政治，指战略，为实现重要目标而制定的长期连贯的计划，例如：economic game plan，Vietnam game plan。美国前总统尼克松尤其喜欢用此词语。Game plan 也用作动词，如尼克松说过："We have to game-plan this."

（五）高尔夫球

在标准的 6 000 码（约 5 500 米）长的高尔夫球场上，共有 18 个球穴。球员们打完 18 个球穴后一般都去吃东西。所以高尔夫球手们都戏称高尔夫球俱乐部的酒吧间是第 19 个球穴。后来人们用 The nineteenth hole（第 19 个洞穴）这个习语喻指"（工人下班后）回家吃饭"。

高尔夫球是一种用勺形的棒击球，使球通过障碍进入小圆穴的球类游戏。按规定每一场须将球击入 18 个穴，击球次数最少者为胜。一般运动员击球 72 次就可击入 18 个球穴。这是规定的标准击球次数，要求运动员达到的一般水平，英语中叫作 par。Par 本是拉丁语借用词，意为"同等"或"相同水平"，course 原指"高尔夫球场"，par for the course 就是"（高尔夫球）规定的标准击球次数"，即"一般标准"的意思。

此语始用于 1920 年左右，以后在口语中转义为"意料之中的（事）"、"没什么不寻常的（事）"。Jim was half an hour late,was he? That's just par for the course for him.（吉姆迟到了半个小时吧？他就是这样。）One third of the students failed the exam this time, but it's par for the course.（这次考试 1/3 的学生不及格，不过这种情况是正常的。）The school budget is going to be cut again this year, but then that's par for the course.（学校的预算今年又将再次被削减，不过这是预料中的事。）So he went off and left you? Well, that's about par for the course.He's no friend.（这么说他溜了，把你丢下来？唉，他就是这样，很不够朋友。）The train's late again—I guess that's about par for the course.（火车又晚点了——我认为这几乎是意料之中的事。）

语言中的词汇与民族文化息息相关，而词汇中的习语则是词汇对民族文化的发展和变化最为敏感的部分。社会文化生活中的每一个侧面都会反映到习语中来。在当今全球化经济的迅速发展和人民生活水平以及受教育程度的提高的同时，习语的发展变化也相应加快。随着体育娱乐活动的发展，与之相关的习语还会产生并且还会渗透到社会生活中的方方面面。当我们回顾和探查这些习语来源和含义时，我们犹如翻开了一本厚厚的历史文化画卷，欣赏一幅幅仍栩栩如生的图画，重温昔日的辉煌，品味今天的含义。我们只有随语随义把握英语习语（包括体育习语）及其文化背景和在特定语境中的文化蕴含，才能学好和用好习语，并有效地提高语言交际能力和社会文化能力。

参考文献

[1] 戴卫平 . 词汇与文化 [J]. 山东外语教学，1999（1）：79-82.

[2] 戴卫平，吴蓓 . 英语与英美文化 [J]. 长沙大学学报，2001（3）：62-65.

[3] [美] 迪克•麦卡锡，苏明 . 美国成语俗语 [M]. 北京：中国对外翻译山版社，1997.

[4] 梁淑珍 . 美国习语故事 [M]. 天津：天津人民出版社，1994.

[5] 美国之音中文部 . 美国英语成语俗语续编（一）[M]. 北京：中国对外翻译出版社，1995.

[6] 庄和诚 . 英语语言新说 [M]. 汕头：汕头大学出版社，1994.

第四篇　美国土著印第安

一、美语与印第安文化

谈到美国文化就必然要谈到印第安人，因为印第安人是美国本土上最早的居民。他们世世代代在这里生活劳动、休养生息，是美国真正的主人。和世界各国、各地区的人民一样，土著印第安人为人类的历史发展做出过重大贡献。印第安人是美国历史上不少重大事件的涉及对象或直接参与者。"语言是一种用以传递信息的符号系统。对于每一个人而言，一种语言通常被看作是一种社会化的文化遗产。"（蔡昌卓，2002：26）虽然美国土著印第安人是一个被征服的民族，但他们的语言却作为珍贵的文化遗产保留下来，融进了美语。印第安人的语言为外来殖民者提供了现成的语言素材，填补了早期美语在某些方面表达的词汇空白。

北美大陆土地辽阔，地貌繁复多姿，资源异常丰富。欧洲殖民者从他们踏上这块土地的时刻起，就置身于一个崭新的环境中。他们看到在欧洲从未曾见过的特殊地理，生态环境中的各种事物和现象，以及当地土著人各种各样奇怪的服饰、用品和风俗等。所有这些在欧洲的自然、社会环境里可能是前所未有的事物和现象，使欧洲殖民主义者迫切需要新的语汇来表达眼前的这一切。世代生活在这里的印第安人的语言成了一个直接的语言材料，向当地人借用他们原来用于表达这些事物的词汇就成了创造新词的一个方便方法。在当代美语中，有1 700多个词语来自印第安语，如：

（1）北美大陆的动物名称词：opossum（负鼠），whippoorwill（夜鹰），chipmunk（金花鼠），woodchuck（土拨鼠）；

（2）植物名称词：timothy（梯牧草），sassafras（黄樟），pecan（美洲的核桃），pawpaw（巴婆果）；

（3）人工制品词：toboggan（平底雪橇），peltry（毛皮），kinnikinic（烟草代用品），mackinaw（厚呢短大衣）；

（4）社会风俗、制度的词语：powwow（狂欢典礼），totem（图腾），manitou（自然神）；

（5）生态环境词：bayout（牛扼湖），slew（沼泽）；

（6）交通工具词：canoe（独木舟）；

（7）人物名称词：sagamore（次于酋长的头目），squaw（女人），papoose（与工会会员一起工作的非会员工人），sachem（要人）；

（8）食物名称词：johnnycake（玉米馅肉饼），tapioca（木薯淀粉），pemmican（干肉饼），hominy（玉米粥），succotash（豆煮玉米），pone（玉米面包）。

在《美国特有词词典》中，有关 corn 及其构成的复合词多达 8 页，且每个词条都与早期从印第安语中演绎过来的词 corn 有关。此外，印第安人跟 corn 有关的习语也融入了美国白人生活圈内，最富有代表性的是 1836—1930 年流行于白人中间的 corn dance（玉米舞），这是一种为庆祝玉米丰收的民间舞蹈。美语中，与 fire 相关的复合词和成语特别多，这跟印第安人的民族性格有关，因为他们有火一样的热情、火一样的勇敢。与 fire 的复合词最有代表性的有 fire water（火酒），fire hunt（火光陷阱），fire dance（火舞：夜间举行的一种祈祷死而复生的宗教舞蹈），fire keeper（举火把的头领）。（蔡昌卓，2002：113）

美语中有一些词和短语，是由印第安语意译而成的。如：Medicine Man 在印第安语中原指巫医、咒术语，现在美语中为医生的俗称；Great Father 原为印第安人称呼美国总统的用语，现在美俚语中也用此来称呼美国总统；To Scalp 在印第安语中意为剥取敌人头皮当作胜利品，现在美语中引申为剥夺某人的权力或职务。美国主要的河流、湖泊和著名景观都以印第安语命名。象征美国民族精髓的 The Mississippi（众水之父）就是源于印第安语的。Totem 原为印第安人认为与自己家族有密切关系的天然物，如鹿、狼、蛇、龟等动物，奉为祖先来崇拜，并以之作为本民族的标志，现在美语中为拜物教之意，并已广泛进入英语。Apache（阿帕奇：直升机），Cherokee（切诺基：越野车）则源自于印第安部落的名字。

美语中的印第安语借词还可通过合成的方式构成复合词。大多数印第安语中的名词都能很容易地与别的词组合。Indian 就是一个典型的例子，这个词本身构成了许多复合词，如：Indian millet（高粱），Indian mulberry（桑），Indian nut（松果），Indian pipe（水晶兰），Indian shot（美人蕉），Indian tobacco（黄花烟草），Indian wrestling（卧地角力），Indian Summer（晚秋晴暖宜人的气候），Indian pudding（印第安布丁）等。*The Dictionary of Americanisms* 所列举的由 Indian 一词构成的合成词竟多达 80 个。这说明美国土生土长的印第安人语汇在丰富美语，并使之适应新大陆交际需要方面做出了积极的、不可磨灭的贡献。

北美印第安人对近代美国文明的兴起也做出了重要贡献。这表现为北美印第安人是开发北美的先驱，是近代农业的奠基人。今天在美国的许多种农作物就发源于美洲印第安人的种植，如玉米（maize）来自印第安语 mahiz，马铃薯（potato）来自印第安语 batata。美国的烟草业最初始于印第安人赠送给新大陆移民的烟草。Tobacco（印第安语 tabaco）一词原指印第安人通过鼻孔来吸的烟叶，他们把种植烟草的技术传授给欧洲移民。烟草成了殖民地时期南部的主要产品之一。迄今弗吉尼亚烟草仍名扬世界。

北美印第安人的文化为美利坚文明增添了光彩。美利坚文化发展到今天，吸收了印第安文化的许多精华。美国的自然州名中，有 34 个取自印第安人的名字。如今成为世界首要工商业、金融业中心之一的 Manhattan 依然保留其印第安土著语的名称。美国主要的河流、湖泊和著名景观都以印第安语命名。

二、印第安语与美洲地名文化

地名是人类社会活动在其发展过程中的一定时期的产物。它通常能反映出当时的某些自然特征和历史背景的状况，甚至史事本身的某些侧面或具体细节，从而在一定程度上展现着该地的历史地理特征。

（一）印第安人与美洲文明

美洲大陆神奇美丽而又辽阔富饶，它孕育和滋润了古印第安文明。印第安人是美洲最早的主人，他们在 1492 年哥伦布到达美洲之前就已经生息在整个美洲大陆上，数万年下来生活着以易洛魁人、玛雅人、阿兹特克人和印加人为主的部落众多的印第安人。易洛魁人是北美洲印第安人中最为令人瞩目的。1877 年美国民族学家摩尔根发表了关于易洛魁人的社会制度的著作——《古代社会》，这使得易洛魁人闻名于世。玛雅人和阿兹特克人生活在中美洲。玛雅人享有"美洲的希腊人"的美誉，他们创造的灿烂文明被视为美洲印第安人文化的摇篮。阿兹特克人则因为建造了当时世界上最大的城市之一——铁诺奇蒂特兰和气势恢宏的金字塔而使世人钦羡。印加人生活在南美洲，自国家出现后，很快建立起中央集权制的帝国，具有"新世界的罗马人"的称号。在漫长的历史岁月中，他们创造了辉煌的成就和高度发达而又举世闻名的古代美洲文明，成为世界六大文明之一。

（二）印第安语与美洲国家的名称

美洲印第安文明的丰富与繁荣表现在语言上主要在于它的语系复杂和繁多。印第安民族的语言，大致由 72 个较大的语系构成，其中北美印第安人便有 58 个独立的语系，中、南美洲大约有 14 个较大的语系。因此有很多的美洲国家是以印第安语命名的。在以印第安语命名的美洲诸国中大多是以当地的自然特征或者是外部形状来命名的。

巴拉圭共和国（The Republic of Paraguay），是南美洲中部的内陆国家，境内主要山脉是阿曼拜山和巴兰卡尤山，其南边国境完全与阿根廷接壤，东北与西北角则分别是巴西与玻利维亚。该国境内主要河流有巴拉圭河和巴拉那河。巴拉圭（Paraguay）在印第安古瓜拉尼语中意为"有一条大河的地方"，其国名由于境内有一条叫巴拉圭的大河而得名。河名则来自当地一个印度安部落名称"巴拉瓜"（Paragua）。而部落的名称又源于印度安语中的 para，意为"水"。

巴拿马共和国（The Republic of Panama）简称巴拿马，是中美洲最南部的国家。连接大西洋及太平洋的巴拿马运河位于国家的中央，拥有重要的战略地位，坐拥世界知名的航运要道巴拿马运河。巴拿马（Panama）在印第安语中的意思是"蝴蝶之国"。16 世纪初，哥伦布在巴拿马沿海登陆以后，发现这里到处是成群飞舞的彩色蝴蝶，于是，使用了当地的语言，把这个地方命名为"巴拿马"。

秘鲁孕育了美洲最早人类文明之一的小北史前文明，以及前哥伦布时期美洲的最大国家印加帝国。16 世纪，西班牙帝国征服印加帝国，建立秘鲁总督区，包含西班牙在南美洲的大部分殖民地。秘鲁（Peru）在印第安语中是"玉米之仓"的意思。秘鲁这个名词的来源系根据印第安语，其意为"粮仓"或"玉米秆"，因为该国农作物主要出产玉米。

海地位于加勒比海北部，是加勒比海上的一个岛国。该国的黑人占 95%，因此有"黑人共和国"之称。居民多信奉天主教。官方语言为法语和克里奥尔语，90%的居民使用克里奥尔语，1804 年 1 月 1 日宣告独立，是世界上第一个独立的黑人国家。海地（Haiti）全境 3/4 是山地，它的名字就是印第安阿拉瓦克语里"多山之地"的意思。1492 年，哥伦布在海地登陆，当地印第安居民称这个岛为海地（Haiti）。

乌拉圭位于南美洲的东南部，北邻巴西，西接阿根廷，东南濒大西洋。居民约90% 是白人，其余有 8% 的印欧混血儿。在古印第安瓜拉尼语中，乌拉圭（Uruguay）意即"一条有着甲壳动物的河流"。

牙买加是加勒比海中的一个岛国。牙买加原本是印第安人居住地，但在 1494 年哥伦布发现它不久后就变成了西班牙人的殖民地，1655 年又被大英帝国占领，1962

年 8 月 6 日牙买加宣布独立，目前是英联邦成员国。牙买加（Jamaica）在印第安阿拉瓦克语中意为"泉水之岛"，因岛上水草丰茂、地下水源丰富而得名。该国气候适宜，阳光明媚，遍布山谷与溪流，风景非常美丽。

智利位于南美洲西南部，安第斯山脉西麓。东同阿根廷为邻，北与秘鲁、玻利维亚接壤，西临太平洋，南与南极洲隔海相望，是世界上地形最狭长的国家。智利（Chile）一词源于印第安阿罗克尼亚语 chili，意为"寒冷"、"冬天"。该地名的由来据说是由于占领部分国土的秘鲁印加人发现该地气候较其赤道地带的故土寒冷。

古巴是北美洲加勒比海北部的群岛国家。古巴（Cuba）是以部族名称命的名。"古巴"一词源于印第安语，是岛上一个土著部族的名称。1492 年，哥伦布在巴哈马群岛登陆时，听印第安人说南面有一个既大且富的"古巴岛"，古巴这一国名就是沿袭印第安人的称呼而来的。

尼加拉瓜位于中美洲中部，北接洪都拉斯，南连哥斯达黎加，东临加勒比海，西濒太平洋。印欧混血种人占 69%，白人占 17%，黑人占 9%，印第安人占 5%。尼加拉瓜（Nicaragua）是以酋长的名字而命名的。在尼加拉瓜印第安部落中有一位英勇骁战的酋长叫"尼加鲁"，后来即以此为国名。

墨西哥合众国位于北美洲，北部与美国接壤，东南与危地马拉与伯利兹相邻，西部是太平洋，东部有墨西哥湾的阻隔。墨西哥（Mexico）是以部落的战神所命的名。墨西哥是从印第安语"墨西特里"得来的，"墨西特里"是印第安人阿兹特克神化传说中的战神。在西班牙殖民者踏上墨西哥这片土地之前，当地生活着阿斯特克人。他们崇拜战神的别名叫"墨西特里"。后来人们便以此来命名，指的是"墨西特里臣民居住的地方"。

（三）印第安语与加拿大地名

加拿大（Canada）为北美洲最北的国家，西抵太平洋，东迄大西洋，北至北冰洋，东北部和丹麦领地格陵兰岛相望，东部和法属圣皮埃尔和密克隆群岛相望，南方与美国国土接壤，西北方与美国阿拉斯加州为邻。领土面积达 998 万平方千米，为全世界面积第二大的国家。

印第安文明也影响着加拿大，在加拿大的诸多地名中，有很多是以印第安语命名的。首先国家名称 Canada 就来源于印第安易洛魁语的 kanata，意为"棚屋"或"村庄"。据说，加拿大的国家名称源于 16 世纪的一次误会。1534 年，法国航海家让·卡尔切率领舰队来到北美洲。他们沿一个海湾向内陆驶去，发现岸上住着印第安人。印第安人热情地接待了他们。法国人问这是什么地方，叫什么名字。印第安人以为在问他们的村庄，便回答"加拿大"，后来"加拿大"就成了国名。

　　河流曾孕育了人类的诞生。遍布世界的大大小小的河流是人类生存发展的摇篮，是人类精神与物质文明的发祥地。世界上每一个文明的发源地，都是傍依江河湖泊，并依靠必要的可供水源而发展起来的。古代早期的城市，也都选择在有河流、有水的地方。加拿大的很多河流湖泊都是以印第安语命名的，然后以此命名各个地名。

　　安大略（Ontario）是加拿大中部的一个省及东南边界处的一个湖泊的名称。安大略源于印度安易洛魁语 oniatar-io，意为"美丽的"（指湖）。省名得自安大略湖湖名。萨斯喀彻温（Saskatchewan）加拿大一河名，河名源于印第安语 siskachiwan，意为"急流"。加拿大中南部有一个省因此而得名。渥太华（Ottawa）是加拿大的首都，位于安大略省东南部，因渥太华河而得名，河名则源于印第安阿尔冈金语词 adawe，意即"大河"。育空（Yukon）为加拿大北部一地区，与美国阿拉斯加州毗邻，因育空河而得名。河名源于印第安语，意为"大河"。

　　大奴湖（Great Slave Lake）位于加拿大西北部的马更些区南部，因曾在该湖沿岸居住过的印第安部落而得名。这些印第安部落被印第安人中的克里人赶到了北部地区，并被他们称作"奴隶"。大熊湖（Great Bear Lake）位于加拿大西北部的马更些区。印第安语名是由于在此地曾打死过一只特大的熊而得来的，英译名是由法语译名 Lac du grand ours 转译而来的。克朗代克河（River Klondike）在加拿大育空地区。此河源于印第安语的 throndik，意为"鱼河"。马尼托巴湖（Lake Manitoba）因湖中一岛而得名。岛名是马纳托帕（Manatuapa），为印第安语，意即"伟大的神灵"（为当地的克里人所崇拜），他们视此岛为神灵的住所。加拿大中部的一个省也因此而得名。伊利湖，美国与加拿大之间的大湖泊之一，因北美印第安易洛魁人（Iroquois）而得名。

　　多伦多（Toronto）是安大略省的省会，为加拿大第一大城市。该城创建于1794年，建于一个叫作"多伦多"（Toronto）的印第安人村庄的遗址上。而 Toronto 则源于易洛魁语的 Toron-to-hen，意为"会场"或"富饶的地方"。

（四）印第安语与美国地名

　　美国地名到处有印第安人的遗迹。根据麦肯（1982）的统计，美国至少有54%的州名和15%的湖名起源于印第安语。这些地名拥有比美国本身还要悠久的历史，因而在美国文化中根深蒂固。此外，1 000 多条河流和不计其数的大城小镇都沿用印第安名字，本义多半不为人知。例如，密西西比河（Mississippi）本义为"大河"。弗吉尼亚州的圣南多亚河（Shenandoah），本义为"天女"；加利福尼亚州的莫哈维沙漠（Mohave），由于附近的山脉，取名"三山峰"；现为国家公园的约山美地（Yosemite）本义为"灰熊"。

在美国的州名中有许多是印第安人用来命名河流的，后来又转用作州名。这类州名主要有：俄亥俄（Ohio）源于印第安易洛魁语，意即"美丽的"（指俄亥俄河）。堪萨斯（Kansas）因堪萨斯河而得名。康涅狄格（Connecticut）来源于印第安阿尔冈金语的 Kuenihtekot，意思是"长河"。伊利诺斯（Illinois）因密西西比河的一条支流伊利诺斯河而得名。衣阿华（Iowa）是 1846 年以密西西比的支流衣阿华河命名，河名源于印第安语，含义是"摇篮"。明尼苏达（Minnesota）源于河名，河名由印第安苏语词 minne（水）和 sota（浑浊的）两词组成，意即"浑浊的水"。内布拉斯加（Nebraska）其名由印第安语中的 ni（水）与 bthaska（平缓的）两词组合而成。此名原为普拉特河（Plate）的名称，河名是由法语名 Platte 转写而来，而法语名则由印第安语转译而来。

有些州名是印第安人根据当地的自然特征或是地理风貌来命名的。阿拉斯加（Alaska）位于北美洲的西北端。该名源于阿留申语的 A-la-as-ka，意为"大陆"。亚利桑那（Arizona）名称由印第安帕帕戈语中的 ali（小的）和 shonak（泉）组合而成，意即"有涓涓细流的地方"。肯塔基（Kentucky）源于易洛魁印第安语 Ken-tah-ten，意思是"希望的土地"，或"黑色的沃土"。密苏里（Missouri）意思是"大独木舟之乡"。马萨诸塞（Massachusetts）意思是"伟大的山地"。密执安（Michigan）意思是"大湖"或"广阔的水面"。怀俄明（Wyoming）源自印第安阿尔冈金语的 meche-meami-ing，意思是"起伏的山谷"。阿肯色（Arkansas）意思是"靠近地面的微风"。爱达荷（Idaho）意思是"山中的宝石"。

另外一些州是以印第安人的部落名称来命名的。奥马哈（Omaha）是美国内布拉斯加州最大的城市，位于密苏里河畔。其名源于印第安人部落名，意即"居住在该河上游的人"。达科他（Dakota）为美国北部的两个州，即南达科他州和北达科他州。该地名源自在此居住过的印第安人的一个部落名。该部落名源于印第安奥马哈语的 dokota，意为"同盟者"，即部落联盟的成员。

美洲的诸多地名以印第安语命名充分反映了当时的印第安文明对当时社会生活的影响，反映了当时自然和社会环境的关系，使人们在看到这些名字的同时也能够回想起灿烂的印第安文明，同时对语言的发展也起了一定的作用。以美国英语为例，这些地名在美国英语的形成初期充实了美国英语和文化。与此同时，美国英语在对印第安语言消化吸收的基础上形成自己的风格，促进了语言的发展。

参考文献

[1] Charles L.Cutler.Brave New Words! Native American Loanwords in Current English[M].Norman and London: University of Oklahoma Press, 1994.

[2] Mencken, H. L. The American Language[M].New York: Alfred A. Knopf, Inc., 1982.

[3] 戴卫平.美国文化与美国词汇 [J]. 山东师大外国语学院学报，2000（1）：19-22.

[4] 戴卫平.美国多元文化与美语词汇发展 [J]. 大学外语教学研究，2001，55-60.

[5] 戴卫平，张学忠.美国地名与美国文化 [J]. 中山大学学报论丛，2002（6）.

[6] 邵献图.外国地名语源词典 [Z]. 上海：上海辞书出版社，1983.

[7] 宋瑞芝.走进印第安文明 [M]. 北京：民主与建设出版社，2001.

[8] 葛婧箐.印第安文明读本 [M]. 北京：中国档案出版社，2005.

第五篇 美国黑人英语与文化

一、黑人英语变体

美国黑人英语不同于普通美国英语，是美国英语许多变体中的一种。黑人英语的形成是特定的社会环境、教育背景和经济状态所致，这与民族本身无关。并不是所有的黑人都说黑人英语，也不是说黑人英语的人都是黑人。说什么语言与人所处的社会环境有关，与肤色无关。

语言维系着一个民族的人际感情，语言具有团结和区别的功能，它是团结本民族集团成员的纽带，具有把本语言社团区别于其他语言社团的作用。因此对本族语言的忠诚是人们的一种普遍心理，本族人之间说本族语会增加亲切感。本族语的使用还往往形成一种社团压力，不遵守使用本族语的社会公约的人会受到本社团的冷淡，而语言忠诚在本族语受到歧视时往往表现得更为明显。语言是一种社会身份的象征。

黑人英语是社会语言学家特别感兴趣的一种语言现象。黑人英语与其他语言变体一样是一个民族身份的象征，是一个民族社会文化的象征。一个人的语言变体的改变意味着社会文化身份的改变和社会价值观念的改变。这也是黑人不愿意放弃他们语言模式的原因之一。

黑人英语的形成是由多种因素引起的，它受到时间、地域、种族、社会和社会集团等因素的制约。迄今 300 年来，美国黑人及其祖先非洲人在美洲大陆的血泪史，他们所遭受的种族压迫和种族隔离是促使语言变异的根本原因。黑人英语来源于多种渠道：既跟白人英语有关，也跟非洲语言有关。语言像一面镜子，它深刻地反映了社会、政治、经济、学术思想等诸多方面的情况与关系。人的社会、政治和经济地位始终决定了他的语言地位。美国黑人英语也不例外。

黑人英语在许多方面确实与别的变体有差异，但任何一种变体与别的变体之间总是存在差异的。黑人英语具有其自己的语音、语法、句法特点，也有它自己的某些独特的词汇。此外，说黑人英语的人也与其他社会集团的人一样，具有他们独特的言语交际方式。黑人英语同其他英语变体一样，是有规则支配的、成系统的，富有交际表达力和灵活性。

二、美语词与美国黑人史

美国黑人的历史是一部屈辱史、血泪史。Slave 一词（及其许多复合词）记载了黑人的惨境。从 1704 年起，slave 一词成为 negro 的同义词，奴隶即黑人，黑人即奴隶，这一用法足以显示当时奴隶制的凶貌。其后，奴隶贩卖制盛行，于是有了 slave-trade（1734）；由于奴隶大量逃亡，于是就有专事捕捉逃奴的 slave-catcher（1765）；奴隶主管理奴隶，居然形成了一套法律：slave code 一词首见于 1835 年。奴隶成为商品，也像牛马一样，由奴隶主经营繁殖，于是有所谓的 slave breeding（1840）；南方奴隶主于 1861 年叛乱，竟然创建了奴隶主之国 Slaveownia。南北战争爆发以后，南方白人暴徒用骇人听闻的方式迫害黑人，记载这段臭名昭著历史的词首推 lynch（私刑）。Lynch 来自南方一白人种植园主人名，因对黑人不经司法途径而施以私刑，残酷杀戮，尤指将人非法吊死而载入史册。南方白人不能容忍黑人成为和他们平等的自由人这一现实，他们极力反对给黑人政治自由和人身自由的权利。为了使黑人"安分守己"，他们采用了暴力和恐怖的手段。臭名昭著的 Ku Klux Klan（三 K 党）便是当时的产物。

从 19 世纪初开始，美国北方越来越多的有识之士主张废除奴隶制度，呼吁让黑人奴隶尽快获得自由。1831 年，abolitionist（废奴主义者）创办了反奴隶制报纸 The Liberator（《解放者》）。1833 年 The American Anti-Slavery Socicty（美国反奴隶制协会）在费城成立。不少废奴主义者将其家宅作为营救逃奴的 The Underground Railroad（地下交通网）的 depot（车站），帮助黑奴从南部的 slave state（蓄奴州）送到北部的 free state（自由州）和加拿大。南北战争中，伴随着 Abolition Movement（废奴运动）出现了 emancipation（解放黑奴），free soil（禁止蓄奴的自由土地），free state（不使用奴隶的州）。1854 之后的几年中，北部有些州在人民反奴隶制的革命运动的压力下，通过了 Civil Rights Act（人身自由法）。从此，civil rights 这个用语就与黑人的命运休戚相关。南北战争后，黑人虽然得到"解放"，成为 freedmen，在法律上确立了政治自由和人身自由的权利，当时政府内阁中也曾设有 The Freedmen's Bureau（被解放黑奴事务管理局），但种族主义思想根深蒂固的南方社会并不准备马上给予刚获解放的黑人以平等的政治、社会和经济地位。黑人们得到的只是一纸法律条文，在生活中仍然受到种族歧视。迫于生计，大批黑人不得不离开他们所熟悉的南方农村，四处迁徙，或移居北方各地，或流入南方城市，凡是能使他们安身立命之处，他们都尽力前往。1877 年之后，随着联邦军队的撤走和南方地方政府的重新上台，黑人的政治权利和其他各项民权急剧下降，到处出现了种族隔离和歧视，俗称 Jim Crow。

一部美国黑人的历史，也是他们为争取自身解放和权利平等而斗争的历史。无论是奴隶制时代还是种族隔离时代，抑或是民权运动时代，黑人从来没有放弃过斗争。20 世纪 50 年代，黑人为反对种族歧视进行的声势浩大的民权斗争，是美国历史上最令人瞩目的一页。他们创造了著名的 sit-in，ride-in，kneel-in，lie-in，swim-in，wade-in，lie-in，free ride，freedom March，Boycott of Transit System 等斗争方式。白人当时把要求平等的黑人称之为 uppity，意为"不守身份的黑人"。经过长期不懈的斗争，黑人终于赢得了 integration（取消种族隔离），segregated school（实行种族隔离的学校）被 integrated school（黑白学生同校的学校）所取代。20 世纪 60 年代高潮迭起的黑人运动最后将 Jim Crow Laws（歧视黑人法规）扫进了历史的垃圾堆。

三、美国黑人的称谓

美国是世界上最大的移民国家，拥有世界各地的不同民族和种族的移民，但唯有非洲黑人是带着锁链而来的，常常被冠之为"非志愿移民"（蔡昌卓，2002：165）。

根据美国公布的调查显示，2006 年美国有 37 051 483 黑人，大约占总人口的 12%。在美国内战前，黑人的称呼是 black 或 negro。内战后，美国黑人开始用 colored 这一称呼，因为黑人认为 colored 比 black，negro 显得体面和得体。用 black 来表示黑人已经有多年的历史，早期美国黑人就讨厌这种称呼，这种厌恶到了内战结束后就更加明显，内战后获得自由的黑人奴隶抛弃了 black 和 negro，他们选择用 colored 来称呼自己。

到了 20 世纪中叶，首先是大写的 Negro 替代了 colored，后来 black，Afro American 逐渐占了上风，这种变化主要与 20 世纪 60 年代的 Black Power 运动有关。当时，黑人歌手在歌中是这样宣传自己的种族的：Say it loud, I am black and I am proud. 而此前使用的 Negro，colored 等几乎同时不再使用。而在同一时期很快被接受的 Afro American 所表示的是对黑人自身和其非洲起源的一种自豪，到了 20 世纪 70 年代 Afro American 的使用达到了顶峰。但是到了 20 世纪 70 年代末，Afro American 这一称呼又开始遭唾弃。与此同时，African American 开始使用。美国黑人政治家杰西·杰克逊（Jesse Jackson）以及其他一些黑人领袖对该名称的使用起了关键的作用。该称呼的使用已经完全在文学、新闻媒体、学术界和政治领域里广泛使用。但是，African American 的出现并没有完全替代 black 这一称呼。因为美国的黑人并不全部是来自非洲的后裔，有些还来自非洲之外的国家和地区，例如加勒比海地区。更多的情况下，一些媒体同时使用 African American 和 black。

值得一提的是 nigger 的使用。Nigger 一词已经变成英语中最忌讳的词之一。在美国黑人看来，nigger 是英语中最具侮辱性、煽动性的种族蔑称。Nigger 一词充满了种族仇恨、暴力和傲慢。Nigger 一词是美国黑人多年受侮辱和抗争的痛苦的写照。（王威，2006：89-90）

四、美国黑人英语的冠名

由于历史的原因，有很多的黑人生活在美国，成为了美国社会的一个令人瞩目的社会阶层，他们所使用的语言也由于带有鲜明的黑人民族特色而享有了一个独特的名字——黑人英语。

在美国，所谓"黑人英语"是指那些居住在美国南部和其他地区大城市里、处于社会下层的黑人所讲的英语。民族的差别是引起语言变异的一个重要因素。在美国，由于历史、社会等因素形成的美国英语变体主要有黑人英语（Black English）、墨西哥美国英语（Chicano English）、亚洲美国英语（Asian-American dialects）、波利尼西亚美国英语（Polynesian dialects）等。从形式差异上看，美国英语变体真正值得注意的是黑人英语。黑人英语是一种社会方言，其使用者遍及美国大部分黑人社区。

黑人英语主要是指由非洲裔美国人后裔所使用的语言变体的名称，其名称也随着时间的发展而发展。美国黑人英语曾被视为一种次等或低级的语言变体。美国黑人英语从早期形成到现在发展被赋予了各种不同的名称，如：Negro Pidgin（黑人洋泾浜语）、Negro Creolc（黑人克里奥尔语）、Negro Dialect（黑人方言）、Negro English（黑人英语）、Non-standard Negro English（非标准黑人英语）、Vernacular Black English（美国本土黑人英语）、African American English、Afro-American English（非裔美国英语）、Black English（黑人英语）等。从黑人英语的不同冠名中可以看出这种语言变体如同黑人的社会地位一样走过了从歧视到被承认的发展历程。（蔡昌卓，2002：175）Ebonics（黑人方言）一词由 Ebony 和 phonics 缩写而成，它尤其指黑人英语的口语特征，如非标准用法、中下阶层、街道文化不被尊重等特征的总称。

美国黑人英语又称为 Black English Vernacular，即黑人英语方言，在社会学中被定义为具有非洲黑人背景的大多数美国市民使用的英语。虽然黑人英语随地域、社会阶层的不同会有差别，但是黑人群体之间交谈和与其他黑人群体交流时语体会有明显的变化。黑人与黑人之间尤其喜欢用黑人方言交谈。黑人方言是黑人民族性的语言，二者水乳交融，不可分离。

Vernacular 这个词通常解释为"方言、本土的、本族的"。在美国艺术领域，vernacular 指本族的和外来传统的创造性融合。黑人方言是沦为奴隶的非洲黑人对本族语和后天习得的奴隶主语言的创造性组合。黑人英语既包含标准英语和西非的语言成分，又含有美国黑人独特的语言特色，黑人英语的语言结构的分析可以追溯到非洲语言结构和黑人在美洲的经历。美国黑人英语是 16 世纪后期至 19 世纪中期盛行于美国南部的奴隶制的产物，后来随着黑人北迁扩展到遍布美国各州受到种族隔离的贫民群落。非洲本土语言同奴隶主的语言混杂一起就形成了承袭非洲血统的美国黑人从奴隶制时期开始就使用的黑人英语。

然而，近几十年来对黑人英语的进一步研究表明，黑人英语这个名字实际是不甚确切的，因为它不是单纯由民族差异而形成的语言变体，它的使用是与经济地位、教育水准等社会因素密切有关的，由此可见，近年来美国的黑人英语已逐步成为了一种重要的社会方言，而不是单纯的民族方言。一方面并不是所有的美国黑人都使用黑人英语，黑人英语作为一种英语变体使用于美国社会中那些经济地位低下的黑人中，或者是那些虽然已上升到中等收入水平，但与原来的阶层仍保持着密切联系的黑人中。

五、美国黑人英语的来源

美国的黑人英语是美国英语中的一种变体。由于社会历史原因，黑人英语同美国的标准英语和其他英语变体产生了较大的差异。作为社会方言，黑人英语直到 20 世纪 80 年代才被广泛承认。"1979 年底特律法庭决定承认黑人英语，这是黑人英语在法律上的一个里程碑。"（潘绍嶂，1990：17）

美国黑人英语有别于标准的白人英语，而且它的语言、语法及用词都自成体系，因而被称作一种方言。这与黑人英语产生的历史背景有关。众所周知，现今美国的黑人多数是从非洲掳来的黑奴的后裔，他们继承了父辈们的非洲洋泾浜英语和加勒比黑白混血种黑人英语。由于语言是在不断运用着的，所以，任何语言都是动态的，黑人英语也不例外。根据其基本特征进行划分，黑人英语大致经历了洋泾浜语阶段、克里奥尔语阶段、克里奥尔语解体化阶段。

洋泾浜语是指操不同语言的群体为完成某种有限的交际需要而发展起来的一种

辅助语言。克里奥尔语是指已成为某一言语群体母语（本族语）的洋泾浜语，已用于该群体（部分或全部）日常交际的一种语言。洋泾浜语是黑人英语的初始形式，形成于 17 世纪。17 世纪时，欧洲贩奴者把黑人从西非船运到加勒比海岛屿和美洲海岸为奴。奴隶交易持续了近 200 年，数百万的非洲奴隶被贩运卖到了美国。因为怕奴隶们组织谋反，贩奴者经常故意把来自不同种族、操不同语言的奴隶安排在一起贩运。这些奴隶为了交流，创造了几种洋泾浜语，其中，最普遍使用的是奴隶们的非洲语与英语混合而成的洋泾浜语。黑人奴隶到达加勒比海岛屿或北美海岸后，在工作和生活中继续使用这种洋泾浜语来互相交流或与庄园主进行沟通。

　　非洲黑人作为奴隶被贩卖到美洲各地之后，与自己的民族、部落完全失去联系，失去了使用自己母语的交际环境。在这种情况下，他们不得不从其主人、监工以及白人劳动群众那里学习一种新的语言——英语。黑人洋泾浜语的词汇大多来自英语，但其发音和连词成句的方式则取自非洲语。其主要使用者是黑人，因为白人主人和黑人奴隶之间的交际是有限的，并且，如无特殊需要没有白人愿意学习它。

　　随着时间的推移，英语的影响逐渐加深，使得黑人奴隶的语言越来越具有英语的特征，进而演变为克里奥尔语。在美国内战前，黑人英语属于一种克里奥尔语。当非洲奴隶的第二代长大后，不能说其父母的本族语，因为这样无法与外人进行交流。他们也学不到白人标准的英语，因为白人为保持其高度的民族优越感而限制黑人接受教育。加之他们与白人的接触很少，只能接受这个洋泾浜语为母语，使其成为他们的本族语。黑人英语就这样转变为克里奥尔语。虽然克里奥尔语延续了洋泾浜语的简单结构，二者还是有明显区别的。洋泾浜语的正确度和纯度没人过多地关注，其功能也很有限。而发展了的洋泾浜语——克里奥尔语，却能表达人类全部生活经验，并逐步形成自己常用的词汇、句法和规范的发音模式。

　　克里奥尔语解体化是克里奥尔语与标准语变得更接近的过程。黑人英语在美国内战后进入克里奥尔语解体化阶段。美国内战多少改变了美国黑人的状况。他们第一次获得民权，可以自由地到处行走了。在 20 世纪早期，由于连续灾年和北方对劳动力的需求，南方黑人开始移居到北方，特别是东北城市。最重要的是许多学校被要求对黑人开放。黑人们得到接受正规教育和学习规范英语的机会。在社会活动中，他们也开始与白人融合。因此，这一时期的黑人克里奥尔语处于解体化过程。巨大的变化出现在语法和词汇上。对其他人来说，黑人英语比之前更好理解了。

　　语言学习中存在着母语向非母语的转移现象，即语言迁移。迁移可分为正迁移和负迁移。正迁移是指一种学习对另一种学习产生积极影响的迁移；负迁移是指一种学习对另一种学习产生消极影响的迁移。当母语的表达形式与目的语相同或相似时，有助于目的语学习习惯的形成，就促进学习。当母语对非母语学习起阻碍作用时，这种阻碍就叫母语干扰。黑人被当作奴隶最初被贩卖到美洲时，基本上已经熟练掌握了他们各自的母语，他们的非洲母语的语法已经根深蒂固。当他们学说白人的英语时，母语的语法规则与思维习惯就自然地迁移到英语的学习中，正迁移和负迁移都同时存在。

现在的美国黑人英语和当时的克里奥尔语相比较已经是变化了许多。尽管美国黑人英语保持一定的自身特征，但从早期的克里奥尔语到旧黑人英语以至到当下黑人英语却无不留下标准英语影响的烙印。这种变化是符合语言发展规律的，因为民族在相互接触中，其语言势必互相影响，并且随着各国各民族经济、文化的交往越来越频繁，一些交际功能大的民族语言越来越多地用于族际交往，越来越普及。一国之内小民族使用大民族的语言，一个区域内小国使用大国的语言已成为一种趋势。在社会中处于较高地位的民族对社会地位较低的民族的语言所起的影响更大些。

六、美国黑人英语与英语变体

黑人英语是一种社会方言，其使用者遍及美国大部分黑人社区。据 Dillard 调查，大约有 80% 的黑人使用黑人英语。（颜治强，2002：34）

因为在语音、语法等方面不同于美国的标准英语，黑人英语曾被视为次等的或低劣的英语变体。这在语言学上是没有根据的。黑人英语具有其鲜明而系统的语言特征。但这些特征不是混乱的和任意的，它们呈现出一定的规律性。

黑人英语到底是一种方言（dialect）还是一种语言（language）？有人认为，（方久华、熊敦礼，2003：114）"美国黑人英语本质上是一种独立的体系。它与标准英语之间的关系远比一种方言与其标准语之间的关系复杂得多。应该将它作为一种独立的语言进行研究"。

另一种观点则认为黑人英语是一种语言及副语言的特征。这种特征在一个同心的连续体上代表了西非人、加勒比人，以及从非洲被贩运到美国的黑奴的后裔的交际能力。它包括黑人，尤其是那些被迫接受殖民环境的黑人的各种惯用语、行话、黑话、个人语言，以及社会方言。（方久华、熊敦礼，2003：111-112）

过去，西方许多语言学家常把黑人英语有别于标准美国英语这一事实归咎于黑人种族低劣，他们拒绝将黑人英语作为英语的一种变体进行考察与研究。今天情况不同了。许多语言学家认为：黑人英语的确有别于白人英语，但这丝毫不能说明黑人种族比白人低劣卑贱，因此不能以种族歧视的偏见去探讨黑人英语，而应将黑人英语作为一种独特的英语变体进行研究。

黑人英语作为英语的一个子系统，它有自己特殊的语言规则，又继承了很多南方方言和其他英语方言的语音、词形和句法特征。黑人英语虽不规范，但并非杂乱无章，它有一些与标准英语不同的语法规则。

Labov（1972）等把黑人英语划定为标准英语的一种变体，他们认为无论千变万化，黑人英语的核心语音语法规则都和标准英语保持一致。那么何为语言变体呢？语言在社会语言学家的眼中是一个"有序的异质体"。"有序"使得社会交往正常进行；"异质"则让同在一个社会中的芸芸众生"人以群分"。中国人说中国话，美国人说美国话，这就是"有序"。各个局部的"有序"就形成了以言语差异为显著区别特征的不同的言语社团或者叫作言语共同体（speech community）；在一个"有序"的言语社团中，又可以不同时代、不同地域、不同行业、不同身份、不同性别等标准区分出不同的"变体"，这就是所谓的"异质"。

根据"异质"程度的差异，社会语言学把语言的异质变化区分为三个层次：

语言变异（linguistic variation）——整体宏观变迁，比如唐朝的中国话跟宋朝的中国话；

语言变体（linguistic variety）——局部宏观差异，比如当代汉语中北方话跟南方话；

语言变项（linguistic variable）——局部微观调整，比如我国南方话中下层女性使用的"小姐妹"。

黑人英语已是成熟而又重要的英语变体之一，随着黑人地位的上升，黑人英语在社会中将发挥着越来越大的作用。

七、美国黑人英语对标准美国英语的影响

第一次世界大战后，美国劳动力出现短缺，很多非洲裔黑人来到北部的工厂，他们的文化也开始影响白人文化，特别是源于非洲的音乐词汇。19世纪早期，美国出现了jazz、blues、cakewalk、jitterbug、break dancing等音乐形式。20世纪50年代rock and roll风靡美国，非洲裔美国黑人的音乐受到越来越多的关注和喜爱，Michael Jackson的专辑 *Bad* 一经发行就受到大众的追捧和欢迎。非洲裔美国黑人的日常用语也受到白人的喜爱，如apple（money）、blood（brother）、bread（money）、man（fellow）、babe（baby）等已进入标准美国英语。Sambo原指黑人奴隶，现在经常出现在儿童故事里。John原指受剥削的人，现在用来指花花公子。Okay and uh等词也受到白人的喜爱。非洲裔美国黑人英语词汇对美国文学的影响也很显著。很多非洲裔美国黑人作家的语言深深影响了白人文学、文化。Langston Hughes是比较杰出的诗人，他用非洲裔美国黑人英语创作诗歌来表现黑人的处境和生活方式。他的作品中的语言深

受读者的喜爱。以下诗节选自他的 *Weary Blue*（1925）。

> Thump, thump, thump, went his foot on the floor.
> He played a few chords then he sang some more——
> "I got the Weary Blue
> And I can't be satisfied.
> Got the Weary Blues
> And can't be satisfied——
> I ain't happy no mo'
> And I wish that I had died."

这个诗节中，blues 是非洲裔美国黑人英语词汇，同时也是一种源于非洲裔黑人的一种音乐形式。作者通过 blues 来表达对自由、平等和简单生活的渴望，展现了其语言词汇、句法特色。总之，非洲裔美国黑人英语的词汇对美国的音乐、日常生活、文学都有广泛而深刻的影响，而且深受白人的喜爱。

在标准美国英语中，很多词汇源于非洲裔美国黑人英语，如 awesome，neat，tubular，vicious，phoney，rooty，toot，lam，sock，bug，dirt，babe，guy，okay 等。一些词汇源于美国南方，如 before-day，call the hogs，bo-dollar，outside baby。另外，很多标准英语词汇在非洲裔黑人赋予它们新的意义后又进入标准英语，如 rap。18 世纪中期，rap 的意思是责备或反驳。19 世纪晚期，它通常被用于一些短语。例如，to take the rap 意思是接受指责（被骂，是罪魁祸首）。南北战争后，美国黑人使用该词来谴责白人，试图取得与其平等的地位。Cookie 开始指 sweet biscuit，非洲裔黑人赋予它新的含义——pretty woman that are attractive to men。一些词汇，如 apple、blood、bread、babe、cool/hot 等，经过黑人的使用都获得了新的意义。

非洲裔美国黑人英语词汇填补了标准英语表达的空白，使后者更加生动、形象。以强烈节奏为鲜明特色的爵士乐产生于美国南部黑人聚居地。20 世纪 30 年代，爵士乐开始流行，黑人用 hot 来形容它，后来用 cool 来形容它。随着爵士乐的发展，cool 一词的意思更加形象、生动，成为 handsome，wonderful 的同义词。

八、美国黑人英语的贡献

作为一种英语变体或社会方言，黑人英语自然同标准英语有差别，但同时它又与日俱增地影响和丰富后者的词汇和用法。举 cool 一词为例。Cool 一词原本属于正宗盎格鲁-撒克逊标准英语的基本词汇，含义为"凉快、冷静"。用于赞扬喝彩，相当于"好极了、绝了"以及"酷"等的新义，则始于20世纪50年代美国音乐界的黑人英语。Cool一词的新义现早已跳出了黑人英语的小圈子，转而代表一种精神和心态，赞扬一切标新立异的思想和与众不同的形象被广泛使用在大众英语中。20世纪的90年代被人戏称为cool再生的时代。

在当今美国，cool不仅是青少年首选的颂扬之词，而且越来越频繁地出现在日常会话、歌坛影视、报刊杂志、商业广告里，无论是新媒体还是旧媒体都广泛使用cool这个典型的黑人英语词。Cool词义的历史演变和广为流行使用，从一个侧面反映了黑人英语对标准英语的影响。

黑人所用的英语对美国社会的影响正逐渐增大。黑人在娱乐业占有越来越重要的地位。黑人戏剧短小精悍、妙趣横生，经常在媒体上播出。好莱坞大片黑人英语可谓是大行其道。黑人歌星更是起到了推波助澜的作用，其曲目中常使用黑人英语词汇。黑人表演业的崛起，把黑人英语带给了千家万户。黑人英语的影响集中反映在词汇上，特别是黑人占优势的娱乐圈里流传出来的时髦词。如果单从jazz这个英文单词的汉语音译"爵士"来看，许多不明内涵的中国人往往会把爵士乐当成是一种高雅的，属于上流社会的音乐，其实并不尽然。这种以大段即兴演奏为标杆的音乐，事实上与美国的黑人文化密不可分。Jazz（爵士乐）的发源地，就是美国南部新奥尔良的黑人聚集区，而早期生活在那里，备受白人奴役的非裔黑人的生活经验，则是爵士乐最早的灵感来源。与jazz一同被接受的词语还有blues（布鲁斯）、cakewalk（步态舞）、break dancing（霹雳舞）、jitterbug（吉特巴舞）、rock n' roll（摇滚舞）等，它们早已成为标准英语而扎根于美国文化之中，并在美国社会生活中占有一席之地。

很多历史经验证明，对少数民族的文化越是压制，它就越是发展，或早或晚会争取到自己应有的地位。19世纪的美国黑人文化无疑是受压迫最深的文化，然而，恰恰是这一文化中的爵士乐改变了美国的音乐，继而又改变了整个世界的音乐。美国黑人音乐家用的很多词语受到了白人的认同和喜爱，如a solid sender指an outstanding person；a hip chick指的是a beautiful woman；hall a ball表示to enjoy yourself；hip表示wise, sophisticated。那些常去夜总会的jazz babies（爵士迷），包括flappers（女爵士迷）和sheiks（男爵士迷）在他们的言谈中总要说上几个Jive talk（黑人南方家乡话）以显示他们的潇洒和时髦；报道爵士乐演出的记者们出于同一目的也在他们的专栏里加上几个Jive talk，这使得Jive talk飞速传播，并进入了美国英语。美国白人乐队也演唱黑人音乐，如白人组合"后街男孩"的歌曲 *It ain't no life, I won't cry no more*。

全美的各种体育比赛和体育联赛中，黑人球员、运动员占了一大半。美国拥有篮球神话之称的黑人篮球巨星迈克尔·乔丹，正是他将 NBA 推介给了全世界。美国黑人还在田径、垒球、棒球、网球、拳击等项目上拥有众多的黑人世界冠军。青少年对球星、冠军十分崇拜，因此也就模仿他们的一言一行。

美国的普通大众，特别是草根阶层很容易认同黑人英语所表现出的愤世嫉俗和对传统的蔑视，像 baby kisser（政客）、fat cat（富人）等早已经成了美国英语里的时髦词汇。在美国社会，只要深入民间，就会发现不仅 awesome、babe、chick、dude、get busted 之类黑人英语词汇是美国青少年的口头禅，而且像 apple（苹果—钱）、blood（血—兄弟）、bread（面包—钱）、man（男人—伙计、）hot（热—好极了）、babe（婴儿—年轻女子）、cookie（小甜饼—漂亮女子）这样典型的黑人词汇，也往往被看成标准英语而得到肯定。19 世纪和 20 世纪的黑人小说家在寻求素材和创作时把注意力投向了黑人族群的文化之根，同时在他们的作品中都大量采用了黑人白话。

美国英语里的许多俚语表达法来源于黑人英语。美国黑人英语中丰富多彩的俚语已经成为美国英语的一大特色。例如：schlub（蠢货）、schnook（笨蛋）、bunk（假话）、bunglesome（拙劣的）、ass-kisser（马屁精）、wonk（死记硬背的学生）、yardbird（未经训练的入伍新兵）等。

美国黑人英语对美国语言影响同样富有说服力的是黑人的许多谚语、格言在美国社会中的传诵与引用。例如：The blacker the berry, the sweeter the juice.（她既成熟，又逗人喜爱。）You aren't got a pot to piss in or a window to throw it out of.（你已穷困潦倒。）If I tell you a hen hip snuff, look under its wing and find a whole box.（我说的是真的，完全可靠。）You never miss yo water till yo well run dry.（你不口渴时是想不到水的。）这些富有代表性的警句、格言生动形象，寓意深刻，生活气息浓厚，是黑人智慧的结晶。

在美国政治生活和对外交往中有句著名的谚语，即 speak softly and carry a big stick（轻声讲话，拿着一根大棒），它也是源于黑人英语。美国前总统罗斯福在一次会上谈论美国的对外关系时说："Speak softly and carry a big stick, you will go far."（轻声讲话，拿着一根大棒，你就能征战全球。）这就是人们所熟知的美国"大棒"（big stick）政策。

美国黑人英语中的词汇相当奇特。黑人英语词汇的产生绝非因为英语已有的词汇不够丰富，而是缘于黑人在美国的特殊经历，所以黑人词汇蕴藏着深刻的社会内涵。黑人英语词汇丰富了英语的表达。黑人英语的词汇还在不断地推陈出新。

黑人文化丰富了美国英语。黑人的方言在与英语的长期交往中形成了自己独特的风格，它既为英语输出了丰富的营养，同时又从英语中吸取新鲜血液，进而形成了美国最大的移民群体语言——黑人英语。黑人英语是美国英语的一部分。具有独特风格的美国黑人英语与白人的标准英语一起使美国文化更加丰富多彩。

随着黑人教育水平的提高，以及黑人英语对美国社会各领域影响力的进一步增强，美国黑人在美国社会的发言权和话语权也越来越大，这必定促进美国黑人社会地位的进一步提高，这种迹象现在已经凸显出来了。如今美国联邦和地方政府已经有越来越多的黑人被选入各级权力机构甚至最高权力机构。随着美国黑人社会地位的提高和接受教育水平的不断上升，黑人英语还将会继续对美国甚至世界英语的发展产生深远的影响。

参考文献

[1] Algeo, J. Fifty Years among the New Words: A Dictionary of Neologisms[M]. Cambridge: Cambridge University Press, 1941.

[2] Allen, J. & J. Turner. We the People, An Atlas of American Ethnic Diversity[M]. New York: McMillan Company,1988.

[3] Green, L.G. Afro-American English[M].Cambridge: Cambridge University Press, 2000.

[4] Labov, W. Language in the Inner Circle: Studies in the Black English Vernacular[M].Philadelphia: University of Pennsylvania Press, 1972.

[5] Melville, H. On American Bloodline[J].The Pacific Historic Studies,1982(5):57-62.

[6] Mencken, H. The American Language, an Inquiry into the Development of English in the United States[M].New York: A.A.Knopf, 1936.

[7] Russell, R. Spoken Soul: The Story of Black English[M].New York: John Wiley and Sons, Inc., 2000.

[8] Smitherman, G. Talking and Testifying: The Language of Black American[M]. Detroit: Wayne State University Press,1977.

[9] Tottie, G. An Introduction to American English[M]. 北京：北京大学出版社，2005.

[10] Wentworth, H. & S.B.Flexner. Dictionary of American Slang[M].New York: Thomasy Growell Publishers,1975.

[11] 蔡昌卓. 美国英语史 [M]. 北京：北京大学出版社，2002.

[12] 陈安. 新英汉美国小百科 [M]. 上海：上海译文出版社，2000.

[13] 陈原. 语言和人 [M]. 北京：商务印书馆，2003.

[14] 董小川. 美利坚民族认同问题探究 [J]. 东北师范大学学报，2006（1）：48-55.

[15] 董小川. 美国文化概论 [M]. 北京：人民出版社，2006.

[16] 端木一万. 美国社会文化透视 [M]. 南京：南京大学出版社，1999.

[17] 方久华，熊敦礼. 美国黑人英语语言特点探讨 [J]. 华中科技大学学报，2003（4）：111-114.

[18] 冯利. 黑人英语与标准美国英语差异之探讨 [J]. 内蒙古农业大学学报，2009（4）：205-206.

[19] 侯维瑞. 英国英语与美国英语 [M]. 上海：上海外语教育出版社，1992.

[20] 刘元珍. 美国社会透视 [M]. 东营：石油大学出版社，1995.

[21] 牛道生. 英语与世界 [M]. 北京：中国社会科学出版社，2008.

[22] 潘绍嶂. 黑人英语中的否定句 [J]. 外语教学与研究，1990（4）：17-21.

[23] 潘绍嶂. 美国黑人英语中 be 的语法特点 [J]. 山东外语教学，1992（1-2）：105-108.

[24] 王恩铭. 当代美国社会与文化 [M]. 上海：上海外语教育出版社，1997.

[25] 王威. 现代英语中美国不同种族称呼的探讨 [J]. 苏州大学学报，2006（4）：88-92.

[26] 王妍. 美国英语中黑人英语变体的研究 [J]. 江苏外语教学研究，2005（1）：64-67.

[27] 熊金才，李淑芬. 论美国英语的独立趋势及其影响 [J]. 外语教学，1995（2）：24-29.

[28] 许国璋. 许国璋文集 [M]. 北京：商务印书馆，1997.

[29] 颜治强. 世界英语概论 [M]. 北京：外语教学与研究出版社，2002.

[30] 杨玉圣. 从移民的视角探索美国 [J]. 美国研究，1993（1）：153-161.

[31] 郑立信，顾嘉祖. 美国英语与美国文化 [M]. 长沙：湖南教育出版社，1993.

第六篇　美利坚与联邦

全球人口的 40% 生活在联邦制国家。28 个实行联邦制政府体系的国家不仅包括美国这样的超级大国、强国，也包括密克罗尼西亚与圣基茨和尼维斯这样不发达的小岛国。

在当今世界近 200 个国家中，联邦制国家有 20 多个，除了众所周知的美国和俄罗斯外，还包括加拿大、澳大利亚、印度、巴基斯坦、墨西哥、巴西、阿根廷、德国、奥地利、比利时、瑞士、尼日利亚、苏丹等。全球 10 个人口最多国家中的 6 个以及 10 个面积最大国家中的 8 个都是联邦制国家。多中心、自治、非集权，尊重多样性，保护少数以及维护国家的统一是联邦制的基本特征。实行联邦制的国家都是同一种政治制度的联合体。例如，前苏联、解体前的南斯拉夫曾是社会主义的联邦制。现有的联邦制国家都是资本主义联邦制。联邦制的优点：既像一个小国那样自由和幸福，又像一个大国那样光荣和强大。

一、"联邦" 与 "邦联"

（一）何谓 "联邦"

《现代汉语词典》（汉英双语）对 "联邦" 的释义为："由若干具有国家性质的行政区域（有国、邦、州等不同名称）联合而成的统一国家，各行政区域有自己的宪法、立法机关和政府，联邦也有统一的宪法、立法机关和政府。国际交往以联邦政府为主体。"（federation; union; commonwealth; union of administrative regions with the power of a state, each administrative region having its own constitution, legislative body, and government, but the union also having its central constitution, legislative body and government. International contacts are made mainly with the federal government.）

《新世纪汉英大词典》在"联邦"这一词条下面的英语释义为"federation; union; commonwealth"; "联邦共和国"中"联邦"的英语释义为"federal/federated"。

(二)何谓"邦联"

《现代汉语词典》(汉英双语)对"联邦"的释义为:"两个或两个以上的国家为了达到某些共同的目的而组成的联合体。邦联的成员国仍保留完全的独立主权,只是在军事、外交等方面采取某些联合行动。"(confederation; league or alliance formed by two or more countries for some common purposes, with member countries maintaining total independence and sovereignty, but taking certain combined actions in defense and foreign affairs.)

邦联是"国家的联合",而联邦是"联合的国家"。

(三)例   句

下面为《新世纪汉英大词典》在其附录中对世界各国家和地区全称中所使用的"union, federal, federated, federative, federation, confederation, commonwealth"的汉语释义:

1.Union

The Union of Myanmar(缅甸联邦)是多民族的国家,全国分7个省和7个邦。省是缅族主要聚居区,"邦"多为少数民族聚居地。旧首都是仰光,新首都是内比都。

2.Federal

The Federal Republic of Germany(德意志联邦共和国)

The Federal Democratic Republic of Ethiopia(埃塞俄比亚联邦民主共和国)

埃塞俄比亚人口为5 800万,全国共有80多个民族,按照各民族聚居的情况,全国划分为9个州和2个特别市。

埃塞俄比亚联邦民主共和国(The Federal Democratic Republic of Ethiopia),是位于非洲东北部的一个内陆大国。埃塞俄比亚这个国家皇帝被推下台后,成为共和国,厄立特里亚分离出去后,为了国内各部族的权利分享,只好把国家改建成了联邦。

The Federal Islamic Republic of the Comoros(科摩罗伊斯兰联邦共和国)在西方殖民者入侵之前长期由阿拉伯苏丹统治。1912年科摩罗正式沦为法国殖民地,1946年成为法"海外领地",1961年取得内部自治。1975年7月6日独立,成立"科摩罗共和国",1978年10月22日改国名为"科摩罗伊斯兰联邦共和国"。

The Federal Republic of Nigeria(尼日利亚联邦共和国)

3.Federation

The Russian Federation（俄罗斯联邦）

The Federation of Saint Kitts and Nevis（圣基茨和尼维斯联邦）

4.Federated

The Federated States of Micronesia（密克罗尼西亚联邦）

5.Federative

The Federative Republic of Brazil（巴西联邦共和国）

6.Confederation

The Swiss Confederation（瑞士联邦）

7.Commonwealth

The Commonwealth of Australia（澳大利亚联邦）

The Commonwealth of the Northern Mariana Islands（U.S.）（北马里亚纳群岛自由联邦 [美]）

The Commonwealth of Puerto Rico（U.S.）（波多黎各自由联邦 [美]）

多米尼克国（The Commonwealth of Dominica）（曾译"多米尼加联邦"，由于英语 commonwealth 为多义词，故改译为"多米尼克国"。）多米尼克于 1918 年 11 月 3 日宣布独立，属于英联邦国家。

多米尼加共和国：The Dominican Republic，来源于 Dominican，在西班牙语中为"星期天、休息日"的意思。哥伦布于 15 世纪末的一个星期日到此，故名。

虽然都是西印度群岛上的岛国，但并不是同一个岛，更不是同一个国家。一个原来是英国属地，一个原来是西班牙属地。

在英语、西班牙语、法语、俄语甚至阿拉伯语中，The Commonwealth of Dominica 中的 Dominica 都为名词，而 The Dominican Republic 国名中的 Dominican 都采用形容词形式。为此，在西文中两个"多米尼加"在书写上不会产生混淆现象。我国有关部门经研究决定，自 1993 年 10 月起将 The Commonwealth of Dominica 中的"Dominica"按其英语发音改译为"多米尼克"，以避免在加勒比地区出现两个"多米尼加"的重名现象。

多米尼加共和国的英文拼写为 Dominican Republic。中文译名最初是从英语 Dominican 一词中省去形容词 -n 而译作"多米尼加共和国"。在国际上，为了避免产生混淆现象，The Dominican Republic 一律全称而无简称形式，而 The Commonwealth of Dominica 除全称外，在适当场合可简称为 Dominica。

（四）State——"邦"或是"州"

《新世纪汉英大词典》和《现代汉语词典》（汉英双语）对"邦"的释义均为：nation，state country。英语中的 state 一词，既可表示"邦"也可表示"州"。

The United States of America（美利坚合众国）中的"States"其实也可以翻译成"邦"。根据《现代汉语词典》（2002：56）"邦"即"国" = nation，state，country。"美利坚合众国"也就是"美利坚合众邦"。美国是一个从邦联制到联邦制演变的国家。

State 的含义在美国历史上却有极大的差别，这与 18 世纪美国的立国特点密不可分。在 1776—1781 年的独立战争中，13 个殖民地演变为 13 个独立自主的共和国，并以此为基础组成以邦联制为基础的合众国。《美国宣言》生效后，美国成为联邦制共和国，state 在邦联制下的主权国家地位被改变，由"邦"演变为联邦制下的基本政治实体"州"。因此，在邦联制下的 state 应翻译为"邦"，在联邦制下的 state 应翻译为"州"。

美国的《独立宣言》的英文全称为 The Unanimous Declaration of the Thirteen united States of America，注意 united 为小写。《独立宣言》颁布之后，北美出现了 13 个各自独立的 states（国家），但其内部政治模式与殖民地时期仍无多大差别，state 可称为"邦"，而北美这时尚无一个统一的国家及其名称。

二、单一制—联邦制—邦联制

（一）国家的结构形式

国家的结构形式可分为三种类型，即单一制、联邦制和邦联制。"邦联"与"联邦"，表面上看只是字序的颠倒，但事实上，两个概念所包含的内容确有着本质的不同。"邦联"和"联邦"从本质上讲都属于国家的政治体制，但二者在结构上都有极大的差别。"邦联制"就是"国中有国"。邦联的组成分子几乎都有国家的独立性，例如，解体以前的苏联由许多独立的国家组合成一个"邦联"的形式，各有各的国号，各有各的国旗，外交、国防均可自主，司法有终审权，可以拥有自己的军队，也可以为联合国会员。前苏联的乌克兰和白俄罗斯就分别在联合国占有一席之地。乌克兰和白俄罗斯为 1945 年联合国的创始国之一。

"邦联"只是主权国家的联合，而"联邦"则是一个完整的国家。英文中用"confederation"表示"邦联"，而"federation"则是表示"联邦"。

"邦联"是两个或两个以上的国家为了达到共同目的而组成的一种国家联合。在邦联中，各成员国保持自己的主权以及内政和外交上的独立。"邦联是各个独立主权国家通过一个特定时期缔结的条约或协议而联合在一起的松散联盟。"经由邦联而建立起的联邦制国家有美国、德国、瑞士等。历史上，1707 年的英格兰和苏格兰曾是邦联。

　　1777 年 11 月 15 日，在美国独立战争的进程中，出于对英战争的需要，第二届大陆会议通过了"邦联和永久性联合条例"，即《邦联条例》。《邦联条例》共 13 条，第一条就声明"《独立宣言》发表之后出现的政治联盟（邦联）就叫美利坚合众国，它是永久性的联合。"《邦联条例》生效之后，地方机构仍可称为"邦"，美国国名可合法地称为 The United States of America，但其国体为"联盟"，可以"邦联"称之。1787 年，美国制定了一部新宪法——《联邦宪法》，开始从邦联制变为联邦制。《联邦宪法》序言的开篇中有这样一句话："We, the people of United States."《联邦宪法》生效后，国名仍为"美利坚合众国"，但地方机构丧失作为独立国家的主权，可称为"州"。

　　1781 年美国通过并颁布了 *The Articles of Confederation*（《邦联条例》），成为取代英国的合法主权实体，但 1776—1787 年的美利坚合众国实际上是一种比较松散的国家联合体，因为她没有强有力的中央集权。从 1776 年 7 月《独立宣言》宣布独立之日起，state 是最基本的、最重要的政治单位，《邦联条例》生效也未改变当时美利坚人的国家概念，无论在情感上，还是在政策上，都未能使各邦的联系更紧密。美国史学家布尔斯汀一针见血地指出，在美利坚合众国这个联盟里，state 的概念是如此的根深蒂固，以至于 confederation 与各 state 之间情牵一线、若即若离。这也导致了美利坚合众国这一新生国家，因邦联政府的软弱无能，而在世界各国眼中形同乞丐。"邦联政府是一个头脑听从四肢指挥的怪物。"这极大地辜负了殖民地人民长期追求 The Union of States 的政治热情。

　　1789 年 4 月 30 日，华盛顿就任美国联邦的第一任总统，标志着美国完成了由邦联到联邦的转变，由"脑袋听从四肢指挥"邦联制演变为"四肢听从脑袋指挥"的联邦制。从邦联到联邦是美国政治制度史上的一次重大变革。在 18 世纪末期，当时绝大多数国家（至少是大国）是中央集权的专制主义国家，而唯有美国创造了"联邦制"。"联邦制"标志着一个完全意义上的、新的现代主权国家的诞生。

　　邦联制不具有稳固性，无论其存在的历史或长或短，最终都是人类历史上不成功的尝试。"联邦"则是由几个成员国（邦或州）联合而成的统一国家。各成员国（邦或州）将主权交给联邦的最高权力机构，一般只保留一定的自治权。"联邦"是国际交往中的主体。与联邦不同，邦联不是国家主体，它本身没有最高立法机关和行政机关，也没有统一的军队、国籍等。一个邦联中的各成员国各自保持内政、外交上的独立，是不同的主权国家。

1787 年至现在的美国，1922—1990 年的苏联，1949 年成立的德意志联邦共和国，以及解体前的南斯拉夫联邦共和国等都是"联邦"。此外，独联体、加勒比共同体、欧盟都可视为"邦联"。当今世界一些国家为了共同的经历利益，组成了"邦联"，如：欧共体、独联体、东非共同体、西非共同体等，都是邦联制的组织形式。

"邦联"和"联邦"是一种时代的产物，这两种国家体制随着政治经济的发展，政府与非政府交往的日益增多，将会自行消失或被新的体制所替代。

（二）联邦制与联盟制

"联邦制"与"邦联制"和"联盟制"国家是有区别的。联邦制国家中联邦政府（中央政府）权力比较集中。"邦联制"是两个或两个以上的主权国家为了特定的目的而结成国家联合的一种组织形式。"联盟制"国家是指由两个或更多的国家合并成一个单一的新国家，或者若干主权国家的同盟，中央政府的权力有限。英文中一般用 union 来表述"联盟制"国家，它与 confederation（邦联）相近。1922—1990 年的苏联（The Soviet Union）就是这样一个"联盟制"国家。苏联的全称为"苏维埃社会主义共和国联盟"，英文为"Union of Soviet Socialist Republics"。1990 年 6 月 12 日，俄联邦率先发表主权宣言，宣布脱离苏联独立。独立之后的俄罗斯是一个由 89 个主体、100 多个民族组成的多民族的联邦制国家。根据宪法，俄罗斯的国家权力由俄联邦总统、联邦议会、联邦政府和联邦法院行使。

邦联制不是真正意义上的国家结构形式，邦联制国家也不是真正意义上的近现代国家，但它的确在历史上存在过。后来，随着各成员国政治、经济联系的加强，邦联制国家逐渐解体或被联邦制的国家所取代。

美国常被视为典型的联邦制国家，但其构成单位是"州"，而不是民族国家意义上的享有国家主权的"国"。因此，我们不能说今天的美国作为联邦制国家是由若干个享有国家主权的成员国所组成的。

参考文献

[1] 褚乐平 . 联邦党人与反联邦党人关于宪法批准问题的争论 [J]. 史学月刊，2003（7）：60-66.

[2] 董晓璐 .《邦联条例》与早期美国政治体制的确立 [J]. 文学选刊，2011（4）：61-62.

[3] 房乐宪 . 邦联主义与欧洲一体化 [J]. 欧洲研究，2003（4）：73-85.

[4] 侯学华. 邦联国会在美国宪政体制变动中的作用 [J]. 贵州社会科学，2011（9）：112-118.

[5] 惠宇主编. 新世纪汉英大词典 [Z]. 北京：外语教学与研究出版社，2003.

[6] 马万利. 反联邦党人与1787年费城制宪会议 [J]. 中国政法大学学报，2008（1）：103-111.

[7] 现代汉语词典（汉英双语）[Z]. 北京：外语教学与研究出版社，2002.

[8] 苑晓光. "联邦"还是"邦联" [J]. 科教文汇，2006（7）：113-115.

[9] 郑宗太，林书渊. 从邦联到联邦 [J]. 福建广播电视大学学报，2006（3）：24-27.

[10] 朱政梅. 试析美国从邦联制到联邦制的转变 [J]. 苏州大学学报（哲学社会科学版），1989（1）：132-134.

第七篇　美国英语中的"白宫用语"

美国总统既是美利坚合众国国家元首又是政府首脑，同时也是美军的总司令。另外，美国总统还享有立法创议权和对国会通过的法案进行否决的权限。美国总统对国家政治、外交、经济、军事、社会等方面所起的举足轻重的影响在新闻报道中得到充分的体现。

一、"总统名 + doctrine"词

在美国政治中，总统扮演着最重要的核心角色，集内政、外交、行政、立法、司法、军事大权于一身。随着美国总统的更迭，美国政局不断变幻，不但一朝天子一朝臣，而且一朝天子一朝政，每个总统都有自己的一套班子和一套政策。因此，就有了以总统名字命名的各种主义（doctrine）。美国英语中用"总统的名字 + doctrine"的公式来概括和说明美国外交政策或政策主张的某些特征或新动向，将历任美国总统提出的施政蓝图，冠以"doctrine"，成为影响美国外交政策的一些基点。这些不同历史阶段以总统名字命名的"doctrine"往往成为当时美国对外政策的重要指导原则，影响当时甚至其后很长一段时期美国整体的或某一领域的对外政策。

一个主义就像一个武器库。它的使用是出于战略的考虑。在美国历史上，以总统名字命名、而且影响巨大的"doctrine"还不在少数。例如：

19 世纪 20 年代，欧洲"神圣同盟"试图干预美洲，进行领土扩张。为此，当时的门罗（James Monroe）总统在致国会的咨文中提出了著名的"门罗宣言"。称"美洲是美洲人的"，实质是"美洲是美国人的美洲"。这些原则经过引申和发展，最终被命名为 Monroe Doctrine（门罗主义），长期指导着美国对拉美各国的政策。

20 世纪初，威尔逊（Woodrow Wilson）总统提出了他称之为"世界和平纲领"的主张，阐述了美国对于第一次世界大战后世界秩序的构想，力图建立起一个新的

国际体制，这就是 Wilson Doctrine（威尔逊主义）的主旨。

提起冷战，我们就不能不提 Truman Doctrine（杜鲁门主义）。它的实质就是美国必须遏制所谓的共产主义扩张。这是美国政府实行遏制政策的开始，也是美苏两国长期冷战的开始。

Eisenhower Doctrine（艾森豪威尔主义）的实质是要求国会在必要的时候动用美国军队反对所谓共产主义的侵略，以保护那些请求援助的国家的领土完整和政治独立。

20 世纪 60 年代末期，尼克松（Nixon）看到美国因越战等问题使美国的实力大大削弱，所以他对美国的全球战略做了由进攻转入防守的重要调整，避免再参加越战式的地面战争，这一战略变化被称为 Nixon Doctrine（尼克松主义）。尼克松主义的出台，标志着美国已经开始进行重大战略调整，从战略进攻态势转为战略收缩。

卡特（Carter）政府对外极力推行人权外交，试图用政治和经济手段来对抗苏联。然而，随着苏联入侵阿富汗，卡特政府被迫调整对外政策。1980 年 1 月，卡特总统在向国会发表的国情咨文中警告：任何外来力量企图控制波斯湾地区的尝试将被视为对美国重大利益的侵犯，美国将采取一切必要的手段，包括动用军事力量加以回击。这就是后来所称的 Carter Doctrine（卡特主义）。

Reagan Doctrine（里根主义）的核心是遏制苏联扩张主义，防止苏联渗透。而 Clinton Doctrine（克林顿主义）的核心则是公开宣扬"人权高于主权"，打着"维护人权"的幌子干涉别国内政。

在经历了单边主义、"9·11 事件"、阿富汗战争和伊拉克战争之后，Bush Doctrine（布什主义）正式登上历史舞台。所谓"布什主义"，是指布什政府从共和党保守主义和现实主义思想出发，以实力为手段、反恐为重点、单边主义和先发制人为核心、追求国家利益和"绝对安全"进而称霸世界。

以"美国总统名字＋ -ism（主义）"合成的词，则用来指内政尤指经济政策或主张。例如：Jeffersonianism（杰斐逊主义）是杰斐逊总统的政治原则和思想，指相信国家的权力、严格解释联邦宪法和相信平民等的原则、思想和政策主张；Carterism（卡特主义），指卡特在国内推行的一套自由派或中间偏左的政策；Reaganism（里根主义）指里根提出的如减税、小政府、自由企业、控制货币供应等的经济政策；Clintonism（克林顿主义），指克林顿在竞选中和执政之初提出对国内经济进行改革的主张。

二、"New ＋施政蓝图"词

历任美国总统都曾提出自己的施政蓝图，如：塔夫脱（Taft）的 Dollar

Diplomacy（金元外交），西奥多·罗斯福的 Big Stick Policy（大棒政策），杜鲁门的 Fair Deal（公平施政），艾森豪威尔的 Modern Republicanism（现代共和党主义），约翰逊的 Great Society（伟大社会），里根的 Containment（遏制政策），克林顿的 Engagement（接触政策），以及小布什一度实行的 Congagement（遏制—接触战略）、Unilateralism（单边主义）和后来的 Pre-emption（先发制人）的打击战略。

历任的美国总统们在施政蓝图上几乎都搞过创"New"：例如：

New Freedom（新自由）是威尔逊在 1912 年总统竞选运动中提出的口号，意为政府要对大企业的垄断进行干预，以保护小企业的民主权利。

New Nationalism（新国家主义）是西奥多·罗斯福（Theodore Roosevelt）总统在 1910 年提出国家利益高于集团利益和个人利益的进步党的计划，旨在使共和党走更加开明的道路。

始于 1929 年的大萧条造成美国经济崩溃的情势使得富兰克林·罗斯福（Franklin D.Roosevelt）宣称美国必须采取与过去截然不同的新的方案来解决国家危机。这就是罗斯福 New Deal（新政）名称的由来。New Deal 之所以为"New"，主要系罗斯福政府空前扩大了它在经济领域的角色，大政府理念成为解决一切政治、经济、社会问题的答案。罗斯福新政的核心是三个 R：Reform（改革）、Recovery（复兴）和 Relief（救济）。

Frontier（边疆）是美国历史的特产。美国之成为美国，离开 frontier 的推进或领土的扩展，是无从谈起的。美国人倾向于把美国历史上的边疆经历、边疆生活及边疆上生活的人，看作是他们基本价值观念的来源。多少年来，frontier spirit（边疆精神）一直是美国人引以为自豪的民族文化特征的一个重要成分。New Frontier（新边疆）是 1960 年美国大选时肯尼迪（Kennedy）提出的竞选口号。他要用拓荒精神来处理国内外问题，并决心在宇宙空间赶超前苏联。肯尼迪的这个 New 字是仿富兰克林·罗斯福的 New Deal（新政）的 new 字，frontier 使美国人缅怀起祖先开国时的拓荒精神。

New era（新时代）是尼克松总统提出的施政纲领。尼克松和里根都曾先后提出过 New Federalism（新联邦主义）这个想法。New Federalism 的实质就是想将联邦政府的巨大负担转嫁给州政府。卡特执政期提出了 New Populism（新平民主义），里根执政期间执行的是 New Conservatism（新保守主义）。

New Paradigm（新典范）是在老布什领导下经过大大修改后革新的美国共和党政纲，主张政府分散权力，使个人有更多的权力。老布什执政时还用过 New world order（世界新秩序）这个政治口号，意为非西方国家必须按美国意志行事。

New Partnership（新伙伴关系），New Covenant（新契约）以及 New Economics（新经济学），是克林顿提出的施政纲领。

三、"美国总统词"

作为美国政坛的核心人物，美国总统对美利坚合众国所起的举足轻重的影响体现在社会、政治、经济等诸多方面。这一点可以从美国英语中与美国总统有关的词语中得到验证。

Clinton（克林顿）自 1993 年任职至 2001 年卸任，不仅他的名字变得家喻户晓，而且在新闻报道中还出现了不少 Clinton 的派生词，例如：Clintonian 和 Clintonspeak，前者当形容词用时指"跟克林顿政策有关的"，用作名词时表示"克林顿政策的支持者"；后者则被定义为闪烁其词、犹抱琵琶半遮面的说话方式。Clintonize（使克林顿化，使适合或适应克林顿的政策），Clintonmania（克林顿热），Clintonomics（克林顿的经济政策或主张），Clintonite（克林顿派的），Clinton Republican（投克林顿票的共和党人），Clinton-lingo（克林顿官话），Clinton's compromise（克林顿式的妥协）等词语都与 Clinton 有关。

Ronald Reagan（里根）在任期间，根据幕僚与顾问的建议，独创了一套经济政策，其中心思想是以减税来刺激供给，即所谓的 Reaganomics（里根经济学）。与 Reaganomics 一同进入美国政治词语库的还有 Reaganomic（按照里根的经济理论的），Reaganite（里根主义分子），Reaganology（里根政策研究），Reagan Democrat（里根民主派），Reaganaut（里根宇航计划的支持者 [由 Reagan 和 astronaut 拼缀而成]）和 Reagonesque（里根式的）等 Reagan 词语。

Nixon 执政期间进入美国英语的 Nixon 词语有：Nixologism 尼克松惯用语（例如：restructure，options，delivery systems，firm up，time frame），New Nixon（新尼克松，指改变政治策略，树立自己新形象的尼克松），Nixonian（尼克松的），Nixonization（尼克松化），Nixonomics（尼克松经济政策）。

Hooverize（使贫困化，使绝望），取自美国前总统胡佛的姓 Hoover。在他任期内，美国出现了经济大萧条，因此 Hooverize 成为"贫困化"和"绝望"的同义词。与此同时出现的 Hoover Village，Hoover Soup，Hoover prosperity 等均由此而来。Hoover Village ＝ Hooverville（胡佛村）是贫民窟的意思。穷人装破烂东西的袋子叫 Hoover bag（胡佛袋），由于无力购买燃料而改由畜力拉动的汽车叫 Hoover carts（胡佛车），流浪汉在公园长凳上遮体用的报纸叫 Hoover blanket（胡佛毯），乞丐翻在外头的空口袋叫 Hoover flag（胡佛旗），农夫逮来充饥的野兔叫 Hoover hogs（胡佛肉）。Hoover soup（胡佛汤）意思是政府对贫民微不足道的救济。Hoover prosperity（胡佛式的繁荣），指盲目乐观的繁荣。而 Hoover 这个名字本身则是"经济萧条"的同义词。

新闻英语中与其他历届总统派生出的词语还有：Bushie（布什的支持者），

Bushism（布什用语），Eisenhower syntax（艾森豪威尔句法，意为"错误的书面语言"），Kennedy Round（肯尼迪回合，指的是美国和一些欧洲国家从 1964—1967 年在日内瓦举行的一系列关于降低关税壁垒的谈判，因肯尼迪政府在 1962 年通过了扩大贸易法使美得以参加谈判，故名），Carterize（使卡特化，使总统优柔寡断），Carterite（卡特的支持者），Johnson Treatment（约翰逊手法，指美国前总统约翰逊惯于采取的对人软硬兼施、进行讨价还价的手法），Fordonomics（福特经济政策，美国前总统福特是尼克松因水门事件下台而继任总统的，他的经济政策有名无实，不过是 Nixonomics 的衣钵而已）。

四、"总统选举"词

根据美国宪法，美国实行总统制，总统制的规矩是美国的开国元勋们定下来的。总统选举每四年举行一次。

Donkey 是民主党的党徽，Elephant 是共和党的党徽。四年一次的美国总统选举又称为"驴象之争"或"驴象赛跑"。凡想登上美国总统宝座的人，必须先经过提名，这一总统候选人提名阶段称为 primary（预选）。

在美国，参加总统竞选少不了演讲。历史上，美国式的总统竞选演讲方式可谓是五花八门，有 whistle-stop（站台演讲），stump speech（树桩演讲），barnstorm（谷仓演讲），soap box（街头竞选演讲），bandwagon（乘宣传车演讲），swing around the circle（旅行演讲），front-porch campaign（前廊竞选），political blitz（闪电般到各地搞竞选活动），buscapade（bus，campaign 和 motorcade 之缩合，大客车竞选活动），sound bite（电视上竞选演讲）等。

美国选民的结构虽然复杂，但仍以中间立场的选民占大多数。像"总统大选"这样竞争激烈的选举，候选人一定要设法迎合多数选民的胃口，才有机会当选。所以，能符合中间大多数选民的立场，就称为 politically correct（政治立场正确）。当几个竞选者相持不下时，政客和政党的领袖们为保持政治势力平衡，常出乎意料地推出一名新的总统候选人，并使其成功，这种总统候选人就是人们平常所说的 dark horse（黑马）。决定参加总统竞选的人来自各州。各州举行初选时，本州的候选人被称作 favorite son，即本州人所拥护的总统候选人。一个受欢迎的当选的总统候选人在一个州或一个国会选区得到的大量选票，有助于他的党的参、众议员候选人取得胜利。这种影响在美国政治中称为 coattail（上衣后摆效应）。

五、"奥巴马"词汇

随着四年一度的美国总统大选尘埃落定,奥巴马成为众人瞩目的焦点的同时,应运而生的奥巴马词汇也迅速地进入了英语词汇。

奥巴马在其就职演说中将自己的理想、面对的挑战及公众的希望融为一体。他就职演讲中使用频率最高的词汇,包括"国家"、"美国"、"新"、"人民"及"每个人"等。

在总统大选期间,"变革"这个词汇与奥巴马联系最为紧密,而在他的就职演讲中却只说过一次;奥巴马在大选中极力提倡的"希望"一词,也仅仅使用了三次。

可是像"国家"、"美国"、"新"、"人民"、"每个人"、"繁荣"以及"世界"这样的词汇却频频出现。在本次就职演讲中,奥巴马几乎没有涉及任何与政策有关的词汇,相反却更多集中于大众和鼓励类词汇。此外,他在演讲中对全球经济现状也略过不提,只有三次提到过"经济",关于"经济衰退"更是没有涉及。

奥巴马显然意识到他的就职具有非常重大的历史意义,在他的通篇演讲中,多次提到"历史"、"共同"、"一代人"、"代代"及"时代"等类似的词汇。

相比之下,在前总统小布什的第二次就职演讲中,多次强调"自由"、"解放"以及"国家",反复使用"美国"和"每个人"。

(一)奥巴马演讲时常用词汇

Restored our reputation——恢复我们(美国)的声望

Job creation——创造工作机会

Fiscal restraint——财政限制

Win-win——双赢

Affordable health care——支付得起的医疗保险

Previous Administration——之前的政府(指小布什政府)

At the end of the day——最终(我们能够达成……)

Empower (or empowerment)——赋予……的权力;使……有能力实现……

Touch base——与……接触(以达成共识)

Mindset——思维定式

Bipartisan——不分党派的

Inherited as in "I inherited this mess"——继承下来的,如"从前一届政府继承下来的问题和混乱"

Relief for working families——为一般工薪家庭解除……

Unprecedented——前所未见的

Accountable（or held to account）——负有责任的（或为……负责）

Free market——自由市场

Reform——改革

Strategic fit——战略适宜

Let me be clear——让我明确这一点

Make no mistake——绝不犯错

Back from the brink——从……的边缘回到……

Signs of recovery——经济复苏的迹象

Out of the loop——（公众、或官员不能）不知情

Benchmark——比较指标

（二）例　　句

1.If there is anyone out there who still doubts that America is a place where all things are possible, who still wonders if the dream of our founders is alive in our time, who still questions the power of our democracy, tonight is your answer.（如果现在仍然有人在那里怀疑美国是不是任何事情都可能发生的地方，疑惑于我们国家的缔造者们的梦想是否还鲜活地存在于这个时代，对我们民主的力量打上问号的话，今夜就是你的答案。）

2.It's the answer spoken by young and old, rich and poor. It's the answer that led those who've been told for so long by so many to be cynical and fearful and doubtful about what we can achieve to put their hands on the arc of history and bend it once more toward the hope of a better day.（这是美国人共同说出的答案，无论老还是少，富还是穷，长久以来，很多人一再被告知，要对我们所能取得的成绩极尽讥讽、担忧和怀疑之能事，但这个答案让这些人伸出手来把握历史之弧，并再次使它朝向美好明天的希望延伸。）

（三）一些直接派生出来的奥巴马词汇

Obama 这个词被信手拈来、演变、组合成许许多多的新词。例如：

Obamacare——奥巴马保健

Obama-nomics——奥巴马经济

Obamacize——如奥巴马一样去行事

Obamania——奥巴马狂热

Obamafy——使……具有奥巴马特色

Obamaspeak——奥巴马词汇

Obamanation——奥巴马集团

Barack star——奥巴马的气质

Obamabot——奥巴马粉丝

Obama——酷：You so obama.（你真酷。）

参考文献

[1] 陈安 . 新英汉美国小百科 [M]. 上海：上海译文出版社，2002.

[2] 戴卫平 . 美国总统与美语"总统"词 [J]. 中国科技翻译，2006（1）.

[3] 陆谷孙主编 . 英汉大词典补编 [Z]. 上海：上海译文出版社，1997.

[4] 萨本望 . 论"布什主义"[J]. 外交学院学报，2003（2）.

[5] 周学艺 . 英汉美英报刊词典 [Z]. 北京：外语教学与研究出版社，2002.

第八篇　美国"货币"

一、美国通用货币

通用货币是指法律规定的具有强制通用力的货币，又称为法定货币。美国通用货币是纸币和硬币。纸币共 11 种。美钞的纸张、大小、颜色完全一样，唯有面值和所印的人像有一定的规定，即：

George Washington（1 元）	Benjamin Franklin（100 元）
Thomas Jefferson（2 元）	William McKinley（500 元）
Abraham Lincoln（5 元）	Grover Cleveland（1000 元）
Alexander Hamilton（10 元）	Jam Madison（5000 元）
Andrew Jackson（20 元）	Salmon Chase（10000 元）
Ulysses Grant（50 元）	

美钞背面是绿色，所以我们对美钞总称为 greenback。不同纸币又有不同的名称：

1 元纸币为 ace	20 元为 double sawbuck 或 double saw
2 元为 deuce	100 元为 century 或简称 C 或 yard
5 元为 fiver	1 000 元为 grand 或简称 G
10 元为 sawbuck 或 tenner	

5 000 元为 five grands 或简称 five G's。

美国硬币共有 6 种：1 分、5 分、1 角、2 角 5 分、5 角和 1 元。

硬币上都铸有拉丁文 motto（众多之一）的字样。

1 分是铜币，正面是林肯的像，还铸有 IN GOD WE TRUST（我们信仰上帝）及

LIBERTY（自由）的字样，另外还铸有发行的年号。背面有 ONE CENT 的金额，有 UNITED STATES OF AMERICA 字样。

5 分是镍币，故称 nickel，正面是第 3 届美国总统杰弗逊的头像及其在他的家乡弗吉尼亚州夏洛茨维尔市的邸宅蒙蒂塞洛（Morticello）的图景。

1 角是银币，正面原为女人头像神，现改为富兰克林·罗斯福总统的侧面头像。背面铸有火炬和树，以及面额 ONE DIME 的字样，通称 dime。

2 角 5 分也是银币，上面铸有华盛顿总统像和鹰（eagle），又有 QUARTER DOLLAR 的字样，所以通称为 quarter，有时也称为 two bits。

5 角也是银币，一面有女人立像，印有 IN GOD WE TRUST（我们信仰上帝），一面有 HALF DOLLAR 的字样，通称为 half dollar，又称 four bits。

1 元硬币通称 silver dollar，又称 buck 或 ace，can，slug，dough，smacker 等，虽现在已不再铸造，在西南部一带，至今还流通。

美国的 money 俗称 Jack 和 dough。

二、美元下跌（The Falling Dollar）

The falling Dollar: Who gains, Who loses, Who cares, and Why?

美元下跌：谁得益，谁受损，谁关心，为什么？

（1）What does the U.S. trade deficit have to do with the falling dollar?

The U.S. government wants the dollar to fall because as the dollar declines in value against the yuan, the euro and the yen, U.S.goods become cheaper. U.S.companies then sell more at home and abroad, and the U.S.trade deficit declines.Cries for trade protection abate, and the global free-trade system is preserved.

美国贸易赤字同美元汇价下跌有什么关系？

美国政府希望美元下跌，因为美元对人民币、欧元、日元的价值下跌，美国的货物就会变得更为便宜，美国的公司就能够在国内外销售更多的货物，美国的贸易赤字就会下降，贸易保护的呼声也会随之减弱，全球性自由贸易体系也将得以保持住。

（2）Is there a connection between the falling dollar and the rising stock market?

美元下跌同股票市场价格上升之间有联系吗？

There are several links, but they are neither symmetrical nor guaranteed to work at all times.

有几个有关系的地方。但是这些关系既不是对称的，也不保证总会发生。

First, the cheaper dollar makes it cheaper for many foreign investors to snap up

U.S.stocks. That prompts heavy buying from abroad.

首先，比较便宜的美元使得许多国外投资者得以比较便宜地抢购美国股票。这个情况造成外国大量买进。

Also, if the trade picture is improving, that means U.S.companies eventually will be more competitive.

还有，如果贸易情况好转，那就意味着美国的公司最终将更具有竞争力。

Consequently, many investors are buying shares of export-oriented U.S.companies in anticipation of better profits in the next year or so.

因此，许多投资者正在买进出口导向的美国公司的股票，期望在下一年左右的时间里得到较多的利润。

But that is a rather faddish notion right now; if corporate earnings are disappointing in the next few quarters, the buying spree might disappear.

从目前来看，那仅仅是一时流行的概念，如果公司的收益在今后几个季度里令人失望的话，这种买进股票的狂热行为就可能消失。

And, finally, if a plummeting dollar leads to a rise in interest rates, the stock market rally could stall.

最后，如果美元价格的直线下跌导致利率上升，股票市场价格的回升就会停顿。

（3）Could the falling dollar get out of hand?

美元下跌会不会失去控制？

If the dollar falls too far, investors might lose confidence in U.S.investments, especially the government bond market.The money to finance the federal budget and trade deficits could migrate elsewhere. Inflation could flare up, too.

如果美元下跌太多，投资者可能会失去对美国投资的信心，特别是对美国政府债券市场。对联邦政府预算和贸易赤字提供的资金可能移向其他市场，从而使通货膨胀再次发生。

The U.S.Federal Reserve then might need to step in and stabilize the dollar by raising interest rates. And higher interest rates could cause the U.S.economy to slow down and end the Wall Street rally.

美国联邦储备委员会这时可能介入，提高利率来稳定美元。而较高的利率将会导致美国经济减慢，华尔街的繁荣景象也将随之消失。

三、美联储：央行（The Fed: Central Bank）

The Federal Reserve System is the central bank of U.S..

联邦储备系统是美国的中央银行。

Congress created the Fed Reserve through a law passed in 1913, charging it with a responsibility to foster a sound banking system and a healthy economy.

国会在 1913 年通过的一条法律创建了联邦储备，交给它促进一个健全的银行系统和兴旺发达的经济的责任。

This remains, today, the broad mission of the Fed and its component parts.

这个今天仍然是联邦及其组成部分的综合性的任务。

The 12 federal reserve banks nationwide, each serving a specific region of the country; and the Board of Governors in Washington, D.C., set up to oversee the fed system.

全国 12 家联邦储备银行，每一家都在一个特定的区域履行其职责；和为监督联邦系统而设在华盛顿的联邦储备委员会。

To accomplish its mission, the fed serves as a bank's bank and as the government's bank, as a regulator of financial institutions and as the nation's money manager, performing a vast array of functions that affect the economy, the financial system, and ultimately, each of us.

为了完成它的使命，作为银行的银行和作为政府的银行，作为金融机构的调节者和作为国家的货币管理者，联储履行着影响经济、金融系统，和最终影响到我们会每一个人的广泛大量的职责。

Another important federal reserve responsibility is serving the nation's largest banking customer—the U.S.government.

联储的另外一项重要的责任是向这个国家的银行主顾——美国政府提供服务。

As the government's bank or fiscal agent, the fed processes a variety of financial transactions involving trillions of dollars.

作为政府的银行或者财政代理人，联储处理涉及数以万亿计的各种各样的财务交易。

The Fed reserve also issues the nation's coin and paper currency.

联储还发行这个国家的硬币和纸币。

The U.S.Treasury, through its Bureau of the Mint and Bureau of Engraving and Printing, actually produces the nations' cash supply; the fed banks then distribute it to financial institutions.

实际上美国财政部是通过它的造币局和雕版和印刷局生产国家的现金；然后联储银行把现金分发给各金融机构。

The currency periodically circulates back to the fed banks where it is counted, checked for wear and tear, and examined for counterfeits.

这些货币周期性地流转回各联邦银行，进行点数、检查破损，并且细查假钞。

If the money is still in good condition, it is eventually sent back into circulation as institutions order new supplies to satisfy the public's need for cash.

如果一个钱币仍然完好，它在金融机构为了满足公众对现金的需要而提出订单时会最终被送回流通。

Worn-out bills, however, are destroyed by shredding.The average $1 bill circulates for approximately 18 months before being destroyed.

而不能再用的钞票则通过切碎予以销毁。1元面值的钞票在销毁前，平均流通大约 18 个月。

第九篇　美国的政府组织

　　美国是联邦制国家。美国政府由国会、行政机构和最高法院三部分组成，见图9-1。根据美国宪法，国会是美国的最高立法机关，由参议院和众议院两院组成。国会两院的议员由各州选民直接选举产生。联邦行政机构可分为三大类，即白宫直属机构、政府各部门及独立机构。白宫直属机构——白宫办公厅、国家安全委员会、行政管理和预算局。政府各部门——国务院、财政部、国防部、司法部、内政部、农业部、商务部、劳工部、卫生与公众服务部、住房及城市发展部、交通部、能源部、教育部。独立机构——邮政总局、原子能委员会、国家航空和宇宙航行局、国际交流署、联邦储备局。

```
┌──────────────────┬──────────────────┬──────────────────┐
│  LEGISLATIVE     │  EXECUTIVE       │  JUICIAL         │
│  BRANCH          │  BRANCH          │  BRANCH          │
│  立法部门         │  行政部门         │  司法部门         │
└──────────────────┴──────────────────┴──────────────────┘
```

图 9-1　美国政府结构图

　　最高法院是联邦司法系统的最高机关，由一名首席法官和 8 名法官组成。按照美国宪法规定，最高法院对关于大使、公使、领事及一州为当事人的案件"有权审批"；有管理下级法院所审理案件的上诉裁判权。无论是初审还是复审，最高法院的判决都是最终的判决。最高法院不仅有最高裁判权，而且还有监督立法和解释立法的权力。

一、Congress（国会）

（一）Senate（参议院）

President 主席（副总统兼）
President Pro Tempore 临时主席
Majority Leader 多数党领袖
Minority Leader 少数党领袖
Majority Whip 多数党督导
Minority Whip 少数党督导
Standing Committees of the Senate 参议院常设委员会

（二）House of Representatives（众议院）

Speaker 议长
Majority Leader 多数党领袖
Minority Leader 少数党邻袖
Majority Whip 多数党督导
Minority Whip 少数党督导
Standing Committee of the House 众议院常设委员会
House of Special Committees 众议院特别委员会
Congressional Joint Committee 国会联合委员会

二、The Administration（政府）

（一）The Cabinet（内阁）

Secretary of State 国务卿
Secretary of the Interior 内政部长
Secretary of Labor 劳工部长
Secretary of Agriculture 农业部长
Secretary of Defense 国防部长
Attorney General 司法部长
Secretary of the Treasury 财政部长
Secretary of Energy 能源部长
Secretary of Health and Human Services 卫生与公众服务部长

Secretary of Transportation 运输部长

Secretary of Housing and Urban Development 住房和城市发展部长

Secretary of Commerce 商务部长

Secretary of Educ6tion 教育部长

Secretary of Veterans Affairs 退伍军人事务部长

（二）Executive Office of the President（总统办事机构）

White House Office 白宫办公厅

Office of Management and Budget 行政管理和预算局

Council of Economic Advisers 经济顾问委员会

National Economic Council 国家经济委员会

National Security Council 国家安全委员会

Office of Policy Development 政策制定办公室

Office of the U.S. Trade Representative 美国贸易代表办公室

Council on Environmental Quality 环境质量委员会

Office of Science and Technology Policy 科技政策办公室

Office of Administration 行政管理办公室

Office of National Drug Control Policy 国家药品政策管制办公室

National Critical Materials Council 国家重要物资委员会

National Space Council 国家空间委员会

（三）White House Office（白宫办公厅）

Chief of Staff 办公厅主任

Assistant to the President for Economic & Domestic Affairs 负责经济和国内事务的总统助理

Assistant to the President for National Security 负责国家安全事务的总统助理

（四）Department of States（国务院）

Secretary of State 国务卿

Deputy Secretary 第一或常务副国务卿

Under Secretary 副国务卿

Assistant Secretary 助理国务卿

Deputy Assistant Secretary 助理国务卿帮办

（五）Others（其他）

Department of the Treasury 财政部

Department of Defense 国防部

Chairman of the Joint Chiefs of Staff 参谋长联席会议主席

Secretary of the Amy 陆军部长

Secretary of the Navy 海军部长

Secretary of the Air Force 空军部长

Department of Justice 司法部

Attorney General 司法部长

Deputy Attorney General 第一或常务副部长

Department of the Interior 内政部

Secretary of the Interior 内政部长

Deputy Secretary 副部长

Department of Health and Human Services 卫生与公众服务部

Department of Housing and Urban Development 住房和城市发展部

Department of Transportation 运输部

Department of Energy 能源部

Secretary of Energy 能源部长

Deputy Secretary 第一或常务副部长

Under Secretary 副部长

Department of Veterans Affairs 退伍军人事务部

Secretary of Veterans Affairs 退伍军人事务部长

（六）Local Government（地方政府）

State Legislature 州议会

State Government 州政府

Governor 州长

Lieutenant-Governor 副州长

District of Columbia ＝ Washington, D.C. 哥伦比亚特区

County 县

三、Judiciary（司法执构）

Supreme Court of the United States 美国最高法院

District Court 地方法院

Claims Court 索赔法院

Court of Appeals for the Federal Circuit 联邦巡回上诉法院

Court of International Trade 国际贸易法庭

Territorial Courts 属地法院

Court of Military Appeals 军事上诉法院

Court of Veterans Appeals 退伍军人上诉法院

Administration of the Courts 法院行政管理局

Federal Judicial Center 联邦司法中心

参考文献

[1] 陈安 . 新英汉美国小百科 [M]. 上海：上海译文出版社，2002.

[2] 惠宇主编 . 新世纪汉英大词典 [Z]. 北京：外语教学与研究出版社，2003.

[3] 陆谷孙主编 . 英汉大词典 [Z]. 上海：上海译文出版社，1999.

[4] 周学艺 . 英汉美英报刊词典 [Z]. 北京：外语教学与研究出版社，2002.

[5] 周学艺 . 美英报刊文章阅读 [M]. 北京：北京大学出版社，2004.

第十篇　美国的节日

　　节日是生活中值得纪念的重要日子。节日是世界人民为适应生产和生活的需要而共同创造的一种民俗文化，是世界民俗文化的重要组成部分。各国、各民族和各地区都有自己的节日。一些节日源于传统习俗，如中国的春节、中秋节、清明节、重阳节等。有的节日源于宗教，比如基督教国家的圣诞节。有的节日源于对某人或某件事件的纪念，比如中国的端午节、青年节。另有国际组织提倡的指定日子，如劳动节、妇女节、母亲节。在美国，每年人们欢度许多节日。这些节日按时间顺序先后有：

一、元旦（New Year's Day）

　　每年 1 月 1 日庆祝新的一年的开始。人们举办各种各样的新年晚会，到处可以听到"辞旧迎新"的钟声，为美国的联邦假日。

二、林肯诞辰（Abraham Lincoln's Birthday）

　　每年 2 月 12 日，庆祝林肯诞辰，为美国大多数州的节日。

三、圣瓦伦丁节（St.Valentine's Day）

　　每年 2 月 14 日，是 3 世纪殉教的圣徒圣华伦泰的逝世纪念日。情人们在这一天互赠礼物或贺卡，故又称"情人节"（The Lovers' day）。

四、华盛顿诞辰（George Washington's Birthday）

　　每年 2 月 22 日，庆祝美国开国总统华盛顿诞辰，为美国的联邦假日。

五、圣帕特里克节（St.Patrick's Day）

每年 3 月 17 日，是悼念爱尔兰的守护神圣帕特里克的节日。很多美国人为爱尔兰人后裔。

六、复活节（Easter Day, Easter Sunday）

一般在每年春分后月圆第一个星期天，约在 3 月 7 日。该节是庆祝基督（Jesus Christ）的复活，过节人们吃复活节彩蛋（Easter Eggs），为美国的联邦假日。

七、愚人节（April Fool's Day）

每年 4 月 1 日，该节日出自于庆祝"春分点"的来临，在 4 月 1 日受到恶作剧愚弄的人成为"四月愚人"（April Fools）。

八、母亲节（Mother's Day）

每年 5 月份的第 2 个星期日，政府部门和各家门口悬挂国旗，表示对母亲的尊敬。在家里，儿女们和父亲给母亲买些礼物或做些家务。

九、阵亡烈士纪念日（Memorial Day）

每年 5 月份的最后一个星期一，纪念为美国献身的阵亡烈士，为美国的联邦假日。

十、国旗日（National Flag Day）

每年 6 月 14 日，庆祝国旗的升起。

十一、父亲节（Father's Day）

每年 6 月的第 3 个星期天，表示对父亲的尊敬。在家里，儿女们和母亲给父亲买些礼物。

十二、国庆节（Independence Day）

每年 7 月 4 日，庆祝美国建国，为美国的联邦假日。

十三、劳动节（Labor Day）

每年 9 月的第 1 个星期一，表示对劳工的敬意，为美国的联邦假日。

十四、哥伦布日（Columbus Day）

每年 10 月 12 日，纪念哥伦布在北美登陆，为美国的联邦假日。

十五、万圣节（Halloween; Eve of All Saint's Day）

每年 10 月 31 日，孩子们多化装成鬼，打着灯笼或点燃篝火尽情地玩耍。

十六、万灵日（All Soul's Day）

每年 11 月 2 日，祭悼所有死者灵魂之日。

十七、退伍军人节（Veterans Day）

每年 11 月 11 日，表示对退伍军人的敬意。

十八、感恩节（Thanksgiving Day）

每年 11 月最后一个星期四，感谢上帝所赐予的秋收，为美国的联邦假日。

十九、大选日（Election Day）

每年 11 月的第 1 个星期一后的星期二，选举美国总统。

二十、清教徒登陆纪念日（Forefather's Day）

每年 12 月 21 日，纪念清教徒在美洲登陆。

二十一、圣诞节（Christmas Day）

每年的 12 月 25 日，基督徒庆祝耶稣诞生的日子，是美国最隆重的节日。

第十一篇　美军军衔

一、军　　衔

军衔，是国家最高权力机关根据军人的职务、军事素养和业务素养、资历贡献以及军兵种或勤务区分，授予军人的一种衔称。军衔在 15—16 世纪产生于西欧一些国家，所以习惯上称为西欧式军衔。它是在欧洲新兴资产阶级反对封建等级制的过程中，随常备军的发展而逐渐形成的军事制度。到了 17—18 世纪，军衔制为世界大多数国家的军队所采用。

军衔分为永久军衔和临时军衔两类。一般称的军衔指永久军衔。永久军衔又分军官军衔与士兵军衔两大类。军衔按获得者的兵役状况和所在部队的专业性质，在横向上又区分为不同的类别。

士兵军衔一般分"士"和"兵"两类，"兵"可以分为列兵（二等兵）、一等兵（上等兵）等几级。"士"即"士官"，一般由拥有专业技术者担任或从资深士兵中选出，各国把士官分为上士、中士、下士、军士长（或称士官长）等。

军官军衔一般分将、校、尉三个级别，每个级别内又分上、中、下三等，有的还会加上"大"这一等，如中国有大校、俄罗斯有大尉。

有的国家在将官之上还设有元帅，在尉官与士官之间还设有准尉。军衔等级设置的数量，每个国家各不相同，最多的设 20 多级，最少的只设十几级。军衔等级设置多少，总体上受本国军队的规模和编制体制的制约。欧洲早期的军队最大编制是团，所以当时最高军衔只到上校，将军则是代表君主或元首指挥作战的首领。以后，随着军队组织编制的扩大，将军逐步区分为若干等级，以指挥不同规模的军队。各国军官军衔同军队职务之间有一定的对称关系，通常是少尉对应排长、中尉对应副连长、上尉对应连长、少校对应营长、中校对应副团长、上校对应团长、准将对应旅长、少将对应师长、中将对应军长、上将对应方面军司令官。

二、美军军衔

美国的兵种包括陆军、空军、海军、海军陆战队,每个兵种都有自己的军衔制度,几乎每个兵种都有:五星上将、上将、中将、少将、准将、上校、中校、少校、上尉、中尉、少尉、一级准尉、二级准尉、军士长、上士、中士、下士、一等兵、二等兵、三等兵,但各自却有不同的叫法。

任何一个国家都不会缺少陆军(Army),美国也一样,陆军是美国武装力量的组成部分之一,主要负责陆地上的作战。美国的陆军军衔较为复杂,然而却分得清楚明白。

General of the Army 五星上将

General 上将

Lieutenant General 中将

Major General 少将

Brigadier General 准将

Colonel 上校

Lieutenant Colonel 中校

Major 少校

Captain 上尉

First Lieutenant 中尉

Second Lieutenant 少尉

Chief Warrant Officer 一级准尉

Warrant Officer 二级准尉

Master Sergeant 军士长

Sergeant First Class 上士

Sergeant 中士

Corporal 下士

Private First Class 一等兵

Private 二等兵

Basic Private 三等兵

海军部设于五角大楼内,又称为"华盛顿海军大院"。美国海军有自己的军衔制度。

Fleet Admiral 五星上将

Admiral 上将

Vice Admiral 中将

Rear Admiral 少将

Commodore 准将

Captain 上校

Commander 中校

Lieutenant Commander 少校

Lieutenant 上尉

Lieutenant Junior Class 中尉

Ensign 少尉

Commissioned Warrant Officer 一级准尉

Warrant Officer 二级准尉

Chief Petty Officer 军士长

Petty Officer First Class 上士

Petty Officer Second Class 中士

Petty Officer Third Class 下士

Seaman First Class 一等兵

Seaman Second Class 二等兵

Apprentice Seaman 三等兵

美国空军（Air Force）的任务是"通过空中和太空中的武力保护美国及其利益"，它于1947年9月18日正式成立。美国空军的作战单位由数个主司令部、野外作业机构和直接报告单位组成。联队是编号空军卜属的指挥层。一个联队有1 000—5 000人，它可以完成一个相当大规模的任务。它有维持装备的任务，其下可有数个大队和中队。一个联队可以是一个作战联队、一个空军基地联队或一个特别任务联队。

General of the Air Force 五星上将

General 上将

Lieutenant General 中将

Major General 少将

Brigadier General 准将

Colonel 上校

Lieutenant Colonel 中校

Mayor 少校

Captain 上尉

First Lieutenant 中尉

Second Lieutenant 少尉

Chief Warrant Officer 一级准尉

Warrant Officer 二级准尉

Master Sergeant 军士长

Technical Sergeant 技术军士

Staff Sergeant 参谋军士

Airman First Class 一等兵

Airman Second Class 二等兵

Airman Third Class 三等兵

美国海军陆战队（Marine Corps）由地面部队、航空兵和后勤部队三部分组成。它是美国的四大兵种之一，也是美国快速反应部队的主要作战力量。

General 上将

Lieutenant General 中将

Major General 少将

Brigadier General 准将

Colonel 上校

Lieutenant Colonel 中校

Major 少校

Captain 上尉

First Lieutenant 中尉

Second Lieutenant 少尉

Commissioned Warrant Officer 一级准尉

Warrant Officer 二级准尉

Master Sergeant 军士长

Technical Sergeant 技术军士

Staff Sergeant 参谋军士

Sergeant 中士

Corporal 下士

Private First Class 一等兵

参考文献

[1] 陈安 . 新英汉美国小百科 [M]. 上海：上海译文出版社，2002.

[2] 惠宇主编 . 新世纪汉英大词典 [Z]. 北京：外语教学与研究出版社，2003.

[3] 陆谷孙主编 . 英汉大词典 [Z]. 上海：上海译文出版社，1999.

[4] 周学艺 . 英汉美英报刊词典 [Z]. 北京：外语教学与研究出版社，2002.

[5] 周学艺 . 美英报刊文章阅读 [M]. 北京：北京大学出版社，2004.

第十二篇　美国（世界）顶级品牌

一、美国的世界顶级品牌

品牌是制造商或经营商加在商品上的标志。品牌由名称、名词、符号、象征、设计或它们的组合构成。品牌一般包括两个部分：品牌名称和品牌标志。品牌是人们对一个企业及其产品、售后服务、文化价值的一种评价和认知，是一种信任。当下，品牌已是一种商品综合品质的体现和代表，当人们想到某一品牌的同时总会和时尚、文化、价值联系到一起。企业在创品牌时不断地创造时尚、培育文化。当品牌文化被市场认可并接受后，品牌便产生其市场价值。

（一）Tiffany 蒂芬尼——珠宝

蒂芬尼的设计焕发出浓郁的美国特色，卓越的设计并非完全的奢侈，更不是轻浮的夸耀，而是真正能震撼心灵的作品。蒂芬尼的每一款珠宝都有属于自己的精神空间。

（二）American Express 美国运通——旅行信用卡

美国运通成立于 1850 年。经过 150 多年的推陈出新和逐步成长，美国运通已成为全球最受信赖的顶尖旅游服务商标。

（三）Armani 阿玛尼——时装

乔治·阿玛尼现在已是在美国销量最大的欧洲设计师品牌。他以使用新型面料及优良制作而闻名。就设计风格而言，其服装似乎很少与时髦两字有关。在两性性别越趋混淆的年代，服装不再是绝对的男女有别。

（四）Calvin Klein 卡尔文·克莱恩——服装

卡尔文·克莱恩是美国第一大设计师品牌，曾经连续四度获得知名的服装奖项。卡尔文·克莱恩的品牌因为年轻、快节奏和机能性，反映着其特有的民族自由精神，被看成美国时尚的代表人物。

（五）Harley·Davidson 哈雷·戴维森——摩托

1903 年，在美国威斯康星州的密尔沃基，诞生了一辆由自行车改装的具有动力装置的摩托车，这就是第一辆哈雷·戴维森摩托车。一个多世纪过去了，哈雷早已不再是一般意义上的交通工具，它已经成为一个将机器和人性完美融合为一体的金属明星，成为男人们的精神图腾。

（六）Starbucks 星巴克——咖啡店

星巴克已发展成在多个国家拥有几千多家全球连锁店的、国际最著名的咖啡零售品牌。

（七）Cadillac 凯迪拉克——名车

凯迪拉克商标图形主要由"冠"和"盾"组成。"冠"象征着凯迪拉克家族的纹章，冠上 7 颗珍珠喻示皇家的贵族血统。"盾"象征着凯迪拉克军队的英勇善战。

（八）Hummer 悍马——名车

军用悍马诞生于 1980 年。1992 年悍马民用版问世。如今通用公司拥有这个品牌销售权。驾驶悍马越野车会使你明白一个汽车传奇是怎样诞生的。

（九）Coach 寇兹——皮具、手袋

成立于 1941 年的寇兹是美国资格最老和最成功的皮革制品公司之一。其凭借着耐久的质量、精湛的制作工艺，在一代美国女性消费者中建立起坚实的声望。

（十）Donnakaran 唐那凯伦——服装、眼镜

美国目前首屈一指的当红知名世界品牌，其服装商品出自名设计师 Donnakaran 之手笔。销售对象是名人政要，高阶主管和艺人。

二、人名、地名命名

"品牌"是商品经济高度发展的产物，是当今经济社会的一个主要方面。"品牌"

是识别商品的一种标记。对于广大消费者而言，品牌是其选购商品的无声向导。企业借助品牌推出产品，消费者通过品牌购入商品。对于企业而言，品牌是投资的凝聚、心血的结晶，是产品质量、信誉和知名度的载体，是企业走向市场的签证。英语中有"Name is the game."（决胜于品牌）。毋庸置疑，品牌是产品的"黄金名片"。著名的国际电脑公司 IBM 的总裁曾说过，IBM 公司的所有资产就是 IBM 三个字母，它是"前卫、科技、智慧"的象征。可见优秀的品牌对于企业是多么的重要。正因为如此，无论是东方还是西方国家的品牌设计家们绞尽脑汁、想方设法推出各种妙趣横生、生动活泼、独特新奇的商标牌名，以吸引目标受众者的眼球和刺激消费欲望。

品牌是由词语构成的为消费者认知特定商品的语言符号，其语义是牌子在消费者心目中的形象以及消费者对形象的态度。商家选择暗含商品效能并具有一定形象性的词语作品牌标名，可以激起消费者心中的民族文化积淀，从而产生丰富的语义联想并形成品牌意识，最终达到赢得消费者好感、认可进而购买商品的目的。品牌的语义内容是品牌意象的重要组成部分。一个好的品牌名应当具有美好、积极、耐人寻味的语义内容，而且语义的内容越丰富，就越能诱发人们的联想，联想越丰富也就越有助于品牌意象的确立。

品牌的命名不同于人名、地名等专有名词，乃有意为之，人为创意。人们在生活中也为人取名、为地易名，但不会如为品牌择名那样精心，常常是悬赏微求，万里挑一。

英语商标名称中有用地名命名的现象。美国的 Kentucky Fried Chicken（肯德基炸鸡，快餐连锁店），就是以肯德基州命名的。Avon 是英国剧作家莎士比亚的家乡附近的一条河的名称，1939 年，一位美国人将 Avon 用来命名他的化妆品公司及其产品，来纪念他喜欢的英国剧作家莎士比亚。Marlboro（万宝路香烟）是美国西部一个小镇名，这个香烟名反映了美国西部壮美的景色：红色的延绵的沙漠、苍凉的大峡谷、远方的群山、奔驰的骏马，以及剽悍自信的牛仔，很适合美国人追求新奇、富于冒险和追求浪漫的大众心理。

西方以其企业创始人名字作为商标的居多，这尤其表现在时装业。时装体现了设计师独有的理念和风格。时装常常使人联想起其创始人，而大多数时装公司的名称和时装品牌都以创始人名称命名，使得创始人与其创办的公司和生产的时装更加有名，如美国的 Ralph Lauren（拉尔夫·劳伦）。世界著名的化妆品、香水、珠宝和箱包品牌中有美国的 Calvin Klein（卡尔文·克莱恩）。

西方的一些公司名称和品牌也是以其创始人名称作为命名理据的。著名的例子有美国的 Ford（福特汽车公司）、Fox（福克斯公司）、Disney（迪斯尼电影公司）、Dell（戴尔电脑公司）。美国名牌化妆品 Revlon 是其创始人姓氏 Revson 的变体。有一些商标是以其他有关人士的名字命名的。Gillette（吉列）是美国吉列公司生产的刀片品牌，它源自该公司的第一任经理 Camp Gillette 的姓氏。

西方喜欢用创始人名字做商标与其社会重视、尊重个人努力、成功、发明创造有关，品牌创始人不惧怕"抛头露面"，"好大喜功"，因而伴随产品知名度的扩大，创始人的名字也为消费者所牢记，有的名字让人产生的联想还不仅仅于此。Goodyear Tire and Rubber Company（固特异轮胎及橡胶公司），是美国最大的载客汽车轮胎制造商。Goodyear 看起来像一个商家煞费苦心想出来的名称，由 good 和 year 两个词组成，一来表示产品的质量非常好、信得过，二来也暗示了产品可以经年累月使用，经得起时间的考验，确实是个绝佳的品牌名。但事实上，这只不过是个巧合而已，Goodyear 是公司创始人 Charles Goodyear 的姓。Charles Goodyear 是出生在美国的发明家，他发明了硫化法，使橡胶应用于工业。有些西方公司名称和品牌是以其若干创始人名称的首字母合成的缩略词作为命名理据的。著名的例子有美国的 P&G（宝洁洗涤剂公司），创始人为 Procter 和 Gamble；惠普电脑公司的牌子 HP，创始人为 Hewlett 和 Packard；美国的 Dreamwork SKG（梦幻工厂电影公司），SKG 分别代表公司的三位著名人物 Spielberg，Katzenberg 和 Geffen。

总而言之，以姓名作为商品的商标有以下三大优越性：

（1）名人效应。被用作商标使用的自然人的姓名，大多在相关行业内具有一定的知名度，为人所共知。现代社会，市场的竞争异常激烈，相同质量、用途的商品并不必然能够赢得相同的经营业绩，商家必须在其经营活动中独辟蹊径，才能够吸引消费者对其商品的注意力。以姓名作为商标，即商家充分利用人们对名人的崇拜心理，采取人们喜闻乐见的方式推出自己的商品。这样既可节省广告宣传投入，又可缩短商品被公众接受的时间。

（2）被作为商标的姓名往往蕴含着巨大的经济价值。这是名人效应的必然结果。人们喜欢某位名人，更乐意接受用其姓名作为注册商标的某种商品，因此必然会给商家带来可观的经济回报。姓名商标作为企业宝贵的无形资产，能够凭其品牌影响力为企业创造更多的财富。

（3）以姓名作为商标使用的商品，一般具有较高的质量和良好的信誉。质量和信誉是企业的生命。企业要长久的生存并发展，必须具备这一品质。姓名商标之所以存续远古至今，正是由于它所代表的商品具备很好的质量与信誉。

三、青睐吉祥、高雅字眼

英语属于印欧语系，在这个语系当中，古典拉丁语、希腊语是科学术语、宗教用语的主要来源，因而这两种语言具有"高贵"、"典雅"的意味。用这两种语言的词汇命名的商标，常有"名牌"的含义。美国施乐公司的著名商标 Xerox 源自希腊语，它的意思是"干、干性的"，作为科学术语，它指一种特殊的"干性复印工艺"。这个商标既表现了复印机的特性，又暗示出了"名牌"的意思。

一种新型的汽车出租服务近年来在欧美等国家发展，供客户租车，自行驾车遨游。美国有一家从事这种租车服务的公司名叫 Avis。Avis 这个词就源自拉丁语，意为 bird，旨在说明公司向顾客提供速度与旅程，让顾客展翅高飞，无远弗届。Avis 这个字无论形、音都远较 bird 为佳，而且还富有古典色彩。

四、暗示产品信息

商标，顾名思义，就是商品的标志，因此，商标往往具有标志性，让人一看便知是何种商品，具有何种功能与特性。在商品琳琅满目的当代社会，人们的认知日趋多元化、表层化。由表"测"里，顾名思义。好包装里装好东西，好名字代表好商品。"以貌取物，因名购物"。消费者的这种认知习惯在今天表现得尤为充分。商品品牌作为商品投给社会的第一印象，已成为能促进销售的有效手段。在质量好的前提下，好牌子的商品常成为消费者情有独钟的畅销货。好名字至少应符合两个条件：①好记。好记的名字通常是易懂易念，简短而富有形象。②合乎人情事理。名字既要切中消费者心理，又要注意名实大致相符。

各类产品根据其原料、质量、型号、用途、价格等都有较明确的消费层次和销售对象。将产品的特性巧妙地概括在商标中，使消费者从商标中就可以获得有关产品本身的信息，是一种常用的命名策略。品牌作为特定商品的专用名称，在商品宣传中有很重要的作用。人们从接触商品信息到发生购买行为要经历知道、了解、信服、欲望和行动的心理过程，如果品牌名称反映产品的某些属性，消费者就能迅速认知该产品的类型、功能或目标消费者等信息。

英语商标中有很多利用产品功能作为商标命名的理据。Clean & Clear（可伶可俐洗面奶），是一种洗面乳的品牌，暗示经常使用可以去掉脸上的痤疮和粉刺，达到面部 clean and clear（干净、清爽）的效果。Head & Shoulder（海飞丝），是一种洗发香波的品牌，暗示洗完后头发上和双肩上没有头皮屑。男性药品 Viagra（伟哥）的 via 表示 life（生命），而 gra 表示 energy（能力）。这个品牌名称暗示了这种药品的功能。Vicks Cough Silencer（维克斯止咳水），不仅把止咳的意味表达出来了，而且用 make cough silence，使得品牌名听起来幽默诙谐，不像一般的药名那样严肃、呆板，让人"听"而却步。Safeguard（舒肤佳香皂），含有保护的意思，暗示能达到彻底清洗污垢，保证安全、健康的效果。Scrabble，一种拼字游戏板的商标名，就是用来让人胡乱拼凑的，用 scrabble（乱涂、乱抹）来命名就很生动地表现出产品的性能。

诚然，商标是商品的标志性符号，商标命名不能完全脱离商品，商品自身的特点或性质当是商标命名的客观依据。但是有些特定商品（例如卫生保健类）的命名就不能过于直白，而应该采用暗示命名策略，这样可以避免商标名过于直白甚至粗俗，以致在消费者心中产生不良的印象。

五、植物命名

植物命名往往选取那些人们很熟悉并能唤起美好联想的植物，通过丰富的联想产生商标意象，最终使商品在消费者心目中留下美好的印象。例如：Apple（苹果牌计算机）、Tulip Jaune（黄郁金香牌香水）都是著名的商标名。西方国家采用植物命名成功的例子，应属 CocaCola（可口可乐），世上很少有人不知道 CocaCola。CocaCola 是 Coca 和 Cola 两种植物的名字。在 Cocacola 这个世界级的商标中，coca 代表南美洲的一种草药，cola 代表非洲的一种果子。比较而言，西方国家采用动物命名的产品要比植物多，比如像 Tiger（虎牌啤酒）；Bull Durham（一种烟丝）；Hush Puppies（一种轻便软底鞋）；Sno-cat（雪猫拖拉机，一种在深雪中行驶的拖拉机商标名）。

六、招牌命名

国内外很多企业为了建立稳固的品牌和企业形象，常常将企业名称和产品合二而一，这样做可以一举两得，既宣传了商品，同时又宣传了该产品的生产者。例如：International Business Machine Corp（国际商业机器公司）—IBM，Procter & Gamble（美国宝洁公司）—P&G，Pond's（旁氏化妆品），Johnson's（强生婴幼儿产品）。这种简洁的缩写名称随着其产品的普及而深入人心，广为人们所接受，对产品起着巨大的宣传作用。

七、文学作品命名

一个民族的经典文学作品是该民族宝贵的文化遗产，民族文学作品体现出该民族的精神风貌，其中的优秀代表还会流传到其他国家和地区，成为全人类的共同财富。各国商标中都有许多来源于本民族或外族优秀作品中的人物和作品名称本身。

我们所熟悉的 Shangri-la（香格里拉）是美国一家著名酒店的营业商标，其名称来源于美国作家詹姆斯·希尔顿的小说《消失的地平线》。希尔顿在书中描绘了一个地方，位于中国西藏，叫"香格里拉"，类似于我国晋代陶潜笔下的《桃花源》。美国的 Popeye's（大力水手波佩，快餐连锁店），原是美国漫画家 Elzie C.Segar 创作的连环画中的一个人物，吃菠菜后力大无穷，曾拍成动画片；美国的 Mickey Mouse（米老鼠），原是著名的卡通人物，现在也被用作商标名。

八、形象命名

利用形象作为命名依据，也是一种间接的，但是常用的品牌命名策略。人们利用商品的外形、特点与某些动物相似的表象特征来做商标名称，使商标名具有形象感。Caterpillar 本义是指一种蠕动的毛毛虫，被用作一种履带拖拉机的商标名，因为这种拖拉机行驶起来酷似一条爬行的毛毛虫。许多汽车制造商都用动物的名称给自己的产品命名，因为他们想借用这些动物来再现自己产品的灵巧和快速等特点，从而在市场上建立一个良好的品牌形象。再如有一种品牌名为 Puma 的著名运动服就是以此来命名的。Puma 是一种生活在美洲的大型猫科动物，在《简明不列颠百科全书》中的译名为"美洲狮"。用它作为运动服品牌名使人联想到穿着这种运动服的运动员跑得像 puma 一样飞快。Puma 的飞快形象是深受运动员欢迎的。Puma 的中文译名是"彪马"，这种动物纯系杜撰的动物名称，但"彪"的意思是"小老虎"，能让人想到是一种像虎仔一样健壮的马，穿上该运动服的人会给人如虎一样勇猛、如马一样矫健的联想。汽车商标以动物命名的有：Cougars（美洲狮），Branco（烈马），Mustang（小野马），Viper（蟒蛇），Thunderbird（雷鸟），Jaguar（美洲虎），Bobcat（短尾猫），Lynxes（大山猫）等。美国长途客运公司的标志用车商标为 Greyhound（灰狗），该名称体现了该车快速的性能，同时也给人以生动的形象：一只飞奔的狗，无疑有助于乘客产生一种新奇欲试的心理。

九、造字冠品牌

品牌名称一般来说不能重复，企业也不愿重复别人使用过的商标。有抱负的企业家都希望其产品名称能够在全球通行，而又没有任何读音、拼写、文化上的陷阱。因此，许多西方品牌命名多采用新创词构成。英语文字很大程度上是依据语音的任意性符号，音素组合的任意程度很大，对语义表达的依赖性相对很小。汉语文字具有较大的理据性，对语义表达的依赖性很大。因此，英语商标词常使用杜撰的词汇，注意语音的表现；汉语商标总是充分利用现有词汇，注重语义的表达。

一般来说，西方人对品牌名称的要求比较单纯：①简单易记；②不重复；③在别国语言里不会产生误解；④对宗教信仰不要有侮辱性含义。有时为了达到这样的目的，同时为了安全起见，造新词就是一个权宜之计，如康柏公司 Compaq（美国电脑生产商）来源于 compact（计算机术语，意思是密集的、压紧的），把词尾变成 q，就构成一个新词。Axion Presoak（美国一种畅销洗衣粉商标名），将 axiom（原则，公理）的词尾 m 换成 n，soak（浸透，浸泡）加上前缀 pre，暗示购买者如果将衣物事先浸入该类洗衣粉里，便会收到很好的效果，这是一个"公理"，让人不得不信。Pepsi-Cola 是 1898 年由美国的一名药房经理创制的。他意欲制造一种饮料，以减轻 dyspepsia（消化不良）的症状。他掐头去尾剪取了 dyspepsia 的中间几个字母 pepsi，作为新饮料的品牌名。美国老牌指甲油 Cutex 源于拉丁文 Cuticle（表层）和商标常用结尾 -ex。OXO 为一种美国牛肉精品牌。它也许是品牌中最干净、最简洁、最富美学意味的。此词的创意，可谓一目了然：来自 OX 再加上 19 世纪非常流行的词尾 -O。类似这样的词很容易使人联想到源词，使公司的行业特征凸显。

　　人造新词是西方品牌的一个显著特点，这种由一个词的一部分与另一个词的一部分结合而构成的新词形式新颖、结构紧凑，所含意义明确。但还有一种构成是由完全不含意义的词语构成，它同样具有很强的独特性和显著性，能大大加强商品的新鲜感和吸引力。如 Kodak，Rolex 等品牌就是人工合成的，它们的独创性大大加强了商品的知名度。Kodak 诞生于 1888 年。作为一个专有名词，Kodak 却没有词义，它并不企图提示某个已存在的词义，比如 Compact，也不是某个词的派生词。它是由美国摄影先驱 George Eastman 生造出来的。他认为一个好的商品名必须简短、有力，不致错拼、错写，以免破坏它的同一性。他很喜欢字母 K 发音干脆利索，强而有力。Kodak 5 个字母中竟然有两个 K（以 K 开头、结尾），是理想的品牌名。Kodak 还有拟声作用——让人联想到相机快门的"咔嚓"声，让人易读易记，常存脑海。

　　西方国家大都使用拼音文字，其基本结构单位是字母。大体上每个字母代表语言中的一个语音单位。这就使人们有可能根据自己的意思将某些字母拼合在一起，组成一个有音有形而无实在意义的字来。例如，Exxon（美国埃克森石油公司的商标）之所以用作商标，是因为它有两个 X，非常醒目。

　　如果把营销比喻成一场战役，那么成功的品牌名称就像一面不倒的军旗。当一种品牌的旗帜猎猎风中，构成一道独特的风景线时，其他同类产品实际上已在竞争中惨遭淘汰。品牌产生的影响有时候远远超出人们的想象，有的成功品牌甚至能跨越时空，作为语言的一部分被永远保留下来。例如 kleenex（纸巾）是 1924 年美国威斯康星州 Kimberley Klarke 公司首次生产的一种可当手帕或擦脂粉用的柔软手纸。由于在日常生活中被人们反复使用，以后逐渐转化为"纸巾"的俗名；jello（果子冻）来源于美国 General Foods 生产的果冻甜食的商标名 Jell-O；Kodak 本是一种小型照相机的商标名，后被用作普通名词，泛指小型照相机，现在这个商标词又转化为动词，即"用小型照相机拍摄"。

美国的 Odis 电梯公司于 1900 年申请专利的 Escalator 这个商标是由 escalade ＋ elevator 构成，这种电梯原来专为旅客登上曼哈顿高架铁道而设计，后成为商标名。1949 年此词广泛为大众所用，失去专属特性，派生出 escalatory，变成公众财产。Escalator 也就永久地留在英语里面，泛指一切自动扶梯。模仿 escalator 的结构，1966 年衍生出 travolator。这个词是由 travel ＋ elevator 构成。Travolator（变体为 travelator，travellator）是一种自动人行道，设置于机场、车站及购物中心。就是这些商标名，以其独有的魅力、影响力渗透到了人们的日常生活中，最终作为语言的一部分留存了下来。

参考文献

[1] 戴卫平，张志勇 . 英文品牌命名特色刍议 [J]. 唐山师范学院学报，2005（4）：29-32.

[2] 顾参林 . 英语中的 Trade Name[J]. 外国语，1995（2）：71-74.

[3] 贺川生 . 国际品牌：命名案例及品牌战略 [M]. 长沙：湖南人民出版社，2000.

[4] 胡开宝，陈在权 . 商品名称的美学特征与英语商品名称的翻译 [J]. 中国翻译，2000（5）：51-53.

[5] 谭卫国 . 中西文化与广告语言 [J]. 上海师范大学学报（哲社版），2003（2）：107-112.

[6] 朱亚军，张云秋 . 商标命名的暗示策略 [J]. 修辞学习，2002（3）：26-27.

第十三篇　美国人姓名成因

英语是世界上最为活跃、具有空前庞大词汇量的语言。其原因之一是英语从其他语言中引进了大量的外来语。在英语产生后的 1 500 多年中，它广泛地从世界上的其他语言中直接借用了大量词汇。1978 年出版的《英语百科全书》就列举了现代英语吸收了包括以下语种的词汇：希腊语、意大利语、西班牙语、葡萄牙语、荷兰语、俄语、斯拉夫语、波斯语、梵语、希伯来语、阿拉伯语、土耳其语、马来语、汉语、埃及语、北非语、西非语、北美土著语等。其原因之二是英语如同任何别的语言一样，通过各种渠道和方式构成了大量的新词，极大地丰富了英语语言。通过人的姓名转换为单词就是其中之一，即"人名名称"（eponyms），指的是某个时代或运动的代表人物、某种理论的创始人、某种物品的发明人、某种现象的发现人，以及宗教神话和文学作品中出现的人物等等。

一、科学家的名字

人类社会的发展是与科学技术分不开的，人类的历史，同时又是一部科学技术发展的历史。19—20 世纪是现代科学技术迅猛发展的时期，在科学和技术领域中发生了历史上空前的、有深远影响的重大突破，大大加快了人类历史的进程，改善了人类的社会生活，坚定了人类改造自然、改造社会的信心和决心。同时，科学技术的惊人发现也造就了一批科学巨匠，产生了一系列伟大的发明和发现。人们为了缅怀他们，就以这些科学巨匠的姓名来命名他们的新发明、新发现以及创新成果。当然，这也与西方，包括美国人崇尚个人的价值观是分不开的。

例如，有关电的术语，瓦特和电压单位伏特分别是以英国科学家 James Watt（1736-1819）和意大利科学家 Alessandro Volta（1745-1827）的姓氏命名的。两个单位名称可以分别缩略为 W 和 V；派生词 kilowatt（千瓦）、kilovolt（千伏）、

megawatt（兆瓦）、megavolt（兆伏）都是常用的词；复合词 watt-hour meter（电表）、voltmeter（电压表）, voltaic battery（伏打电池组）等都是人们所耳熟能详的。再看以下的例子。

电流强度单位 ampere（安培）是以法国科学家 Andre Marie Ampere（1775-1836）的姓名命名的。

电阻单位 ohm（欧姆）是以德国科学家 Georg Simon Ohm（1787-1854）的姓氏命名的。

电感单位 henry（亨利）是以美国科学家 Joseph Henry（1797-1878）的姓氏命名的。

电磁感应强度单位 gauss（高斯）是以德国科学家 Karl Froedrich Gauss（1777-1855）的姓氏命名的。

磁通量单位 weber（韦伯）是以德国科学家 Wilhelm Eduard Weber（1804-1891）的姓氏命名的。

磁通势单位 gilbert（吉伯）是以英国科学家 William Gilbert（1540-1603）的姓氏命名的。

磁通量单位 maxwell（麦克斯韦）是以英国科学家 James Clerk Maxwell（1831-1879）的姓氏命名的。

磁场强度单位 oersted（奥斯特）是以丹麦科学家 Hans Christian Oersted（1777-1851）的姓氏命名的。

磁通量密度单位 tesla（特斯拉）是以美国科学家 Nikola Tesla（1856-1943）的姓氏命名的。

电量单位 faraday（法拉第）是以英国科学家 Michael Faraday（1791-1867）的姓氏命名的，以他的姓氏构成的复合词也有一大批：Faraday cage（法拉第罩、静电屏蔽）、Faraday cup（法拉第筒）、Faraday effect（法拉第效应）、Faraday rotation（法拉第旋转）、Faraday's constant（法拉第常数）。

力的单位 newton（牛顿）是以英国物理学家 Isaac Newton（1642-1727）的姓氏命名的。

能量和功的单位 joule（焦耳）是以英国物理学家 James Prescott Joule（1818-1889）的姓氏命名的。

放射线强度单位 curie（居里）是以波兰物理学家 Marie Curie（1867-1934）的姓氏命名的。

长度单位 fermi（费米）是以意大利物理学家 Enrico Fermi（1901-1954）的姓氏命名的。

光谱线波长单位 angstrom（埃）是以瑞典物理学家 Anders Angstrom Angstrom

（1814-1874）的姓氏命名的。

压强的国际制单位 pascal（帕斯卡）是以法国物理学家 Blaise Pascal（1623-1662）的姓氏命名的。

Marchese Guglielmo Marconi（1874-1937）是意大利人，他发明的无线电报使英语增加了几个跟他的姓氏有关的词：marconi（发无线电报）、marconigram（无线电报）、marconigraph（无线电报机）。

Luigi Galvani（1737-1798）在解剖青蛙时发现了生物电现象，许多有关电的术语都来自他的姓氏：galvanic（电流）、galvanise（给……通电）、galvanism（伏打电）、galvanometer（电流计）、galvanistical（电疗的）等等。有的词已经转义成为普通词语，例如：galvanic 还可以作 "惊人的、富有感染力的" 解，galvanise 可以作 "使兴奋、激起" 解，galvanism 还可以作 "感染力、吸引力" 解，这些词在日常生活中也是常用词。

二、原创者的名字

人们在日常的工作和生活中，发现或发明了一些新的东西，结果人们就用他们的姓名来命名其新发现和新发明。

Pinebeck（冒牌货、便宜货），源出英国宝石商 Christopher Pinchbeck。他发明了一种铜和锌的合金用来假冒金质饰物。

Levis（李维斯牛仔裤），得名于布商 Leis Strauss（1829-1902）的大名。

Macadam（碎石路、柏油碎石路），源自碎石路面的发明者，英格兰工程师 John.L.MacAdam（1756-1836）的姓氏。

Biro（圆珠笔）是匈牙利记者 Ladislas Biro（1900-1955）在 1938 年发明的。

Hansom（双轮双座马车），它是由英国建筑师 Joseph A.Hansom（1803-1882）所设计。

Derby 源出 12 世纪 Derby 伯爵，他是现代赛马运动的首创人。人们为了纪念他，就把赛马称为 derby。

Derringer（大口径短筒小手枪）为美国费城一军械工人 Henry Deringer 于 1835 年发明。

Diesel（柴油机）是由德国热机工程师 Rudolf Diesel（1858-1913）发明的。

Shrapnel（榴霰弹）为英国一位将军 Sharpnel 发明，由此而得名。

Mackintosh（防水胶布）源出苏格兰发明家 Charles Mackintosh。

Babbitt（巴氏合金）是根据美国发明家 Isaac Babbitt（1799-1862）的姓氏命名的。

Braille（盲文）是法国盲童学校教师布莱叶 Louis Braille（1809-1852）于 1824 年创制的。

Magnolia（木兰花），是以法国植物学家 Pierre Magnol（1638-1715）的名字命名的，是他首先发现了这种植物。

Lobelia（半边莲）是佛兰芒植物学家 Matthias de l'obel（1538-1616）发现的。

三、医生的名字

人类的历史在某种程度上讲就是同各种疾病顽强抗争的历史。作为人类的白衣天使，大夫始终战斗在与疾病抗争的第一线，他们总是第一个接触到首发病例的人。其中不少医生就发现或首次诊断了某种疾病，结果这些疾病以它们的发现者的姓名来命名。

Addison's disease（艾迪生氏病）是肾上腺性青铜色皮肤病，由英国医生 Thomas Addison 于 1855 年发现。

Alzheimer's disease（阿耳茨海默氏病）是早年性痴呆病，由德国医生 Alois Alzheimer（1864-1915）于 1900 年发现。

Aujeszky's disease（奥耶斯基氏病）是伪狂犬病，由匈牙利病理学家 Aladar Aujeszky（1869-1933）于 1902 年发现。

Bright's disease（布赖特氏病）是肾上球肾炎，由英国医生 Richard Bright（1789-1858）于 1827 年发现。

Grave's disease（格雷夫斯氏病）是甲状腺机能亢进，由爱尔兰医生 Robert James Graves（1796-1853）发现。

挪威医生 Armauer Gerhard Henrik Hansen（1841-1912）发现的 Hansen's disease（汉森氏病）是麻风病。

英国医生 Thomas Hodgkin（1789-1866）发现的 Hodgkin's disease（何杰金氏病）是淋巴肉芽肿病。

法国医生 Prosper Meniere（1799-1862）发现的 Meniere's disease（梅尼埃尔氏病）是内耳性眩晕病。

英国医生 James Parkinson（1775-1824）发现的 Parkinson's disease（帕金森氏病）是震颤麻痹。

Cushing'syndrome（库兴氏病）是美国医生 Harvey Williams Cushing（1869-1939）发现的。

Down's syndrome（唐氏综合征）是英国医生 John Langdon 发现的。

Bell's palsy（贝耳氏麻痹）是面神经麻痹，是苏格兰医生 Charles Bell（1774-1842）发现的。

Huntington's chorea（亨廷顿氏舞蹈病）是遗传性慢性舞蹈病，由美国医生 George Huntington（1851-1916）最早诊断出来。

英国医生 Thomas Sydenham（1624-1689）发现的一种舞蹈病 Sydenham's chorea（西登哈姆氏舞蹈病），是儿童和青年人所患的一种舞蹈病。

四、食客的名字

民以食为天。饮食在任何一个民族文化中都是一个重要的因素。美国英语中有许多家喻户晓的"食物"名称就取自于人名名称。

取自人名的食品名称，最普及的莫过于 sandwich（三明治，夹肉面包），这个名称是从 John Montagu Fourth Earl of Sandwich（1718-1792）而来。这位伯爵是个赌徒，为不影响打牌而吩咐侍者在两片面包中夹一片火腿给他在牌桌上吃，作为一种食品因此而得名。

Garibaldi biscuit（葡萄干饼干）是以意大利民族解放运动领袖 Giuseppe Garibaldi（1807-1882）的姓氏命名的。

澳大利亚歌剧演员 Nellie Melba（1861-1931）一次上饭馆吃饭，点了一道菜，店里却没有，老板在冰激凌上放了块桃子，再浇点草莓酱给她，为讨她喜欢而把这种甜食称为 peach melba。一种新甜食和一个英语新词就这样诞生了。

Francois Rene de Chateaubriand（1768-1848）是法国著名作家，他喜欢吃的一道菜烤里脊牛排就成了 Chateaubriand steak，或者干脆简称为 Chateaubriand。至于消毒牛奶被称为 pasteurised milk，是因为牛奶经过了法国科学家 Louis Pasteur（1822-1895）发明的巴氏杀菌法处理。

有几种酒的名称来历就更有意思了。英国海军上将 Edward Vernon（1684-1757）的外号叫 Old Grog，因为他总是披着格罗兰姆呢（grogram，一种丝与马海毛织成的粗松斜纹织物）制成的斗篷，他规定水手喝的朗姆酒（rum）应该兑水，这种兑水的朗姆酒于是得名为 grog。英国名将 Nelson 在海战中牺牲后，其遗体被浸泡在朗姆酒里并被运回英国，从此，朗姆酒又名 Nelson's blood。

五、历史人物的名字

（一）风云人物

历史上的一些政治经济风云人物，不少人会因为他们所扮演的不同角色而进入词汇。例如：John Hamcock，喻义为"签上你的大名"，John Hamcock 因在美国《独立宣言》上签名时字迹遒劲，令人瞩目，而被引申为"某人的亲笔签名"。

第二次世界大战时，希特勒（Adolf Hitler, 1889-1945）因其实行法西斯专政，发动第二次世界大战，他的姓氏 Hitler 就成为"独裁者"的代名词。

挪威的法西斯党魁吉斯林（Vidkun Quisling, 1887-1945）在纳粹入侵后当傀儡政府头子，他的姓氏成了普通名词 quising，作"卖国贼"解。

英国战时首相丘吉尔（Winston Churchill, 1874-1965）的拥护者成了 Churchillian，他的纪念品成为 Churchilliana。

第二次世界大战期间，为了防备德国飞机空袭，英国内务大臣 John Anderson（1882-1958）于 1939 年提倡在各家后院建造波纹铁防空掩蔽所，大小足以容纳一家人，这种防空掩蔽所遂以他的姓氏命名为 Anderson shelter，在战时共建了 300 万个。他的继任 Herbert Stanley Morrison（1888-1965）又推出一种建在室内、可容纳 2—3 人的钢壁防空室，于是以他的姓氏命名为 Morrison shelter。

劳工大臣 Ernest Bevin（1881-1951）为了解决战时劳动力问题，把达到服兵役年龄的部分青年选去当矿工，这些青年被称作 Bevin boys。

食品部长 Frederick James Marquis，The first Baron Woolton of Liverpool（1883-1964）为了解决食品问题，号召大家吃一种以土豆、胡萝卜、防风根、甘蓝等当馅的蔬菜馅饼，叫作 Woolton pie。

交通大臣 Leslie Hore-Belisha（1898-1957）在任职期间采用了发琥珀色闪光的人行横道指示灯。这种指示灯被称作 Belisha beacon。

外交大臣 Anthony Eden（1897-1977）并不是因他的外交业绩而得名，而是由于在 1935 年刚上任时戴的一种黑色软毡帽后来风行一时，这种帽子就叫 Anthony Eden。

美国前总统克林顿（Bill Clinton）的政策带有克林顿的色彩 Clintonian，他执行的政策是 Clintonism，他执行的经济政策是 Clintonomics，他的支持者被称为 Clintonite。

Laffer curve（拉弗曲线）是供应派学者 Arthur Laffer 用来表达供应关系的解说图。

Keynesian（凯因斯主义的）来源于英国经济学家 John Maynard Keynes。

（二）历史人物

在人类历史的长河中，总有一些历史人物因其某一特征或某一事件而为人们所记住，其姓名就因其喻义而进入普通词汇。例如：

Croesus 是吕底亚的末代国王，他敛聚了大量财富，后来人们就把富有比喻为 as rich as Croesus。

　　Pyrrhic victory 是"得不偿失的胜利"的意思。Pyrrhus 是前三四世纪时希腊西北部 Epirus 国的国王。当时罗马帝国恶势力正在兴起，因而与 Epirus 产生了冲突。在意大利南部有一个希腊移民建立的城市 Tarentum 和罗马交战，该城向 Pyrrhus 王请求援助。双方打了两仗。结果 Pyrrhus 获胜，可 Pyrrhus 已经元气大伤，后人们就把他的胜利称之为"得不偿失的胜利"。

　　Guy 源出于 Guy Fawkes，他为火药阴谋案的主犯，每年 11 月 5 日焚烧其模拟像以示庆祝，后来表示"好笑的人"，"令人瞧不起的笑柄"，当动词用表示"好笑"。在现代英语中，guy 已失去了过去的贬义，现指"男子"，表示"伙计"、"家伙"、"朋友"等。

　　Caesar 源出于拉丁文 Julius Caesar（罗马将军，政治家）的小名，因其是剖腹产生。Caesar 一词后来被其侄子 Octavius（第一位罗马教皇）霸占，Caesar 一词后来就发展成 emperor 的同义词。与 Caesar 有关的词和词组还有：Caesarean birth（剖腹产）、Caesardom（恺撒辖地）、Caesarism（专制独裁）、Caesarist（专制独裁鼓吹者）、Caesar's wife（不容怀疑的人，源自 Plutarch《恺撒》中恺撒的话："I thought my wife ought not even to be under suspicion."）、appeal to Caesar（向最高权威者申诉）、Great Caesar！（天哪！好家伙！糟糕！）、render to Caesar the things that are Caesar's（把现世事交给现世君王，尽公民义务，语出基督教《圣经》，意指别让宗教信仰影响公民责任）。

　　Silhouette（剪影）来自 18 世纪中期法国作家 Etiennede Silhouette，他爱好剪影。

　　Chauvinism（极端的、盲目的大国主义或者大男人主义）来自 Nicolas Chauvin，他是盲目崇拜拿破仑的一名法国军人。由此引申的词语有 male-chauvinism、white-chauvinism。

　　Draconian 是"严厉的、苛刻的"的意思。Draco 是前 7 世纪的雅典政治家。亚里士多德说他写了几部宪法，缺点是立法太苛刻，几乎什么罪都处死刑。

　　Martinet（严格执行纪律的人），源自 17 世纪法国一位名叫 Jean Martinet 军事教官。

　　Bowdlerize（删改），源出 Thomas Bowdler，此人以删改莎士比亚作品而得名。

　　Comstockery（严禁败坏道德和社会风俗的书刊出版成剧本上演），源出美国一位自封的书刊审查员 Anthony Comstock。

　　Philippic（猛烈的抨击），指古希腊（Demosthenes）痛斥马其顿国王腓力三世（Phillip Ⅲ）。

（三）特异人物

　　除了以上历史人物因其某一特征或某一事件而为人们所记住之外，一些普通人的名字也因其特征而转化为与此有关的普通名词。例如：

Malkin 意为"淫荡的女人"，来源于从前一位淫荡的女子 Malkym。

Moll 为美国俚语"女流氓"、"流氓的姘妇"，源出同一女子 Malkym。

Doll 是一女子名 Dorothy 的缩写，该女子身材矮小，后来用于描写个子小而漂亮的女子和"洋娃娃"。

Hooligan（流氓恶棍）来源于流氓恶棍 Patrick Hooligan。

Annie Oakley（免费入场券、优待券）源于 Annie（1860-1926），美国的神枪手。她的神枪绝技，令全美国的人倾倒，她的名字家喻户晓，妇孺皆知。美国人看比赛时，持优待券入场，剪票后在票上留一小孔，使人想起她神枪穿孔，于是人们渐把"优待券"叫作 Annie Oakley。

六、文学作品中人物的名字

西方文化异彩纷呈。文学作品，特别是小说、戏剧或电影中总会出现一些具有典型性格的人物。随着时间的推移以及人们长期的传诵和引用，这些人物的名字就被赋予一定的深层含义，逐渐转为普通名词。例如：

Jim Crow laws（歧视黑人的法规）。Jim Crow 是南北战争之前某台戏的里的一个角色，他非常歧视黑人。

Muckraking（揭发丑闻）典故出自 John Bunyan 的作品 *The Pilgrim's Progress*，书中有一个拿着铁扒在扒粪的角色，叫作 muckraker，比喻有些人将时间浪费在一些龌龊的事情上，而不做心灵的修养。

Robot（机器人）来自捷克小说家 Karel Lapek 的科学幻想剧 *Rossum's Universal Robots*。

Shylock 意为"狠毒的放高利贷者"。Shylock 是莎士比亚《威尼斯商人》中的一个狠毒的放高利贷者。

Masochism（受虐狂），是以奥地利小说家 Leopold Von Sacher-Masoch（1836-1895）的名字命名的。

Orwellian 源自英国小说家 George Orwell，其著作有 *Animal Farms* 和《1984》等，都是影射前苏联的政治讽刺小说。Orwellian 的释义为"受严格统治而失去人性之社会的"、"严格控制的"。

Malapropism 意为"近音词的荒唐误用"。英国剧作家（Richard Brinsley Sheridan 1751-1816）于 1775 年问世的第一部喜剧《情敌》（*The Rivals*）中有一人物名叫 Mala Prop 夫人，她饶舌健谈，但却矫揉造作，性喜炫耀。她好用多音节词，但却不解其意，屡屡荒唐地误用发音相似而意思迥异的词语，以致笑料百出。

Gatsby 源自美国小说家 F. Scott Fitzgerald 的 *The Great Gatsby*。Gatsby 是个由穷军官暴发致富的人物，后转指"靠个人奋斗由穷变富的暴发户"。

Bumble（妄自尊大的小官吏），是 Dickens 小说 *Oliver Twist* 中的人物。

Odyssey 意为"漫长而艰难的历程"，古希腊荷马写的一部英雄史诗，描写 Odysseus 在古城特洛伊（Troy）陷落之后所经历的一段漫长而艰难的历程。

Micawber 为 Charles Dickens 的小说 *David Copperfield* 中的人物，此人充满幻想，总希望有朝一日时转运来，后喻指"幻想突然走运的乐天派"。

Tartuffe 是法国作家 Moliere 所著的同名喜剧中的人物，此人是十足的伪君子，现指"伪善的人"。

Pollyanna 为 Eleanor Porter 所著小说中的人物，此人遇事老是过分乐观，以主观善良的愿望看待一切事物，现指带有这种性格特征的人。

Fagin 意为"教唆儿童犯罪的教唆犯"，来源于 Charles Dickens 的小说 *Oliver Twist* 中的一个角色。

Scrooge（吝啬鬼）来源于 Charles Dickens 的小说 *Christmas Carol* 中的一个人物。

Babbitt 原为美国小说家 Sinclair Lewis 所著的同名小说中的主人公，现指"当代典型的市侩，美国资产阶级实业家"。

Mrs. Grunny 意为"拘泥于常规的人"。Mrs. Grundy 是英国剧作家 Thomas Morton 的喜剧 *Speed the Plough* 中的一个从未出现的人物，只因其邻居 Mrs. Ashfield 老是担心自己举动会遭到她的非议，总是在嘴边挂着她。Mrs. Grundy 因此成为"爱管闲事的人，拘泥于常规的人"。

Paul pry 意为"爱打听别人隐私的人"。英国剧作家 John Poole 在 *Paul pry* 这篇喜剧中为主人公取名 Paul Pry，他整日无所事事，游手好闲，好打听别人的隐私。

Sad Sack 意为"不中用的人、不称职的人"。英国军队漫画家 George Baker 在其漫画中塑造了一个笨拙无能，头脑糊涂的士兵 Sad Sack。

Elmer Gantry（神棍）是美国小说家 Sinclair Lewis 在其同名小说中所刻画的一个人物。Gantry 是一个伪善的牧师，他利用宗教欺骗信徒，收敛钱财，以满足个人的私欲，后成为"伪善的宗教人士"代名词。

Walter Mitty（具有英雄式幻想的人）是美国作家 James Thurber 在其 *Secret Life of Walter Mitty* 中创造的一个人物，他可以随时随地脱离现实生活，沉浸到英雄式的幻想中去。心理医生甚至用 Walter Mittyism 来称呼这种英雄式的幻想症。

Munchausen 是德国人 R.E.Raspe 所编虚夸的冒险故事集中的一位主人公，现可当名词用表示"吹牛大王"，也可当形容词用表示"虚夸的"。

Mentor 意为"恩师、保护人"。在荷马史诗 *The Odyssey* 中，Mentor 是主角 Odysseus 的好朋友。Odysseus 在攻打特洛伊城时，将自己的儿子 Telemachus 托付给 Mentor。

七、古希腊、古罗马神话、历史传说中的人物姓名

作为西方文明的滥觞，古希腊、古罗马文化起着举足轻重的作用。而神话作为文化的一种载体，对语言的发展影响很大，尤其是英语。美国英语词汇其中就有许多是源自神话中的人物。除此之外，历史传说对英语词汇的贡献也很大。

（一）古希腊神话中的人物

Heitor（战争之勇士），Heitor 是古希腊神话中 Trojan 之战的英雄，希腊人做好木马，将士兵藏于木马中，进入特洛伊城。

Pandora's box （灾祸之源），希腊神话中 Pandora 是神创造的第一个女人，类似夏娃的角色。Pandora 好奇心作祟，打开了一个盒子，结果给人类带来苦难。

Siren（汽笛、警报器）来自希腊神话中半人半鸟的女海妖 Siren。

Morphine（吗啡）是以希腊神话中的睡梦之神 Morpheus 的名字命名的。

Narcissus （水仙花）来自希腊神话中的 Narcissus。

Ocean （海洋）来自希腊神话万水之神 Oceanus。

Panacea （灵丹妙药）来自希腊神话 Panacea，她是医药之神 Asclepius 之女，能治百病。

Peony/paeony（芍药、牡丹）来自希腊神话中的一个人物名 Paeon。

Nemesis （报应），Nemesis 来自希腊神话女神。

Hygiene（卫生、保健法），希腊神话中有一女神叫 Hygeria，被人奉为健康之神。

Tuesday（星期二）是以北欧战神（Tyr）的名字命名的，相当于拉丁语中的 diesmartis （day of Mars）。

Wednesday（星期三）是以北欧的风暴之神（Woden）的名字命名的，Woden 是 Tyr 的父亲，相当于拉丁语中的 Mercurii dies（day of Mercury）。

Thursday（星期四）是以北欧的雷神（Thor）的名字命名的，相当于拉丁语中的 dies jovis（day of Jupiter）。

Friday（星期五）是以北欧的婚姻神（Frigg）的名字命名的，Frigg 是 Woden 的妻子和 Thor 的母亲，相当于拉丁语中的 dies veneris（day of Venus）。

Saturday （星期六）是从拉丁语 Saturni dies 借译过来的，Saturn 是罗马神

话中的农神。

Pygmalion 是希腊神话中塞浦路斯国王 Pygmalion 用象牙精心雕琢的一尊塑像，他情不自禁地爱上了这尊塑像。现在人们用 pygmalion 来比喻用某种技巧和才能塑造某人而后又爱上后者的那种人。

（二）古罗马神话中的人物

Volcano（火山）是因古罗马宗教所信奉的火与锻冶之神 Vulcan 而得名，拉丁文为 Vulcanus 或 Volcanus。

Money（金钱）来自罗马神话中主神 Jupiter 之妻天后 Juno Moneta.mercury（水星、水银），是由罗马神话里 Mercury 的名字演变过来的，他是商人、盗贼等的保护神，也是诸神的使者。

Diana（保持独身主义），来自罗马神话中的月亮神，也是狩猎女神与处女的保护神。

January（一月）以罗马神话中的两面神（Janus）的名字命名，Janus 的一张面孔朝着过去，一张面孔朝着未来，用于一年之始再恰当不过了。

February（二月）以罗马神话中的天后（Juno）的名字命名，Juno 的另一个称呼是 Februaria。

March（三月）是以罗马神话中的战神（Mars）的名字命名的。

May（五月）来自拉丁语 Maius，女神迈亚（Maius）是罗马神话中赫耳墨斯的母亲。

June（六月）是以天后 Juno 的名字直接命名的。

July（七月）是以恺撒大帝（Julius Caesar）的名字命名的。

August 是以恺撒大帝的侄子 Augustus 的名字命名的。

Tantalize 现为动词，意为"折磨"、"使对乞求之物可望而不可即"、"诱发某人希望而后之失望"，是由 Tantalus 加后缀构成。Tantalus 是古希腊神话中 Zews 之子，因泄露天机而被贬，站在齐头水中，渴时欲饮而水退之，饥时欲摘头顶树上升，仍不得饮食。

（三）历史传说中的人物

Don Juan 是西班牙传奇人物中一个专门玩弄女性的荒淫贵族，现喻指"调戏妇女的人"。

Damon and Pythias 是"生死之交"的意思，来自意大利古代的一个传说故事。青年 Pythias 因触犯国君 Dionysius 而被判处死刑，他要求回乡告别，国君不同意他的要求，唯恐他逃走。这时 Pythias 的好朋友 Damon 挺身而出，愿在 Pythias 回乡期间代为服刑。Pythias 因暴风雨延误，Damon 被押往刑场，他们的友情感动了国君。后来他们的名字连在一起，就用来表示"患难之交、生死之交"。

Faust 是中世纪传说中的人物，此人为了获得知识和权力不惜向魔鬼出卖自己的灵魂。后出现了 Faustian spirit，指"一种为了获得知识可牺牲一切的精神"。

A Roland for an Oliver 意为"不分胜负"。相传法国国王查理曼大帝身边有 12 名勇士，其中最著名的有 Roland 和 Oliver。一次两人比武，五天五夜未决胜负，后逐渐衍生出以上喻义。

美国英语中还有好多普通名词（还有少数动词、形容词）来源于人名名称，每个词都含有不同的社会文化、历史背景和典故。社会创造了语言，这些词的转换是在漫长的语言发展历史过程中自然形成的，它使得美国英语词汇更加形象生动活泼。这种词的转换仍在继续。如美国 *Newsweek*（1995 年 10 月 30 日）就把记者必须服从联合国"公众信息"的规定称之为"Journalists are subjected to an Orwellian flow of public information."。Orwell 就是本章中提到过的一个小说家，他的两部作品 *Animal Farms* 和《1984》都是影射前苏联独裁、专断的政治体制的讽刺小说。后来，他的名字就被转喻为"严格控制的"。作者采用了这个词，确实给文章增添了几分新意。随着社会和科学的发展，英语词汇，包括美语词汇会越来越多。词汇的喻义引申必须遵照约定俗成的原则，不能随意胡编乱造；对一个词的学习，不仅要知其然，而且要知其所以然。

参考文献

[1] 陈勇.英文人名非指称用法的特点及语用翻译[J].四川外语学院学报,2003（1）.

[2] 李半池.英美报刊选读[M].上海：上海复旦大学出版社，2001.

[3] 陆国强.英语词汇学[M].上海：上海外语教育出版社，1983.

[4] 汪榕培.英语词汇学高级教程[M].上海：上海外语教育出版社，2002.

[5] 汪榕培.英语词汇学研究[M].上海：上海外语教育出版社，2000.

[6] 汪榕培.英语词汇学探胜[M].上海：上海外语教育出版社，1999.

[7] 杨庆旺.科技上下五千年[M].哈尔滨：哈尔滨船舶工程学院出版社，1994.

[8] 张韵斐.英语词汇学概论[M].北京：北京师范大学出版社，1985.

[9] 张志勇,戴卫平.论英语民族姓名的文化涵义[J].唐山师范学院学报,2004（1）.

[10] 庄和诚.英语词源新说[M].汕头：汕头大学出版社，1994.

第十四篇　美国人青睐的美语词汇

　　某些词语，虽然作为英语通用语应用的很广泛，但美国人似乎特有癖好，例如 generation 一词。美国历史学家把林肯一代人称为 blundering generation（粗鲁的一代）。美国内战后出生的人叫作 missionary generation（传教士的一代）。美国人把第一次世界大战后的青年叫作 lost generation（迷惘的一代），接下来又出现了 GI generation（大兵一代）。GI 是 government issue 的缩写。20 世纪 50 年代对政治持怀疑观望态度的青年被称为 silent generation（沉默的一代）或 uncommitted generation（不介入的一代），把 20 世纪 50 年代知识界出现的颓废派叫作 beat generation（垮了的一代）。第二次世界大战后美国出生率猛增产生了 boom generation（婴儿潮一代）。美国的报刊杂志对这代人有各种各样的别称：now generation（注重现在的一代），me generation（以我为中心的一代），protest generation（动辄抗议的一代），Vietnam generation（越战的一代），rock generation（摇滚的一代）。20 世纪 70 年代又出现 expressway generation（高速公路一代）。美国建国至 20 世纪 60 年代共经历了 13 代人，因此 20 世纪 60—80 年代出生的这代人被称为 Thirteenth generation，亦称 X generation。1946—1964 年的生育高峰期过后，美国出现了一段生育低谷期，因此"第 13 代人"又被称作 bust generation（生育低谷期的一代）。20 世纪 80 年代至 2000 年出生的一代称为 millennial generation（千年的一代）。不同时代的人具有显著的性格特征和行为规范上的差异，同时这种性格行为和道德取向上的差异必然造成代与代之间的 generation gap。

　　1826 年前后起，美国的许多州出现了 prohibition movement（禁酒运动），并一度通过了 prohibition laws（禁酒法），还有一大批 prohibitionist（禁酒党人）。有些州自行宣布为 dry state（禁酒州），至 1918 年全国有 3/4 以上的人生活在 dry state，dry city 或 dry county 里。禁酒在当时成为现代改革运动的重要组成部分。1919 年联邦议会通过的宪法修正案第十八条，即 The Prohibition Amendment（禁酒修正案）以国法形式禁止酿造、运输和销售一切酒精饮料。美国正式成为一个 dry country（禁酒国）。但禁酒运动却导致出现了 speakeasy（非法酒店）和 bootlegger（非法酒商）。许多嗜酒的人嘲弄禁酒法，成为 scofflaw（嘲弄法律者）。这场被称为 the noble experiment（高尚实验）的禁酒运动最终以失败而告终。然而，prohibition 一词却深深地印上了美国历史上"禁酒"的烙印。

在通用英语中，administration 指"管理"、"经营"，但在美语中则用作"政府"、"一位总统任内的政府"、"行政官员"、"（行政官员的）任期"。在 19 世纪初叶，administration 还被美国人当作形容词用，如 administration paper（报纸，1808 年），administration man（行政官员，1810 年），administration candidate（政府候选人，1827 年），administration party（政党，1837 年）。大写的 Administration 早在 1803 年就开始用来专指"总统及其内阁，即政府"。作为"任期"用，它最早见于乔治·华盛顿总统 1796 年的《告别词》中所出现的 first administration（第一届政府）。Campaign 在英语中原是战争术语，指"战役"，后在美语中则用作"运动"、"竞选活动"，且用得十分生动而形象。与 administration 等大多数名词术语一样，campaign 也常用作形容词，如 campaign paper（竞选简报），campaign document（竞选文件），campaign speech（竞选演说），campaign manager（竞选经纪人），campaign orator（竞选演说者）等。此外，该词还常用作动词，指"参加竞选活动"、"竞争"。（蔡昌卓，2002：265-266）

美利坚民族的一个突出特色就是多种族性。因此，美国面临的最突出的问题就是种族关系。美国历史上的种族问题主要涉及各种肤色的人是否拥有平等的社会地位和权利。其中，与种族直接和经常联系在一起的词是 discriminate。Discriminate 这个词的英语意思是说以不同的方式对待其他人，这种方式可能是好的也可能是坏的。例如：It is unjust to discriminate against people of other races.（歧视其他种族的人是不公平的。）；discriminate in favor of white people（优待白人）（《英汉语大词典》）。但是，自从 discriminate/ discrimination 与黑人权利地位问题联系在一起以后，就被引申为歧视。在英语中与中文"歧视"的含义完全相同的另一个词是 prejudice，主要是瞧不起的意思。在美国，常常同时使用这两个词来说明黑人问题。如果只用 prejudice 而不用 discrimination，只能说明瞧不起，无法说明权利和地位的不平等；只用 discrimination 而不用 prejudice，则只能说明权利和地位的差别而无法说明种族歧视。另一与有色人种，主要是与黑人有关的词是 racism（种族主义）。种族主义不仅仅是歧视问题，它还是一种建立在种族之上的优越系统。在美国，主要表现在白人种族优越。事实上，种族主义是歧视加权利。民权运动兴起之后，种族主义遭受抨击，种族隔离制度在美国最终解体，race（种族）被 ethnic/ethnic group 所取代。但事实上，ethnic 这个词本身的使用就是一种种族歧视。

　　Ethnic 一词源自希腊语中的 ethnos（民族）。Ethnos 是一个古老的词语，在古希腊时代，该词主要是一个与 people 或 city 的名称相对应的 nationality 的称谓，是古希腊城邦国家的产物。古希腊时代是欧亚非大陆处于不同社会发展阶段的社会群体、各种族群体第一次大规模交汇的时期。所以，ethnos 这一词语也彰显了 tribe 或 race 的含义。在纪元以后的几个世纪中，该词出现了用以指称"非希腊部落"的含义。Ethnos 在现存的古希腊词典中主要指那些在血统、体貌、族体、宗教等方面的"异己"群体。Ethnos 在进入英语后，被用来形容那些非基督教的"异教徒"、"民族"、"未开化的人"、"野蛮人"等。源自 ethnos 的 ethnic 和 ethnic group 等术语的含义在西方发达国家从早期指称宗教异类、非白人种族、民族、非英裔移民等含义到 20世纪 60 年代泛指基于种族、民族、宗教、语言和文化背景的群体。20 世纪 60 年代后，ethnic 在美国开始在法律中用以指称犹太人、意大利人和其他较小的种类人的用语，反映主要用于某些在宗教、语言等方面"固执己见"而有别于美国主流社会的其他移民群体的特点。美国的盎格鲁 - 撒克逊英裔被称为 white，但 white ethnics 则意指"意大利裔或波兰裔或东南欧裔白人而非英裔人"。可见，在 white 之后加上 ethnics，也就成为区分"美国白人"的一种称谓，可见其应用对象是明确的，是 WASP 白人对非 WASP 白人的歧视。

　　Ethnic group "通常被指称在一个社会中居于文化上非主流地位、人口规模属于少数的群体，包括移民群体"。美国曾是一个以 WASP 为主体的社会，WASP 是White Anglo-Saxon Protestant 的缩写，意思为盎格鲁 - 撒克逊白人新教徒，其含义是指美国人认定自己的民族是以白人、英裔、新教徒这三个特征为标志的。种族上的盎格鲁 - 撒克逊种族是美国的民族认同二个原则之一。因此，美利坚民族自然是WASP 民族。在 WASP 思想流行时代，白人、英裔、新教徒这三个特征是美国人的民族认同标准，而其他人种，即 ethnic group，则处于从属地位，成为非主流文化。Ethnic group 一词语在美国流行与美国移民现象直接相关。就移民而言，任何脱离其族体（nationality）或民族（nation）母体的群体，也就不再是族体或民族，而成为美国的 ethnic group。

　　"语言与社会的关系是密不可分的。语言既是社会交往的工具，又是社会生活的记录者。在充当工具和记录者的过程中，语言也会受到社会的影响。社会上所发生的一些事件（如历史事件、政治事件等）往往会引起语言符号意义的变化。"（张克定，2001：11）随着美国历史的发展，美语中一部分词汇的意义变得"狭窄"。词义的"缩小"是指词从原先表达外延较宽广的概念缩小到表达外延较狭窄的概念，即从泛指转为特指。Prohibition 的广义是"禁止"但由于美国历史的原因，prohibition 在美国常常不言而喻特指"禁酒"。

同 prohibition 情况相类，由于历史原因，美语中由广义变为狭义的词还有不少，例如：

abolition 废除——美国黑奴制度的废除；废奴运动

confederacy 联盟——（1860—1861 年南北战争时南部 11 州的）南部联邦

containment 控制——（里根政府实施的）遏制政策

reservation 保留——印第安人保留地

civil rights 公民权——美国黑人民权

congress 代表大会——国会

signer 签字者——《独立宣言》签字者

elector 选举者——总统选举团成员

freeman 自由人——被解放的黑奴

integration 综合——取消种族隔离

secession 脱离——（南方 11 州的）脱离联邦

segregation 隔离——（对黑人实行的）种族隔离

伴随上列词语，还出现了相应的词语，如 abolitionist（废奴主义者），abolitionism（废奴主义），confederate（南部联邦居民），integrationist（主张或赞成取消种族隔离的人），secessionist（主张脱离联邦者），segregationist（种族隔离主义者），prohibitionist（禁酒主义者），prohibitionism（禁酒主义），federalist（联邦党人），federalism（联邦主义）等。

跟词义变"窄"相反，有一部分词汇随着美国历史的发展，出现了由本义引申出来的独特意义。换句话说，这些词的词义"扩大"了，产生了新的意思。由于禁酒运动，使 dry 和 wet 这两个本来很平常的词语在美语中的词义扩大了，产生了新的意思。Dry 的本义为"干的"，引申为"禁酒的"，如 dry law（禁酒法）；wet 的本义为"湿的"，引申为"反对禁酒的"。于是，禁酒的州成了 dry state，不禁酒的州成了 wet state。截止 1918 年全美国有 3/4 以上的人生活在 dry state，dry city 或 dry county 里。而且，dry 和 wet 都可以用作名词，drys 成了"禁酒论者"，wets 成了"反对禁酒的人"。类似这样词义扩大的词语还有 veteran（老兵）——退伍军人；grapevine（葡萄藤）——小道消息；ticket（票）——候选人名单。

词的本义可以是有理据的（motivated），也可以是无理据的。但词的转义总是有理据的。美国英语词语的转义受制于美国历史的诸多因素。美语词的转义无论是变"窄"或是变"宽"都是对美国历史现实的客观反映。

参考文献

[1] 蔡昌卓 . 美国英语史 [M]. 北京：北京大学出版社，2002.

[2] 陈安 . 新英汉美国小百科 [M]. 上海：上海译文出版社，2000.

[3] [美] 丹尼尔·布尔斯延 . 美国人建国的历程 [M]. 上海：上海译文出版社，1997.

[4] 董小川 . 美国文化概论 [M]. 北京：人民出版社，2006.

[5] 端木义万 . 美国社会文化透视 [M]. 南京：南京大学出版社，1999.

[6] 顾嘉祖 . 语言与文化 [M]. 上海：上海外语教育出版社，1990.

[7] 刘元珍 . 美国社会透视 [M]. 山东东营：石油大学出版社，1995.

[8] 汪榕培，卢晓娟 . 英语词汇学教程 [M]. 上海：上海外语教育出版社，1997.

[9] 严维明 . 美国史与美国语 [J]. 外国语，1984（1）：24-28.

[10] 杨玉圣 . 美国历史散论 [M]. 沈阳：辽宁大学出版社，1994.

[11] 郑立信，顾嘉祖 . 美国英语与美国文化 [M]. 长沙：湖南教育出版社，1993.

[12] 张克定 . 语言符号衍生义理据探索 [J]. 解放军外国语学院学报，2001（6）：9-12.

[13] 仲掌生 .20 世纪美国文化断想 [J]. 解放军外国语学院学报，2000（3）：99-101.

第十五篇　美国的艺术奇才

一、Helen Keller（海伦·凯勒）

The name Helen Keller has special meaning for millions of people in all parts of the world. She could not see or hear. Yet she was able to do so much with life. Her success gave others hope.

海伦·凯勒这个名字对世界各地的数百万人来说都有着特殊的意义。她看不见也听不到，然而她一生中却做到了很多事情。她的成功给其他人带来了希望。

Helen Keller was born on June 27, 1880, in a small town in Alabama. Her father, Arthur Keller, was a captain in the army of the south during the American Civil War. Her mother was his second wife.

1880 年 6 月 27 日，海伦·凯勒出生在阿拉巴马州的一个小镇上。她的父亲，阿瑟·凯勒，是美国内战时期南方军队的一个上尉。海伦的母亲是他的第二任妻子。

Helen Keller was just like any other child until she was a year and-a-half. She was very active. She began walking and talking eagerly. Then, 19 months after she was born, Helen became very sick. It was a strange sickness that made her completely blind and deaf. The doctor could not do anything for her. Her bright, happy world now was filled with silence and darkness. The young child had strong desires. She knew what she wanted to do. No one could stop her from doing it.

在一岁半以前，海伦和别的孩子并没什么两样。她非常活跃，很早就学会走路和说话。但是到她 19 个月大的时候生了一场大病，疾病使她完全失明和耳聋。医生对此爱莫能助。她原本光明、快乐的世界从此充满了寂静和黑暗。这个幼儿有着强烈的欲望，她知道自己想做什么，没有人能阻止她。

Miss Sullivan, her teacher, taught Helen many things, to read and write, and even to use a typewriter. The most important thing she taught Helen was how to think. Helen was able to learn many things, not just languages. She was never willing to have a problem unfinished, even difficult problems in mathematics.

海伦的老师沙利文小姐教会了海伦很多事情，读和写，甚至使用打字机。最重要的是她教会了海伦如何思考。海伦能够学到很多东西，不仅仅是语言。她从不愿意半途而废，甚至对数学上的难题也是如此。

Helen even went to college. She was 16 years old when she began studying at Radcliffe College in Cambridge, Massachusetts. She completed her studies with high honors. It was a hard struggle. Few of the books she needed were written in the Braille language that the blind read by touching pages. Miss Sullivan and others had to teach her what was in these books by forming words in her hands.

海伦还上了大学，她开始在马萨诸塞州的剑桥瑞德克力大学院学习时只有 16 岁。她以优异的成绩完成了学业。这是一场艰苦的斗争，她所需要的书没有几本是用那种供盲人阅读、靠触摸的盲文写的。沙利文小姐和其他的人不得不靠在她手心上拼划来告诉她书上的内容。

All of Helen Keller's knowledge reached her mind through her sense of touch and smell and her feelings. Miss Keller learned to love things she could not hear—music for example. She did this through her sense of touch. When waves of air beat against her, she felt them. Sometimes she put her hand to a singer's throat. She often stood for hours with her hands on a piano while it was played.

海伦·凯勒所有的知识都是通过她的触觉、嗅觉和内心感受传送到大脑的。凯勒小姐学会了去热爱她听不到的事物，例如通过触觉学习音乐，她能通过空气的振动感受音乐。有时，她会把手放在演唱者的喉咙上。她还经常会把手放在被弹奏的钢琴上，在旁边一站就是数小时。

Helen Keller was tall and strong. When she spoke, her face looked very alive. She often felt the faces of close friends when she was talking to them, to discover their feelings. She and Miss Sullivan enjoyed jokes, laughing at funny things that happened to themselves or others.

海伦·凯勒长得又高又壮。当她说话时，脸上的表情非常生动。当与亲密的朋友交谈时，她经常会用手去触摸他们的脸来感受他们的情感。她和沙利文小姐很喜欢开玩笑，她们时常会为发生在她俩身上的或是其他人身上的趣事开怀大笑。

Miss Keller had to work hard to support herself after she finished college in 1904. She worked for several organizations that helped blind people in America and in other countries. She started the Helen Keller Endowment Fund and asked for money from wealthy people. She wrote several books, and made a movie based on her life.

1904 年，凯勒小姐大学毕业后，不得不努力工作来维持生计。她在美国和其他国家的几个帮助盲人的组织工作，创设了海伦·凯勒资助基金，并从富人们那里获得捐赠。她写了几本书，并根据自己的生活经历拍了一部电影。

Miss Keller also worked to improve conditions for the blind in developing countries. After World War Two, she worked with soldiers who had been blinded in the fighting. She spoke in more than 25 countries. Her main goal was to increase public interest in the difficulties of people with physical problems.

凯勒小姐还致力于改善发展中国家盲人生活条件的工作。第二次世界大战过后，她与战争中失明的士兵们一起工作。在超过 25 个的国家和地区发表过演讲。她的主要目的是提高公众对残疾人困难生活的关注。

Helen Keller died in 1968. She was 87 years old.

海伦·凯勒于 1968 年辞世，享年 87 岁。

二、Walt Disney（沃尔特·迪斯尼）

Born on December 5, 1901 in Chicago, Illinois U.S., Walt Disney was raised on a Midwestern farm in Marceline, Missouri, and in Kansas City, where he was able to acquire some rudimentary art instruction from correspondence courses and Saturday museum classes. He would later use many of the animals and characters that he knew from that Missouri farm in his cartoons.

1901 年 12 月 5 日，迪斯尼出生在美国伊利诺伊州的芝加哥市。他在密苏里州马塞林中西农场里长大，在堪萨斯市，他从相关课程和星期六博物馆培训班上获得一些初步的艺术教育。他后来在卡通片中使用了他在密苏里州农场上了解到的许多动物和人物。

He dropped out of high school at the age of 17 to serve in World War I. Disney returned in 1919 to Kansas City for an apprenticeship as a commercial illustrator and later made primitive animated advertising cartoons.

17 岁时他从高中辍学，到第一次世界大战战场上服役。迪斯尼于 1919 年回到堪萨斯市，学习商业广告插图绘画，后来制作了原始的广告卡通片。

His first success came with the creation of Mickey Mouse in *Steamboat Willie*.

Steamboat Willie was the first fully synchronized sound cartoon and featured Disney as the voice of a character first called "Mortimer Mouse". Disney's wife suggested that Mickey sounded better and Disney agreed.

他的第一次成功来自于在《汽船威利号》中创造的米老鼠。《汽船威利号》是第一部声像完全同步的卡通片，展现了迪斯尼给首次被称作"莫蒂默老鼠"的形象所配的声音。迪斯尼的妻子建议米老鼠的声音听起来应更悦耳，迪斯尼同意了。

The invention of such cartoon characters as Mickey Mouse, Donald Duck, Minnie, and Goofy combined with the daring and innovative use of music, sound, and folk material made the Disney shorts of the 1930s a phenomenon of worldwide success. This success led to the establishment of immensely profitable, Disney-controlled sidelines in advertising, publishing, and franchised goods, which helped shape popular taste for many years.

卡通形象的塑造，如米老鼠、唐老鸭、米尼、古菲等，加上对音乐、配音以及民间题材的大胆创新的应用，让 20 世纪 30 年代迪斯尼的电影短片风靡全球。这一成功使他建立了在广告、出版和授权产品生产方面，由迪斯尼控制的、利润极为可观的副业，并在很多年里影响着大众品味。

In 1954, Disney successfully broke into television. By the time of his death, the Disney studio's output amounted to 21 full-length animated films, 493 short subjects, 47 live-action films, 7 rue-Life Adventure features, 330 hours of Mickey Mouse Club television programs, 78.5 Zorro television adventures, and 280 other television shows.

1954 年，迪斯尼成功地打入了电视界。到他去世时为止，迪斯尼制片厂的产量达到 21 部全长度的动画片、493 部短片、47 部实拍动作片、7 部根据真实故事改编的历险片、330 小时的米老鼠俱乐部电视节目、78.5 小时的佐罗电视历险片，以及 280 部其他类型的电视片。

In addition to his theme parks, Disney created and endowed a new university, the California Institute of the Arts. He thought of this as the ultimate in education for the arts, where people in many different disciplines could work together, dream and develop, and create the mixture of arts needed for the future.

除主题公园外，迪斯尼还创立并捐资兴建了一所新大学——加州艺术学院。他把该校看作艺术教育的制高点，在这里，来自不同学科的人可以协同合作、追求梦想、不断进步，创造出未来所需的艺术合成。

In 1939, Disney received an honorary Academy Award and in 1954 he received four Academy Awards. In 1965, President Johnson presented Disney with the Presidential Medal of Freedom and in the same year Disney was awarded the Freedom Foundation Award.

1939 年，迪斯尼获得 1 项荣誉奥斯卡奖。1954 年，他获得了 4 项奥斯卡奖。1965 年，约翰逊总统授予迪斯尼"总统自由勋章"，同一年，他被授予"自由基金会奖章"。

Disney died on December 15, 1966, in Los Angeles, California. At the time of his death, his enterprises had garnered him respect, admiration, and a business empire worth over $100 million-a-year, but Disney was still remembered primarily as the man who had created Mickey Mouse.

1966 年 12 月 15 日，迪斯尼在加利福尼亚州洛杉矶市逝世。在他去世的时候，他的企业为他赢得了尊敬、钦佩，以及每年产值超过 1 亿美元的商业帝国，但是人们仍然记住他，主要是因为他创造了米老鼠。

三、Lionel Hampton（莱昂内尔·汉普顿）

Lionel Hampton is an American Pioneering Jazz Icon. He is the frenetic jazz vibraphonist, gifted bandleader and storied showman who was the most celebrated musician of the swing era and went on to a six-decade career on the American stage.

莱昂内尔·汉普顿是美国爵士乐的开拓者。他是一位富有激情的爵士乐电颤琴演奏家、天赋极高的乐队领队以及强节奏爵士乐传奇表演家，是爵士乐时代最负盛名的音乐人，一直在美国舞台上活跃了 60 年。

A dynamic showman with an electric personality, Hampton was the giant of jazz. He pioneered the use of the vibraphone as a jazz instrument and single-handedly popularized its use. Hampton has cut hundreds of records. He was known for tremendous energy and for directing bands that were among the most long-lived and consistently popular large ensembles in jazz. His work has been hailed by everyone from presidents to jazz critics and endorsed by the public through enthusiastic attendance of his performances and unending sales of his records.

汉普顿是一位个性非常鲜明的表演艺术家、爵士乐巨匠。他是将电颤琴作为爵士乐演奏器乐的第一人，并独自一人将其推广开来。汉普顿已录制数百张唱片。他因精力充沛并组建爵士乐坛上存在时间最长且颇受欢迎的大型乐队之一而闻名遐迩。他的作品受到从总统到爵士乐评论家的广泛赞誉，并受到公众认可，公众充满热情地观看他的演出且持久地购买他的唱片。

Hampton began working as a drummer when he was a teenager. He spent many of his formative musical years in Los Angeles, playing with top local bands and some great national figures as they came through town. Among them were Louis Armstrong—who first encouraged him to play the vibraphone—and, later, Benny Goodman. He was one of the first musicians to bridge the racial gap between blacks and whites in jazz. He joined drummer Gene Krupa and pianist Teddy Wilson to form the multiracial quartet in the 1930s. Hampton later recalled, "I didn't recognize that it was a social advancement, but it was the first time blacks and whites ever played together out in public".

汉普顿十几岁时开始成为一名鼓手。他的音乐风格是在洛杉矶度过的数年中形成的，当时他与当地顶级的乐队和一些来小镇演出的美国著名音乐人同台演出。其中包括路易斯·阿姆斯特朗，正是他第一个鼓励汉普顿演奏颤音琴的。后来他又遇到了本尼·古德曼。汉普顿是第一个打破爵士乐中种族隔阂的音乐人。在 20 世纪 30 年代，他与鼓手吉恩·克鲁帕和钢琴演奏家特迪·威尔逊联手组建了多种族的四重奏乐团。汉普顿后来回忆道："我当时并没有意识到这是一种社会进步，但这确实是黑人和白人首次在公众场合同台演出。"

By 1930, he was touring extensively on the West Coast with his own groups, making records and enjoying billing as the"fastest drummer in the world", when he struck his first note on a vibraphone. He played with Armstrong's group for a year, establishing the vibraphone as a jazz instrument and himself as its top interpreter.

到了 1930 年，汉普顿同他的乐队沿西海岸巡回演出，录制唱片，以"世界上最快的鼓手"荣登排行榜，这是他开始第一次演奏颤音琴。汉普顿同阿姆斯特朗的乐队演出了一年，这期间他把颤音琴确定为爵士乐的演奏乐器，同时，他自己也成为该乐器最出色的阐释者。

Hampton played the vibes with lightning swiftness and harmonic and melodic simplicity and the drums with a fierce, driving rhythm. He became a household name after recording hits with Goodman. He kept up a torrid performing pace, appearing at colleges and jazz festivals across the country and on countless television variety shows. He also wrote more than 200 pieces of music of jazz standards. He performed his best-known composition, *Flyin'Home*, more than 300 times a year for more 50 years.

汉普顿演奏颤音琴时轻快、和谐，旋律简洁优美，而击鼓时则节奏强劲有力。在与古德曼共同录制了热门金曲后，汉普顿这个名字家喻户晓。他演出档期爆满，频频现身于全国各地的大学、爵士音乐节和无数的电视综艺节目。汉普顿还创作了 200 多首爵士乐曲。在长达 50 多年的时间里，他那首广为人知的作品 *Flyin'Home*（《飞回家》）每年演奏超过 300 多场。

Later, he left Goodman and started his own big band, featuring a big sound, swinging arrangement. His band specialized in boogie-woogie, jump and later bop, and later it had become as much a rhythm and blues as a jazz attraction. But it nevertheless remained the medium for the introduction of many jazz talents.

后来，汉普顿离开古德曼而创建了自己的大乐队。该乐队演奏高昂，节奏强劲有力。他的乐队擅长演奏布基伍基乐曲、强节奏爵士乐和博普爵士乐。到后来，乐队以爵士乐和节奏布鲁斯而闻名。但它一直是许多爵士乐天才的摇篮。

四、 Jim Davis（吉姆·戴维斯）

Jim Davis, is an American cartoonist who created the popular comic strip Garfield in 1978.As an Art and Business major at Ball State University, Davis distinguished himself by earning one of the lowest accumulative grade point averages in the history of the school. Prior to creating Garfield, Davis worked for a local advertising agency. Garfield is now one of the most popular cartoon characters in the world. The Garfield character is a selfish, overweight orange and black cat with drooping eyelids.

吉姆·戴维斯是美国的一位漫画家，他于 1978 年创造了家喻户晓的卡通人物加菲猫。作为博尔大学艺术与经济专业的学生，他的累积平均积分点成绩可以排在学校历史上倒数几位，也因此而出了名。在加菲猫诞生之前，吉姆在当地一家广告公司工作。如今，加菲猫——这个自私自利、黄黑相间的大眼皮肥猫——早已成为全世界最受欢迎的卡通人物之一。

Jim was born on July 28, 1945, in Indiana, where he grew up on a small farm with his parents and brother Dave. His love of cartooning emerged during the time he would normally be doing chores, but couldn't due to asthma. Davis' inspiration for Garfield probably came from his childhood on the farm, where he was surrounded by some 25 cats.

吉姆生于 1945 年 7 月 28 日，从小与父母和弟弟戴夫一起生活在印第安纳州的一个农场。他本该忙于农场劳动，但由于哮喘不能干活。就在这段时间里，他萌发了画漫画的理想。也许是农场上的 25 只猫给了吉姆最初的创作灵感。

Davis now lives in Muncie, Indiana where he and his staff continue to produce Garfield under his own company, Paws, Inc., which started in 1981. He is married to Carolyn, a singer and teacher whom he met while both were attending college, and has a son. Oddly, Davis did not have cats when he started Garfield and still does not today, as his wife is allergic to them. He does, however, have a dog.

1981 年戴维斯在印第安纳州的蒙西市创办了自己的保时公司，现在他仍在那里和同事们致力于加菲猫的漫画创作。其妻卡罗琳是一名歌手兼教师，两人在大学里相识，他们养有一子。有趣的是，戴维斯创作加菲猫的时候并没有养猫，现在也没有——因为卡罗琳对猫过敏。不过，他的家里倒是养了条狗。

Garfield is a lazy, fat, self-indulgent cat who thinks he's a human. He is wry and quick-witted and makes no apologies for himself. When he's not napping or eating, he's kicking Odie. If he were a human, he'd be despicable. Somehow, though, he's lovable.

加菲猫是一只懒惰、肥胖、自我放纵的猫，它认为自己是一个人。它固执己见，反应迅捷，而且从来不认错。当它不打瞌睡、不吃东西的时候，它就踢欧迪（漫画故事中的一条呆狗，是加菲猫的忠实朋友和嘲讽对象）。如果加菲猫真是一个人的话，它会是一个卑劣的人。然而不管怎么说，它是惹人喜爱的。

Everyone can relate to Garfield in some way because most of the humor is about eating or sleeping, something we all do. Also, he's a pet and most people can relate to the pet-owner relationship. It's funny. Look at what humans put up with—shredded furniture, broken lamps, chewed-up shoes—it's a comical situation. Pets get away with murder.

每个人都能在某一方面与加菲猫联系在一起，因为该形象大部分的幽默都是关于我们人类少不得的吃和睡。而且，它是一个宠物，大部分人都会由此想到宠物与主人的关系。这很有趣。看看谁能忍受这些：撕咬家具、损坏灯台、嚼碎鞋子，这是一个滑稽的场面。宠物犯事后却总能逍遥法外。

Davis was raised on a farm and there were always cats around, so he drew on all of catdom to come up with Garfield. Garfield's name and personality are partly inspired by his grandfather, James Garfield Davis, who was a big man, and sort of a curmudgeon. Odie is a stereotype of a dumb dog, and Jon Arbuckle is more or less, him. He is inspired by everything—books, TV, movies, but mainly, he is a good observer of people.

戴维斯是在一个农场长大的，那里有很多猫，于是他汇集所有猫的举止习性，创作出了加菲猫。加菲猫的名字和个性部分源于他祖父的启发，他叫詹姆斯·加菲·戴维斯，是一个身材魁梧然而脾气不太好的人。欧迪是一只呆狗的定型，而乔恩·阿巴克尔（漫画故事中加菲猫的主人）或多或少有一些戴维斯的影子。书、电视、电影，所有的东西都能给戴维斯启发，但主要是由于戴维斯善于观察人。

Garfield's looks have changed some. In the very early years, Garfield had much smaller eyes and his body was more or less a big blob. Over the years, his eyes got bigger. Davis needed readers to see his eyes better because his eyes were capable of telling so much. His body is more rounded and his legs are longer now, too. All these changes took place pretty gradually and for the most part, the changes were made to help move story lines along. He thinks Garfield is more appealing graphically now than he was in 1978, and even though his looks changed, his personality did not.

加菲猫的长相有一些变化。在刚开始那几年，加菲猫的眼睛要小得多，身子差不多就是胖乎乎的一大团。这些年，它的眼睛变大了。戴维斯需要读者更清楚地看见它的眼睛，因为它的眼睛能够传达出很多东西。它的身子更匀称了，腿也更长了。所有这些变化都是一点一点地逐渐发生的，而且设计这些变化大都是为了帮助推动故事情节向前发展。他认为现在的加菲猫比 1978 年在绘图上更具有吸引力；尽管它的外表变了，但它的个性没有变。

五、Christopher Reeve （克里斯托夫·里夫）

Christopher Reeve, the cinematic Superman who became a real-life inspiration for people with spinal injuries through his painstaking struggle to overcome total paralysis while continuing to speak out for stem cell research, died on October 10, 2004 at his home in New York. He was only 52.

克里斯托夫·里夫，于 2004 年 10 月 10 日在纽约的家中去世，年仅 52 岁。这位荧屏超人在现实生活中是脊椎病患者的精神榜样，他虽然全身瘫痪但仍与病魔斗争，并且不断呼吁支持胚胎干细胞研究。

A horseback riding accident in 1995 left the actor paralyzed from the neck down. After briefly pondering suicide, Reeve became a powerful proponent of causes ranging from insurance coverage for catastrophic injuries to unleashing the possibilities some scientists believe lie in using embryonic stem cells for research.

1995 年，一次骑马事故导致这位演员从颈部以下瘫痪。放弃了自杀的念头后，里夫开始关注一些例如灾难性受伤保险的建立或胚胎干细胞的研究活动，并成为了这些活动强有力的支持者。

As a young unknown actor, Reeve propelled himself to the status of instant myth in 1978 by starring in *Superman*: The Movie, a hugely popular film, then going on to do three successful sequels. Many critics said he brought humor and sensitivity to his portrayal of the Man of Steel.

他一直是一名默默无闻的青年演员，直到 1978 年，里夫主演了电影《超人》，这部电影受到了极大的关注，里夫迅速成为一个神话，随后他继续主演了三部续集并大获成功。很多评论家说，他给铁血男儿这个角色注入了他本身的敏感和幽默。

He was tall, with a strikingly handsome, square-jawed face and a strong athletic build. Even before Superman, he looked like Superman. Enhancing the image, he performed his own stunts; off-screen he piloted his own plane. There were numerous other roles, including substantial leading parts on Broadway.

他个子很高，有着极其英俊的方下巴和强壮的体格。在扮演超人之前，他看起来就已经很像超人了。电影中，为了提高画面感，他自己表演惊险动作；银幕外，他亲自驾驶飞机。他还扮演了许多其他角色，其中还有在百老汇出演的大量主角。

But it wasn't Reeve's 6' 4", 225 pounds. Physique that made him so convincing as Superman and Clark Kent. He brought a true duality to the role, making you believe not only that he could bend steel with his bare hands, but that Lois Lane and Jimmy Olsen didn't recognize that Clark and Superman were one and the same. Reeve played Clark Kent as a slightly pitiable everyman, a very square peg who just couldn't seem to fit into the world's round holes.

使他成为令人心悦诚服的超人和克拉克·肯特的，并不是里夫6英尺4英寸（约2.11米）、225磅（约102千克）的体格，而是因为他能使角色的双重身份充满真实性，使你相信他不但能赤手空拳地掰折钢铁，而且无法认出克拉克和超人是同一个人，即便是洛伊斯·莱恩或者吉米·奥尔森。里夫把克拉克塑造成一个可怜的普通人，一个似乎不适合在这个世界上生存的普通人。

When the horn rims and blue suit came off to reveal the Superman uniform underneath, everything fell into place. But unlike the actors portraying superheroes before him, Reeve played Superman with something that had previously been lacking: humility. Reeve was smart enough to know that: the iconic costume of Superman would do most of the acting for him, so he played it low-key. This was not a god, standing with puffed chest, arms akimbo and brow furrowed, lording over the inferior humans he could conquer if he desired.

在摘掉角质架眼镜，脱去蓝色的西服露出里面的超人制服后，一切都变得井井有条。但与之前扮演超级英雄的演员不同的是，里夫扮演的超人有着某种以前一直欠缺的东西——谦卑。里夫十分聪明，他知道，超人标志性的服装会为他表演增色不少，所以他低调地扮演这个角色。超人不是神，挺胸站立、双手叉腰、眉头紧皱，主宰着只要他想便能征服的下等人类。

It was Reeve's personal courage in dealing with his paralysis that transcended both his causes and profession, making him a real-life superhero in the minds of many. By tirelessly exercising and using electrical shocks to stir his numb nervous system, he was beginning to recapture—twitch by tiny twitch —the use of his body.

里夫在对付瘫痪时自身的勇气甚至超越了他的事业和职业，使他成为许多人心中真实的超级英雄。经过坚持不懈的锻炼和电击刺激麻木的神经系统，他开始能够一点一点地扭动，重新获得运用身体的能力。

In September 2000 he moved an index finger and the news startled scientists who had not expected to see such progress so long after so severe an accident. Reeve expected nothing less and continued to improve.

2000 年 9 月，他的一根食指可以动了，这个消息令科学家们吃惊不已，他们没有想到在发生如此严重的意外之后这么久还能看到康复到如此程度。而里夫的期望更多，他的身体状况继续得以好转。

Reeve in February 2003 decided to have surgery to free him from the respirator that had enabled his paralyzed lungs to breathe. Electrodes were implanted in his diaphragm so that breathing could be regulated electronically. But infections ultimately trumped technology, intensive exercise and even iron determination. The slim luck that had nurtured Reeve ran out. Even as he worked at recovery, he had produced a string of accomplishments since his accident that included writing two books and directing and acting in movies. At the same time, he lobbied extensively for public health issues.

2003 年 2 月，里夫决定借助手术摆脱他瘫痪的肺，取而代之的，将是他借以呼吸的呼吸器。通过手术他的横膈膜被植入电极，这样他的呼吸就能用电来控制。但感染最终击败了一切——技术、不懈的锻炼和铁一般的意志。原本支撑着里夫的小小运气终于还是用尽了。在他努力康复期间，他取得了自从意外发生以来一系列的成就，写了两本书，执导和参演了电影。同时，他还为公共健康问题进行了广泛的游说活动。

第十六篇　美国的财经大亨

一、John Rockefeller（约翰·洛克菲勒）

John Rockefeller was born on farm at Richford, New York, on July 8, 1839. Rockefeller was one of the first major philanthropists in the U.S., donating a total of $540 million to charitable purposes. Rockefeller was 57 years old in 1896 when he decided he should focus his efforts on philanthropy, giving away the bulk of his fortune in ways designed to do the most good as determined by careful study, experience and the help of expert advisers.

1839 年 7 月 8 日，约翰·洛克菲勒出生在纽约州里奇福德农场。洛克菲勒是美国主要的早期慈善家之一，总共为慈善事业捐献了 5.4 亿美元。1896 年，当洛克菲勒 57 岁时，他决定把精力集中在慈善事业上，于是投入大部分资金，通过仔细研究，凭借经验，再辅以专家意见以期实现最佳成效。

As his wealth grew in the 1870s and 1880s, Rockefeller came to favor a cooperation and conditional system of giving in which he would agree to supply part of the sum needed for a particular project if the others interested in it also would provide substantial financial support. It was on such a conditional basis that Rockefeller participated in the founding of the University of Chicago. Rockefeller offered to give $600 000 of the first $1 million for endowment, provided the remaining $400 000 was pledged by others within 90 days. Thus, the University of Chicago was incorporated in 1890, and over the next twenty years Rockefeller contributed to help build up the institution, always on condition that others should join in its support. In 1910 he made a farewell gift of $10 million, which brought his total contributions to the university to about $35 million.

在 19 世纪 70—80 年代，随着财富的积累，洛克菲勒开始青睐一种合作性和有条件的捐赠体系，只要有人乐于提供可靠的财政支持，他愿意为特定项目提供所需的大量资金。正是在这种有条件的基础上，洛克菲勒参与了芝加哥大学的建立，捐赠了首批 100 万美元捐款中的 60 万美元，其余的 40 万美元在其他人的保证下 90 天内提供。这样，芝加哥大学于 1890 年开始组建，在接下来的 20 年里，洛克菲勒总是在其他人也加入资助的条件下，帮助建设该学府。1910 年，他捐献了最后一笔 1 000 万美元的礼物，这样，他对芝加哥大学的总捐资达 3 500 万美元。

Rockefeller donated a large of money to help the poor. He also donated much love to his family. In 1864, he married Laura Spelman, whose father was a prosperous businessman. Eventually, they had four children who lived to adulthood: three daughters and a son. The family lived in a large, comfortable, but not ostentatious house in Cleveland until moving to New York in the 1880' s. Rockefeller instilled a sense of industry and public responsibility in his offspring that extended down to the third and fourth generations, producing one vice president and three state governors. Of all the leading American industrial families, the Rockefeller dynasty became the most remarkable.

洛克菲勒捐赠了一大笔钱来帮助穷人，他还向家人奉献了许多爱。1864 年，他娶劳拉·斯贝尔曼为妻，劳拉的父亲当时是一个成功的商人。他们一共有 4 个子女长大成人，三女一男，全家生活在克利夫兰市的一座巨大、舒适却又不显卖弄的房子里，一直到 19 世纪 80 年代，洛克菲勒举家迁往纽约。洛克菲勒向子孙后代灌输勤奋和社会责任的意识，这种意识延续到第三代、第四代后人，培养出了一位副总统和三位州长。在美国所有的实业家庭中，洛克菲勒王朝是最为突出的。

In the 1870s Rockefeller began to make business trips from Cleveland to New York. After a time he started bringing along his family for lengthy stays and, in 1884, he bought a large brownstone house at 4 West 54th Street, the land of which is now part of the garden of the Museum of Modem Art. Beginning in the 1890s, the family spent part of their time at Pocantico Hills, about 25 miles north of New York. Rockefeller died on the morning of May 23, 1937, at his home in Ormond Beach. He was 97 years old.

19 世纪 70 年代，洛克菲勒开始从克利夫兰到纽约做商业旅行。过了一段时间，他带着家人在纽约做较长久的逗留。1884 年，他在西 54 街 4 号购买了一幢较大的褐色砂石建筑的房子，这块地现在成了现代艺术博物馆花园的一部分。从 19 世纪 90 年代开始，洛克菲勒一家还在纽约以北 25 英里（1 英里≈1609 米）处的薄砍迪柯山度过一段时光。1937 年 5 月 23 日上午，洛克菲勒在奥锰蒙德海滩的家中逝世，享年 97 岁。

二、Henry Ford （亨利·福特）

Henry Ford was born on July 30, 1863 in Wayne county, Michigan, U.S.. He was the son of the Irish immigrants. When he was young, in addition to helping his father with the harvest, Ford also attended school in a one-room school house. However, Ford disliked both school and farm life, and at the age of 16, he walked to Detroit in search of employment.

1863 年 7 月 30 日，亨利·福特出生在美国密歇根州韦恩县。他是爱尔兰移民的儿子。小时候，除了帮助父亲收割以外，福特还要到一所只有一间校舍的学校上学。然而，福特既不喜欢上学，也不喜欢农场，16 岁时，他步行到底特律去找工作。

Ford was employed as an apprentice in a machine shop, where he learned about the internal combustion engine. After several years of learning his trade, Ford returned to the family farm and worked part-time for an engine company. Ford set up a small machine shop on the farm and began tinkering with engines and machines.

福特在一家机械修理店当上了学徒工，在那里，他学到了内燃机的知识。在此行业学习几年后，他回到家庭农场，并在一家发动机公司做兼职工作。福特在农场上开办了一家小型的机械修理店，开始摆弄发动机和机器。

Several years later, Ford moved back to Detroit when Ford was made chief engineer at the Detroit Edison Company. The position required Ford to be on-call 24 hours a day, but the irregular hours allowed him time to experiment. He had experimented with gasoline-powered vehicles and horseless carriages for several years before his first vehicle was completed. The "Quadricycle", a vehicle with a buggy frame mounted on four bicycle wheels was completed in 1896. Ford sold the "Quadricycle" to raise capital for more creations.

几年后，福特搬回底特律，之后，他当上了底特律爱迪生公司的总工程师。这一职位要求福特 24 小时随时待命，但这种不规则的时间安排反而使他有空从事实验。在做成第一辆汽车之前，他用几年时间试制了汽油发动机车和不用马拉的车。1896 年，他的"四轮车"竣工了，这是一辆安装在四对轮子上的、马车形状的机车。福特卖掉了这辆"四轮车"，并为制造更多的车提供了资金。

During the following several years, Ford continued to fine-tune his passenger vehicles. In addition, he built racing cars and even drove them himself. In 1903, Ford produced an automobile he was ready to market, and he formed the Ford Motor Company. In 1908, Ford introduced the successful Model T, which had been manufactured for 19 years.

在接下来的几年里，福特继续改良他的载客汽车。此外，他还制造赛车，甚至还自己驾驶赛车。1903 年，福特制造了准备投向市场的汽车，他组建了福特汽车公司。1908 年，福特成功研制了福特 T 型车，该型号车生产了 19 年。

Ford was able to market the Model T to the general public just because of his advanced production technology. At the Ford Motor Company's plant in Highland Park, Michigan, Ford introduced the first assembly line in 1913, which drastically reduced production time. As a result, more automobiles were made available at a lower cost. Ford also instituted the $5/day minimum wage, which he claimed increased productivity.

正是由于先进的制造技术，福特才有可能将 T 型车推向普通的公众。1913 年，在位于密歇根州海兰公园里的福特汽车公司制造厂里，福特引进了第一条组装线，这大大地缩短了制造时间，结果，更多的车可以以低成本制造出来。福特还制定了每天 5 美元的最低工资制，他声称这一制度大大提高了生产力。

By 1920, Ford built a huge plant in River Rouge, and the company became almost entirely self-sufficient. In 1926, Ford began losing sales to General Motors because the Model T was becoming outdated. The Ford plants were shut down for five months, after which Ford introduced the Model A and later the V-8. Both models received moderate success but were outsold by General Motors and Chrysler.

到了 1920 年，福特在胭脂河兴建了一家大型制造厂，公司几乎完全自给自足。1926 年，由于 T 型车变得过时了，福特公司的销售开始输给通用汽车公司。福特汽车厂关闭了 5 个月，之后，福特引进了 A 型以及后来的 V-8 型汽车。这两款车取得了一定的成功，但是销售不及通用汽车公司和克莱斯特汽车公司。

The problems Ford Motor Company encountered can be attributed to Ford's stubborn and authoritarian management style. Although Ford's only child had been named president in 1919, Ford remained in strict control. When General Motors and Chrysler signed contracts with the United Automobile Workers, Ford refused to follow suit. He employed spies and company police to prevent his workers from unionization. Ultimately, Ford was persuaded to sign a contract with the United Automobile Workers in 1941. Ford's only son died in 1943, and Ford resumed the presidency. However, he had experienced two strokes by that time, and two years later handed over the presidency to his grandson. Ford died at his home in 1947 at the age of 87.

福特汽车公司遭遇的难题可归咎于福特固执、独裁的管理模式。虽然福特唯一的儿子于 1919 年被任命为董事长，但是福特仍然牢牢地控制着公司。当通用汽车公司和克莱斯特汽车公司与汽车工人联合会签订协议时，福特拒绝照着干。他雇佣了间谍和公司警察来阻止工人们组成工会。最后，福特终于被说服，并于 1941 年与汽车工人联合会签订协议。1943年，福特的儿子去世，福特继续担任董事长。然而，到了那时，他已经患了两次中风，两年后，他将董事长一职交给了孙子。1947年，福特在家中去世，享年84岁。

三、Walter P. Chrysler（瓦尔特·克莱斯勒）

Chrysler was born in Ellis, Kansas U.S., in 1875. His first job as a janitor brought him 10 cents an hour. In 1893 he took a cut in pay to 5 cents an hour in order to enter a four-year machinist apprentice program. By the second year he was earning 10 cents an hour, then 12.5 cents in the third year, and finally 15 cents an hour in the fourth year. During this time he studied air brakes before the Union Pacific Railroad installed them, and he studied steam heat that was replacing the coal stoves in passenger ears.

克莱斯勒1875年出生于美国堪萨斯州的埃利斯市。他的第一份工作是当一名看门的，每小时10美分。1893年，为了上一个四年制的机械师学徒课程，他将收入减到每小时5美分。到了第二年，他每小时赚10美分，第三年12.5美分，最后第四年15美分。在这段时间里，他学习了"气刹"，那时，太平洋联合铁路公司还没有安装气刹，他还学习了正在汽车上取代煤炉的蒸汽热。

In 1897 Chrysler moved to Wellington, Kansas to work for Santa Fe Railroads and to learn new things. After two weeks he was at the top of the pay scale—27.5 cents an hour. So he went back to Ellis, Kansas for 30 cents an hour and then on to Denver, Colorado where a job at Colorado & Southern lasted two weeks.

1897年，克莱斯勒搬到堪萨斯州的惠灵顿市，为圣达菲铁路工作，并学习新东西。两个星期后，他就在工资单上排第一位——每小时27.5美分。于是，他又回到堪萨斯州的埃利斯市工作，每小时30美分，然后，他去了科罗拉多州的丹佛市，在科罗拉多南方铁路公司工作了两个星期。

Chrysler was earning $90 a month as a foreman over 90 men in 1902. He took more correspondence courses and moved on to the Colorado and Southern Railroad in Trinidad, Colorado for $105 a month as general foreman. In 21 months he became a master mechanic; only 29 years old, yet the boss of 1 000 men and earning $140 a month.

1902年，克莱斯勒当上了管90人的工头，每月挣90美元。他参加了更多的函授课程的学习，并转到科罗拉多州特立尼达市的科罗拉多南方铁路公司当总工头，每月薪金105美元。21个月后，他当上了总机械师。尽管只有29岁，但是他已经成了1 000人的老板，每月挣140美元。

At 34 years of age he was in charge of thousands of men and millions of dollars worth of equipment, stilt at $350 a month. Chrysler took more correspondence courses in engineering and after an unpleasant meeting with the new President, Chrysler took a cut in pay to $275 a month in order to work for American Locomotive Company as a foreman in the Allegheny shop in Pittsburgh. Here he bought a 6-cylinder car.

34 岁的时候，他负责几千人和几百万美元的设备，每月工资高达 350 美元。克莱斯勒学习了更多管理方面的函授课程，在与新总裁的一次不愉快会面后，他把月薪降到 275 美元，以便在美国机车公司位于匹兹堡的阿勒格尼厂房担任工头。在那里，他买了一部六缸车。

Chrysler was promoted to works manager at the age of 36. Chrysler was earning $12 000 a year but accepted a job as works manager at Buick for $6 000 a year. He was finally in the automobile business. Chrysler was general manager of Buick in 1916 when he was offered the presidency of Buick. Chrysler accepted and received $120 000 a year. 32 000 Chryslers were built in 1924 and sold for $1 595 the same as Buick. This car was a true 70 mph performer with four wheel hydraulic brakes and a replaceable oil filter.

36 岁时，克莱斯勒被提升为工厂经理。克莱斯勒那时年薪 12 000 美元，但是他接受了年薪 6 000 美元的别克工厂经理一职，终于走进了汽车行业。1916 年，克莱斯勒当上了别克公司的总经理，并担任别克公司的董事长。克莱斯勒接受了这一职位，年薪为 12 万美元。1924 年，生产了 32 000 辆克莱斯勒车，售价为每辆 1 595 美元，与别克车同价。该款汽车时速真正达到了 70 英里，并安装有四轮液压刹车器和可替换滤油器。

四、Sam Walton（萨姆·沃尔顿）

Sam Walton was born on March 29, 1918. As Walton grew up he was always an ambitious boy. He wasn't the smartest person at school but he was determined to do good so with hard work and lots of studying he became an honors student. Right after his graduation he entered the retail world working as a management trainee.

萨姆·沃尔顿 1918 年 3 月 29 日出生。在沃尔顿的成长过程中，他是个雄心勃勃的男孩。他在学校里不是个最聪明的学生，但他下决心要学好，所以，他勤奋学习，终于获得"优等生"称号。刚一毕业，他就进入零售业，做了一名管理见习员。

As time passed he went from being a poor town boy to the richest man in the world. He gained experience at friend's store. Soon after he got married, Sam decided to own his own department store. This dream came to a reality when he purchased a store in Newport with the help of his father-in-law.

随着时间的推移，他从一个贫穷的城镇男孩成为世界上最富有的人。他在朋友的商店积累了经验。结婚后不久，他决定拥有一家属于自己的百货商店。这一梦想变成现实，他在岳父的帮助下购买了纽波特市一家商店。

With the assistance of the friends, his store led in sales and profits in the six-state region. Sam made this possible by properly stocking all the shelves with a wide range of goods with very low prices, keeping his store centrally located so it was easily accessible to many customers, stayed open later than most stores especially during Christmas seasons, and experimented with discount merchandising. All these ideas were new to businesses but Sam caught on fast and was able to use them to his advantage.

在朋友的帮助下，他的商店在 6 个州地区的销售和利润排行榜上名列前茅。萨姆恰当地在货架上摆放种类繁多的廉价商品，把店址安在中心地带以方便顾客光顾，其打烊时间比多数商店更晚，尤其在圣诞节期间，他还尝试过折价销售。这些做法使上述愿望成为可能。所有这些创意对于当时的商业来说都是崭新的，但是萨姆掌握得很快，并能够很好地运用它们。

In 1950, he purchased a store in Arkansas, which ended up being called Walton's 5 & 10. Before this store opened it needed many improvements but to Sam that was no problem. He was never discouraged for a second. To introduce his store to the new town in July 1950, Walton staged his first sales promotion, called the"Remodeling Sale" and then the following year he had the grand opening.

1950 年，他在阿肯色州购买了一家商店，叫作"沃尔顿 5 分和 10 分店"。在商店开办之前需要许多改进，但对于萨姆来说，这不是个问题。他从没有片刻的气馁。1950 年 7 月，为了将商店介绍给这座新城，沃尔顿举行了第一次促销活动，叫作"重塑形象销售"，第二年，他的商店隆重开业。

Most people would not have time to do anything else but Sam did, he decided to start a second store. This was also named Walton 5 & 10, and it was just as successful as the other Walton 5 & 10. Walton knew though he needed a qualified manager to run the store so it would be as successful as his other store. He hired a manager, offering him a percentage of the store's profits, now known as profit sharing. Even with this new manager, Sam did not neglect the new store. He visited once a week to make sure everything was running smoothly.

多数人不会花费时间做其他事情，但是萨姆做了，他决定开办第二家商店。该店也叫作"沃尔顿 5 分和 10 分店",它同其他的"沃尔顿 5 分和 10 分店"一样成功。然而,沃尔顿明白他需要一个合格的经理来经营商店,以便于它跟其他的商店一样成功。他雇佣了一位经理,向他提供一定百分比的利润,这一形式现在称作"利润分成"。即便有了这位新经理,萨姆也没有忽视这家新店。他每个星期去一次,看看是不是万事顺利。

To keep his stores running in tip top shape, Sam was always trying to find new ideas to improve business. The next new thing he found was a concept known as Self-service. This is that the cash registers that were located at the counters throughout the store would be replaced by checkouts located in the front of the store where customers would pay for everything at one time. The cashier would unload the new light weight baskets and ring the goods up and put them in bags and then the customer was ready to exit the store.

为了使商店的运作处于巅峰状态,萨姆总是在寻找新创意来改善经营。接下来他发现的新方法被冠以"自助"这个概念,这是指分布在店内的收银台将被前置于商店的结账台所代替,这样,顾客就可一次性支付所买的全部商品。收银员卸下新型轻便购物篮里的商品,将商品记入现金记录机,并装进袋子,然后,顾客就可以走出商店了。

As time passed, Sam opened more stores with the help of his brother, father-in-law and brother-in-law. In 1954, he opened a store with his brother in a suburb near Kansas City in a shopping center. This store was quite profitable, too. Later, Sam decided to just concentrate on retail business instead of the shopping center business. Sam opened larger stores which were called Walton's Family Center. To keep management on their toes and on top of the game, Sam offered them the opportunity to become limited partners. This kept the managers always trying to keep profits at a maximum and kept them improving their manager skills. His ways were proven to be successful because by 1962 Sam and his brother owned 16 variety stores in Arkansas, Missouri, and Kansas. That was how Wal-Mart got it start and that was why they were different from any other store today.

逐渐的,萨姆在兄弟、岳父和内弟的帮助下开办了更多的商店。1954 年,他与弟弟在临近堪萨斯市郊的购物中心开办了一家商店,该商店也非常赢利。后来,萨姆决定集中精力做零售生意,而不是做购物中心业务。萨姆开办了叫作"沃尔顿家庭中心"的大型商店,为了让管理跟上去,并处于经营的顶端,萨姆给经理们提供了成为有限合伙人的机会,这使得经理们总想赢得最高利润,并不断提高经营技能。他的方法被证明是非常成功的,因为到了 1962 年,萨姆和弟弟在阿肯色州、密苏里州和堪萨斯州拥有十六家杂货店。这就是沃尔玛的发端,这也是它们与今天其他商店不同的原因。

Wal-Mart first opened in 1962 and became the world's number one retailer. Wal-Mart's success has also given many people today an opportunity for a bigger job market. More than 600 000 Americans work at Wal-Mart. The reason for its popular success is Sam Walton's values. Wal-Mart goes according to what Sam Walton believed, "Each Wal-Mart store should reflect the values of its customers and support the vision they hold for their community".

沃尔玛开办于 1962 年，成了世界上头号零售店。沃尔玛的成功也给了今天许多人更多的工作机会，60 多万美国人为沃尔玛工作。它大获成功的原因在于萨姆·沃尔顿所倡导的价值理念。沃尔玛按照萨姆·沃尔顿的理念走下去："每一个沃尔玛商店都应该反映顾客的价值观，支持他们对社区的想法。"

五、Alan Greenspan（阿兰·格林斯潘）

Greenspan took the job as the Chairman of Federal Reserves in 1987. Months after taking the job, Greenspan faced the October market crash. He stopped panic dead the next morning with a well-timed announcement that the Fed would back loans by banks caught short.

格林斯潘于 1987 年就任联邦储备委员会主席一职。接任工作后几个月，他就面临 10 月份的股市暴跌。他适时地宣布，联邦储备委员会将保证处于不利地位的银行正在放出的贷款，在第二天早晨就完全消除了人们的恐慌。

"This is a wonderful economy," the former Chief of the Fed said in New York. Asked what he might have done differently over the years, he laughed."I would have probably screwed it all up."

美联储前主席在纽约说："经济形势好极了。"当被问及这些年来他如果担任主席，做法和格林斯潘会有什么不同时，他笑道："我也许会把事情都弄糟了。"

In fact, the Fed chairman has only one of 12 votes on the Federal Open Market Committee, which gathers around a 2-ton mahogany table to decide the proper level for interest rates that will determine the borrowing costs for millions of American consumers and businesses. But Greenspan is persuasive. With artful obfuscation in public and devastating clarity behind closed doors, he nudges an unwieldy economy in directions his foresight suggests it ought to go.

事实上，联邦储备委员会主席在联邦公开市场委员会的 12 票中只占 1 票。委员会成员聚集在两吨重的红木桌子边，决定适当的利率水平。这一利率水平将决定上百万美国消费者和工商企业的借款成本。但是格林斯潘很有说服力。在公众面前，他很有技巧地装糊涂，私下里头脑却惊人地清醒。他促使运转不灵的经济朝着他预见的方向发展。

When the then President Clinton nominated Greenspan to a fourth term, however, he seemed hardly coerced. The Senate quickly and enthusiastically gave Greenspan an overwhelming confirmation victory.

当时任总统克林顿总统提议让格林斯潘进入第四任期，他似乎没有受到什么压力。参议院很快就通过了这项提议，以压倒多数票批准格林斯潘连任。

Inflation is down to trace levels, with unemployment at its lowest in generations. The once-huge budget deficit is now a surplus, offering the potential for tax cuts and also treasured Democratic social programs. U.S. markets keep rising, attracting capital from around the world. Sen. Phil Gramm, the Texas Republican who conducted confirmation hearings, declared Greenspan "the greatest central banker in the history of the world".

通货膨胀下降到了极低的水平，失业率也跌至几代人以来的最低水平。一度出现的巨额预算赤字现在变成了盈余，这为减税提供了可能，也为民主党的社会计划提供了资金。美国的市场继续呈上升趋势，吸引了来自世界各地的资金。得克萨斯州的共和党参议员菲尔·格拉姆主持了批准格林斯潘连任的听证会。他宣称格林斯潘是"世界上有史以来最伟大的中央银行家"。

All of this success feeds a personality cult that disappoints people used to reading intimate details about their heroes' personal life. "He is a very, very private person, and all of this attention embarrasses him," said his wife. "For fun, he likes baseball and Mozart. It's too bad he can't indulge in both at once."

所有这些成功加深了人们对格林斯潘人格魅力的崇拜，而他的个性却使那些喜欢阅读偶像私人生活细节的人感到失望。格林斯潘的妻子说："他是个非常非常不喜欢抛头露面的人，人们对他的所有关注都使他感到尴尬。在娱乐方面，他喜欢棒球和莫扎特的音乐，但遗憾的是，他不能同时沉浸在这两种爱好中。"

Greenspan, up at dawn, spends two hours in his bathtub absorbing economic data and writing speeches. That started as therapy for a bad back, but now it is purely sport. "He doesn't really appreciate fine food and wine," his wife said. "He used to love thrillers but no longer has time. What he really enjoys is pondering some math problem. I often come home to find him scribbling differential equations."

格林斯潘在黎明时起床，花两个小时泡在浴缸里阅读经济数据和准备发言稿。

这曾经是他治疗背痛的方法，但现在纯粹变为一项运动了。他的妻子说："他并不真正喜欢美食和好酒，过去他喜欢读惊悚小说，但是现在没有时间读了。他真正喜欢的是思考某个数学问题。我回家后常常发现他正在纸上涂写微分方程。"

Greenspan learned tennis at 48 and threw himself into doing well at it. Once he joked that at the progress he was making, according to his projections, he would be touring with the pros at age 104.Tennis partners describe him as highly motivated to win. Line calls can be heated.

格林斯潘在 48 岁时学会打网球，从此热衷于此。他曾经开玩笑说，据他推算，按照他现在的进步速度，他在 104 岁时能和网球职业选手一起参加巡回比赛。他的网球搭档描述说，他想赢取比赛的积极性很高。边线得分竞争得很激烈。

"His humor is very dry, and he tends toward puns, for which I forgive him, but he keeps me laughing all the time,"his wife said. The couple breaks for occasional tennis vacations or visits friends out West. When relaxed at a good party, Greenspan does a mean jitterbug. At home, he is Sweetie Pie.

他的夫人说："艾伦的幽默是干巴巴的，他喜欢用双关语，这一点我原谅他，但他能使我笑个不停。"他俩偶尔会休假、打网球或是拜访住在美国西部的朋友。在晚会上处于放松状态时，格林斯潘的吉特巴舞跳得极为出色。在家里，他是"亲爱的人"。

After 12 years of dating, they held a glamorous wedding at the Inn at Little Washington in Washington, Virginia, She wore a designer gown. Rather than shop for a tux, he selected a blue suit from his closet.Guests are still talking about the passionate, unbankerly kiss.

经过 12 年的约会，他们在弗吉尼亚州华盛顿的"小华盛顿旅馆"举行了盛大的婚礼。新娘穿一款由设计师专门设计的礼服，格林斯潘却没有购买礼服，而是从衣柜里选了一套蓝色的西装。宾客们如今还在谈论那热情似火、与他银行家的风格不相符的一吻。

He owns no stocks or mutual funds, preferring to avoid any appearance of profiting from the rich market conditions he has created. Greenspan speaks to reporters only off the record. He abandoned TV talk programs after a single appearance when misunderstood remarks spooked the Dow Jones index.

格林斯潘没有股票或共同基金，希望避免任何从自己创造的有利市场条件中获利的嫌疑。格林斯潘只对记者做非正式的谈话。有一次，他与电视记者的谈话被误解，引起道·琼斯股票指数波动，此后他不再接受电视记者的专访。

六、Paul Allen（保罗·艾伦）

While attending a school in Seattle, Paul Allen, born in 1954, in Seattle, capital city of Washington, U.S.,met Bill Gates, a fellow student. Less than a decade later, in June 1975, Allen and Gates were both college dropouts with the intention of designing software for the new wave of personal computers. Gates and Allen reinvented Q-DOS as MS-DOS and installed it as the operating system for IBM's PC offering, which dominated the market after its release in 1981.

1954 年，保罗·艾伦出生在美国华盛顿州首府西雅图市。在西雅图一所学校读书时，艾伦遇见了同校同学比尔·盖茨。几年之后的 1975 年 6 月，艾伦和盖茨双双从大学中途退学，目的是为个人电脑的新浪潮而设计软件。盖茨和艾伦将 Q-DOS 改造成微软磁盘操作系统（MS-DOS），并将它安装在 IBM 个人电脑上作为它的操作系统，1981 年该系统发行之后就占领了市场。

In 1983, Allen resigned from Microsoft after being diagnosed with Hodgkin's disease, and undergoing several months of radiation treatment. Allen's share in the company he co-founded made him a billionaire at just over 30 years of age.

1983 年，艾伦在被诊断患有何杰金氏病后，辞职离开微软，进行了几个月的放射治疗。后来，艾伦在他合伙创办的公司里的股份使他在刚过 30 岁的时候就成为亿万富翁。

Meanwhile, Allen began to concentrate on other projects, hoping to find the next big idea lurking somewhere just out of sight. In 1986, he set up a company called Vulcan Ventures in order to research possible investments; to that end, he founded a Silicon Valley think tank in 1992 called Interval Research. Through Interval Research and Vulcan Ventures, Allen began to put into practice his long-term dream of wiring the world into a society in which virtually everyone is online.

与此同时，艾伦开始关注其他项目，期待着发现潜藏在视野外某一个地方的下一个重大构想。1986 年，为了研究可能性的投资，他创办了武尔坎风险公司，那以后，他又于 1992 年创办了名为间隙研究（Interval Research）的硅谷智囊团。通过间隙研究和武尔坎风险公司，艾伦开始为他的长期梦想付诸行动，即将整个世界连成一个社会，让每一个人都在线。

His investments were diverse: America Online, SureFind (an online classified ads service), Teluscan (an online financial service), Starwave (an online content provider), hardware, software, and wireless communications. Allen built an infrastructure of well over

30 different companies in pursuit of his wired world strategy. In 1999, he invested nearly $2 billion in the RCN corporation, bringing his total holdings in the cable and Internet businesses to over $25 billion. He has also invested a good deal in the production of interactive media and entertainment. In total, Allen has major investments in over 100"new media"companies. Allen, with a net worth of around $30 billion, is variably reported to be from the second to the fourth richest man in the world. He now lives on an Island, near Seattle.

他的投资也是多样的：美国在线、SureFind（一个在线分类广告服务网络公司）、Teluscan（一个在线财经服务网络公司）、Starwave（一个在线信息提供商）、硬件、软件和无线通信。为追求他联通世界的战略，艾伦在 30 个以上不同公司里建立了一个基础结构。1999 年，他向 RCN 公司投资了将近 20 亿美元，使得他在有线业务和因特网业务中的总财产超过 250 亿美元。他还在互动媒体和娱乐业生产中有大量的投资。总的来说，艾伦在超过 100 家"新媒体"公司占有主要投资。各种报道声称资产净值达 300 亿美元的艾伦是世界上排名第二到第四的富豪，他现居住在西雅图附近一个岛上。

七、Meg Whitman（梅格·惠特曼）

Born in 1957, the Long Island native graduated from Princeton University in 1977, then got her MBA at Harvard in 1979. She started her career in brand management at Procter & Gamble, a great breeding ground for future Internet executives. Whitman then worked for eight years at consulting firm Bain & Co. From 1989 to 1992, she was an executive at Walt Disney, where she opened the first Disney stores in Japan and learned the basics of how to make a business run smoothly. She then moved to shoemaker Stride Rite, where she helped revive the Keds brand. Whitman oversaw FTD's conversion from a money-losing, florist-owned cooperative to a profitable private company, and she rejuvenated the FTD brand.

这位 1957 年出生的长岛人于 1977 年从普林斯顿大学毕业，然后在 1979 年从哈佛大学获得工商管理硕士学位。她的事业开始于在宝洁公司里的商标管理，这为她日后担任互联网经理打下基础。她在一家咨询公司——贝恩公司——工作了 8 年，1989—1992 年，她到沃尔特·迪斯尼公司当经理，其间，她在日本开办了第一家迪斯尼商店，并学会了如何使得公司运转平稳的基本知识。然后，她去了斯特来德·来特制鞋公司，在那里，她帮助拯救了"科兹"品牌。在惠特曼的管理下，花商全球递送公司（FID）由一个亏本的花商合作社转变为赢利的私人公司，FTD 这一商标也恢复了生机。

Since taking over as CEO in May 1998, she kept eBay focused on its core competencies. Any expansion was gradual and auction-related. She kept the company concentrated on what users would want. From the start, she understood what makes the company tick. She said "What is really interesting about eBay is that we provide the marketplace, but it is the users who build the company. They bring the product to the site, they merchandise the product and they distribute it once sold". Indeed, Wall Street observers claim that eBay runs so smoothly, it's difficult to point to what management has done. Whitman's contribution is, to some extent, taken for granted. Her low-voltage but efficient style is precisely what makes Whitman a business executive worth praising.

1998 年 5 月担任首席执行官以来，她一直让电子海湾集中于核心的所能之事。公司的发展壮大是循序渐进的，并与拍卖挂钩。她让公司专注于用户所要的东西，从一开始，她就懂得什么使得公司运转起来。她说过："电子海湾真正有趣的，是我们提供市场，但正是用户建立了该公司，他们将产品带进网站，推销产品，一旦售出，他们就送走它。"实际上，华尔街观察员声称，电子海湾运转平稳，很难指出已经进行了何种管理。在某种程度上，惠特曼的贡献是理所当然的。正是惠特曼低压高效的工作作风使她成为了一名值得称赞的商业执行官。

When Meg Whitman took over as chief executive of eBay, she set about her work with her usual know-how and curiosity. She knew she had to build the eBay brand. Her style—collaborative yet decisive, serious but loose—at the tone for the company.

当梅格·惠特曼接过电子海湾首席执行官一职时，她凭着她已有的知识和好奇心着手工作。她知道她必须建造电子海湾的品牌。她的风格——具有协作精神，也不乏明确果断，严肃认真但又放松自由——为公司确定了基调。

Yahoo has slipped from profitable to unprofitable, and Wall Street wonders if the never-profitable Amazon. com will survive. But eBay is doing fine; Wall Street complains that its stock is too expensive, but the company is worth more than four times as much as Kmart, and Whitman is leading it into its sixth very profitable year in a row.

雅虎从赢利机构下滑成不赢利机构，华尔街怀疑从来不赚钱的亚马逊网站是否还能继续生存下去。但电子海湾做得很好，华尔街抱怨它的股票太贵了，而该公司的价值超过了开玛连锁店的 4 倍多，惠特曼领导着它连续 6 年盈利丰厚。

The down-to-earth Whitman is starting to get her due. *Worth* magazine named her No. 5 on its list of"best"CEOs. *Fortune* magazine ranked her the second most powerful woman in business, behind Hewlett-Packard chief Carly Fiorina. While dot-com bubbles are bursting all over, Whitman runs an international e-commerce giant whose customers use eBay's person-to-person auctions. Meg Whitman stands as the most successful Internet executive of all.

脚踏实地的惠特曼开始收获她应该得到的东西了，《财产》杂志将她评为第五位"最佳首席执行官"，《财富》杂志将她列为商业界第二女强人，排在惠普公司总裁卡莉·菲奥莉娜之后。在各种网站遍地开花的时候，惠特曼经营着一家国际电子商务巨型网站，顾客们使用电子海湾进行人对人的拍卖，梅格·惠特曼成了最为成功的互联网经理。

八、Ted Turner（特德·特纳）

Ted Turner, the founder of Cable News Network and Turner Network Television, set an independent course early in his career. Turner built a communications empire from his father's over-stretched billboard business and is now creatively engaged in giving away the fortune he earned from it.

特德·特纳是有线电视新闻网和特纳网络电视的创始人，在创业初期就走上了独立之路。特纳继承父亲的广告业务，建立了一个通信帝国，如今他正专注于把从中获得的财富有创意地捐赠出去。

Turner demonstrated his individuality early on."Terrible Ted"is remembered for his odd habits. Brown University asked him to leave after he was caught with a woman in his private quarters. He won the America's Cup in 1977 with his yacht and then showed up drunk to collect the prize. He has worn a Confederate officer's uniform, complete with sword, to corporate negotiations; managed the Atlanta Braves which he owns, along with the NBA's Atlanta Hawks during a particularly bad season; and challenged his arch enemy, fellow media mogul Rupert Murdoch, to a televised boxing match in Las Vegas.

特纳很早就表现出了个性，人们就因为他的古怪习惯把他称呼为"可怕的特德"。布朗大学发现特纳在自己的住处与一个女人鬼混后，劝其退学。1977年，他划着自己的皮划艇夺得了美国冠军，然后喝醉了酒出现在领奖台上。他曾穿着美国内战时南部邦联的军官制服，配上剑，参加公司谈判。在特别差的赛季里，他管理过自己所拥有的亚特兰大勇敢者队以及NBA亚特兰大鹰队，在电视直播的拉斯维加斯拳击赛上挑战过劲敌媒体大亨鲁珀特·默多克。

Taking the helm of the family business upon his father's death, Turner expanded into television, purchasing an Atlanta UHF station in 1970. Just a decade later, he used the profits from that station, now the flagship of his nationwide Turner Broadcasting System—to launch CNN. Despite widespread predictions of disaster, the 24-hour all-news cable channel soon proved its worth with minute-by-minute coverage of such events as the space shuttle Challenger disaster in 1986 and the Persian Gulf War in 1991.

父亲死后，特纳接手掌管家庭企业，并扩张进入电视界，于 1970 年购买了亚特兰大 UHF 电视台。仅仅 10 年后，那个电视台成为了特纳广播公司在全国的旗舰，他利用电视台的利润开办了有线电视新闻网。尽管人们普遍认为这一举措会失败，但对 1986 年"挑战号"航天飞机失事和 1991 年波斯湾战争等事件进行的追踪报道，很快证明了这个 24 小时全新闻有线频道的价值。

Beginning in the mid-1980s, Turner began focusing on his personal brand of philanthropy. His much-maligned Goodwill Games, first held in Moscow in 1986, were both a publicity stunt for Turner Broadcasting and a genuinely-intended contribution to world peace. The Turner Foundation, founded in 1990, gives millions to environmental causes, and in 1994, Turner himself gave $200 million to charity. His gift of $1 billion to a new foundation to support the United Nations, announced in 1997, may be the largest single donation by a private individual in history.

从 20 世纪 80 年代中期起，特纳开始关注自己的慈善形象。1986 年，他在莫斯科举办了受到广泛指责的首届友好运动会，这次运动会既是特纳广播公司的宣传表演，也是真想为世界和平有所贡献。1990 年成立的特纳基金会为环保事业捐出了几百万美元。1994 年，特纳本人就为慈善事业捐献了 2 亿美元。1997 年他宣布为一个新的基金会捐赠 10 亿美元来支持联合国，这可能是历史上最大的一笔个人捐款。

Although Turner never earned a university degree, he is widely read, particularly in history and the Bible. He has several residences, including a several-thousand acre ranch in Montana.

尽管特纳没有获得过大学文凭，但是他读了很多书，尤其是历史和圣经。他有多处住宅，其中包括在蒙大拿州的几千英亩的大牧场。

九、Larry Ellison（拉里·埃利森）

Oracle is the world's leading supplier of software for information management and the world's second largest independent software company, boasting revenues of more than $9.7 billion. The huge success of the company makes Larry Ellison one of the richest people in America. Ellison's success is proof that business is not something learned through academic textbooks, but rather an innate gift. A college dropout, Ellison is renowned for his business sense, drive and ambition. In order to achieve Ellison's success, one must take huge risks and learn from mistakes made along the way.

甲骨文公司是世界上最大的信息管理软件供应商，世界第二大独立软件公司，公司收入超过 97 亿美元。甲骨文公司的巨大成功使得拉里·埃利森成为美国最富有的人之一。埃利森的成功证明了做生意并不是从学校课本上学来的东西，而是天生的才能。埃利森，一个大学辍学者，以其商业头脑、干劲和抱负而闻名于世。为了取得像埃利森那样的成功，你就得承担巨大的风险，边犯错误边学习。

Oracle underwent some changes before becoming the multibillion dollar corporation it is today. When first founded by Ellison, it was known as Soft-ware Development Laboratories and then reincarnated into Relational Technologies until it finally took on the name it is known as today: Oracle.

甲骨文公司在成为今天的拥有几十亿美元的公司之前也经历过变化。埃利森开始创立它的时候，称其为"软件开发实验室"，后来摇身变成"相关科技"，最后才采用现在的名称：甲骨文。

Ellison demanded at least 100 percent growth in sales of his company's software, a near impossible feat for a company that already boasts $100 to $500 million in sales. It would have been impossible for Oracle and Ellison, if it wasn't for some dodgy sales practices. This may be considered one of Ellison's mistakes as it negatively affected Oracle's business reputation. Although Ellison's high demands led to a highly stressful work environment, it also led to high productivity and Oracle's present success.

埃利森要求公司软件销售至少增长 100%，这一业绩对于销售额已达 1 亿—5 亿美元的公司来说几乎是天方夜谭。如果不是使出巧妙的销售术，这对于甲骨文公司和埃利森是不可能的。也许有人认为巧妙的销售术是埃利森的错误，因为它对甲骨文公司的商业声誉产生了负面影响。尽管埃利森的苛刻要求营造了一个高度紧张的工作环境，但它却带来了高生产率，并促成了甲骨文公司现在的成功。

As well as a billionaire, Ellison is also believed to be quite a multi-faceted character: playboy, world champion sailboat racer, sports nut, jet pilot, ruthless businessman, marketing genius, and avant-garde thinker.

除了亿万富翁的身份外，埃利森还是一位多面人物：花花公子、世界帆船比赛冠军、体育迷、飞行员、冷酷的商人、营销天才和前卫思想家。

十、Jeff Bezos（杰夫·贝索斯）

Jeff Bezos is the founder and CEO of Amazon. Com, which is headquartered in Seattle, Washington, and ranked as the world's largest e-tailer. He is not exactly your typical CEO. In fact, everything about him and his company Amazon. Com challenges convention. How else can you explain how a man who had an extremely successful career in Wall Street would leave his job, move across the U.S. to Seattle, and start an e-company that would soon amass over 10 million customers in cyberspace?

杰夫·贝索斯是亚马逊公司的创始人及首席执行官。亚马逊公司是世界上最大的网络零售商，其总部位于华盛顿州的西雅图。确切地说，贝索斯不是传统意义上的首席执行官。事实上，有关他和他的公司的一切都是离经叛道的。否则，他离开自己在华尔街极为成功的事业，千里迢迢来到西雅图，创办了一家很快拥有 1 000 多万网络消费者的电子商务公司，对此又做何解释呢？

Bezos seems as comfortable stealing ideas as he does inventing them. eBay is the rage? Amazon begins holding auctions. Google is getting the headlines and Web searching is the hot business? Bezos starts Amazon's own search engine. And he is determined to make his company the Wal-Mart of the Internet. Bezos has admitted to his copycat skill. He said, "We watch our competitors, learn from them, see the things that they were doing for customers and copy those things as much as we can".

贝索斯将自己"窃得"的想法视为己出，用得一样心安理得。时下网上交易平台电子港湾不是正火爆吗？亚马逊公司也开始举办网上拍卖。谷歌不也上了头版头条吗？网上搜索不也很热门吗？贝索斯便启动了亚马逊自己的搜索引擎。他决心要使自己的公司成为网络世界的沃尔玛。贝索斯坦言自己是在效仿他人。他说："我们关注着竞争对手，向他们学习，看看他们为客户提供什么服务并尽可能地去效仿。"

Bezos would rather interview 50 people and not hire anyone than hire the wrong person. "Company cultures aren't so much planned as they evolve from that early set of people. New employees either dislike the culture and leave or feel comfortable and stay." says Bezos.

贝索斯宁愿面试 50 人而不录用一人，也不愿错用一人。这是为什么呢？贝索斯说："企业文化与其说是人为规定的，倒不如说是从最早的一批员工身上逐步发展起来的。新员工要么不喜欢这种文化而离开，要么觉得轻松愉快而留下来。"

"If you're not stubborn, you'll give up on experiments too soon, "Bezos says. "But if you're not flexible, you'll go against the wall and you won't see a different solution to a problem you're trying to solve.""There are many ways to be externally focused that are very successful,"Bezos says. "You can be customer-focused or competitor-focused."But he warns that "some people are internally focused, which may hurt the whole company".

　　贝索斯说："如果你不固执，就会过早地放弃试验。可如果你不灵活，就会撞上南墙不回头，就看不到解决问题的新方法。"贝索斯说："以外部为关注焦点的种种方法是很成功的。你可以把客户或是竞争对手作为关注焦点。"但他警告说："一些人以内部为焦点，这样会损害整个公司。"

Bezos loves making decisions based on hard data，but when that's not possible, he believes in the power of being "simple-minded", relying on common sense about what would be in the best interests of his customers. "Sometimes we measure things and see that in the short term they actually hurt sales,"says Bezos. "But we do it anyway, because we believe that the short-term results probably aren't indicative of the long-term."

　　贝索斯喜欢依据可靠数据做决定。但当不可能获得可靠数据时，他便相信头脑简单、力量无穷。他靠常识来决定什么对客户是最有利的。贝索斯说："有时，经过权衡，我们认为某些事情在短期看来会有损销售额。但我们还是会去做，因为我们相信短期内的成效可能并不说明长期结果。"

十一、Michael Dell （迈克·戴尔）

Michael Dell is the chairman and CEO of Dell, the company he founded in 1984 with $1 000 and an unprecedented idea in the computer industry: sell computer systems directly to customers. The latest global innovation to come from Dell is its leadership on the Web. Dell is acknowledged as the largest online commercial seller of computer systems. The company also is redefining the role of the Web in delivering faster, better and more convenient service to customers.

　　迈克·戴尔是戴尔公司总裁兼首席执行官，他于 1984 年用 1 000 美元和计算机行业中史无前例的思想创立了该公司：将计算机系统直接销售给客户。戴尔公司的最新全球创新是在网络领域的领军力量，它被公认为是最大的计算机系统在线经销商，公司为了做到更快、更好、更方便地为顾客提供服务而重新定义了网络的作用。

The company's corporate customers include many of the companies in the *Fortune* 500 list of the largest American companies. With the addition of Dell to this list in 1992, Mr. Dell became the youngest CEO of a company ever to earn a ranking on the *Fortune* 500.

　　公司的团体客户包括了许多《财富》杂志上"美国 500 强"的公司。1992 年，戴尔公司也被列入 500 强，戴尔先生也因此成为进入《财富》500 强的最年轻的首席执行官。

Because of the phenomenal success of the company, Mr. Dell has been honored many times for his visionary leadership, earning a spot on *Time*/CNN's list of the 25 most influential global executives in 2001 and being named the 2001 *Chief Executive* of the Year by Chief Executive Magazine, "Entrepreneur of the Year"from Inc. magazine, "Man of the Year"by *PC* Magazine, "Top CEO in American Business"from *Worth* magazine and "CEO of the Year"by *Financial World and Industry Week* magazines. In 1997, 1998 and 1999, he was included in *Business Week's* list of "The Top 25 Managers of the Year".

由于公司取得了巨大的成功，戴尔也因其具有远见卓识的领导才能多次获奖，被《时代》、有线新闻网列入"2001 年全球最有影响的经理"，被《首席执行官》杂志提名为"2001 年年度首席执行官"，还被评为 *Inc.* 杂志"年度企业家"、*PC* 杂志"年度风云人物"、《价值》杂志"优秀美国企业首席执行官"以及《财经世界和商业周刊》杂志"年度首席执行官"。1997、1998、1999 年连续列入《商业周刊》的"年度最优秀二十五位经理"。

十二、 Warren Edward Buffett （沃伦·爱德华·巴菲特）

Warren Edward Buffett was born on August 30, 1930 in U.S.. A young Buffett was always fascinated by numbers and always had a keen eye for business. By age 11, young Buffett had purchased his first stock at his father's brokerage—three shares of Cities Service Preferred—at $38 a share. Even at age 11, he wasn't too young to learn that patience is a virtue, and could have made the difference between his $5 profit (from selling too early) to hundreds more, after the stock soon rose to $200.

1930 年 8 月 30 日，沃伦·爱德华·巴菲特出生在美国。年幼的巴菲特总是对数字着迷，总有敏锐的商业目光。到了 11 岁，小巴菲特就首次在父亲的证券经纪业务中购买股票——"良好城市服务公司"的三股，每股 38 美元。甚至在 11 岁时，他也没有因为年龄太小而不了解忍耐的益处，他能分辨出 5 美元（抛出太早）和几百美元利润之间的差异。不久股票就涨至 200 美元。

Since he was rejected from Harvard Business School, Buffett studied Economics at New York's Columbia University, to learn from his idol Graham, and eventually become his protege. Working with Graham as his mentor turned out to be a life-altering decision.

由于上哈佛大学商学院遭拒，巴菲特就到纽约哥伦比亚大学学经济学，师从他的偶像格雷厄姆，并最终成为他的门生。把格雷厄姆当成自己的导师被证明是改变他人生的决定。

What eventually became a billion-dollar fortune started out with his childhood earnings. He used the money earned from his soda pop and pinball machines to make his first investment partnership; with the money of investors and his own $100, Buffett began purchasing stocks, aiming to beat the Dow Jones Industrial Average by 10% a year. He did just that, from the start in 1957, until the end of the partnership in1969.

最终成为亿万富翁的历程始于他儿时赚的钱，巴菲特使用从贩卖汽水和弹球机中赚的钱做了第一笔合伙投资。凭投资者的钱和自己的 100 美元，巴菲特开始买股票，目标是从道琼斯工业指数中年获利 10%，从 1957 年开始到 1969 年合伙结束为止，他就是那样做的。

One of his biggest career moves was his investment in Berkshire Hathaway, a textile mill in New Bedford, MA, in 1962. He used Berkshire's capital by investing it in other businesses, amongst them insurance companies.

他最大的创业举动之一是 1962 年投资位于马萨诸塞州新贝德福德市的纺织厂贝克夏·哈瑟维，他使用贝克夏的资金，投资其他企业，其中包括保险公司。

Buffett, with the millions of dollars Berkshire was making thanks to him, began to fill his portfolio with stocks of companies that were undervalued, and inexpensive at the time. By sticking to companies such as American Express and Coca-Cola, companies with solid brand names rather than the latest Wall Street trend, Buffett has become one of the wealthiest men in the United States.

多亏了巴菲特，贝克夏赚了几百万美元。巴菲特用这笔钱开始在他的公文包里装上当时贬了值的、便宜的公司股票。他坚持购买诸如美国运通、可口可乐以及品牌可靠的公司的股票，而不是华尔街最新流行的公司的，这使他成为美国最富有的人之一。

But despite being known as the greatest stock market investor of the day, and having the kind of wealth only Bill Gates is familiar with, Buffett lives the kind of down-to-earth life familiar to many. He eats at Dairy Queen, loves Coca-Cola and burgers, still lives in the same house he purchased for $31 000, and doesn't dress like the billionaire he is.

尽管巴菲特享有"当今最伟大的股票市场投资者"的美誉，拥有仅比尔·盖茨才熟悉的那种财富，但他却过着大众熟知的平实生活。他在普通餐馆吃饭，喜欢喝可口可乐，吃汉堡包，仍然住在他用 31 000 美元购买的房子里，穿着并不像亿万富翁。

第十七篇　美国的总统

一、George Washington（乔治·华盛顿）

George Washington is the first President of the United States. He was born in 1732 into a Virginia planter family. From 1759 to the outbreak of the American Revolution, Washington managed his lands around Mount Vernon and served in the Virginia House. After he got married, he devoted himself to a busy and happy life. But like his fellow planters, Washington felt himself exploited by British merchants and hampered by British regulations. As the quarrel with the mother country grew acute, he moderately but firmly voiced his resistance to the restrictions.

乔治·华盛顿是美利坚合众国的第一任总统。1732 年，华盛顿生于弗吉尼亚一个种植园主的家庭。从 1759 年到美国革命爆发，华盛顿一直在经营弗农山周围的土地，并在弗吉尼亚庄园干活。他结婚后过着忙碌而幸福的生活。但是和其他的种植园主一样，华盛顿感到自己受到了英国商人的盘剥和英国法规的限制。当与宗主国的争端变得越来越激烈的时候，他适度而坚决地表达了对这些约束的抵抗。

When the Second Continental Congress assembled in Philadelphia in May 1775, Washington, one of the Virginia delegates, was elected Commander in Chief of the Continental Army. On July 3, 1775, at Cambridge, Massachusetts, he took command of his ill-trained troops and embarked upon a war that was to last 6 grueling years.

1775 年 5 月，当第二次大陆会议在费城召开时，华盛顿作为弗吉尼亚州的代表之一被选为大陆军司令。1775 年 7 月 3 日，在马萨诸塞的剑桥城，他指挥着这支训练不佳的军队，开始了长达 6 年的艰苦战争。

He realized early that the best strategy was to harass the British. Ensuing battles saw him fall back slowly, then strike unexpectedly. Finally in 1787 with the aid of French allies—he forced the surrender of the British troops at Yorktown.

他很早就意识到最好的战术就是困扰英军。在随后的战争中，他慢慢撤退，然后又出其不意地反击。最后在 1781 年，在法国盟军的帮助下，他在约克镇迫使英军投降。

Washington longed to retire to his fields at Mount Vernon. But he soon realized that the Nation was not functioning well, so he became a prime mover in the steps leading to the Constitutional Convention at Philadelphia in 1787. When the new Constitution was ratified, the Electoral College unanimously elected Washington President.

华盛顿渴望退休，回到弗农山。但他很快意识到国家此时运转不利，于是成为了 1787 年费城宪法大会的发起人。当新宪法经过批准后，选举团一致同意推选华盛顿为总统。

He did not infringe upon the policy-making powers that he felt the Constitution gave Congress. But the determination of foreign policy became preponderantly a Presidential concern. When the French Revolution led to a major war between France and England, Washington refused to accept entirely the recommendations of either pro-French, or pro-British. Rather, he insisted upon a neutral course until the United States could grow stronger.

他并不侵犯宪法给予国会的决策权。但是，外交方针是总统的事务。当法国革命发展成英法大战时，他既不采取亲法路线，也不采取亲英路线，相反，他坚持中立的立场，一直到美国变得强大。

To his disappointment, the two parties were developing by the end of his first term. Wearied of politics, feeling old, he retired at the end of his second term. In his Farewell Address, he urged his countrymen to forswear excessive party spirit and geographical distinctions. Washington enjoyed less than 3 years of retirement at Mount Vernon, for he died of a throat infection on December 14, 1799.

使他失望的是，在他第一届任期结束前，两党各自为营。华盛顿对政治感到厌倦，觉得自己已经老了，于是在第二届任期结束后就退休了。在他的告别演说中，他力劝人们放弃过强的政党精神，淡化区域差异。华盛顿在弗农山享受了不到三年的退休生活于 1799 年 12 月 14 日死于咽喉感染。

二、 Abraham Lincoln（亚伯拉罕·林肯）

Abraham Lincoln(1809-1865), 16th president of the United States and one of the greatest men of history. A humane, farsighted statesman in his lifetime, he became a legend and a folk hero after his death. Lincoln rose from humble backwoods origins to become one of the great presidents of the United States. In his effort to preserve the Union during the Civil War, he assumed more power than any preceding president. A superb politician, he persuaded the people with reasoned word and thoughtful deed to look to him for leadership.

亚伯拉罕·林肯（1809—1865），美国第十六任总统（1861—1865），人类历史上最伟大的人物之一，一位仁慈而有远见的政治家，在去世后成为一代传奇英雄。他出身寒门却成为美国最伟大的总统之一。为了让美国在战争后仍然保持统一，林肯做出了任何一任总统都难以企及的努力。一位优秀的政治家，他用令人信服的语言和周到的行为使得美国人民依赖他的领导。

Lincoln was born on Feb. 12, 1809, in Hardin County, Kentucky. He was born in the undistinguished family—second family. His mother died in his tenth year His father removed from Kentucky to Indiana in his eighth year. It was a wild region, with many bears and other wild animals still in the woods. There he grew up. Lincoln made extraordinary efforts to attain knowledge. He was a captain in the Black Hawk War, spent eight years in the Illinois legislature. His law partner said of him, "His ambition was a little engine that knew no rest".

林肯生于 1809 年 2 月 12 日肯塔基州哈丁县的一个二等家庭，母亲在他 10 岁时去世，他 8 岁时父亲移居到印第安纳州，那里到处是熊和其他野生动物，林肯就在那里长大。林肯花大量时间来学习知识，在黑鹰战争中他是上尉，并在伊利诺斯立法机关工作 8 年。与他在法律机关共事的人曾经说过："林肯的雄心壮志就像是一个从来不知道休息的发动机。"

In the American Civil War, his chief concern was the preservation of the Union from which the Confederate (Southern) slave states had seceded on his election. In 1863 he announced the freedom of the slaves with *The Emancipation Proclamation*. He was reelected 1864 with victory for the North in sight, but was assassinated at the end of the war.

在美国内战中，他最关心的问题就是战后美国的统一问题，因为在他当选为美国总统时南部奴隶制各州已经脱离了美国。1863 年林肯颁布了《解放奴隶宣言》，正式宣布了奴隶的自由。1864 年当北部胜利在望时，林肯再次被选举为美国总统，但是却在内战结束时被暗杀。

As President, he built the Republican Party into a strong national organization. Further, he rallied most of the northern Democrats to the Union cause. On January 1, 1863, he issued *The Emancipation Proclamation* that declared forever free those slaves within the Confederacy.

作为一名总统，林肯把共和党建设成为一个强大的国家组织。另外，他联合北部大部分民主党派来共同完成统一大业。1863 年 1 月 1 日，林肯颁布了《解放奴隶宣言》，宣布在联邦内奴隶获得永久性自由。

Abraham Lincoln is considered one of our greatest, if not the greatest President, and is also one of, if not, the greatest American president. Lincoln's achievements were so great that till now the following presidents in the history of the United States could not catch up with. He saved the Union and freed the slaves. The spirit that guided Lincoln was evident in his second Inaugural Address. This speech is inscribed on one wall of the Lincoln Memorial in Washington, D.C.

如果不能说亚伯拉罕·林肯是位最伟大的总统，他也是最伟大人物中的一位；并且如果不是最伟大的美国总统，也是其中的一员。林肯的成就非常伟大，后任的美国总统都不能企及。他拯救了联邦也解放了黑奴。他在第二次就职演说中明显地显示出了指引他前进的精神。这次演讲的内容被刻在华盛顿林肯纪念碑的一侧墙壁上。

Lincoln never let the world forget that the Civil War involved an even larger issue. This he stated most movingly in dedicating the military cemetery at Gettysburg: "that we here highly resolve that these dead shall not have died in vain—that this nation, under God, shall have a new birth of freedom—and that government of the people, by the people, for the people, shall not perish from the earth."

林肯从来没有让世界忘记内战还有更大的意义，这一点他在盖茨堡军事公墓的演说中动情地表现出来：“我们应该在这里下定最大的决心，一定要让那些死难者不要白白牺牲，我们要让这个民族在上帝的庇佑下，获得自由的新生，让这个属于人们、依靠人们、为了人们的政府与世长存！”

三、Franklin Roosevelt（富兰克林·罗斯福）

When Franklin D. Roosevelt assumed the Presidency the United States was at Great Depression. Roosevelt was born in 1882 at Hyde Park, New York. He attended Harvard University and Columbia Law School. Following the example of his cousin, President

Theodore Roosevelt, whom he greatly admired, Franklin D. Roosevelt entered public service through politics, but as a Democrat. He won election to the New York Senate in 1910. President Wilson appointed him Assistant Secretary of the Navy, and he was the Democratic nominee for Vice President in 1920.

富兰克林·罗斯福就任总统时，美国正处于经济大萧条的低谷。罗斯福 1882 年出生在纽约海德公园，曾就读哈佛大学和哥伦比亚大学法学院。富兰克林·罗斯福一向佩服他的堂兄西奥多·罗斯福总统，并有意以他为榜样，但他却以民主党人的身份参与政治，进入公益事业。1910 年，富兰克林成功地当选为纽约参议院议员，威尔逊总统任命他为海军部长助理，1920 年他还获得民主党副总统的提名。

In 1921, when he was 39, disaster hit—he was stricken with poliomyelitis. Demonstrating indomitable courage, he fought to regain the use of his legs. In 1928 Roosevelt became Governor of New York. He was elected President in November 1932, to the first of 4 terms.

1921 年，在富兰克林 39 岁那年，灾难袭来，他患上了脊髓灰质炎。他显示了不屈的勇气，与病魔抗争。1928 年罗斯福当选为纽约州州长。1932 年 11 月，富兰克林当选为美国总统，这是他四次当选中的第一次。

By March of next year there were 13 000 000 unemployed, and almost every bank was closed. In his first "hundred days", he proposed, and Congress enacted, a sweeping program to bring recovery to business and agriculture, relief to the unemployed and to those in danger of losing farms and homes, and reform.

第二年三月，全国共有 1 300 万人失业，几乎所有的银行倒闭。在他执政头 100 天，由他提议，国会制定并通过了一个全面复兴的计划用于复兴商业和农业，救济失业人口及面临失去农场和家园的人们，进行改革。

By 1935 the Nation had achieved some measure of recovery. Roosevelt had a new program of reform launched: Social Security, heavier taxes on the wealthy, new controls over banks and public utilities, and an enormous work relief program for the unemployed. In 1936, Roosevelt was reelected by a top-heavy margin.

1935 年政府复兴计划初见成效。罗斯福出台了一个改革新策略：建立社会保险体制，对富人征重税，改变对银行和社会公用事业的控制策略，并建立巨大的失业救济工程。1936 年，罗斯福以极大的优势再次当选美国总统。

Roosevelt had pledged the United States to the "good neighbor" policy, transforming the Monroe Doctrine from a unilateral American manifesto into arrangements for mutual action against aggressors. He also sought through *neutrality legislation* to keep the United States out of the war in Europe, yet at the same time to strengthen nations threatened or attacked. When the Japanese attacked Pearl Harbor on December 7, 1941, Roosevelt directed organization of the Nation's manpower and resources for global war. As the World War II drew to a close, Roosevelt's health deteriorated, and on April 12, 1945 he died of a cerebral hemorrhage.

在外交政策上，罗斯福主张放弃"门罗主义"，采用"睦邻友好"政策，这样就使得美国由单边防卫转为双边合作防卫。他还敦促国会通过了《中立法修正案》，使美国远离欧洲战争，与此同时却支持被威胁与被攻击的国家。1941 年 12 月 7 日，日本偷袭珍珠港，罗斯福立刻组织全国人力、物力加入这场世界战争。第二次世界大战临近尾声时，罗斯福身体也每况愈下。1945 年 4 月 12 日，罗斯福因脑溢血而病逝。

四、Richard Nixon（理查德·尼克松）

Born in California in 1913, Nixon had a brilliant record at Whittier College and Duke University Law School before beginning the practice of law. During World War II, Nixon served as a Navy lieutenant commander in the Pacific Fleet. On leaving the service, he was elected to Congress from his California district. In 1950, he won a Senate seat. Two years later, Eisenhower selected Nixon, aged 39, to be his running mate.

1913 年，尼克松生于加利福尼亚。在从事律师行业前，他在威特尔学院和杜克大学法学院学习，成绩优异。第二次世界大战期间，尼克松在太平洋舰队担任海军中尉。服完兵役后，他从加利福尼亚区被选入国会。1950 年，他入选参议员。两年后，艾森豪威尔推举 39 岁的尼克松作为他的竞选伙伴。

As Vice-President, Nixon took on major duties in the Eisenhower Administration. Nominated for President in 1960, he lost by a narrow margin to John F. Kennedy. In 1968, he again won his party's nomination, and went on to defeat Vice President Humphrey and third-party candidate George C. Wallace.

担任副总统期间，尼克松承担了艾森豪威尔政府的主要职责。1960 年，他被提名为总统候选人，但以微小的差距败给了约翰·肯尼迪。1968 年，尼克松再次获得他所在党的提名，并战胜了副总统汉弗莱和第三政党候选人乔治·华莱士。

Some of his most acclaimed achievements came in his quest for world stability. During visits in 1972 to Beijing and Moscow, he reduced tensions with China and the Soviet Union. His summit meetings with then Russian leader Brezhnev of Soviet Union produced a treaty to limit strategic nuclear weapons.

尼克松最令人称道的成就在于他寻求世界的稳定。1972 年访问北京和莫斯科期间，他缓解了美国同中国和前苏联的紧张局势。他和前苏联领导人勃列日涅夫在峰会上缔结了一个限制核武器的条约。

In 1972, his administration was embattled over the Watergate scandal, stemming from a break-in at the offices of the Democratic National Committee during the 1972 campaign. The break-in was traced to officials of the Committee to reelect the President. A number of administration officials were forced to resign; some were later convicted of offenses connected with efforts to cover up the affair. Nixon denied any personal involvement, but the courts forced him to yield tape. The Watergate scandal brought fresh divisions to the country and ultimately led to his resignation. He died on April 22, 1994.

1972 年，尼克松政府卷入了"水门事件"的丑闻。"水门事件"是指 1972 年大选期间对民主党全国委员会办公室的一次闯入（事件的起因是在 1972 年大选期间，尼克松的竞选班子成员擅自闯入了民主党在水门大厦的全国委员会办公室）。这次闯入牵扯到了致力于重选总统的该委员会的官员们。许多政府官员被迫辞职，有的后来还因为企图掩盖真相被定罪。尼克松矢口否认和事件有任何个人联系，但法院迫使他交出了证明他企图干扰调查的录音带。水门丑闻给国家带来了新的分歧，并最终导致尼克松的辞职。尼克松于 1994 年 4 月 22 日去世。

五、George W. Bush（乔治·W·布什）

George W. Bush was born on July 6, 1946. He was almost destined to follow in the footsteps of his father, in one way or another. Bush Junior attended Philips Andover Academy in Massachusetts, and continued his studies at Yale as part of the Class of 1968, both his father's alma maters. Before going on to receive his MBA from Harvard University in 1975, Bush entered the military service.

乔治·W·布什生于 1946 年 7 月 6 日。小布什几乎是注定要以某种方式步其父的后尘。小布什曾就读于马萨诸塞州的菲力普·安多佛学院，后于 1968 年进入耶鲁大学继续学习，而这两所大学都是他父亲的母校。在 1975 年从哈佛大学取得工商管理硕士学位之前，小布什服了兵役。

Once his military days were over and he became a Harvard graduate. Entering the oil and gas industry just like his father, Bush invested $17 000 to set up Arbusto Energy (arbusto means Bush in Spanish), and even ran for the U.S. House of Representatives in 1978, but lost the race.

兵役一结束，小布什就成为哈佛大学的研究生。同他父亲一样，小布什也进入了油气行业。他投资 17 000 美元建立了阿布斯托公司（"阿布斯托"在西班牙语里是"布什"的意思）。1978 年他参加了美国众议院的竞选，但以失败告终。

While the 1970s are referred to as Bush's "nomadic days"(marked by heavy drinking and possible drug use), the1980s were a moneymaking time for Bush. He changed the name of his oil company to Bush Exploration and merged with an oil-investing fund, due to the fact that oil prices experienced a sharp decline in the early 1980s.

20 世纪 70 年代被称为布什的"游牧岁月"（那时他总是酗酒，还有可能吸毒）。20 世纪 80 年代是布什人生中一段赚钱的时期。由于在 20 世纪 80 年代早期，油价急剧下跌，小布什把他的公司改名为布什勘探公司，并与一家石油投资基金会合并。

Putting his business skills to good use, Bush made a considerable profit. With the end of his oil business days, Bush reached a crossroads in his life, and took a turn towards politics. Turning away from the bottle and looking more towards religion (he is now a practicing Methodist, but was born Episcopalian), he moved to Washington D.C. to help George Bush Senior on his presidential campaign.

小布什极好地发挥了他的商业才能，获得了可观的利润。在他从事石油业的最后的日子里，小布什来到人生的十字路口，然后转向了政治。这时，小布什不再酗酒，在信仰上下了更多的工夫（尽管他生来是圣公会教徒，现在已成为一个地道的循道宗信徒了）。小布什迁往华盛顿特区，帮助老布什竞选总统。

As his number one confidante and right-hand man, Bush's tasks on his father's campaign included speech-writing and serving as chief liaison to Christian conservatives. George Bush Sr. was elected, while Junior moved to Dallas with his family and ventured into another business opportunity and made a profit of nearly $15 million. Now in his home state of Texas, Bush reentered politics—as the candidate for a second time—and won the 1994 election. After defeating his tough opponent, Bush was named Governor of Texas and succeeded in meeting most of his campaign's promises in the terms he served.

作为他父亲的第一知己和得力助手，小布什在父亲的竞选中的任务包括撰写演讲稿和充当与基督教保守派之间的首席联络员。老布什当选了，小布什举家迁往达拉斯，从事另外的商业投资，赢得了将近 1 500 万美元的利润。在他的家乡得克萨斯州，布什再次参与政治——第二次充当候选人——并于 1994 年在选举中获胜。在打败了一个相当强硬的对手之后，布什被任命为得克萨斯州的州长，并在任职期间成功地兑现了他许下的大部分诺言。

As the first Texas Governor to be elected to a second term, Bush announced that he was running for President—just like his father. The race between Republicans Bush and Cheney versus Democrats Al and Joe was too close to call. George W. Bush was finally named the 43rd President of the United States, making history for a second time as the first son of a former President to make it to the White House.

作为第一个连任的得克萨斯州州长，布什宣布他要竞选总统——就像他的父亲一样。共和党的布什和切尼与民主党的艾尔和乔之间的竞争十分激烈，难分胜负。最后布什成为美国第四十三届总统。作为前总统的长子，小布什又一次创造了历史，入主了白宫。

六、Barack Obama 巴拉克·奥巴马

Barack Obama was born in Hawaii on August 4th, 1961. His father was born and raised in a small village in Kenya, where he grew up herding goats with his own father, who was a domestic servant to the British.

巴拉克·奥巴马 1961 年 8 月 4 日出生于夏威夷。他的父亲出生于肯尼亚的一个小村庄，长大后和他父亲在那里一起牧羊。奥巴马的爷爷曾是英国人的家仆。

Barack's mother grew up in small town Kansas. Her father worked on oil rigs during the Depression, and then signed up for World War. Ⅱ after Pearl Harbor, where he marched across Europe in Patton's army. Her mother went to work on a bomber assembly line, and after the war, they studied on the G.I.Bill, bought a house through the Federal Housing Program, and moved west to Hawaii.

巴拉克的母亲是在堪萨斯市长大的。在大萧条期间她的父亲在石油钻井台工作。珍珠港事件后，他便报名参加了第二次世界大战，随巴顿将军的军队征战了整个欧洲。她的母亲去了一家轰炸机装配厂工作。战争结束后，他们研究了士兵福利法，通过联邦住房计划购买了一套住宅，往西搬到了夏威夷。

It was there, at the University of Hawaii, where Barack's parents met. His mother was a student there, and his father had won a scholarship that allowed him to leave Kenya and pursue his dreams in America. Barack's father eventually returned to Kenya, and Barack grew up with his mother in Hawaii, and for a few years in Indonesia. Later, he moved to New York, where he graduated from Columbia University in 1983.

巴拉克的父母是在夏威夷大学认识的。他的母亲是夏威夷大学的一名学生，他的父亲获得了奖学金，这使他得以离开肯尼亚来到美国追求他的梦想。巴拉克的父亲最后回到了肯尼亚。巴拉克跟着母亲生活在夏威夷，在那儿长大成人。他们还在

印度尼西亚生活了几年。后来，他搬到了纽约，1983 毕业于哥伦比亚大学。

Remembering the values of empathy and service that his mother taught him, Barack put law school and corporate life on hold after college and moved to Chicago in 1985, where he became a community organizer with a church-based group seeking to improve living conditions in poor neighborhoods plagued with crime and high unemployment. The group had some success, but Barack had come to realize that in order to truly improve the lives of people in that community and other communities, it would take not just a change at the local level, but a change in laws and in politics.

巴拉克牢记母亲同情和服务于人的价值观的教诲，1985 年大学毕业后他将在法学院的学业和企业中的工作搁置一边，来到芝加哥，在那里成为一个社区组织者，与一个以教会为基础的团体一起寻求改善深受犯罪困扰和高失业率的贫困社区的生活条件。该团体取得了一些成功，但巴拉克已逐渐认识到为了真正改善该社区及其他社区人们的生活，不应仅仅是改变当地水平，而是要改变法律和政策。

He went on to earn his law degree from Harvard in 1991, where he became the first African-American president of *The Harvard Law Review*. Soon after, he returned to Chicago to practice as a civil rights lawyer and teach constitutional law. Finally, his advocacy work led him to run for the Illinois State Senate, where he served for eight years. In 2004, he became the third African American since Reconstruction to be elected to the U.S. Senate.

1991 年他继续攻读哈佛大学的法学学位，并成为《哈佛法学评论》首位非裔美国人社长。不久之后，他回到芝加哥，做了一名民权律师并教授宪法。最后，他的宣传工作促使他竞选伊利诺伊州参议院议员，并在参议院工作了 8 年。2004 年他当选为美国参议院议员，这是自南北战争以来担任这一职务的第三位美国黑人。

It has been the rich and varied experiences of Barack Obama's life—growing up in different places with people who had differing ideas—that have animated his political journey. Amid the partisanship and bickering of today's public debate, he still believes in the ability to unite people around a politics of purpose—a politics that puts solving the challenges of everyday Americans ahead of partisan calculation and political gain.

巴拉克·奥巴马的生活经历一直是丰富多彩的——成长在不同的地方，与有着不同思想的人一同生活——这使他的政治之旅更富有活力。在当今党派和公开辩论的争执中，他仍然相信自己有能力团结民心并致力于共同的政治目标———一种解决美国人每天面临的挑战高于党派利益和政治利益的政治目标。

In the U.S.Senate, he has focused on tackling the challenges of a globalized, 21st century world with fresh thinking and a politics that no longer settles for the lowest common denominator. His first law was passed with Republican Tom Coburn, a measure to rebuild trust in government by allowing every American to go online and see how and where every dime of their tax dollars is spent. He has also been the lead voice in championing ethics reform that would root out corruption in Congress.

在美国参议院任职期间，他一直注重处理全球化的挑战问题，21 世纪的全球新思维和不再满足于最低的共同标准的政治信条。他与共和党人汤姆·科本提议的第一部法案获得通过，这是一项重塑对政府信任的措施，即允许每一位美国人上网查看他们缴税的每一分是如何使用的，用在何处。他还带头倡导道德的改革，由此可根除国会的腐败。

But above all his accomplishments and experiences, he is most proud and grateful for his family: his wife, Michelle, and his two daughters, Malia and Sasha.

除了他所有的成就和经历外，他最为骄傲的和最要感谢的就是他的家人：他的妻子，米歇尔和他的两个女儿，玛利亚和萨莎。

七、A Black President and Significance in History（黑人总统与历史意义）

On August 27, 1963, Waldo Martin, Jr. was glued to the television at home in Greensboro, N.C. It wasn't an unusual spot for a 12-year-old to be found, but August 28, 1963 was different. On-screen stood Martin Luther King, Jr., delivering his"I have a dream"speech from the steps of the Lincoln Memorial.

1963 年 8 月 27 日，小瓦尔多·马丁正在北卡罗来纳州绿区的家中聚精会神地看电视。对于一个 12 岁的孩子来讲，看电视并非什么稀奇的事情，但是 1963 年的 8 月 28 日却与众不同。电视屏幕上的马丁·路德·金正在林肯纪念堂前的台阶上发表他的那篇著名演说——"我有一个梦想"。

Fast forward to the present at U.C. Berkeley, where Martin is a history professor co-teaching a course about civil rights in the United States. The other night, he watched Sen. Barack Obama, the nation's first black major party presidential nominee, give his nomination acceptance speech in Denver, Colo.

时光快速切换到今天的加州大学伯克利分校，马丁现在已是该校的历史学教授，与他人合作在讲授美国的民权运动史。几天前，他在电视上看到巴拉克·奥巴马参议员成为这个国家历史上第一个被提名为总统候选人的黑人，并且在科罗拉多州的丹佛发表了接受提名的演讲。

For Martin and many other professors, Obama's candidacy and subsequent election to Presidency opens a new and often personal chapter in their study of American politics, race relations and life.

对于马丁和其他研究美国政治、种族和社会的教授而言，奥巴马获得总统候选人提名以及后来当选为总统揭开了他们个人研究生涯中崭新的一页。

"I was thrilled,"Martin said."The whole idea of his nomination and being elected is thrilling. In my lifetime, I would not have predicted this could happen."

马丁说："我非常激动。无论是他获得提名还是当选都非常激动人心。我这一生都无法想象会有这样的奇迹发生。"

"America, we are better than these last eight years,"Obama said."We are a better country than this."

奥巴马说："与过去的8年相比，我们美国人民在进步，美国也在进步。"

The senator gave his acceptance speech 45 years to the day after King addressed some 250 000 civil rights activists marching in the nation's capitol. It also came 53 years after the day 14-year-old Emmett Till's body was found brutally beaten and drowned in a Mississippi river.

奥巴马参议员发表接受提名演讲的当天恰好也是小马丁·路德·金对在国会大厦前游行的250 000万民权运动者前发表演讲45周年。也恰好是14岁的埃默特·提尔在遭受毒打并沉尸密西西比河后遗体被人发现53周年。

For Robert Allen, a professor of African American studies and ethnic studies, the changes between 1963 and 2008 seem astonishing.

对于专门研究非洲裔美国人和种族问题的教授罗伯特·艾伦而言，1963—2008年的变化简直令人难以置信。

"While I thought we were making great progress with the March on Washington, I thought we were also generations away from the possibility of electing a black president,"said Allen, who grew up in racially segregated Georgia."For me, history has been speeded up."

艾伦是在宗族隔离制度盛行的佐治亚州长大的，他说："虽然我一直以为从'向华盛顿进军'的游行活动结束至今美国取得了巨大的进步，但是要选出一位黑人总统至少还需要几十年的努力。而对于我来说，历史进程已经大大加快了。"

The syllabus for Allen's fall seminar, Men of Color in the United States, includes for the first time Obama's memoir *Dreams from My Father: A Story of Race and Inheritance*.

Allen said he plans to use it to study the politician's background as a community organizer.

艾伦在他秋季学期开设的研讨课"美国的有色人种"的教学大纲中首次收录了奥巴马的回忆录《父亲的梦想：种族与继承的故事》。艾伦说他计划利用这个材料来研究这位政治家的社会背景。

Mark Brilliant, an assistant professor in history and American studies who is co-teaching with Martin in a class titled "Civil Rights and Social Movements in U.S. History: Struggles for Racial Equality in Comparative Perspective, World War Ⅱ -Present", said he wants to examine how Obama has built a multifaceted coalition that includes young voters, African Americans and Democrats.

马克•布赖恩特是历史学和美国研究助理教授，与马丁共同教授一门叫作"美国历史上的民权与社会运动：二战后美国争取种族平等斗争比较研究"的课程。他希望研究一下奥巴马是如何建立一个全方位的联合政府的，这里面有年轻选民、非洲裔美国人和民主党人。

"One thing that Obama talks a lot about is hope,"Martin said. "How do you sustain hope, possibility? How do you create change? "

马丁说："奥巴马谈论最多的是希望。如何使希望永存？如何带来变革？"

Jack Glaser, an associate professor in the Goldman School of Public Policy, said that Obama won the election, and his victory would serve as a"powerful stimulus"in reducing prejudice and discrimination.

古尔德曼公共政策学院的副教授杰克•格拉泽说，奥巴马赢得了这场大选，他的胜利将会极大地减少种族偏见和歧视。

"It will be a constant reminder of the ability of African Americans to achieve at the highest level."Glaser said.

格拉泽说："这将永远表明非洲裔美国人有能力取得最高成就。"

Obama's rise also carries significance for U.C. Berkeley scholars of early American history. One such individual is associate professor Mark Peterson, whose History class will largely focus on slavery.

奥巴马的崛起对于加州大学伯克利分校研究美国早期历史的学者而言意义也十分重大。主要讲授奴隶制的历史学副教授马克•彼得森也是其中之一。

"(Obama) is an African American who is somewhat statistically or historically in the minority in that the vast majority of African Americans in the U.S. have ancestors who were brought to the New World as slaves,"he said. "It gives him an interesting perspective on the variety of the American historical experience."

他说："从统计学和历史学的角度看，奥巴马在非洲裔美国人中都属于少数，因为大部分非洲裔美国人的祖先最初来到美国时的身份都是奴隶。这一点不同使他能够从一个崭新的角度来审视美国历史的多样性。"

Peterson said he has known about the senator since before his keynote address at the 2004 Democratic National Convention—all the way back to the mid-1980s, when he saw a "tall, striking-looking"figure walking around the Harvard Law School campus.

彼得森说，早在20世纪80年代中期，他就在哈佛大学法学院看见过这位十分引人注意的高个子在校园里散步，而2004年在民主党全国代表大会上这位参议员发表的主旨演讲更是使他声名鹊起。

"I never met him,"Peterson said. "There are common people on campus that you just sort of recognize."

彼得森说："我在校园里从未看见过他，校园里有很多普通人，也就是面熟而已。"

八、Lessons for Business from Obama's victory（奥巴马获胜之启示）

This topic is about the lessons business leaders can take from Obama's win. Because even with the differences between running a campaign and a company, three critical leadership principles overlap. And it was upon those principles that Obama's decisive victory was built.

本议题是关于企业的领导者能够从奥巴马的获胜中所得到的启示。因为即使竞选和经营公司有所差别，三个指导原则也会交叉，并且正是基于这些原则奥巴马才取得了决定性的胜利。

Start with the granddad of leadership principles: a clear, consistent vision. If you want to galvanize followers, you simply cannot recast your message. Nor can you confuse or scare people. Obama's message was simple and aspirational. He talked about the failings of George W. Bush. He talked about change and hope and health care for all. Over and over, he painted a picture of the future that excited people. He also set a perfect example for business leaders: Stick to a limited number of points, repeat them relentlessly, and turn people on.

首先，指导原则的第一点是：清晰、始终如一的愿景。如果你想激励你的支持者们，你当然不能改变你的信息。你也不能让人迷惑或者惊恐。奥巴马传递的信息简单而振奋人心。他谈论小布什的失误。他谈论到改变、希望和所有人的医疗。一次又一次，他向人们展示了一个激动人心的美好愿景。他也为商业领袖们树立了一个完美的榜样：就坚持几点，不懈地坚持，并让人们为之振奋。

The next leadership principle should sound familiar: execution. The execution isn't the only thing a leader needs to get right, but without it little else matters. This election proves their point. In nearly two years of steady blocking and tackling, Obama's team made few mistakes. From the outset, his advisers were best in class, and his players were always prepared, agile, and where they needed to be.

下一个指导原则听起来应该很熟悉：执行力。执行力并不是领导者需要了解的唯一一件事，但是没有了执行力一切都无关紧要。本次大选印证了这一点。在近两年稳扎稳打的竞选中，奥巴马的团队几乎没有犯过错。从一开始，他的顾问就鹤立鸡群，他的表现一直是有备而来、灵活并且恰到好处。

Another, perhaps bigger, execution lesson can be taken from Obama's outmaneuvering of Hillary Clinton for the Democratic nomination. She thought she could win the old-fashioned way, by taking the big states of New York, Ohio, California, and so on. He figured out an unexpected way to gain an edge—in the usually overlooked caucuses.

另外，也许更为重要的是，有关执行力的启迪可以从奥巴马策略性地在民主党的提名中战胜希拉里·克林顿中获得。她认为她能够按照过去的传统通过攻克诸如纽约、俄亥俄、加利福尼亚等大选而获胜。奥巴马想出了与众不同的方式获得优势——关注常被忽略的秘密会议。

The business analog couldn't be more apt. So often, companies think they've nailed execution by doing the same old "milk run" better and better. But winning execution means doing the milk run perfectly—and finding new customers and opening new markets along the way. You can't just beat your rivals by the old rules; to grow, you have to invent a new game and beat them at that, too.

这样的情形与企业几乎如出一辙。公司常常认为越来越好地完成例行工作就是贯彻执行力。但获得执行力意味着完美地做好例行工作——在其中来寻找新的客户和开拓新的市场。你不能用过时的规则来击败你的竞争对手。为了发展，你就得发明一种新的游戏并用它来击败你的竞争对手。

Finally, this election reinforces the value of friends in high places. From the start, Obama had support from the media, which chose to downplay controversies involving him in the end, no one could dispute that Obama's relationship to the media made a difference.

最后，本次大选再次证明了位居高层的朋友的价值。从一开始，奥巴马就赢得了媒体的支持。众媒体选择避而不谈有关奥巴马的争议。但奥巴马与媒体的关系对于此次大选获胜至关重要，这一点毋庸置疑。

As a business leader, you can't succeed without the endorsement of your board. Every time you try to usher in change, some people will resist. They may fight you openly in meetings, through the media, or with the subterfuge of palace intrigue. And you'll need to make your case in all those venues. But in the end, if your board has your back, defeat can be turned into victory.

同样地，若在企业中得不到董事会的支持，企业领导人是不可能成功的。每一次试图变革都会有人反抗。他们可能会在会议中通过媒介与你公开对抗，或者找一个冠冕堂皇的理由来逃避问题。你必须针对这些情形来说明你的情况。可最后如果有了董事会的支持，那就可能反败为胜。

That's why you need to start any leadership initiative with your"high-level friends"firmly by your side, convinced of the merits of your character and policies. But that's not enough. If you want to keep your board as an ally, don't surprise them

这就是为什么你需要主动地和你的高层朋友创建友好关系的原因。用你的人品和策略使他们信服。但是这样做还远远不够，如果你想让你的董事会成为你的联盟，不要让他们震惊。

Surely pundits will scrutinize this election for years to come. But business leaders can take its lessons right now. You may have winning ideas. But you need much more to win the game.

毫无疑问，权威人士将会在未来的几年仔细观察这场选举。而企业领导者却可以马上从中受益。你可能有获胜的想法，但是要赢得游戏，你要做的还有很多。

If his is an America for all people, as Barack Obama has so passionately promised, then surely it will also serve the interests of the millions of hard-working small-business owners and entrepreneurs who are so much a part of this country's strength and future.

如果巴拉克·奥巴马任期内的美国像他在选举中承诺的那样是献身于全人类的美国的话，那么它也一定会为构成这个国家力量和未来的数百万辛勤的小业主和企业家的利益服务。

第十八篇　美国的国务卿

一、Henry Alfred Kissinger（亨利·艾尔弗雷德·基辛格）

Henry Alfred Kissinger spent the first years of his life in Germany. His father was a teacher in a girl's school and his mother was a devoted middle-class hausfrau. He grew up in the turbulent years under the Weimar Republic with anti-Semitism galloping and inflation out of control. Kissinger denies that his father's dismissal from his job and his own expulsion from the school, followed by forced entry into an all-Jewish school, have had the profound effect upon his outlook on the world that some people attribute to them, but inevitably they must have left some indelible marks.

基辛格的童年是在德国度过的。父亲是一所女子学校的教员，母亲是一个贤淑的中产阶级家庭妇女。他是在魏玛共和国反犹主义甚嚣尘上、通货膨胀不可控制的动乱年代中成长起来的。有些人认为，基辛格的父亲被解职，以及他自己在中学被开除，随后又被迫进了清一色犹太人的学校，这些经历对他的世界观有深刻的影响，虽然基辛格否认这点，但这些经历必然给他留下了一些不可磨灭的烙印。

When he and his family finally succeeded in getting out of Germany and to New York via London, Kissinger was fifteen years old. It was not an easy transplantation, but he and his family eked out enough of a living not only for their survival, but even for their basic contentment. Kissinger soon found mentors who sensed his talents and wanted to help him succeed. Nobody, of course, wanted it more than Kissinger himself, though for a long time shyness kept him from giving his ambitions freer rein.

基辛格15岁的时候，他们一家终于设法离开了德国，经由伦敦来到纽约。这次迁居并不是轻而易举的，但他们全家含辛茹苦，终于不但维持了生计，而且还能满足生活中的基本享受。基辛格不久就找到了赏识他的才智并愿帮助他取得成功的恩师。当然，基辛格本人更是求成心切，只是由于他的腼腆习性，很久之后才实现了他的抱负。

One of those who perhaps had a greater influence on his career than any other individual was Dr. Fritz Kraemer, also a German-American, whom he met in the Army in 1943. Kissinger was then nineteen and a buck private in the U.S. Infantry. Dr. Kraemer, a former lawyer, was also a private. Kraemer became a lieutenant and helped to install Kissinger in Germany, in charge of reorganizing its municipal government, a job he carried out well. It was Kraemer, too, who next steered him—Kissinger was by this time a sergeant—to the European Command Intelligence School. There he gave instruction in legal procedures against former Nazis and did it so satisfactorily that his superiors offered him, on demobilization, a job at $10 000 a year to remain on the school staff. But Kraemer thought that Kissinger's talents deserved better use and persuaded him to undertake study at a university. Harvard was among the few willing to accept Kissinger. He not only graduated there, but returned to teach at its School of International Studies.

有一个人对基辛格的前程产生了也许比谁都大的影响，这就是弗里茨·克雷默博士。他也是个美籍德国人，1943 年基辛格在陆军里初次认识了他。当时基辛格 19 岁，是美国步兵中一名新入伍的小兵。克雷默博士以前当过律师，那时也只是个士兵。后来克雷默当了陆军中尉，帮助基辛格在德国谋到了一个负责改组市政府的差事。基辛格干得很不错，当上了军士。后来克雷默又指引他到欧洲司令部情报学校去教书，在那里讲授关于检举前纳粹分子的司法程序的课程。他干得非常令人满意，以至在他复员时上级仍然聘请他继续留校任教，年薪 10 000 美元。但是克雷默认为基辛格的才能应该得到更好的发挥，便劝他进大学去学习。只有几所大学愿意录取基辛格，其中之一是哈佛。基辛格不但在那里毕了业，而且后来还回到哈佛的国际问题学院任教。

Harvard became his intellectual home: It taught him a lot, but not a Bostonian accent—more than a dash of his native German accent remains. This did, in fact, trouble him for many years, but he is self-conscious about it no longer and even jokes about his accent.

哈佛大学成了他的知识之家，教给了他好多东西，但就是没有教会他波士顿的口音，他讲英语时，德国口音依然很重。事实上这确实使他苦恼了好多年，但是后来也就不在乎了，甚至还拿自己的口音开玩笑。

Kissinger gradually established a reputation as a foreign policy expert and military strategist. He traveled far and wide, and became a member of that ingrown world establishment of foreign policy experts. His work for the Council on Foreign Relations and on the Rockefeller reports gave him an added cachet. What catapulted him into public controversy was his book *Nuclear Weapons and Foreign Policy*, which was an attempt to prove that the limited use of tactical nuclear weapons was a practical possibility. It gave him a hawkish reputation and by becoming a best seller it earned him money and also entry into many governmental inner sanctums.

基辛格逐渐树立了他作为外交政策专家和军事战略家的声誉。他周游世界，成为世界上门户极深的外交政策专家集团的一员。而他为对外关系协会写的著作以及为洛克菲勒写的报告更提高了他的声望。他的《核武器与对外政策》一书，使他突然成为了一位议论纷纭的名人。他在这本书里试图论证，战术核武器的有限使用在实际上是有可能的。这本书使他得到了鹰派的名声。而由于该书获得畅销，他不仅赚了钱，而且使他从此得以出入政府内部的许多机密部门。

The amount of human tragedy Kissinger saw around him during his formative years accounts for his being a man given to occasional melancholy, and for being a convinced pessimist beneath a certain playfulness and levity. It is rather apocalyptic gloom that possesses him: thoughts about the inevitability of injustice and some sort of inescapable ultimate doom. He admits to a belief in the tragic element of history:"There is the tragedy of a man who works very hard and never gets what he wants. And there is the even more bitter tragedy of a man who fully gets what he wants and finds out that he doesn't want it."

基辛格早年目睹了周围大量的人间悲剧，这使他时常显得很忧郁，或许可以叫作多愁善感，他成为彻底的悲观主义者，虽然表面上爱开玩笑，有点放荡不羁。可以说，他有着一种悲天悯人的阴郁情绪，忧虑非正义是无法避免的，担心某种无可逃遁的最终末日。他相信历史中的悲剧成分："有的人的悲剧是，终日孜孜不倦，却永远得不到他所向往的东西；还有的人的悲剧更为惨痛，他获得了他所向往的一切，结果却发现原来他根本不需要它。"

Kissinger as a part-time consultant in Kennedy's White House was edged out early, because as one-time assistant for National Security Affairs to Presidents Kennedy and Johnson, said, "He tried to be a private consultant and a public soothsayer at the same time, and the two are incompatible". Kissinger himself admits that his behavior in those days left something to be desired. However, he returned to the government sidelines in 1965 when he was sent to Vietnam, and later on he acted as a go-between in one of the peace feelers between the Johnson administration and Hanoi. The discretion and the skill with which he carried out these missions aroused much admiration inside the Johnson administration.

在肯尼迪执政时，基辛格是白宫中的一名兼职顾问，但很快就被排挤出去。一位曾任肯尼迪和约翰逊两位总统的国家安全事务助理说，这是因为"他既想当秘密的顾问，又想当公开的预言家，这两者是不可兼得的"。基辛格本人也承认，在那些日子里，他的行为是有缺点的。然而，1965年他又回到政府去任兼职，被派去越南，后来就充当了约翰逊政府与河内之间一次试探和平的中间人。他在执行这些使命时所表现出来的足智多谋，在约翰逊政府内部博得了许多人的赞赏。

When Mr. Nixon was elected president, he asked Kissinger whether he would be prepared, at least in principle, without specifying the job he would offer him, to work in his Administration. Kissinger was then Rockefeller's foreign policy adviser. Nevertheless, he got another call to see Mr. Nixon two days later. This time he was offered, unequivocally, the job of National Security Adviser to the President. Kissinger decided to accept and actually called Nixon before the week was over, after only three days' delay.

尼克松先生当选总统后，问基辛格，是否至少在原则上同意参加政府工作；当时并没有具体谈到将请他担任什么职务。基辛格当时是洛克菲勒的外交政策顾问。然而，基辛格又接到了一个电话，要他两天之后去见尼克松先生。这次总统明确地约请他担任总统的国家安全事务顾问。基辛格决定接受邀请，而且实际上不到一个星期，只隔了3天就去拜访了尼克松。

Kissinger still admits, however, that he remained distrustful until he actually began to work for the President; from then on their relationship grew into something unprecedented in American history: Kissinger became the President's de facto Secretary of State. Never before had a President depended on a foreign policy adviser who, in fact, did not hold that office. For a German-born Jew, it was a unique rise to power and fame.

然而，他仍然承认，在他真正开始为总统工作之前，他一直是抱不信任态度的；从开始工作以后，他们的关系就发展成为可以说是美国历史上前所未有的关系了：基辛格成了总统事实上的国务卿。过去从来没有哪个总统这样依靠一个实际上并未担任国务卿这一职位的外交政策顾问。对一个德国出生的犹太人来说，这样青云直上，又有实权又有盛名。

Kissinger has come to enjoy celebrities. Having become one himself, he can meet them on equal terms. He loves the power and fame of which he acquired more than he had ever dreamed, but he still chews his nails. His inner tensions and some of his insecurities persist behind a deceptively casual facade of geniality, self-deprecation, easy humor and aphoristic conversational skill.

基辛格逐渐喜欢起社会名流来了。他自己既已成名，就可以同他们平起平坐了。

他热爱他获得的那种做梦也想不到的那么多的权力和功名，但他仍然忐忑不安。表面上他装得和蔼可亲，十分谦逊，轻松幽默，谈起话来满口警句，然而在这一切的背后，他的内心一直是紧张的，而且有些缺乏自信。

二、 Colin Powell（科林·鲍威尔）

Colin Powell was born on April 5, 1937, in Harlem, New York. Both of his parents emigrated from Jamaica, so Powell was exposed to a multicultural mosaic when he was young. After his 1954 graduation from high senior school, Powell set off to study geology at City College of New York, and graduated in 1958. With a bachelor's degree under his belt, Powell was commissioned as a second lieutenant in the infantry, as he had joined a training program for the U.S. Army, while in college.

科林·鲍威尔 1937 年 4 月 5 日出生于纽约的哈莱姆。他的父母都是牙买加的移民，所以鲍威尔从小就受到多元文化的熏陶。1954 从高中毕业后，鲍威尔进入纽约市立学院学习地理专业，1958 年毕业。在校期间，他参加了一个美国陆军培训项目，获得学士学位后，被授予步兵少尉军衔。

After several years in the military, he is most notable as advisor in Vietnam in 1962, and returning for a second tour of duty as a battalion executive officer for the 23rd Infantry in Vietnam and the American Division in 1968. Powell returned to George Washington University in Washington D.C. in order to receive his MBA in 1971. A recipient of the Purple Heart for his military service in Vietnam, Powell was granted a White House Fellowship in 1972.

在其后的军旅生涯中，鲍威尔最显著的成就是 1962 年成为越南战争的顾问，第二次返回越南战场时任驻越南第 23 步兵营长，1968 年任驻越美军的师指挥官。1971 年，为了攻读工商管理硕士学位，他进入首都华盛顿的乔治·华盛顿大学深造。鲍威尔因参加越战而被授予紫心勋章，并于 1972 年获得白宫奖学金。

He returned to the military in 1973 as Commander of 1st Battalion in the 32nd Infantry in South Korea and 3 years later as Commander of 2nd Brigade of the 101st Airborne Division. Off the battlefront and into the White House, Powell served as an executive assistant in the Energy and Defense Departments during the Carter Administration.

他于 1973 年回到军中，任驻韩国第 32 步兵团第 1 营指挥官，3 年后升至 101 空降师第 2 旅旅长。从战场下来，进入白宫，在卡特政府中，鲍威尔担任能源与国防部门的行政助理。

Powell was named Senior Military Assistant to Deputy Secretary of Defense from 1977 to 1980, during the Reagan Administration was promoted to National Security Advisor in 1987. When Powell was named Chairman of the Joint Chiefs of Staff in 1989, he made history twofold, as the youngest person and the first Afro-American to work in the position. His 35-year military career has granted Powell a long list of honors and foreign military awards in his rise to four-star Admiral.

1977—1980 年，鲍威尔被任命为国防部副部长的高级军事助理。1987 年，在里根总统任期内担任国家安全顾问。1989 年，鲍威尔被任命为参谋长联席会议主席，他创造了两方面的历史：成为美国历史上任该职最年轻的而且是首位非裔美国人。35 年的军事生涯给鲍威尔带来了无数的荣誉和国外军事奖项，使他逐步晋升为四星上将。

Making history once again, Powell was sworn in as U.S.Secretary of State in January 2001, as nominated by then-President, George W. Bush. As Secretary of State, Powell had earned the trust of the American people, and had been strongly encouraged to run for the next Presidency, but he refused.

2001 年 1 月，在时任总统小布什的提名下，鲍威尔宣誓就职美国国务卿，又一次书写了历史新篇章。任美国国务卿期间，鲍威尔赢得了美国人民的信任，曾被力举竞选下任总统，但他拒绝了。

三、Condoleezza Rice（康德莉莎·赖斯）

Condoleezza Rice was born on November 14, 1954 in Birmingham, Alabama, which was then still officially segregated. Growing up during the tumultuous days of the civil rights movement, Rice attended a segregated school in Birmingham and lived in a world inhabited almost exclusively by black people. On September 15, 1963 she was just a few miles away when a bomb planted in a Baptist church by white supremacists exploded, killing four black girls, one of whom was Rice's friend.

康德莉莎·赖斯 1954 年 11 月 14 日生于阿拉巴马州伯明翰市。当时该州官方仍在实行种族隔离政策。成长于民权运动激烈动荡时期的赖斯就读于伯明翰的一所种族隔离学校，生活在几乎清一色的黑人世界里。1963 年 9 月 15 日，一颗由白人至上主义者安放在一个浸礼会教堂的炸弹炸死了 4 名黑人姑娘，其中一个是赖斯的朋友。当时赖斯仅在几英里之外。

Her father, an ordained Presbyterian minister and dean of Stillman College, a predominantly black school, and her mother, an accomplished pianist and teacher of music and science, imparted to their only daughter the sense that—in spite of the racism all around her—she could do anything she desired with her life.

赖斯的父亲是长老会的委任牧师和黑人占多数的学校——斯第尔曼学院的教务长。母亲是位有造诣的钢琴家并且是位音乐和理科教师。他们传授给独女这样一种观念：尽管种族主义肆虐周围，她依然可以倾其一生做自己想做的任何事情。

Rice graduated with a degree in international relations in 1974, then entered the master's program in economics at the University of Notre Dame, in Indiana. She later returned to the University of Denver, where in 1981 she earned a Ph.D.in international studies, with a specialty in Soviet politics and culture.

1974 年赖斯毕业，获国际关系学位，接着进入印第安纳州圣母大学研习经济学硕士课程，后又回到丹佛大学，1981 年获该校国际关系学博士，专业是苏联政治和文化。

In 1981 Rice became an assistant professor at Stanford University. She spent her entire academic career there, an unusual figure in the school's Department of Political Science not only because she is black and female in a field that is predominantly white and male, but also because she is a political conservative on a campus that has historically been liberal.

1981 年，赖斯成为斯坦福大学的一位助理教授，在那儿度过了她的全部学术生涯，成为该校政治科学系杰出的一员，这不仅因为她是在众多白人和男性的领域中的一名黑人女性，也是因为她是政治自由传统校园中的一位保守派。

In the classroom, Rice has often employed what she terms "applied"teaching methods, including simulations of national-security crises in which students prepare strategic responses in real time. She is known as a demanding teacher, one who pushes her students to excel and encourages heated debate.

在课堂上，赖斯常常运用自己所说的"应用"教学模式，其中包括国家安全危机模拟系统。模拟中，学生准备在危机时做出实时战略反应。赖斯以要求严格闻名，促使学生胜过别人，鼓励学生热烈讨论。

Rice made national headlines in 1993, when she was named Stanford's provost, or chief financial and academic officer, a powerful position that placed her second in rank to the university president. Rice was the youngest provost in the university's 103-year history, as well as the first woman and first African-American.

1993 年，赖斯被任命为斯坦福大学教务长，即首席财务和学术行政领导，权力仅次于校长，这使她登上了全国头条新闻。她是该校 103 年历史中最年轻的教务长，也是第一次任此职务的女性、第一个美籍非洲人。

As an academic star and Soviet expert, Rice attracted the attention of Washington policymakers during the Cold War, and in 1986 she was awarded a fellowship from the Council on Foreign Relations to work on nuclear strategic planning with the director of the Joint Staff of the Joint Chiefs of Staff. After the election of George Herbert Walker Bush as president, in 1988, Rice accepted several concurrent, high-level appointments in Washington: director of Soviet and East European affairs with the National Security Council, special assistant to the president for national security affairs, and senior director for Soviet affairs.

作为学术明星和苏联问题专家，赖斯引起了冷战时期华盛顿政策制定者的注意。1986 年，她被聘为对外关系委员会成员，与参谋长联席会议中的参谋长们共同制定核战略规划。1988 年，乔治·布什当选总统后，赖斯同时兼任华府的几个高级职务：国家安全委员会苏联与东欧事务主任、总统国家安全事务特别助理和苏联事务高级专员。

Through her relationship with the former president, Rice developed a friendship with the Bush family. In July 2000, at George W. Bush's request, Rice took a leave of absence from Stanford to become chief foreign policy adviser in his presidential campaign. She briefed him once a week on world developments, offering advice about situations likely to arise over the next few years.

因为与前美国总统的关系，赖斯和布什家族建立了友谊。2000 年 7 月，应乔治·W·布什之邀，赖斯请假离开斯坦福大学担任小布什总统竞选班子的首席外交政策顾问。她每周向小布什汇报世界最新发展情况，并就以后几年可能发生的情况提出建议。

Rice, who has claimed not to make career plans very far in advance, has nonetheless said that her dream job would be commissioner of the National Football League. She is called "Condy" by her friends and close associates. She has never been married.

尽管赖斯宣称对未来职业无长远规划，不过，她说过最想做的工作就是全国橄榄球联合会的总干事。朋友和亲密同事亲切地称她为"康迪"。赖斯至今未婚。

Former U.S.Secretary of State Condoleezza Rice has made a key step in her post-Bush administration career: The William Morris Agency (WMA) announced on Wednesday that it has signed her as a client.

威廉·莫里斯经纪公司于本周三宣布，美国前国务卿康德莉莎·赖斯为其签约客户，这是赖斯在布什政府的任期结束后迈出的重要一步。

The former professor and Stanford University provost has been in the Bush administration since its beginning, first as national security adviser and then as Secretary of State. Her appointment ended, after Barack Obama was sworn in as president.

曾经做过大学教授以及斯坦福大学教务长的赖斯在布什政府组建之初就为其效力，起初担任国家安全事务顾问，之后成为国务卿。巴拉克·奥巴马宣誓就职后，她的任期也随即结束。

Although most other members of the Bush administration might have trouble finding such a wide-ranging deal, Rice found a strong market among talent agencies.

布什政府的大多数成员可能都不太容易能找到如此好的一个归宿，不过赖斯在经纪人公司那里倒是颇有市场。

"It was certainly a competitive situation,"said Jim Waitt, chairman and CEO of the William Morris Agency. "She was very thorough about the process and who she would feel most comfortable with and who would be speaking on her behalf."

威廉·莫里斯经纪公司总裁兼首席执行官吉姆·韦特说："当时竞争很激烈。她对整个选择的过程、跟谁合作最轻松，以及谁会成为她的代理人等环节要求都非常细致。"

It's unlikely that Rice will turn up as a talking head on television, however. The deal includes William Morris representation for books, lecture appearances and philanthropic initiatives, as well as business initiatives in media, sports and communications.

不过，赖斯不太可能以电视节目主持人的身份现身。双方签署的合约项目包括威廉·莫里斯公司所做的书籍代言、出席讲座，以及慈善活动，另外还包括媒体、运动和社交方面的一些商业活动。

WMA co-chief operating officer Wayne Kabak said that the agency was struck not only by Rice's well-rounded resume. In addition to her political career, Rice is an accomplished concert pianist as well as a big-time National Football League fan.

威廉·莫里斯经纪公司联席执行官韦恩·卡巴科称他们看中的并不仅仅是赖斯无懈可击的个人履历。除其从政经历以外，赖斯还是一位出色的音乐会钢琴演奏家，同时还是国家足球联赛的超级球迷。

"It's more than just books, it's much more than just lectures,"Kabak said."We're here to help her create and enhance an agenda that is very important to her in her post-government career."

卡巴科透露说："她要参与的活动不仅限于书籍和讲座。我们要帮她制作并实现她从政生涯结束之后另一个重要的发展规划。"

That agenda will include philanthropic efforts involving classical music and college educations for disadvantaged students, as well as initiatives to help U.S.children become global citizens.

这个规划将包括推动古典音乐以及贫困学生大学教育等方面的慈善活动，还会在帮助美国儿童成为世界公民方面有一些举措。

In support of those efforts, Rice might appear on camera, but she won't be traveling the well-worn path as a news or policy analyst.

为了宣传这些活动，赖斯可能需要出镜，但肯定不会走大家已经很熟悉的那种新闻分析师或政策分析师的路线。

"She's not interested in being a shadow Secretary of State,"Kabak said."It's not her goal to go on morning talk shows the day after something happens. That's not what she wants to do."

卡巴科说：“她不想活在国务卿的影子里。她的目标不是每天一早上在脱口秀节目中评论头一天发生的事情。那并不是她想做的事情。”

四、Hillary Clinton（希拉里·克林顿）

Hillary Clinton was born in Chicago, Illinois, on October 26, 1947. Her father was a small businessman and her mother a homemaker. She is a graduate of Wellesley College and Yale Law School. She is married to former President William Jefferson Clinton. They have one daughter, Chelsea.

希拉里·克林顿 1947 年 10 月 26 日出生于美国伊利诺伊州芝加哥市。她的父亲是个小商人，母亲是位家庭主妇。她毕业于韦尔斯利学院和耶鲁法学院，嫁给了前总统威廉·杰斐逊·克林顿，并有一个女儿名叫切尔西。

Hillary Clinton was the Secretary of the State under Obama Administration. She was elected to the United States Senate by the people of New York on November 7, 2000. She was then the first First Lady of the United States elected to public office and the first woman elected independently statewide in New York State. A strong advocate for New York, Senator Clinton worked with communities throughout the state to strengthen the economy and expand opportunity. The Senator supported a return to fiscal responsibility.

希拉里·克林顿曾为美国奥巴马政府的国务卿。2000 年 11 月 7 日希拉里·克林顿被纽约人民选举为美国参议院议员。她当时是美国首位成功当选公职的第一夫人，也是纽约州全州第一位独立竞选公职的女性。任参议员期间，希拉里·克林顿积极支持纽约，与全州各社区一起为促进经济、拓展机遇而工作。她支持政府重新负起财政责任。

She served on the Health, Education, Labor, and Pensions Committee; the Environment and Public Works Committee; the Special Committee on Aging; and she was the first New Yorker ever to serve on the Senate Armed Services Committee.

她曾任职于美国卫生、教育、劳工和福利委员会，环境和公共事务委员会，老龄特别委员会，她还是第一个在美国参议院军事委员会任职的纽约人。

After the terrorist attacks of September 11, 2001, Senator Clinton worked with her colleagues to secure the funds New York needed to rebuild. She fought to provide compensation to the families of the victims, grants for hard-hit businesses. She continued to work for resources that enabled New York to grow, to improve homeland security for New York and other communities, and to protect all Americans from future attacks. She had introduced legislation to provide for direct and threat-based homeland security funding to ensure that first responders and high-target communities have the resources they need.

2001 年 9 月 11 日恐怖袭击后，希拉里·克林顿与她的同事们一起争取重建纽约的资金。她为遇难者家属提供补偿金，为受到重创的企业争取捐款。她为确保纽约的发展资金，改善纽约及其他社区的国土安全，保护所有美国人未来不再遭受袭击而持续努力工作。她提议立法机关提供直接的和防备威胁的国土安全资金，以确保应急人员和重要目标社区有所需的资源。

In 2004, Senator Clinton was asked by the Department of Defense to serve as the only Senate member of the Transformation Advisory Group to the Joint Forces Command. She was an original sponsor of legislation that expanded health benefits to members of the National Guard and Reserves.

2004 年，希拉里·克林顿应国防部的请求作为唯一的参议员出任联合部队司令部军事转型咨询小组顾问。她首先倡议立法机关立法，提高国民警卫队和后备队人员的医疗福利待遇。

In the Senate, she continued her work for children and families by leading efforts to ensure the safety of prescription drugs for children, with legislation now included in the Pediatric Research Equity Act; working to strengthen the Children's Health Insurance Program, which increased coverage for children in low income working families; and helping schools address environmental hazards.

在参议院，她继续为儿童和家庭工作，努力确保儿童处方药的安全，将法规写入儿科研究平等法，努力加强孩子们的健康保险计划，增加低收入工人阶层家庭的儿童保险项目，并帮助学校解决环境危害。

Senator Clinton continues to work to increase access to health care. She authored legislation that has been enacted to improve recruitment and retention of nurses, to improve quality and lower the cost of prescription drugs, and to protect food supply from bioterrorism. She sponsored legislation to increase America's commitment against Global AIDS.

希拉里·克林顿参议员不断地为加强卫生保健而不停地工作。她亲笔起草的改善招聘和挽留护士，提高处方药的质量和降低其成本，保护食品供应免遭生物恐怖主义的袭击的立法已经颁布实施。她向立法机关倡议，增加美国对全球艾滋病承担的义务。

To encourage business expansion, Senator Clinton cosponsored legislation enacted in 2004 to extend tax credits to communities in regions designated as Renewal Communities. She had sponsored conferences and business development tours throughout the state aimed at attracting new investment; introduced legislation to increase access to broadband technology in rural areas; and served as chair of the advisory board for New Jobs for New York.

为支持企业发展，希拉里·克林顿参议员倡导的专为重建社区的地区扩大税收抵免的立法于 2004 年实施。她倡议在全州范围内召开商务会议，开展商业发展巡游，吸引新的投资项目；她提议立法以使农村地区宽带技术使用得以扩大；她还曾担任纽约新的就业机会咨询委员会主席。

Senator Clinton had spoken clearly about the importance of protecting constitutional rights, respecting such landmark Supreme Court decisions as Roe v. Wade. She was committed to supporting Roe and working to reduce the number of abortions, by reducing the number of unwanted pregnancies.

希拉里·克林顿对保护宪法权利，尊重最高法院划时代的罗伊诉韦德案的判决重要性观点非常明确。她承诺支持罗伊并通过减少不想怀孕的人数，继续努力减少堕胎的数量。

Strongly committed to making sure that every American has the right to vote in fair, accessible and credible elections—and that every vote must be counted, Senator Clinton introduced *the Count Every Vote Act of 2005*, to provide a verified paper ballot for every vote cast in electronic voting machines; set a uniform standard for provisional ballots, and require the Federal Election Assistance Commission to issue standards that ensure uniform access to voting machines and election personnel in every community.

为致力于确保每一个美国人有权公平地投票，选举简便、可信，必须计入每一票，希拉里·克林顿提出《2005 计算每一票法案》，为电子投票机提供经过验证的投票纸张确保每一票都记录在机；为临时选票制定出一个统一的标准，要求联邦选举协助委员会发布标准确保投票机以及每个社区的选举人有统一的选举模式。

Hillary Clinton is the author of best selling books including *her autobiography, Living History; It Takes A Village: and Other Lessons Children Teach U.S.; Dear Socks, Dear Buddy: Kids' Letters to the First Pets;* and *An Invitation to the White House.*

希拉里还写了很多畅销书，其中包括她的自传《亲历历史》、《举全村之力：以及孩子给我们的其他启示》、《亲爱的袜子，亲爱的朋友：孩子们写给第一批宠物的信》、《应邀到白宫》。

第十九篇　美国的科学之星

一、Thomas Edison（托马斯·爱迪生）

Born on February 11, 1847 in Ohio, U.S., Edison spent 3 months in school, and then was taught at home by his mother. In 1862, he became a telegraph operator and he joined Western Union Telegraph Company in Boston in 1868. Edison's first invention was an automatic telegraph repeater. His first patent was for an electric vote recorder. In 1869, as a partner in a New York electrical firm, he perfected the stock ticker. From 1870 to 1875, Edison invented many telegraphic improvements.

1847 年 2 月 11 日，爱迪生诞生于美国的俄亥俄州。他仅在学校学习了三个月，之后由其母亲在家教育成人。1862 年，他成为一名电信报务员。1868 年他加入波士顿的西部联合电报公司。爱迪生的第一项发明是一台自动的电报转发器。他的第一项专利是一台电动记录投票数的装置。1869 年，他作为纽约电气公司的一位合伙人，完善了股市行情自动收录器。1870—1875 年，爱迪生有很多发明，改进了很多电报装置。

In 1876 Edison's carbon telegraph transmitter for Western Union marked a real advance toward malting the Bell telephone practical. With the money Edison received from Western Union for his transmitter, he established a factory. Again he pooled scientific talent, and within 6 years he had more than 300 patents.

1876 年，爱迪生为西部联合电报公司发明的炭精棒送话器是一个真正进步，它使贝尔电话投入实际使用。他用送话器从西部联合电报公司获得的钱建立了一家工厂，全力投入其中，6 年内他获得了超过 300 项的专利。

Edison's most original and lucrative invention, the phonograph, was patented in 1877.

From a manually operated instrument making impressions on metal foil and replaying sounds, it became a motor-driven machine playing cylindrical wax records by 1887. To research incandescence, Edison and others organized the Edison Electric Light Company in 1878. Edison made the first practical incandescent lamp in 1879. In 1882, the Pearl Street Station in New York City marked the beginning of America's electrical age.

1877 年，爱迪生最有创意、利润最大的发明——留声机——取得专利权。这种手动操作仪器在金属箔片上留下痕迹，并重新播放声音，到 1887 年它已成了一台由发动机驱动推动圆柱体蜡状记录器转动的机器。为研究白炽灯，爱迪生和其他合伙人于 1878 年组建了爱迪生电灯公司。1879 年，爱迪生制造出第一盏实用的白炽灯。1882 年，纽约市珍珠街电站的建成标志着美国电气时代的开始。

In 1883 Edison made a significant discovery in pure science, the Edison effect electrons flowed from incandescent filaments. With a metal plate insert, the lamp could serve as a valve, admitting only negative electricity. Although"etheric force"had been recognized in 1875, the phenomenon was little known outside the Edison laboratory.

1883 年，爱迪生在纯科学领域获得了重大发现，爱迪生效应电子从白炽灯灯丝中流出。以一金属片嵌入，电灯就可以像阀门一样只允许负电子通过，尽管"电阻"于 1875 年就已得到认可，但这种现象除了在爱迪生实验室外几乎不为人所知。

This"force"underlies radio broadcasting, long-distance telephony, sound pictures, television, electric eyes, x-rays, high-frequency surgery, and electronic musical instruments. In 1902 he improved the copper oxide battery, which resembled modern dry cells.

这种"阻力"为收音机广播、长途电话、声像、电视、电子眼、X- 光、高频率手术及电子音乐设备打下了基础。1902 年，他改进了氧化铜电池，就像今天的干电池。

In 1908 his cinema phone appeared, adjusting film speed to phonograph speed. In 1913 Edison produced several"talkies".Meanwhile, among other inventions, the universal motor, which used alternating or direct current, appeared in 1907, and the electric safety lantern was patented in 1914. That year Edison invented the telescribe, which combined features of the telephone and dictating phonograph.

1908 年，爱迪生的有声放映机产生了，它可将胶片速度调节为留声装置的速度。1913 年，爱迪生制作了几部"有声电影"。与此同时，在其他一些发明中，用交流电或直流电的通用发动机于 1907 年问世，保险灯管于 1914 年获得专利。那一年爱迪生发明了结合电话机和授语留声机特征的电话录音机。

His aphorisms are"Genius is 1 percent inspiration and 99 percent perspiration" and "Discovery is not invention". He slept only 4 hours a night, and often worked 40 or 50 hours straight. Edison had more than 10 000 books at home and masses of printed materials at the laboratory. Some 25 000 notebooks contained his research records, ideas, and mistakes. Edison died in West Orange, New Jersey, on October 18, 1931.

爱迪生的格言是："天才就是百分之一的灵感加上百分之九十九的汗水"和"发现不等于发明"。他一晚上只睡四小时，并且总是持续工作 40 甚至 50 个小时。爱迪生家里有 10 000 多本书，实验室里有大量的印刷材料。大约 25 000 个笔记本记载了他的研究记录、想法及错误。1931 年 10 月 18 日，爱迪生在新泽西州西奥兰治去世。

二、The Wright Brothers（莱特兄弟）

When Orville Wright was seven and Wilbur Wright was eleven, their dad brought home a surprise. Before the boys could guess what it was, their father tossed it into the air, and it started to fly. The father told them that it was a toy helicopter that was invented by a young Frenchman. The helicopter was made out of cork, bamboo, and paper. The boys were fascinated by the toy and told themselves that one day they would fly. While the boys were growing up, they were always tinkering with things. Though they were excellent students and loved to read and write, the brothers could not sit too long, because they always wanted to get into action and to invent, design, and build new things. The Wright Brothers were also very determined to do things.

当奥维尔·莱特 7 岁、威尔伯·莱特 11 岁时，他们的爸爸带回家一个惊喜。在他们还未来得及猜出是什么的时候，父亲把它扔向空中，然后它开始飞翔。父亲告诉他们那是由一个年轻的法国人发明的一架玩具直升飞机，由软木、竹子和纸做成。两个男孩被这个玩具深深吸引住了，并且对自己说有一天他们也能飞行。在兄弟俩成长的过程中，他们总是摆弄物件。虽然他们成绩优秀，喜欢读书和写作，但他们不能长时间坐着，因为他们总想参与到实践中去发明、设计和制造新的东西。莱特兄弟非常坚决地去做一些事情。

To make the airplane, the two brothers had to study wind patterns and they also built kites. The kites were an unbelievable sight to see. To keep the kites in air as long as possible the Wright Brothers tries to control them from the ground. They built a kite with warped wing design.

为了制造飞机，兄弟俩必须要研究机翼的特点，同时他们也制作风筝。这些风筝看起来难以置信。为了让风筝尽可能地在空中长时间飞行，莱特兄弟努力从地面控制它们。他们用弯曲翅膀的设计制造了一架风筝。

In 1900, the Wright Brothers built their very first glider that used wing warping. One person could fly this glider. The pilot was supposed to lie face down while holding two ropes that controlled the wing. They tried to fly it northward, where there was good steady wind that blew from the Atlantic Ocean. It was also good because it had a 100-foot sand dune. The brothers took turns in flying the glider and discovered the trill of flying. But the rides only lasted a short time and the longest was only 10 seconds. They were determined to make better gliders.

1900 年，莱特兄弟用翘曲机翼制造了第一架滑翔机，一个人就能操纵滑翔机进行飞行。飞行员面朝下，拉着两根绳子，控制机翼。他们努力朝着北方飞行，因为那里有来自大西洋的平和的风，而且当地一座 100 英尺（1 英尺＝ 0.3048 米）的沙丘也是有利条件。莱特兄弟轮流驾驶滑翔机，并发觉了飞行的颤音。但是几次滑行只持续了很短的时间，最长的仅仅 10 秒钟，于是他们决心制造更好的滑翔机。

In 1901, the brothers improved their glider and gave another try. This time, the improved glider broke the world record by reaching 389 feet, but they were still not satisfied and believed they could make the glider go higher and fly longer.

1901 年，兄弟俩改进了他们的滑翔机并且再次试航。这一次，改进后的滑翔机打破了世界纪录，达到了 389 英尺，但是他们仍不满意，并相信自己能够使滑翔器飞得更高更远。

One year later, the brothers had a new design that had rudder control. With wing warping and proper rudder movement, they could get more stable flight. This time they broke another record and the flight went up more than 600 feet.

一年以后，兄弟俩有了一个用方向舵控制的新设计。有了翘曲机翼和合适的方向舵运动，他们能够更加平稳地飞行。这一次，他们打破了另外一项纪录，使飞行高度超过了 600 英尺。

Meanwhile, the Wright Brothers also dreamed about having an engine-powered flying machine controlled by a pilot. They worked day and night and built the first engine-powered airplane. Since they could not find an engine light enough for flight, they went to the library and studied engine designs, did many experiments and built their own engines, which only weighed 150 pounds. They also designed their own propeller, with a curved top and a flat bottom.

同时，莱特兄弟也梦想有一个由飞行员控制的引擎动力飞机。他们夜以继日地工作，终于制造了第一架有引擎动力的飞机。由于他们找不到重量轻得足以适合飞行的引擎，他们去图书馆研究引擎的设计，做了许多次试验，终于自制出只有 150

磅重的引擎。他们还设计了曲线形上弦杆和平底的螺旋推进器。

In December 17, 1903 the brothers tested their engine-powered machine that they called Flyer 1. At 10:30 a. m. the brothers shook hands as the plane rumbled to life, history was about to be made. Orville went on Flyer 1 and gave the signal to Wilbur that he was ready. Suddenly the plane rolled forward faster and faster, and then finally rose of the ground; Orville was the first person to fly an airplane. The flight carried Orville only 120 feet and the brothers flew their aircraft three or more times that day. Wilbur flew the last flight and it took him 852 feet and lasted 59 seconds. After that they continued building and testing more airplanes.

1903 年 12 月 17 日，兄弟俩测试了他们称作"飞行家一号"的有引擎动力的机器。上午 10 点 30 分，当飞机隆隆启动时，兄弟俩紧握双手，飞行历史即将诞生。奥维尔登上"飞行家一号"，向威尔伯发出准备就绪的信号。飞机突然越来越快地向前滑动，最后从地面升起，奥维尔成为驾驶飞机的第一人。奥维尔只飞行了 120 英尺，那一天，兄弟俩又飞了至少三次。最后一次，威尔伯飞行了 852 英尺，持续了 59 秒。之后，他们继续制造并试验更多的飞机。

In 1908 they perfected an amazing airplane. It could fly 25 miles and stay in the air for 30 minutes; it had a speed of 40 miles per hour. The pilot would have so much control that it could fly in circles and do figures of eight. The Wright Brothers didn't receive much attention until a newspaper reporter witnessed a 1 000-foot flight in 1908. In 1909 the Wright Brothers formed a Wright Co. and opened a factory to manufacture aircraft.

1908 年，他们完美地制造了一架令人惊异的飞机。它能够飞行 25 英里，在空中停留 30 分钟；它的速度能达到每小时 40 英里。由于飞行员可以控制飞机，因此飞机在天空中可以环行，并飞出 8 字型轨迹。但是直到 1908 年，一家报社的记者亲眼目睹了莱特兄弟的飞机能够飞到 1 000 英尺的高空，兄弟俩才引起人们的注意。1909 年，莱特兄弟成立莱特公司，并开办了制造飞机的工厂。

三、Maurice Hilleman （莫里斯·希勒曼）

Maurice R. Hilleman, as the vaccine developer, may have saved more lives than any other scientist of the 20th century. In a remarkably productive career, Hilleman and his team created more than 40 human and animal vaccines, including those for measles, mumps, chickenpox, rubella, hepatitis A and B, and meningitis. His team developed eight of the fourteen vaccines that are routinely given to young children in the U.S.. Those vaccines effectively wiped out many of the most disabling and deadly childhood diseases in the United States and the rest of the world.

莫里斯·R·希勒曼作为一位疫苗研制者，挽救的生命可能比 20 世纪的任何一位科学家都要多。在成就斐然的职业生涯中，希勒曼和他的研究小组研制出 40 多种人类和动物疫苗，其中包括麻疹疫苗、腮腺炎疫苗、水痘疫苗、风疹疫苗、甲肝和乙肝疫苗以及脑膜炎疫苗。美国儿童通常接种的 14 种疫苗中有 8 种是由他的研究小组研制出来的。这些疫苗在美国和世界其他地方有效地消灭了许多令儿童致残和致死的疾病。

Hilleman was also the first to identify how the influenza virus mutates, and he virtually single handedly spearheaded creation of the vaccine that prevented the Asian flu outbreak of 1957 from becoming a repeat of the 1918 Spanish flu pandemic, which killed 20 million people worldwide. He played key roles in the discovery of the cold-producing adenoviruses, the hepatitis viruses and the cancer-causing virus, among others. He was also the first to produce a vaccine against a virally induced cancer.

希勒曼也是确认流感病毒是如何变异的第一人。事实上，他独自一人率先研制出流感疫苗，从而避免了 1957 年爆发的亚洲流感重蹈 1918 年西班牙流感疫情的覆辙，1918 年的那次疫情造成全世界 2 000 多万人死亡。对于导致感冒的腺病毒、肝炎病毒和致癌的病毒以及其他病毒的发现，他起到了关键作用。他还第一个研制出用于预防由病毒引起癌症的疫苗。

Hilleman and his older siblings were raised by relatives on a farm.They tended cattle and chickens, raised vegetables and made brooms that they sold in town. Hilleman took a special interest in the chickens, caring for them, learning about them, even figuring out how to hypnotize roosters. That experience proved invaluable in later years, because many of his creations were produced in chicken eggs.

希勒曼和他的哥哥姐姐都是亲戚一手带大的，他家的亲戚住在一个农场上。他们养牛、养鸡、种蔬菜、制作扫帚并拿到镇上出售。希勒曼对鸡特别感兴趣，他照料鸡群、了解鸡群，甚至琢磨如何给公鸡催眠。日后证明这段经历对他极为珍贵，因为他的很多发明创造都是在鸡蛋里搞出来的。

In 1948, Hilleman went to an army medical center in Washington, D.C., where he began research on the influenza virus. He showed that the virus underwent two major forms of mutation, called drift and shift. drift is the slow, subtle change in surface characteristics that necessitates the production of a new vaccine each year. Shift is a major change in those characteristics that produces, in effect, an entirely new virus to which the population has no resistance. A shift triggered the 1918 pandemic.

1948 年，希勒曼到美国首都华盛顿特区的一家陆军医疗中心工作，在那里他开始研究流感病毒。他证明流感病毒呈现出两种主要的变异形式，称为微变和巨变。微变就是表面特征发生缓慢、细微的变化，使得每年生产新的疫苗成为必要。巨变就是其特征发生重大变化，实际上是产生一种全新的病毒，人类对该种病毒没有抵抗力。巨变引起了 1918 年的流感大流行。

Hilleman's work on the mumps virus was triggered when he came home one evening and found that his daughter, then 5, was in the early stages of the illness. He rushed to his lab to collect swabs and culture media, swabbed her mouth, and placed the swab in beef broth in the freezer to await his return from a business trip the next morning. When he got home, he isolated her strain of the mumps virus and produced the first vaccine against it.

希勒曼研究腮腺炎病毒的起因是，一天晚上他回到家，发现当时只有 5 岁的女儿正处在腮腺炎发病初期。他急忙跑到实验室拿来药签和培养基，用药签擦了一下她的嘴，然后将药签放在冰箱里的牛肉汤里，等第二天上午出差回来再着手研究。回来后，他分离出了她感染的腮腺炎病毒，并研制出第一个对付这种病毒的疫苗。

Hilleman overcame immunological problems to combine several vaccines into single shots, such as the well-known MMR vaccine for measles, mumps and rubella. He also developed a vaccine for hepatitis B, which is one of the primary causes of liver cancer—the first vaccine to protect against cancer.

希勒曼攻克了免疫学难题，将好几种疫苗合为一针，比如著名的麻风腮三联疫苗，即麻疹、腮腺炎和风疹混合疫苗。他还研制出乙肝疫苗，而乙肝是肝癌主要成因之一，这是第一种抗癌疫苗。

第二十篇　美国文学名著

一、*The Scarlet Letter*（《红字》）

Author: Nathaniel Hawthorne 作者：纳撒尼尔·霍桑

Nathaniel Hawthorne (1804-1864) was an American novelist and short-story writer in the 19th century. Nathaniel Hawthorne was born in 1804 in Salem, Massachusetts, the descendent of a long line of Puritan ancestors, including John Hawthorne, a presiding magistrate in the Salem witch trials in 1692, which has a great influence on him. His father was lost at sea when he was only four and he was brought up by his mother.

纳撒尼尔·霍桑（1804-1864），19 世纪美国小说家。1804 年，霍桑出生于马萨诸塞州塞勒姆镇一个没落的清教徒世家。其祖辈曾参与清教徒迫害异端的事件，其中就包括约翰·霍桑，他是 1692 年"塞勒姆驱巫案"的三名主审法官之一。这段历史对霍桑产生了深刻的影响。霍桑的父亲在他 4 岁时在海上遇难，他由母亲抚养长大。

Hawthorne turned to writing after his graduation from Bowdoin College. His first novel was *Fanshawe* and he wrote several successful short stories. He wrote the tales and sketches in the collection *Mosses from an Old Manse* (1843) and gradually gained recognition. In order to earn a livelihood, Hawthorne served as surveyor of the port at Salem (1836-1846), where he began writing his masterpiece, *The Scarlet Letter* (1850), which is often considered the first American psychological novel. He wrote *The House of the Seven Gables* (1851), Then, Hawthorne completed *The Blithedale Romance* (1852).

从博多因学院毕业后，霍桑开始从事写作。他一开始发表了长篇小说《范肖》和几十个短篇作品，后陆续出版短篇小说集《古宅青苔》（1843），逐渐受到认可。为了谋生，1836—1846 年，霍桑在海关任验关员一职，期间致力于他的代表作——

《红字》（1850）的创作。《红字》被认为是美国心理分析小说的开篇。他还写了《带有七个尖角阁的房子》（1851），后又完成了另一部小说《福谷传奇》(1852)。

Plot：*The Scarlet Letter* is set in the 17th century in Boston. Hester Prynne, the heroine of the story, is immigrating with her husband from Old England to Boston, America. Half way her husband is taken slave by the Indians and she arrives in America alone. Forced by poverty, she is tempted by a young minister and becomes pregnant. Such a thing is regarded by the local Puritans as a rebellion and humiliation. They arrest her and put her into prison. She has to wear the letter A (which stands for Adultery) on her chest for all to see her sin. She is made to stand on the platform in the town square waiting for her trial.

《红字》的故事发生在 17 世纪的波士顿。小说描写女主人公海丝特·白兰跟丈夫从英国移居到美国的波士顿。中途丈夫被印第安人俘虏，海丝特只身流落到美国。迫于贫困，她被一青年牧师诱骗怀孕。此事被当地虚伪的清教徒视为大逆不道。当局把海丝特抓进监狱，她还要在胸前佩带 A 字（A 代表 adultery：通奸犯）游街示众，并站在示众台上受审。

The governor comes to preside over Hester's trial. Mr. Arthur Dimmesdale, the local minister, who enjoys a high reputation and is seen as a symbol of morality, is actually the sin man in Hester's love affair. He is also present at the trial and pretends to persuade her to name the father of the child. Hester, however, refuses to give in and would rather suffer from the shame alone. Later when she is released from prison, she moves into a small house outside the town. She struggles to make a living as a seamstress and raises her daughter, Pearl, on her own in spite of all the shame and humiliation.

州长亲自主持了对海丝特的审讯。当地牧师丁梅斯代尔享有盛誉，且被视为道德典范，正是诱骗海丝特的奸夫。他也出席了审判，还假惺惺地劝说她招出孩子的父亲。但海丝特宁愿一人受辱，不肯招供。后来，她从监狱获释，搬到了城外的一间小屋子里。尽管受尽屈辱，海丝特仍顽强地以刺绣为生，独自抚养女儿珠儿。

Dimmesdale is greatly moved by Hester's endurance, persistence and sacrifice. Suffering from inner guilty and outside pressure, He soon falls very ill. Meanwhile, Hester's husband, Doc Roger Chillingworth, is released and is trying to find out secretly who is the father of the child. He pretends to be able to cure the young minister of his disease. Through his contact with Dimmesdale, he gradually knows the truth. Fired by hatred and revenge, he tried every means to torture Dimmesdale to death.

海丝特这种坚忍不拔、自我牺牲的精神，使丁梅斯代尔大为感动。内心的罪恶感与外界的压力令他心力交瘁，不久就病倒了。同时，海丝特的丈夫罗杰·奇林渥斯医生获释归来，一直在暗查到底谁是孩子的生父。他假装能治愈年轻牧师的病，并通过与丁梅斯代尔的接触后逐渐摸清真相。怀着满腔仇恨和报复心理，他要用尽一切手段置丁梅斯代尔于死地。

In order to escape, Hester and Dimmesdale decide to take a ship to go away together with their daughter, Pearl, on the day when the new governor takes office. Unfortunately, their secret decision is seen through by Roger Chillingworth, who threatens to go with them. Seeing there is no way to escape, Dimmesdale on the day of the new governor's arrival holds Hester's arm by one of his hand and takes little Pearl's hand in his other hand. The three of them walk up the stairs to the platform in the town square. Dimmesdale shows people a scarlet letter A on his breast and announces his sin in public. Then he dies in Hester's arms. After he dies, Hester and Peal left Boston. Many years later, Peal grows up and gets married. And Hester is back in Boston again, still wearing the scarlet letter A. She makes clothes and gives them away, trying to turn shameful letter A into a symbol of honor and glory until she dies.

为了逃脱，海丝特跟丁梅斯代尔决定在新州长就职那天，带上他们的女儿珠儿一同乘船出走。但不幸的是此事被奇林渥斯识破，他威胁说要与他们一起走。见无路逃脱，丁梅斯代尔在新州长就职那天，一手挽着海丝特，一手拉着珠儿一起走上小镇广场的示众台，当众露出胸前红色的 A 字，并宣布了自己的罪孽，随后死在海丝特怀抱中。他死后，海丝特与珠儿离开了波士顿。若干年后，珠儿长大成人，也安了家，而海丝特带着那个红色的 A 字再次回到了波士顿。她缝制衣服然后送人，把耻辱的红字 A 变成了道德与光荣的象征，直到死去。

Comment: The author discloses in the novel the cruelty of American law, the deception of religion and the hypocrisy of morality of the nineteenth century. The wide use of symbolism and the large amount of description of the characters' psychology make it both as the first symbolic novel and as the first psychological novel in American literature.

作者揭露了 19 世纪美国法律的残酷、宗教的骗术和道德的虚伪。这部小说以其象征手法以及对人物心理活动的大量描写成为美国文学里第一部象征主义小说，也是第一部心理小说。

二、*The Portrait of a Lady*（《贵妇画像》）

Author: Henry James 作者：亨利·詹姆斯

Henry James (1843-1916), American novelist, playwright, essayist and critic, was born in a rich family in New York. Henry James was the second of the five children. In search of a proper education for his children, Henry senior sent him to schools in America, France, Germany, and Switzerland. Therefore he received a very good education early from his childhood. In 1862 Henry briefly attended Harvard Law School, but his main interest is in literature. In 1864 he began contributing stories and book reviews to magazines. Two more trips to Europe led to his final decision to settle there, first in Paris then in London next year.

亨利·詹姆斯（1843—1916），美国小说家、剧作家、散文家和文学评论家。他生于纽约一个富裕家庭，家里 5 个孩子中他排行老二。亨利的父亲为了使孩子接受良好的教育，曾先后派他到美国、法国、德国和瑞士等地求学。因此他自幼受到良好的教育。1862 年亨利曾在哈佛法学院就读，但他的兴趣却在文学方面。1864 年起，他开始为一些杂志撰稿写故事和书评。他曾两次赴欧洲游历，最后决定移居欧洲。先是在巴黎，次年移居伦敦。

His well-known novel *Daisy Miller*（1879）brought him international fame. *The Portrait of a Lady* is one of his masterpieces. His novels include *The American*（1877）, *Washington Square*（1880）, *The Princess Casamassima*（1886）, and the three late masterpieces, *The Ambassadors*（1903）, *The Wings of the Dove*（1902）, and *The Golden Bowl*（1904）. He also wrote plays, criticism, autobiography, travel books and some of the finest short stories.

亨利·詹姆斯的成名之作《黛西·密勒》（1879）让他享誉世界，而《贵妇画像》则是他另一篇代表作。他的小说包括《美国人》（1877）、《华盛顿广场》（1880）和《卡萨玛西玛公主》（1886）及其后期三部代表作——《专使》（1903）、《鸽之翼》（1902）、《金碗》（1904）。他还曾写过剧本、评论、自传、游记，以及一些优秀的短篇小说。

Plot: Isabel Archer is an American young woman brought to Europe by her aunt, Mrs. Touchette. She meets her uncle, Mr. Touchette, a powerful banker and her cousin, Ralph, and lives with the Touchette family in their home at Gardencourt. Isabel makes a strong impression on everyone at Mr. Touchette's county manor of Gardencourt: her cousin Ralph, slowly dying of a lung disorder, becomes deeply devoted to her and the Touchettes' aristocratic neighbor Lord Warburton falls in love with her. Her friend from America, Henrietta Stackpole, also comes to England to show his affection to Isabel. But when Warburton and Henrietta propose to her, Isabel declines. Later Mr. Touchette's health declines, and Ralph knows that he can't marry Isabel, but he convinces his father that when he dies, he should leave half of his wealth to Isabel. This will protect her independence and ensure that she will never have to marry for money.

聪明美丽的美国姑娘伊莎贝尔·阿切尔随姨妈杜歇夫人来到了欧洲。她见到了姨父大银行长杜歇先生和表兄拉尔夫，并与杜歇一家在"花园山庄"里暂住。伊莎贝尔深得大家的欢心。身患肺病绝症的表兄拉尔夫渐渐爱上了她；杜歇一家的邻居英国贵族沃伯顿爵士因她坠入爱河；伊萨贝尔的美国朋友亨丽埃塔·斯塔克波尔也前来英国向她表达好感。但当沃伯顿和亨丽埃塔向伊萨贝尔求婚时，她都没有轻许。后来杜歇先生的健康每况愈下，拉尔夫知道自己不可能与伊莎贝尔结合，但他劝说父亲分出一半家产让她继承，使她经济独立，可以自由择偶。

After her uncle dies, Isabel comes into a great deal of money and is now independent. She goes to Italy with Mrs. Touchette, where she is introduced to Mrs. Touchette's polished, elegant friend, Madame Merle. Madame Merle is the most fascinating person Isabel has ever met. While enjoying the historical city of Rome and Florence, she also falls into the trap of Madame Merle.

姨父故世后，伊莎贝尔得到一大笔遗产，因此自立了。她和姨妈杜歇夫人去意大利游历。在意大利，伊莎贝尔又结识了姨妈的朋友——高雅华贵、才艺超群的梅尔夫人。她对这位女人十分倾倒。在陶醉于罗马和佛罗伦萨的历史遗迹的同时，伊莎贝尔也渐渐进入梅尔夫人精心布下的圈套之中。

Madame Merle introduces Isabel to a man named Gilbert Osmond, a man of no social standing or wealth, let alone a man with fine taste for art, but whom Merle describes as one of the finest gentlemen in Europe, wholly devoted to art and aesthetics, and his beautiful daughter Pansy. Isabel feels greatly attached to them. Everyone in Isabel's world disapproves of Osmond, especially Ralph, but Isabel chooses to marry him anyway. After some time Isabel finds that her husband is a very mean person and that there is something mysterious about Madame Merle's relationship with her husband. Now she suddenly realizes that Merle is his lover. Merle is attempting to manipulate Isabel into marrying Osmond so that he will have access to her fortune. To her amazement, there is still more to Merle and Osmond's relationship. Merle is Pansy's mother. Pansy was born out of wedlock. Osmond's wife died at about the same time, so Merle and Osmond spread the story that she died in childbirth. The news is such a great blow to Isabel that she falls ill. She feels very depressed. She can choose to leave her husband, but she refuses. She pretends to be very happy and doesn't tell anyone about her misfortune. At this time, Ralph is rapidly deteriorating and Isabel receives word that he is dying. She goes to England to take a last look at him in spite of her husband's objection. After the death of Ralph, Isabel returns to

Rome unexpectedly. She feels unable to break away from her marriage to Gilbert Osmond. She has to fulfill her social duty of being a good wife.

梅尔夫人介绍她认识了一位既无社会地位又无金钱的美国"半吊子艺术家"吉尔伯特·奥斯蒙德，还有他那楚楚动人的女儿。但梅尔夫人却把他描写成一位儒雅斯文、富有教养的艺术家。伊莎贝尔为之动心。尽管她周围的亲戚和朋友，特别是拉尔夫都不喜欢奥斯蒙德，她依然自作主张地下嫁于他。但是不久她就发现丈夫不过是一个平庸浅薄、贪鄙好色的小人，而且觉得他和梅尔夫人关系暧昧。后来才知道他是梅尔夫人的情夫。梅尔夫人极力撮合伊莎贝尔嫁给奥斯蒙德，为的是能够得到她的财产。更令人气愤的是，奥斯蒙德与梅尔夫人的关系还不止这些。梅尔夫人是帕茜的生母，帕茜是私生子。帕茜出生的时候，奥斯蒙德的妻子就去世了。因此梅尔夫人与奥斯蒙德就对外散播他的妻子死于难产的消息。这一事实对伊莎贝尔是一个沉重的打击，她也因此而病倒了。伊萨贝尔痛苦万分。她本可选择离开她的丈夫，但她却没有这样做。她强作欢颜，对外人隐瞒了婚姻不幸的实情。此时她得知表兄拉尔夫病危的消息，不顾丈夫的反对赶去英国看他。拉尔夫死后，伊莎贝尔出乎众人的预料，又回到罗马。她感觉自己无法挣脱掉与奥斯蒙德的婚姻纽带，她必须尽到做妻子的职责。

Comment: The novel is one of the masterpieces of Henry James. It is well-known for its vivid psychological description of the characters. It is regarded as the greatest novel in English and American literature.

本书是亨利·詹姆斯最优秀的作品之一，以细腻的心理描写见称，被认为是英美文学里的上乘之作。

三、*Moby Dick*（《白鲸》）

Author: Herman Melville 作者：赫尔曼·梅尔维尔

Herman Melville(1819-1891), American writer and poet, was born in a wealthy merchant's family in New York. At the age of ten, his father's business went bankrupt and his father died two years later. After the death of his father, he left school and began to make a living by himself. He worked at different jobs such as bank clerk, farm labor, shopping assistant and teacher. In 1841, he shipped aboard the whaler Acushnet and began a series of adventures in the South Seas that would last for three years. He even had the unusual experience of staying with the cannibal.

赫尔曼·梅尔维尔（1819—1891），美国作家、诗人，生于纽约一个富裕的商人家庭。10岁时，他的父亲破产，两年后父亲离开了人世。父亲死后，梅尔维尔辍学并开始独立谋生，先后做过银行文书、农场劳工、店员以及教师等。1841 年他搭乘捕鲸船阿库什尼特号去南太平洋，开始了长达 3 年的探险，甚至有过与食人族相处的奇异经历。

His legendary experience of whaling provided Melville abundant materials for his writings. His masterpiece, *Moby-Dick*（1851）, is just one of them. However, at the beginning the book failed to win the recognition of the readers and didn't sell very well. It wasn't until after his death that *Moby-Dick* began to gain popularity and Melville began to enjoy higher reputation in the American literature. Melville's other novels include *Typee* （1846), *Omoo*（1847）, and *Billy Budd*, completed several months before his death and published in 1924.

传奇式的捕鲸经历，为梅尔维尔的文学创作提供了大量素材。他的杰作——《白鲸》（1851）只是其中一篇。然而，这部杰作起初并未得到读者的赏识，不是很畅销。直到他死后，《白鲸》才被人们所喜爱，梅尔维尔在美国文坛上的声望也与日俱增。梅尔维尔的其他作品包括《泰皮》（1846）、《欧穆》（1847）以及临终前数月写成的《毕利·伯德》直到 1924 年才出版。

Plot: Ishmael is a young sailor. This young man from Manhattan has been to sea four times in the merchant service but yearns for a whaling adventure. Therefore he and his new friend, Queequeg, sign on with the Pequod and sail with Captain Ahab on an exciting and dangerous voyage. Also on the ship are Starbuck, Stubb, and other whalers from different countries. After the ship sets sail, the ship's captain, Ahab, is nowhere to be seen; nevertheless, they hear of him. According to one of the owners of the ship, Ahab is a man of few words but deep meaning, who has been to school as well as among the cannibals.

伊士玛利是个年轻的水手。这个来自于曼哈顿的年轻人已经跟随商船出海过四次，但仍渴望捕鲸的冒险经历。因此他和他新交的朋友魁魁格与"披谷德"号船签了约，跟随其船长亚哈开始了一次激动人心的海上冒险之旅。同船的还有斯达巴克、斯图布以及来自于其他各国的捕鲸手。轮船出海以后，没有人看见过船长亚哈的踪影，然而大家都听人议论他。同行的一位船主说，亚哈是个深沉但却少言寡语的人。他受过教育，也同食人族打过交道。

When Ahab finally appears on his quarter-deck one morning, Ishmael notices that he is an imposing, frightening figure whose haunted visage sends shivers over the crew. A long scar runs down his face and, they say, the length of his body. He has a grim, determined look. One leg is missing and replaced by a white artificial leg made of the polished bone of a sperm whale's jaw.

一天清晨，当亚哈船长终于出现在甲板上时，伊士玛利注意到他威严得令人生畏，可怕的面容令船员们不寒而栗。一道长长的疤痕从他的面部据说是一直延伸到全身，其神色冷峻而坚定。他的一条腿不见了，代之而起的是一条用抹香鲸磨光的颚骨做成的白色假腿。

Ahab finally gathers the crewmen together and, in a rousing speech, solicits their support in a single purpose for this voyage: hunting down and killing the White Whale, Moby Dick, a very large sperm whale with a snow-white head. Captain Ahab hates Moby Dick,"the white devil", because he lost a leg to the white whale in a fight. Now Ahab can only think of one thing. He has to find Moby Dick and kill him. He is prepared to sacrifice everything for this goal.

亚哈把所有的船员们召集到一起，做了一次振奋人心的演讲，并请求他们支持此次航行的唯一目的：追杀一头名叫莫比·迪克的鲸鱼—— 一条头部雪白的巨大抹香鲸。亚哈船长特别痛恨莫比·迪克这个"白色恶魔"，因为在一次搏斗中这头白鲸咬断了他的一条腿。亚哈现在心中只想着一件事，那就是找到莫比·迪克并杀了它。为了达到这一目的，他已经准备好牺牲一切。

There are numerous encounters of two ships on the open sea. On these occasions crews normally visit each other and newspapers and mail are exchanged. The men talk of whale sightings or other news. For Ahab, however, there is but one relevant question to ask of another ship:"Have you seen the White Whale?"Some have. The captain of the Samuel Enderby lost an arm to the leviathan. The Rachel has also seen Moby Dick. As a result, one of its open boats is missing and Captain Garnider's son is aboard. Captain Garnider begs Ahab to aid in the search, but the Pequod's captain Ahab is resolute. He is very near the White Whale now and will not stop to help.

海上航行中，两艘船经常会不期而遇。在这种情形下，两船的船员通常会互访并交换报纸和信件或谈论他们沿途所见到的鲸鱼以及其他一些消息。然而对于亚哈来说，他所要询问其他船只唯一相关的问题就是"你们见到那头白鲸了吗？"有的船只说见过。其中"塞缪尔·恩德比"号的船长被这头庞然大物咬掉了一只胳膊。"雷切尔"号船也看见过莫比·迪克，其结果是它的一只敞舱船失踪了，而船长加德纳的儿子就在上面。加德纳船长恳求亚哈援助搜救工作。但"披谷德"号的船长亚哈决心已定：他现在已非常接近这头白鲸，不会停下来进行援助。

Ahab is the first to spot Moby Dick. For three days, the crew pursues the great whale, who repeatedly turns on the Pequod's boats, wreaking destruction and killing mate Fedallah, sinking the Pequod, and dragging Ahab into the sea and his death. Only Ishmael survives.

He floats for a day and a night before the Rachel rescues him.

亚哈首先发现了莫比·迪克。整整三天，船员们都在追捕这头巨鲸。它一次次出其不意地袭击"披谷德"号的船只，狂暴地肆虐并杀死了大副费德勒，造成"披谷德"号的沉没，船长亚哈也被卷进海里淹死了。只有伊士玛利一人幸存下来，他在海上漂了一天一夜才被"雷切尔"号救起。

Comment: *Moby Dickis* has been considered to be a novel full of symbolism. Through realistic storytelling, symbolic allegory, biblical allusion and figurative language, the author explores the fate of both human being and nature and creates a masterpiece in the world's sea novel. *Moby-Dick* establishes Melville's leading position in American Literature.

《白鲸》被认为是最富有象征意义的小说之一。作者通过写实的故事叙述、象征性的寓言处理，以及圣经典故和意象化语言的运用，探讨了人类与自然的命运，创造出世界海洋文学的经典作品。《白鲸》奠定了作者梅尔维尔在美国文坛上的领先地位。

四、*Uncle Tom's Cabin*（《汤姆叔叔的小屋》）

Author: Harriet Beecher Stowe 作者：哈里特·比彻·斯托

Harriet Beecher Stowe, an American writer, was born on June 14, 1811, in Litchfield, Connecticut. Her father was a preacher. Stowe's mother died when she was four. At the age of twenty-three, Stowe began her literary career and soon she was a regular contributor of stories and essays. Her first book, *The Mayflower*, appeared in 1843.

美国作家哈里特·比彻·斯托夫人于 1811 年 6 月 14 日出生在康涅狄格州的利奇菲尔德。她的父亲是一个牧师，母亲在她 4 岁时就去世了。斯托夫人 23 岁时开始了自己的文学生涯，不久后便开始定期撰写故事和散文。她的第一部作品《五月花号》发表于 1843 年。

Later she and her family moved to live in Cincinnati. In Cincinnati Stowe had come in contact with fugitive slaves. She learned about life in the South from her own visits there and saw how cruel slavery was and what a miserable life the slaves lived. These experiences led Stowe to compose her famous novel, which was first published in the anti-slavery newspaper *The National Era* in 1852 and later in book form. The book had great impact in society and she became famous overnight. Stowe's later works did not gain the same popularity as *Uncle Tom's Cabin*. She published novels, studies of social life, essays, and a small volume of religious poems.

后来她和她的家人迁往辛辛那提市居住。这使她有机会接触到一些逃亡的黑奴。她自己曾多次去过南方，从中了解了那里的生活，也目睹了奴隶制的残酷和奴隶们悲惨的生活。这些经历成就了她的名作——《汤姆叔叔的小屋》。这部小说于1852年首次在《民族时代》刊物上连载，后成本出书并引起了强烈的社会反响，斯托夫人也一举成名。她后来也曾发表过一些小说、社交研究、散文以及少量的宗教诗歌，但都没有《汤姆叔叔的小屋》出名。

Plot: Uncle Tom, a slave on the Shelby plantation, is loved by his owners and every slave on the property for his honesty, hard work and kindness, especially by their son Shelby George, who calls him Uncle Tom. He lives contentedly with his wife and children in their own cabin until Mr. Shelby, deeply in debt to a slave trader named Haley, agrees to sell Tom and Harry, the child of his wife's servant Eliza. Tom is devastated but vows that he will not run away, as he believes that to do so would plunge his master so far into debt that he would be forced to sell every slave.

汤姆是庄园主谢尔比家的一个黑奴，因为他为人忠实、能干，且待人友善、乐于助人，深受庄园主一家和其他奴隶的喜爱，尤其是谢尔比的儿子乔治少爷非常喜欢他，称他为汤姆叔叔。汤姆与妻子和孩子生活在自己的小屋里很满足。后来主人谢尔比由于负债累累，被迫要卖掉黑奴汤姆和他妻子的女仆伊丽莎的儿子小哈里。汤姆虽然很伤心，但誓不逃跑。因为他想如果他逃跑的话会使主人深陷债务之中，从而迫使他卖掉所有的奴隶。

Eliza, however, cannot bear to part with her son and escapes the night before he is to be taken from her. She makes her way to a village, with a family that harbors slaves. There, she is reunited with her husband George, who lived on a neighboring plantation and has also escaped to flee his master's cruelty. Later the three of them escaped to Canada, where they were free completely.

然而，伊丽莎不能忍受与儿子分离，她在儿子被抢走的前一天晚上带着儿子逃跑了。她辗转到了一个村庄。有一户人家专门收留逃跑的奴隶。在那儿她和丈夫乔治团聚了。她丈夫原本在附近一处庄园干活，因为不堪忍受主人的残暴也逃了出来。他们一家三口后来逃往加拿大，从此过上了自由人的生活。

Tom is sold to Haley. Haley takes him to a boat on the Mississippi to be transported to a slave market. On the boat, Tom meets a little white girl named Eva, who quickly befriends him. When Eva falls into the river, Tom dives in to save her, and her father, Augustine St. Clare, gratefully agrees to buy Tom from Haley. Tom has lived with the St. Clares for two years, Eva grows very ill then dies and St. Clare decides to set Tom free. However, before he can act on his decision, St. Clare is stabbed to death while trying to settle a brawl.

汤姆被卖给了哈利。哈利带他上了船，沿着密西西比河而下，准备到奴隶市场上贩卖。在船上，汤姆遇到了一个名叫伊娃的白人小姑娘并很快和她成为了好朋友。后来伊娃掉进了河里，汤姆跳进河里把她救了上来。伊娃的父亲圣·克莱尔为感激汤姆，同意从哈利手里买下他。汤姆和圣·克莱尔一家住了两年。后来伊娃身染重病死了，圣·克莱尔决定为汤姆赎身使他成为自由人。但他还没来得及履行诺言，就在解决一次纠纷中被刺死。

St. Clare's cruel wife, Marie, sells Tom to a plantation owner named Simon Legree, an evil and bitter person whose philosophy is to work his slaves hard and replace them when they inevitably die just a few years later. On Legree's plantation, Tom meets two fellow slaves, Emmeline and Cassy. Emmeline is a young woman sold to Legree at the same time as Tom, and Cassy has suffered at the hands of Legree for several years. Legree soon comes to hate Tom after Tom refuses to beat and discipline the other slaves. Legree had planned to turn Tom into a brutal overseer, and when he realizes that Tom will not participate in cruelty, he becomes enraged and takes out his wrath on Tom. Later when Emmeline and Cassy escape, he demands that Tom tell him everything he knows. Tom admits that he knew of their plans to escape and is aware of their whereabouts, but he refuses to disclose where they are. Legree beats Tom so severely that after a few days, he dies. George Shelby arrives with money in hand to buy Tom's freedom, but he is too late.

圣·克莱尔无情的妻子玛丽把汤姆卖给了一个邪恶凶残的庄园主西蒙·勒格雷。勒格雷的处世原则就是残酷压榨奴隶，一两年死后再换一批。在勒格雷的庄园里，汤姆认识了两位黑奴同伴，埃米琳和卡西。埃米琳是一个年轻妇女和汤姆一样刚刚被卖给勒格雷，而卡西已经受勒格雷奴役好几年了。勒格雷不久就对汤姆恨之入骨，因为汤姆拒绝鞭打和管教其他的奴隶。勒格雷本打算把汤姆培养成一名心狠的监工，当他意识到汤姆拒绝和他合伙时，他恼羞成怒，大发雷霆，对汤姆一顿毒打。后来埃米琳和卡西逃跑了，勒格雷逼汤姆把他所知道的两个女人的全部情况都告诉他。汤姆承认他了解她们的逃跑计划并知道她们逃往何处，但他拒不说出实情。勒格雷最后把汤姆活活地给打死了。乔治少爷带着一笔钱来为汤姆赎身，但为时已晚。

Comment: The novel plays a very important role in arousing people's anti-slavery feelings. It is regarded as one of the reasons of the American Civil War. Later when President Lincoln has an interview with Mrs. Stowe, he refers to her as "a woman who writes a book which leads to a war". This joke reflects vividly the great influence of this novel.

《汤姆叔叔的小屋》在激发民众的反奴隶制情绪上起了巨大作用，被视为美国内战的起因之一。后来林肯总统接见斯托夫人时戏称她是"写了一本书，酿成了一场大战的女人"，这一句玩笑话生动的反映出这部小说的重大影响。

五、*The Last of the Mohicans*（《最后的莫希干人》）

Author: James Fenimore Cooper 作者：詹姆斯·费尼莫尔·库柏

James Fenimore Cooper (1789-1851), American novelist, was born in Burlington, New Jersey. He ranked eleven among the twelve children. He spent most of his childhood in Cooperstown, New York. The forest and the lake nearby and the legend about the Indians made a deep impression on him, which later inspired his Indian stories. Cooper once served in the Navy for five years. The experience later provided materials for his sea stories.

詹姆斯·费尼莫尔·库柏（1789—1851），美国小说家，出生于新泽西州的伯林顿。在 12 个兄弟姐妹中，库柏排行 11。库柏自幼生活在纽约州的库珀斯敦，附近的湖泊、森林以及有关印第安人的传说给库柏留下了深刻的印象，并激发了他日后创作印第安小说的灵感。库柏曾在海军服役 5 年，这为他后来写海上小说提供了素材。

His first published novel *The Spy* brought Cooper instant fame. Of all his novels the most important ones are *The Leatherstocking Tales*, a series of novels about pioneer life. They included such classics as *The Deer-slayer, The Last of the Mohicans, The Pathfinder, The Pioneer* and *The Prairie*. And *The Last of the Mohicans* was the most well-written one. In American literature, Cooper set a precedent in three different types of novels: the first is historical novel represented by *The Spy*; the second is frontier novel represented by *The Pioneer*; the third is sea novels represented by *The Pilot*.

他的第一部长篇小说《间谍》问世后，他迅速成名。在他的所有作品中，占中心地位的是拓荒系列小说——《皮裹腿故事集》，其中包括像《杀鹿人》、《最后的莫希干人》、《探路者》、《拓荒者》和《大草原》这样的经典之作。而《最后的莫希干人》则为其中最出色的一部。在美国文学史上，库柏首开了三种不同类型小说的先河：①以《间谍》为代表的历史小说；②以《拓荒者》为代表的边疆小说；③以《舵手》为代表的海上小说。

Plot: In 1757, the British and French are battling for control of North America. Some Indians help the French and other Indians join the British forces. Among the many tribes in the west of the Hudson River, there is an Indian tribe called the Mohican. Because of the war, there left only three men in the tribe: Chingachgook, his son Uncas, and Hawkeye his adopted white son. Once when British Captain Duncan Heyward is escorting Cora Munro and her sister Alice, the daughter of Colonel Edmund Munro to meet their father at Fort William Henry, they fall into the trap of their guide Magua and are ambushed by a French ally the Hurons. In great danger, they are rescued by the three Mohicans, who eventually escort them to Fort William Henry guarded by Munro.

1757 年，英法两国为争夺北美殖民地而无休止地交战。有的印第安人帮助法军，有的加入了英军。在哈德逊河以西地区的诸多部落中，有一支叫莫希干族的印第安部落，战争使之仅幸存三人：钦加戈、他的儿子恩卡斯以及他的白人养子豪克侬。一次，英军少校邓肯·海沃德在护送上校蒙罗之女科拉和她的妹妹艾丽丝去威廉亨利堡见他们的父亲的途中，中了向导马瓜的圈套，遭到亲法休伦族的伏击。危急之中，三个莫希干人解救了他们，并最终护送他们到达威廉亨利堡上校蒙罗的营中。

When they arrive at Fort William Henry, they find it under siege by the French. Colonel Munro has sent a messenger through to General Webb at nearby Fort Edward for reinforcements. Several days pass, and the aided army still fail to come. As the fort is on the verge of falling, the French commander, General Montcalm offers Munro surrender terms. That is they must return to England and no longer fight in the war. Munro reluctantly accepts.

他们来到威廉亨利堡时，却发现城堡已被法军围困。蒙罗上校早已派人向附近爱德华堡的韦伯将军发出救援。几天过去了，援兵仍迟迟不来。就在城堡即将陷落之际，法军司令蒙特卡姆将军向蒙罗上校提出讲和条件。他们必须返回英国，不再参战。蒙罗无奈只能接受。

As the British march away, they are again ambushed by a much larger force of Hurons led by Magua. And Magua killed Colonel for revenge. Because it is revealed earlier that Magua's village had been destroyed years ago by British soldiers led by Munro, resulting in the death of his children and his wife marrying another man. Hawkeye, Cora, Alice, Uncas, Chingachgook and Duncan Heyward escape and hide in a cave behind a waterfall, but Magua and his men finally find them there. With no choice, Hawkeye and his two companions jump into the falls. Heyward and the two women are captured. The prisoners are taken to a Huron village, waiting for trial. Hawkeye, Uncas and Chingachgook finally find their way there, too.

在英军撤退途中，马瓜带领大批休伦族人再次围攻英军并杀死了蒙罗上校以报家仇。因为小说前面交代马瓜的村庄曾被蒙罗上校率领的英军摧毁。他的孩子被杀，妻子改嫁。豪克侬、科拉、艾丽丝、恩卡斯、钦加戈以及邓肯·海沃德少校得以逃走并躲入一瀑布后的山洞中。但是最终，马瓜他们还是找到了那里。无奈中，豪克依和他的同伴跃入水瀑，而海沃德和两姐妹落入敌手，被带到休伦族营地等待审判。豪克依、恩卡斯和钦加戈最后也赶到了那里。

At last the chief of the Hurons announced his judgment: Cora is to be burned alive in revenge for Magua's dead children; Magua is given Alice to be his wife. In the critical moment, Duncan Heyward pleads to take Cora's place. And Alice is taken away by Magua. While trying to rescue Alice, Chingachgook's son Uncas is killed by Magua. Alice throws herself off the cliff. Chingachgook finally kills Magua and avenges his son. With the death of Uncas, his last blood relative, Chingachgook names himself 'the Last of the Mohicans'.

最后，休伦族酋长宣布决定要烧死科拉，为马瓜死去的孩子报仇；而艾丽丝被赠给马瓜做妻子。关键时刻，邓肯·海沃德自求烧死以替换科拉。而其妹艾丽丝则被马瓜带走。在解救艾丽斯的途中，马瓜杀死了钦加戈的亲子恩卡斯，艾丽丝也跳崖而死。最终，钦加戈杀死了马瓜，为儿子报了仇。至亲恩卡斯死后，钦加戈成了最后一个莫希干人。

Comment: The publication of *The Leatherstocking Tales*, a series of five novels about pioneer life, including *The Last of the Mohicans*, suggests that America begins to break its dependence on English Literature and that real American national literature has come into being. Cooper is one of the representatives who compose *The Declaration of Independence* in literature. He is called"the forefather of American novels".

拓荒五部曲《皮裹腿故事集》，其中包括《最后的莫希干人》的出版表明美国开始摆脱对英国文学的依附，诞生了真正的美国民族文学。而书写这个文学《独立宣言》的代表人物之一就是库柏，他被称为"美国小说的鼻祖"。

六、*The Old Man and the Sea*（《老人与海》）

Author: Ernest Hemingway 作者：欧内斯特·海明威

Ernest Hemingway (1899-1961), American novelist and short-story writer. He was born in the suburb of Chicago in 1899. His father was a country doctor. Hemingway worked as a reporter after graduating from high school. During World War I he served as an ambulance driver in Italy and was seriously wounded. Later, while working in Paris as a correspondent for *The Toronto Star*, he became acquainted with American female writer, Gertrude Stein,

欧内斯特·海明威（1899—1961），美国小说家、短篇小说作家，1899年生于芝加哥市郊橡胶园小镇，父亲是位乡村医生。高中毕业后，海明威曾当过记者。第一次世界大战爆发后，他志愿赴意大利当战地救护车司机，被炮弹炸成重伤。后来他在《多伦多星报》任记者一职，并在巴黎结识美国女作家格特鲁德·斯坦。

Hemingway's first book, *Three Stories and Ten Poems* was published in 1923. With the publication of *The Sun Also Rises*（1926）, he was recognized as the spokesman of the "lost generation"by Stein. His next important novel, *A Farewell to Arms*,（1929）brought him reputation. From his experience as a correspondent in the Spanish Civil War came Hemingway's great novel, *For Whom the Bell Tolls*（1940）. His short novel *The Old Man and the Sea*（1952）won the Pulitzer Prize in 1953, and Hemingway was given the Nobel Prize for Literature in 1954.

1923 年发表处女作《三个短篇小说和十首诗》，1926 年出版了《太阳照样升起》，被斯坦因称为"迷惘的一代"的代言人。1929 年，另一部巨著《永别了，武器》问世，为他赢得赞誉。西班牙内战期间，他以记者的身份创作了《丧钟为谁而鸣》（1940）。1952 年，短篇小说《老人与海》问世，翌年获普利策奖，1954 年获诺贝尔文学奖。

Plot: *The Old Man and the Sea* recounts an epic battle between an old, experienced fisherman and a giant marlin said to be the largest catch of his life. It opens by explaining that the fisherman, who is named Santiago, has gone 84 days without catching any fish at all. He is apparently so unlucky that his young apprentice, Manolin, has been forbidden by his parents to sail with the old man and been ordered to fish with more successful fishermen. Seeing the old man come back empty-handed everyday, the child feels very sad and always helps him with his fishing stuff.

《老人与海》讲的是一位有经验的老渔夫与一条大马林鱼搏斗的故事。故事以渔夫桑提亚哥每天打鱼为开端，他接连打了 84 天，但一条鱼也没有捕到。本来一个叫曼诺林的男孩子总是跟他在一起，可是日子一久曼诺林的父母认为老头悖运，吩咐孩子搭另一条船出海。孩子每次见到老头每天空船而归，心里非常难受，总要帮他拿拿渔具。

Santiago tells Manolin that on the next day, he will venture far out into the Gulf to fish, confident that his unlucky streak is near its end. Thus on the eighty-fifth day, Santiago sets out alone. Eventually the old man catches a giant marlin which is eighteen feet long and weighs one thousand and five hundred pound. The fish carries the boat far into the deep sea but the old man holds on to the fishing-line firmly. He doesn't feel frustrated at all for lack of food, water, weapons or helpers. After two days and two nights, he finally succeeded in killing the fish and headed home.

桑提亚哥告诉曼诺林第二天他将去远处的深海捕鱼，相信这次他一定会时来运转。于是第八十五天他就独自出海了，最终钓到一条身长 18 尺，体重 1 500 百磅的大马林鱼。大鱼拖着船往大海走，但老人依然死拉着不放，即使没有水、没有食物、没有武器、没有助手，他也丝毫不灰心。经过两天两夜之后，他终于杀死大鱼并胜利返航。

On his way home the old man thinks about the high price the fish will bring him at the market. While Santiago continues his journey back to the shore, sharks are attracted to the trail of blood left by the marlin in the water. The old man fights hard with the sharks. In total, seven sharks are slain. But by night, the sharks have devoured the marlin's entire carcass, leaving only its skeleton...

回家的路上，老人盘算着这条鱼在市场上一定能卖上好价钱。可是一个多小时后鲨鱼嗅到了大鱼的血腥味跟踪而至抢吃鱼肉。老人坚持搏斗，总共杀死了 7 条大鲨鱼。但是到了晚上鲨鱼还是吃光了老人两天的辛劳，只剩下鱼骨头……

Ignorant of the old man's journey, a group of fishermen gathers the next morning around the boat where the fish's skeleton is still attached and they are shocked by the size of the big fish. Tourists at the nearby café mistakenly take it for a shark. Manolin comes to see the old man and cries upon finding him safe asleep. The boy brings him newspapers and coffee. When the old man wakes, they promise to fish together once again. Upon his return to sleep, Santiago dreams of lions on the African beach...

第二天早上，一群不知情的渔夫围在老人小船的周围，观看系在船帮上的鱼的残骸。巨大的鱼骨架使他们大吃一惊，附近咖啡馆的游客误以为是鲨鱼。曼诺林来看望老头，见他疲倦得熟睡不醒时不禁放声大哭。孩子给他拿来报纸并端来咖啡。老头醒来后，两人相约再一起去打鱼。老头回来后就睡着了，他梦见非洲海滩上的狮子……

Comment: The author depicts an old man who is unconquerable in spirit and remains graceful under great pressure, which coincides with Hemingway's famous sentence: a man can be destroyed but can not be defeated. The novel conveys to readers a life of struggle. Even if confronted with the powerful nature, man still can get spiritual triumph in spite of the ultimate failure. Hemingway's simple writing style and the depiction of the image of "tough man"have far-reaching influence on European and American literature.

作者塑造了一个在重压下仍然保持优雅风度、在精神上永远不可战胜的老人形象。这正好与海明威的一句名言相符：人能够被毁灭，但是不能够被打败。这部小说表现了一种奋斗的人生观，即使面对的是不可征服的大自然，但人仍然可以得到精神上的胜利，尽管结果是失败的。海明威简洁明了的写作风格和塑造的硬汉形象对现代欧美文学产生了深远的影响。

七、*Sister Carrie*（《嘉莉妹妹》）

Author: Theodore Dreiser 作者：西奥多·德莱塞

Theodore Dreiser(1871-1945), U.S. novelist. Born to poor German immigrant parents in Terre Haute, Ind, Dreiser received his early childhood education in public school. Later he went to study at the University of Indiana. He spent most of his life time as a journalist. He traveled widely to big cities such as Chicago, Pittsburgh and New York and made deep observation about the society, which lay a good foundation for his later writing career.

西奥多·德莱塞（1871—1945），美国小说家，生于印第安纳州特雷霍特镇，父母是贫苦的德国移民。他在公立学校接受了早期教育，后来进了印第安纳大学学习。其一生大部分时间都在从事新闻工作，走遍了芝加哥、匹兹堡、纽约等大城市，广泛深入地观察了解社会，为日后的文学创作打下了坚实的基础。

His first novel, *Sister Carrie*（1900）was denounced as scandalous and was banned for publication. His subsequent novels would confirm his reputation as the outstanding American practitioner of naturalism. After the success of *Jennie Gerhardt*（1911）, he began writing full-time, producing a trilogy consisting of *The Financier*（1912）, *The Titan*（1914）, and *The Stoic*（published 1947）, which was followed by *The Genius*（1915）, one of the most successful novel to him. *An American Tragedy*（1925）, based on a murder trial, was his masterpiece, in which his artistic styles were reflected fully in this novel.

他的第一部小说《嘉莉妹妹》（1900）因被指控"有破坏性"而长期禁止发行。其后续的小说奠定了德莱塞在美国文学界的地位。1911 年，《珍妮姑娘》成功问世后，他开始了全职写作，发表了三部曲——《金融家》（1912）、《巨人》（1914）、《天才》（1915）和《斯多葛》（1947）。《天才》（1915）是德莱塞自己最成功的小说之一。以谋杀案为题材的《美国的悲剧》（1925）是德莱塞的代表作，他的艺术特色统统体现在这部杰作中。

Plot: Leaving her rural Wisconsin home, 18 year-old Carrie heads for Chicago on a train, where she wants to live with her older sister's family. Soon, however, Carrie finds out that working in a sweatshop and living in a squalid and overcrowded apartment is not what she wants. When she meets a man named Drouet, a traveling salesman whose acquaintance she already made on the train to Chicago. Drouet seems to be a man of something and he shows great affection to her. Under his temptation, Carrie moves to live with him. Later she finds that he is not as smart as she expects and loses interest in him. At this time Hurstwood steps into her life.

18岁的嘉莉离开她的家乡威斯康斯，登上了去芝加哥的火车，去投奔她的姐姐，寻求新的生活。但是不久她发现制鞋厂繁重的工作和姐姐家狭小寒酸而简陋的公寓并不是她所向往的生活。有一天她意外路遇杜洛埃——一个她在去往芝加哥的火车上相识的旅行销售商。杜洛埃似乎是个很了不起的人物，对她又那么关切，使她感动。在杜洛埃的诱惑下，嘉丽搬进了杜洛埃的家，开始了另一种生活。同居中嘉丽姑娘发现他并没有自己想的那么聪明，并对他失去了兴趣。这时，赫斯渥走进了她的生活。

Hurstwood, the manager of a respectable bar, is a man of forty years old with a daughter and a son. From the moment he sets eyes on her, Hurstwood is infatuated with the young girl while in the eyes of Carrie, Hurstwood is much superior to Drouet both in social position and appearance. Before long they start an affair. One night, at his job, Hurstwood finds that the safe of the bar is unlocked and he is presented with the opportunity to embezzle a large sum of money. He succumbs to the temptation and decides, on the spur of the moment, to leave everything behind and start a new life with Carrie in New York.

赫斯渥年纪约40岁，有一个女儿和一个儿子，是一家体面酒店的经理。他一见到嘉莉，就迷上了她的美貌，为她神魂颠倒。而嘉莉也觉得赫斯渥更聪明，而且衣着得体、气度不凡、温文尔雅。相比之下，杜洛埃就显得相形见绌。很快的，两个人发展到了情人的地步。一天夜里，赫斯渥无意发现酒店保险箱没有锁上，大有侵吞公款之机，他经不起诱惑，一时之下，什么也不顾了，拿着钱带着嘉丽，来到了纽约，开始了新的生活。

The second part of the book is set in New York City. Hurstwood and Carrie rent a flat where they live as man and wife under an assumed name. Gradually, Hurstwood realizes that finding a new job is not easy at all. As his money is slowly running out, the couple have to start economizing, which Carrie does not like at all. She starts looking for a job herself. After several setbacks she finds employment at one of the many theatres. Owing to her beauty and talent of performance, soon she turns from a little-known person to a popular star. Her rise to stardom is sharply contrasted with Hurstwood's downfall and the difference between them becomes wider and wider. She leaves him, and the rapidly ageing Hurstwood is left all alone, without a job and without any money. At one point, during a strike, he even works as a scab driving a Brooklyn streetcar. He joins the homeless of New York and finally, in a refuge for the homeless, turns on the gas and puts an end to his life in a cold winter night.

本书第二部分场景设在纽约。赫斯渥和嘉莉改名换姓，在附近租了间公寓，以夫妻关系的名义生活在一起。慢慢地，赫斯渥意识到在纽约找到一份工作实在不容易，而他随身携带的钱也快花光了，俩人便开始省吃俭用。嘉莉忍受不了这种生活，便走出家门，几经碰壁之后，她终于在一家戏院找到了工作。由于嘉莉年轻貌美又有表演的天赋，不久就由无名小卒成了当红明星，她逐步地向成功迈进。嘉莉成名了，而赫斯渥却变得穷困潦倒。两人的分歧越来越大，嘉莉决定离开赫斯渥，搬出去住，留下他一个人孤零零的，没有工作，身无分文。一次，布鲁克林的电车工人在罢工，急需招雇司机，赫斯渥也曾前去应聘。他加入了纽约无家可归的人群，最后沦落进无家可归的收留所，在一个严冬的晚上，打开煤气，结束了自己的生命。

Comment: The author discloses the darkness and cruelty of the imperial society and reveals that there is a sharp contrast between the rich and the poor in America. Dreiser has great influence on American literature. His main contribution lies in his breakthrough of the tradition of "elegance"in American literature. His writings mark the beginning of realism in America.

作者揭露和批判了资本主义社会的黑暗和残忍，揭示出美国存在贫富两个对立的世界。德莱塞对美国文学的影响是巨大的，他的主要功绩在于突破了美国文学中的"高雅"传统，他的创作表明了现实主义在美国的开启。

八、*The Great Gatsby*（《了不起的盖茨比》）

Author：F. Scott Fitzgerald 作者：弗兰西斯·司各特·菲茨杰拉德

F. Scott Fitzgerald (1896-1940), American novelist, was born in a merchant's family in St Paul, Minnesota. He showed great interest in writing when he was in high school and once attempted to write playwright. While studying in Princeton University in 1913, he was keen to write stories for the newspaper of the school. He left his studies and joined the army in 1917, where he began to create novels in the camp. He continued his writings after he left the army.

弗兰西斯·司各特·菲茨杰拉德（1896—1940），美国小说家，出生在美国明尼苏达州圣保罗市一个商人家庭。他在高中时代就对写作产生了兴趣，曾尝试写过剧本。在普林斯顿大学学习期间，他也热衷于为学校的刊物写稿，1917 年辍学入伍后，更在军营中开始了长篇小说的创作，退伍后又继续坚持写作。

Fitzgerald published his first novel, *This Side of Paradise*, in 1920 and became famous ever since. In 1924 he moved to Europe. There he became acquainted with such American writers as Gertrude Stein and Ernest Hemingway. With the publication of *The Great Gatsby* in 1925, he established his position in the American literature. He became the spokesman of"the Jazz Age"(the 1920s) and one of the representatives of"the Lost Generation". In his writing career, Fitzgerald also published such novels as *The Last Tycoon*, *Tender is the Night* and many excellent short stories.

　　菲茨杰拉德于 1920 年出版了第一部长篇小说《人间天堂》，并因此而成名。1924 年他移居欧洲，结识了斯泰因、海明威等多位美国作家。1925 年《了不起的盖茨比》问世，奠定了他在美国文学领域里的地位，成了 20 世纪 20 年代"爵士时代"的发言人和"迷惘的一代"的代表作家之一。在他一生的创作生涯中，菲茨杰拉德还发表了《最后一个巨头》、《夜色温柔》等长篇小说，以及许多优秀的短篇小说。

Plot: The setting of *The Great Gatsby* is New York City and Long Island during the 1920s. Nick Carraway, the narrator, is born in the middle-west of America, who later comes to Manhattan, New York and works as a bond broker, dreaming of making a fortune. He lives at Long Island and becomes involved in the life of his neighbor at Long Island, Jay Gatsby, the hero of the novel. The two of them later become good friends. Like Carraway, Gatsby comes from the middle-west as well. Though born of humble origin, he is a man with great ambition who later becomes wealthy through bootleg liquor dealings.

　　《了不起的盖茨比》一书的场景设在 20 世纪 20 年代纽约的长岛，通过尼克·卡拉韦的叙述而展开。卡拉韦出生于美国中西部，后来到纽约曼哈顿做了债券经纪人，并想以此发财。他住在长岛，与故事中的主人公盖茨比是邻居，两人后来成了朋友。和卡拉韦一样，盖茨比也来自中西部。虽然他出身卑微，但雄心勃勃，后因贩卖私酒而暴富。

Gatsby is often entertaining hundreds of guests at lavish parties in order to show off his wealth and gain the attraction of his former lover Daisy and win her back. Daisy was a beautiful young girl. She was his lover five years ago while he was serving in the army. But when he went overseas to fight in World War Ⅰ, Daisy, out of her longing for money, married Tom Buchanan, a rich man of high social position. Gatsby persuades Carraway to help him meet Daisy again. Under the arrangement of Carraway, Gatsby meets Daisy again.

　　盖茨比经常在家举办大型豪华聚会，宴请宾客炫富，目的是为了吸引曾经的恋人黛西回到他的身边。黛西是一位年轻貌美的姑娘，5 年前在盖茨比服兵役时曾是他的恋人。在盖茨比去海外参加第一次世界大战期间，黛西因为利欲熏心嫁给了上流社会的富豪汤姆·布坎南。盖茨比让卡拉韦帮他再见黛西一面。在卡拉韦的安排下，盖茨比与黛西又见面了。

Five yeas ago Gatsby lost Daisy because he had no money. Now he has become rich. He wants to win her love back. But Daisy is no longer the same Daisy. She is not the same innocent girl as Gatsby has expected. She is beautiful and charming in appearance, but foolish, selfish, shallow in her inner world. At the beginning, Daisy is moved by his loyalty and perseverance and tempted by his great wealth and expresses her disappointment at her husband Tom's rudeness and unfaithfulness. Gatsby tries to convince Daisy to leave Tom. However, in the end she shows no courage to leave her home and her husband since she is fully aware that though Gatsby is now very wealthy, he can't offer her the high social position she dreams of.

5年前盖茨比因为没有钱而失去了黛西，现在他富有了，想赢回她的芳心。但黛西已不是原来的黛西，她不再是盖茨比想象中的纯情女孩。她外表漂亮迷人，而内心却变得愚蠢、自私、庸俗。一开始，黛西为他的忠诚和执着感动，对他现有的财富不免动心，也对粗野不忠的丈夫汤姆深感失望。盖茨比劝她离开汤姆。但她最终没有勇气离开她的丈夫，离开她的家，因为黛西深知盖茨比虽然变得富有了，但却不能带她进入她所梦寐以求的上流社会。

After a fierce quarrel, Daisy, in a rotten mood, drives Gatsby's car home. Half way she hits and kills Tom's mistress, Mrs. Wilson, unaware of her identity. Gatsby remains silent to protect Daisy. Tom, out of jealousy, tells Mrs. Wilson's husband it was Gatsby who killed his wife. Wilson murders Gatsby and then commits suicide.While Gatsby's body is still soaked in the swimming-pool, Tom and Daisy are on good terms again and have been out to travel. Carraway is left to arrange Gatsby's funeral, attended only Gatsby's father and one former guest.

在一次激烈争吵之后，心情不宁的黛西在驾驶盖茨比的车回家途中恰好撞死了汤姆的情人威尔逊太太，但她并不知道死者的身份。盖茨比为保护黛西而保持沉默。但嫉妒的汤姆嫁祸于人，告诉威尔逊太太的丈夫是盖茨比撞死了他妻子。威尔逊枪杀了盖茨比后开枪自杀。当盖茨比的尸体浸泡在游泳池水中时，汤姆和黛西重归于好，出门旅行去了。只有卡拉韦留下来操办他的葬礼，而来参加葬礼的宾客唯有他年老的父亲和以前的一位客人。

Comment: *The Great Gatsby* is a novel in which the American dream and their success are conveyed with explicit awareness. The story also reflects the shattering of "the American Dream"in the 1920s. Fitzgerald's great talent and writing style are also fully presented in this novel. *The Great Gatsby* is known as one of the excellent novels in modern America, which establishes his position in the American literature.

小说《了不起的盖茨比》是一部具有鲜明自觉意识的有关美国的成功和理想的小说。小说生动地反映了 20 世纪 20 年代"美国梦"的破灭，同时也淋漓尽致地展现了菲茨杰拉德杰出的才华和写作技巧。《了不起的盖茨比》被誉为当代最出色的美国小说之一，确立了菲茨杰拉德在美国文学界的地位。

九、*The Legend of Sleepy Hollow*（《睡谷的传说》）

Author: Washington Irving 作者：华盛顿·欧文

Washington Irving（1783-1859）, American writer, was born in a rich merchant's family in New York City. Early from his childhood Irving enjoyed reading the works of some English writers such as Scott, Byron, and Burns. After graduating from high school, he obeyed his father to study in a law firm, but his real interest was in literature. In 1802, at the age of nineteen, Irving started to rise in fame after publishing some prose in *The Morning Papers*. He had been to France, Britain, and Italy and took a lot of notes on his journey, thus accumulating abundant materials for his later writings.

华盛顿·欧文（1783—1859），美国作家，出生在纽约一个富商家庭。欧文自幼就喜爱阅读英国作家司各特、拜伦和彭斯等的作品。高中毕业后，他遵从父命在律师事务所学习法律，但他的志趣却在文学方面。1802 年，19 岁的欧文在《早晨纪事报》上发表了几篇散文，崭露头角。他还游历了法国、英国和意大利，做了大量旅途笔记，为以后的创作积累了丰富的素材。

Irving's first work, *A History of New York*, was published in 1809. His talent of humor was fully presented and he became a well-known figure in the literary world of New York. In 1815 Irving again went to England and visited places of interest all over the country, which led him to write his most popular work, *The Sketch Book*. It is one of his representative works and includes short stories, prose and essays. The collection's two most famous stories are *Rip Van Winkle* and *The Legend of Sleepy Hollow*, which are considered to be"the earliest short stories in modern world".

1809 年，欧文发表了第一部作品《纽约外史》，充分显露出他的幽默才能，使他成为纽约文坛风靡一时的人物。1815 年，欧文再度赴英，游遍了英国的名胜古迹，写出了著名的《见闻札记》。《见闻札记》是欧文的代表作，包括小说、散文、杂感等。其中《睡谷的传说》与华盛顿·欧文的另外一篇短篇小说《瑞普·凡·温克尔》被称为"最早的现代短篇小说"。

Plot: *The Legend of Sleepy Hollow* is about a story happened in a valley called Sleepy

Hollow on the Hudson River. It is said that the place is under a spell of some kind, and the whole valley is full of ghost stories, haunted spots and superstitions. The dominant spirit, however, that haunts this valley is the Headless Horseman, whose head is said to be shot off in a battle during the American Revolutionary War and whose spirit often rides to the battlefield at night to look for his head and hurries back to his grave in the churchyard before dawn.

《睡谷的传说》讲述的是发生在哈得逊河畔的一个名叫"睡谷"的地方的故事。据说这个地方被施了魔法，整个山谷鬼气森森，流传着许多恐怖的故事。然而，出没于此最阴森的鬼魂要数无头骑士了。相传在美国独立战争时期的一次战役中，一个骑兵的头被炮弹打飞了。死后，他的阴魂常在夜里骑马飞奔，到战场上去寻找自己的头颅，并在黎明前赶回教堂墓地。

The hero of the story is a schoolteacher named Ichabod Crane. He is a greedy, superstitious, vain and foolish person, who is greatly attracted by Katrina Van Tassel, the daughter and only child of a wealthy Dutch farmer. Ichabod falls in love not only with her beauty but also with her father's property, the vast farm. There were many other young men in the country who wanted to marry her as well. Among them one of the biggest and strongest rivals of Ichabod was Brom Van Brunt. Ichabod's frequent contact with the girl made him feel very jealous.

故事的主人公是一个名叫伊克波德·克莱恩的老师，他是一个贪婪、迷信、自负而又愚蠢的家伙。他看上了当地荷兰富农家的独生女卡特琳娜·凡·塔塞尔，他不仅爱上了她的美貌，还爱上了她父亲的财产——那片广袤的农场。当地有许多年轻人都想迎娶这位姑娘。在这些人当中，对伊克波德构成最大威胁的一个竞争对手是一个叫布朗姆·凡·布朗兹的小伙子。伊克波德与卡特琳娜的频繁接触使他醋心大发。

One afternoon Ichabod was invited to an evening party at Katrina's house. He rode to the party on an old horse named Gunpowder borrowed from his neighbor. Brom Bones was also present. After enjoying a big meal, Ichabod danced with Katrina while Brom Bones leaned against the wall, watching jealously. When the dance was over, Ichabod joined a group of older people telling stories about ghosts and spirits. And most of the stories were about the Headless Horseman. It was just after midnight that Ichabod started home. As he rode deep into the valley, it became darker and darker. Every shape and shadow in the darkness caused him to shiver in fright. Just then he heard clip of horse's hooves. He turned around and was terrified to see that the man on the horse had no head.

　　一天下午，伊克波德应邀晚上去卡特琳娜家参加一个聚会。他骑着一匹从邻居家借来的名叫"黑火药"的老马前去赴宴。布朗姆·凡·布朗兹也出席了晚会。享受了一顿丰盛的晚餐后，伊克波德又邀卡特琳娜跳了一曲舞。布朗姆·凡·布朗兹靠墙站着，妒忌得要命。跳完舞，伊克波德又坐下来听一群老人讲鬼魂幽灵的故事。讲得最多的还是关于那个无头骑士。午夜以后，伊克波德才开始往家走。越往山谷深处骑，夜色越来越深。黑暗中的影影重重吓得他不时地发抖。就在这时他听见一阵马蹄声，回头一看，吓坏了，马背上的人居然没有头。

The Headless Horseman followed close behind him all the way to the bridge which leads to the old white churchyard where the Headless Horseman was said to sleep! Ichabod rode as fast as he could to race across the bridge. Just then he turned around and saw the ghost lifting his head in one hand to throw it at him! He tried to avoid the head, but it hit him square in the forehead. He fell into the dust and the giant horse with its headless rider passed by him like a whirlwind.

　　无头骑士一路紧追着他直到通往教堂墓地的桥边，据说无头骑士就安息于此地。伊克波德使劲儿骑马飞奔越过了桥板。这时他回头一瞥，只见那鬼怪一只手拎起他的头，朝他这边扔了过来。他极力回避，但那个头还是砸中了伊克波德的脑袋，他一头栽在路上。那匹高头大马和幽灵似的骑马者一阵风疾驰而去了。

The next morning Ichabod was nowhere to be seen. Hoof prints were found in the dirt and just across the bridge was a smashed pumpkin. The local people were shocked. They came to the conclusion that Ichabod had been carried off by the Headless Horseman. Soon after Ichabod's disappearance, Brom Bones married Katrina. Whenever the story of Ichabod was mentioned, especially the smashed pumpkin, he would burst into laughter.

　　第二大早晨，伊克波德不见了！人们发现了尘土里的马蹄印以及桥对面一个摔碎的南瓜！整个地区的人都被惊动了，他们得出结论：伊克波德是被无头骑士带走了。伊克波德失踪后不久，布朗姆·凡·布朗兹就与卡特琳娜结了婚。每当人们谈论起伊克波德的故事，特别是那个摔碎的南瓜时，他就会放声大笑。

Comment: Through humorous writing style and imaginative romance, the author describes the old customs of America and its kind and honest people. This work suggests the birth of American national literature. Like Cooper, Irving plays an important role in American Literature. He is called"the father of American literature".

　　作者以幽默风趣的笔调和富于幻想的浪漫色彩，描写了美国古老的风俗以及善良淳朴的人们。这部作品标志着美国民族文学的诞生。欧文与库柏一样，在美国文学史上占有举足轻重的地位，被称为"美国文学之父"。

十、*The Red Badge of Courage*（《红色英勇勋章》）

Author: Stephen Crane 作者：斯蒂芬·克莱恩

Stephen Crane（1871-1900），American novelist, short-story writer and poet, was Born in New Jersey in 1871. He was the youngest of fourteen children. In 1890, he went to New York and began writing for a newspaper. He lived in a poor area of the city and wrote about the people that he met there. In 1893, his first book came out. It was called *Maggie, A Girl of the Street*. He continued working for other newspapers after this.

斯蒂芬·克莱恩（1871—1900），美国著名小说家和诗人，1871 年生于新泽西州。他是家中 14 个孩子中最小的一个。1890 年他来到纽约，并开始为一家报纸撰写文章。他生活在城市的贫民区，写些他在那里遇到的人和事情。1893 年，他的第一本书面世了，书名叫作《街头女郎玛吉》。此后，他继续为其他报纸写稿。

The Red Badge of Courage came out in 1895, and it made Stephen Crane famous. Many people thought that Crane fought in the Civil War. They didn't know that he was born after the war. He was never a soldier, but he described a soldier's life very well. Crane wrote about the fear and suffering of ordinary soldiers. The book was a great success. Later in 1896 Crane's adventurous spirit drove him to Cuba, providing the experience for his most famous short story, *The Open Boat*. He also wrote two books of poems, *The Black Riders*（1895）and *War is Kind*（1899）.

《红色英勇勋章》于 1895 年出版，并使斯蒂芬·克莱恩一举成名。很多人认为克莱恩参加过内战。他们并不知道他生于战后。他从未当过兵，但他对士兵生活的描写却很真实。克莱恩描写了普通士兵的恐惧和痛苦。此书获得极大的成功。1896 年克莱恩喜欢冒险的天性促使他乘船从美国前往古巴。此次经历使他写出了最著名的短篇小说《海上扁舟》。他还写过两部诗集：《黑骑者》（1895）和《战争是仁慈的》（1899）。

Plot: The novel is set in the American Civil War between 1861 and 1865. The hero of the story is Henry Fleming, the only child in his family. He always dreams of going to the war. He thinks that war is an adventure. He wants to be a hero. In spite of his mother's objection, he leaves home and joins the Northern army. He spends several months in army camp, then his regiment is ordered to march to the front. Henry has never heard the sound of gunfire before. Confronted with the first battle in his life, he feels very tense and afraid. The fierce fire in the battlefield stimulates him to fight, but at the same time the fear of death weakens his courage. At one point he shakes off his tension and fights bravely. But when they encounter the enemy's fierce attack, he is terrified. He throws down his rifle and runs away.

小说以 1861—1865 年的美国南北战争为历史背景。 主人公亨利是一个农妇的独子。他认为战争就如同冒险，他想成为英雄。于是他不顾母亲的劝阻，离开家参加了北方军。经过几个月的军营生活，他奉命随军团到前线去作战。亨利从未听过枪炮声，第一次参加战斗，紧张而惶恐。激烈的战斗场面虽然刺激他去作战，但同时死亡的威胁也在动摇着他的勇气。有时他赶走了内心的紧张，勇敢地投入了战斗，但当遭到敌人突袭时，他惊恐万分，扔下枪支逃跑了。

Henry feels incredibly guilty when he learns that his battalion has won and that it wasn't a suicide mission after all. He tries to return to his battalion but is injured by another fleeing soldier who hits him on the head with his rifle. A passing soldier feels pity on him and sends him back to his camp. In his camp, the other soldiers see his wound and think that he is harmed by a bullet. Instead of thinking him as a runaway, they all admire him for his great courage. Henry feels very ashamed of himself and is determined to find a chance to prove himself.

当他听到所在部队获胜的消息时，他悔恨不已，那次使命根本就不是死亡之旅。他试图回到自己所在的部队，但不幸被从火线上溃退下来的一个士兵用枪托打伤了脑袋。一个过路的士兵见他可怜，就把他送回到原来的军营。伙伴们见亨利负了伤，以为他在战斗中负了伤，不仅不怀疑他是逃兵，反而敬佩他的英勇。亨利万分羞愧，决定要寻找机会证明自己。

The next day, the regiment proceeds back to the battlefield. Henry Fleming fights like a lion. Most of the time, he takes the lead in his regiment and his friend Wilson follows him. In an ensuing charge, when his army the 304th Regiment's color bearer falls, Henry takes the flag and carries it proudly before the regiment. At last the enemy soldiers throw down their rifles and surrender. The battle is finished. Henry and Wilson, to their gratification, are considered the best fighters in the regiment, especially Henry Fleming. He is well-known for his bravery and courage. He is famous. He is now a hero. Even the colonel and lieutenant speak highly of him for his extraordinary courage. Though Henry is excited at his recent success in battle, he feels deeply ashamed of his behavior the previous day. But after a moment, he puts his guilt behind him and realizes that he has come through"the red sickness"of battle. He is now able to look forward to peace, feeling a quiet, steady manhood within himself.

第二天，部队返回了战场。亨利像一头猛狮冲锋在部队的最前面，朋友威尔逊紧随其后。特别是当304步兵团的旗手牺牲倒地之后，亨利骄傲地接过了他手中的军旗，最终敌军缴械投降。战斗结束，亨利与他的战友威尔逊成了全团最勇猛的战士。尤其是亨利，他的勇气传遍了全团，他终于一举成名，成了一位英雄，就连团长和副团长也对他的英勇非凡高度赞扬。尽管亨利对战斗中的胜利感到兴奋不已，但内心还是为前一天的行为感到内疚。但不久他就摆脱了这一阴影。他终于领悟到，自己的灵魂经过炮火的洗礼，他已经是一个真正的男子汉了，希望和憧憬又在心中复活了。

Comment: *The Red Badge of Courage* is one of the greatest war novels of all time. It is considered to be the author's masterwork for its perceptive depiction of warfare and of the psychological turmoil of the soldier. It has been called the first modern war novel because, uniquely for its time, it tells of the experience of war from the point of view of an ordinary soldier, including his fear and thought of the war.

《红色英勇勋章》被认为是历史上最伟大的一部战争题材小说。书中作者对战争以及普通士兵矛盾的心理状态刻画得惟妙惟肖、入木三分。作者透过一个普通士兵的眼睛来讲述战争，他对战争的恐惧和思考，具有划时代的意义，是现代第一部战争小说。

十一、*The Call of the Wild*（《野性的呼唤》）

Author: Jack London 作者：杰克·伦敦

Jack London(1876-1916), American writer, was born in California. His family was very poor, and Jack had to leave school early in his childhood and made a living on his own. He worked hard in many different jobs such as shepherd, newspaper boy, porter and sailor. Meanwhile he made full use of his spare time, reading extensively the works of Darwin, Spenser, and Marx. Later, Jack returned to school. But he didn't stay long. In 1897, influenced by the"Gold Rush"in Alaska, he went there to find gold. Instead of getting much gold, he found ideas for his books and stories from this experience.

杰克·伦敦（1876—1916），美国小说家，生于加利福尼亚旧金山，家庭特别贫苦。他从少年起就不得不辍学并独自谋生，当过牧童、报童、搬运工和水手。与此同时，他充分利用业余时间，广泛涉猎达尔文、斯宾塞、马克思等的著作。后来伦敦曾重返学校，但时间不长。1897年他受阿拉斯加淘金热的影响，加入了淘金者的行列。虽然没有淘到多少金子，此次经历却为他的书和小说提供了思想来源。

In his not long writing career, London composes nineteen novels, more than one hundred and fifty long and short stories and some prose and theses. One of the representatives is his well-known novel *Martin Eden*, an autobiography of himself. His famous animal stories include *The Call of the Wild*, *The Seawolf* and *The White Fang*. His famous short stories are *Love of Life* which is appreciated by Lenin and *The Mexican*.

伦敦的创作生涯并不长，期间共写了 19 部长篇小说，150 多篇中短篇小说以及一些散文和论文。其中著名的代表作《马丁•伊登》是部自传体小说。他的动物系列代表作包括《野性的呼唤》、《海狼》和《白牙》。短篇小说代表作是受到列宁赞赏的《热爱生命》和《墨西哥人》。

Plot: The protagonist of the story is a dog called Buck. In California's home, Buck lives a cozy and comfortable life. He is the tallest and strongest dog and has a leading position in his owner's house. He and the children often have a walk together, or play in the water. And in winter, he sits by the side of the heating stoves, warming himself. However, in 1897, people in the Yukon River discovered a gold mine, they needed such dogs as Buck. Buck was then smuggled from home to the North.

故事的主角是一只叫作巴克的狗。在加利福尼亚的家里，巴克过着安逸舒适的生活。他是那儿最高大强壮的狗，地位举足轻重。他经常和孩子们一同散步、一同戏水。冬天，他就坐在炉火边取暖。但是在 1897 年，人们在育空河发现了金矿，他们需要像巴克这样的狗。于是巴克被从家乡偷运到北方。

Buck became a sled dog together with other dogs brought to the North. These dogs were terribly abused by their owners. In order to tame them, they were beaten severely with clubs again and again until they didn't have any strength to resist. And they were constantly subjected to hunger and thirst. Soon, the ill treatment, the harsh weather, the terrible Eskimo dogs, the fights, his dead friend and many other things around him made Buck know he was surrounded by savages. Slowly introduced to the brutality of his new life, Buck was forced to survive and adapt to the tough living conditions in Alaska .

巴克与其他被带到北方的狗一样成了拉雪橇的狗。这些狗受到了主人残酷的虐待。为了驯服它们，主人用棍棒一次又一次地毒打，直到它们没有一丝反抗的力气。它们还得经常忍饥挨饿。这些残酷的虐待、恶劣的气候、凶残的爱斯基摩狗、不断的争斗、死去的朋友，以及身边发生的事不久就使巴克意识到它险恶的处境。渐渐了解了新生活残酷性的巴克迫不得已要学会生存下去，并适应阿拉斯加恶劣的生活环境。

He learns to pull sleds with other dogs, learns to steal food to ease his hunger, and most important of all, learns how to gain a foothold among his group of fierce dogs. Because in order to fight for the lead position in the sled team, the dogs often engage in intense and brutal struggle with each other. His owners soon learn that even though his enemy, Spitz, is "a devil", Buck is "two devils". Because of his incredible strength and unusual wisdom and courage, he becomes the leader of the sled team after defeating Spitz in a battle. There is no longer pity and mercy in Buck's world and there is no fair play. His simple life principle is: kill or to be killed; eat or to be eaten.

他在那里学会了拉雪橇，学会了偷食以慰饥肠，最重要的是他学会了怎样在狗群中占有一席之地。因为为了争夺在雪橇队中的领导权，狗之间也无时不在互相争斗、残杀。巴克的主人不久就意识到，虽然他的对手斯比茨是个恶魔，而巴克却是魔鬼中的魔鬼。由于体力超群、机智勇敢，巴克最终打败斯比茨成为狗群的领队狗。巴克的世界里再也没有怜悯和仁慈，没有公正可言。他信奉的是很简单的原则：杀，或是被杀；吃，或是被吃。

He changes hands many times before he is eventually acquired by a kind and loving owner, John Thornton. When Buck is beaten black and blue by his cruel former owner Harl and is on the very verge of dying, it is Thornton who rescues him and takes good care of him and his injury. Under the tender care of Thornton, Buck recovers quickly. Meanwhile the two of them grow increasingly attached to each other. Buck is very faithful to Thornton. Twice he manages to save Thornton at the risk of his own life. Unfortunately Thornton is killed by the Native Americans in the Gold Rush. Buck goes into a beastly rage and kills several members of the native tribe and takes revenge for his owner. Buck's last tie with people is broken after the death of Thornton. Finally, he is ready to answer to the call of the wild. He returns to the forest and becomes a member of a wolf pack, living a life of wild animals. But he still bears his old friendship in mind and goes to the place where his owner is buried and mourn for him regularly.

他先后换过几个主人，最后被好心的约翰·索顿收留。巴克被残暴的主人哈尔打得遍体鳞伤，就在生死边缘时，索顿救了他，并悉心为他疗伤。在索顿的精心护理下，巴克恢复得很快，由此他们之间产生了真挚的感情。巴克对索顿忠心不二，他两次不顾生命危险救了索顿的命，不幸的是，在淘金的过程中，索顿被土著印第安人杀死。狂怒之下，巴克咬死了几个印第安人，为主人报了仇。索顿死后，巴克觉得与人类再无瓜葛。最终，他回应自身野性的呼唤，重返森林，与狼为伍，过着野生动物的生活。但他不忘旧谊，仍然定期到主人的葬身之处去凭吊。

Comment: In *The Call of the Wild*, the author describes vividly the adventures and wildness in the Gold Rush as well as the struggles of dogs under this special conditions, which reflects deeply the rule in the jungle,"survival of the fittest".

在《野性的呼唤》中，作者将充满冒险和野性的淘金生活以及在这种特殊环境中挣扎的狗的世界表现得淋漓尽致，借此深刻反映了"物竞天择，适者生存"的丛林法则。

十二、*The Adventure of Tom Sawyer*（《汤姆·索亚历险记》）

Author: Mark Twain 作者：马克·吐温

Mark Twain (pen name of Samuel Langhorne Clemens, 1835-1910), was an American writer, journalist and humorist.

马克·吐温（本名塞谬尔·朗赫恩·克莱门斯，马克·吐温是其笔名，l835—1910）美国作家，新闻记者。

Clemens was born on a poor lawyer's family in a small town on Mississippi, Hannibal. After his father's death in 1847, he was apprenticed to a printer and wrote for his brother's newspaper. He later worked as a licensed Mississippi river-boat pilot, joined the Civil War and even dealt with timber, coal business, which lays a good foundation for his later writing career.

克莱门斯出生于密西西比河畔小城汉尼拔的一个乡村贫穷律师家庭。1847 年父亲死后，他就开始出外拜师学徒。他在兄弟的报社当过印刷工，后来当过密西西比河水手，参加过美国内战，还经营过木材业、煤炭业，这为他后来的写作打下了坚实的基础。

He became a writer at the age of twenty-six and began to publish books with the pen name Mark Twain His writings are mainly divided into two periods: ① Short stories. His famous short stories include *Running for Govern*; *The Million Pound Note*; *The Celebrated Jumping Frog of Calaveras County*; ② Long novels. Between 1876 and 1884 he published several masterpieces, including *The Adventures of Tom Sawyer* and *The Prince and The Pauper* and *Huckleberry Finn* et al.. He also writes essays, traveling books, and political comment.

26 岁时，他当上了记者，并采用马克·吐温这个笔名发表作品。他的创作大致可分为两个时期：①以短篇小说为主，著名作品有《竞选州长》、《百万英镑》、《卡县名蛙》等；②以长篇小说为主，1876—1984 年他发表了诸多代表作，有《汤姆·索亚历险记》、《王子与贫儿》、《哈克贝利·费恩历险记》等；他还写一些杂文、游记、政论。

Plot: The story depicts the life of a group of naive children like Tom. Fed up with the boring lessons in school, the hypocritical doctrine and dull living surroundings, they took a series of adventures. Tom is a clever but naughty boy whose parents died early and lives with his aunt. He is very active and can always come up with cunning ideas. He often runs away from school, goes fishing or hanging out with his best friend Huck Finn. He is also fond of playing"pirate games". He even falls in love with a girl named Benci and tries every means to please her.

小说描写的是以汤姆·索亚为首的一群孩子天真浪漫的生活。他们为了摆脱枯燥无味的功课、虚伪的教义和呆板的生活环境，做出了种种冒险经历。汤姆·索亚是一个聪明但调皮的男孩。他父母双亡，住在姨妈家里。他活泼好动，还有着许多精灵鬼点子，总喜欢逃学去钓鱼、和他最好的伙伴哈克贝利·费恩去闲逛、玩扮海盗等等。他甚至喜欢上了名叫蓓琪·撒切尔的女孩，并想尽办法讨好她。

One day at midnight, Tom witnessed a murder—Indian Joe killed a man and claimed the victim Porter to be the murderer. Terrified, Tom and Huck promised to keep it a secret. After Porter was arrested, Tom felt very guilty and often went to prison to see him. Soon the case was brought to court, everyone thought that Porter was the murderer. It is Tom who overcomes his fears and selfishness and tells the judge the truth, thus proving poor Porter to be innocent and Indian Joe was found to be guilty.

一日半夜，汤姆意外地遇上了一场谋杀案——印第安人乔杀了人，并把杀人罪赖到了被打晕的波特身上。汤姆和哈克贝利被吓坏了，承诺会保守秘密。波特被捕以后，汤姆十分内疚，经常去看望他。不久后，法院终于要审理那场凶杀案——大家都以为凶手是波特时，汤姆克服恐惧与自私，向法庭说出了真相，证明了波特的清白，印第安人乔有罪。

Once, Tom attends his own funeral. Because of a quarrel with Benci, he runs away from home in a fit of anger with his friend Harper. Together with Huck, the three of them float on a raft down the river to an island to be"pirates". Not knowing where they go, people in the town assume that they have been drowned and they are trying to search the river for their bodies. One night Tom steals into his aunt's home and finds that aunt Poly is crying desperately for his"death". Feeling guilty about what he has done, the three of them just reappear miraculously while a funeral is being held for them. Tom becomes the hero of the school and Benci is friendly to him again. Another time, Tom comes up with a brave idea: searching for treasure. Tom and Huck find out accidentally that Indian Joe makes a great fortune illegally, but they don't have the slightest idea where he hides the money. At the same time Tom and Benci find themselves trapped in a cave while they are having a picnic. The cave is so deep and complicated that they get lost. The villagers manage to rescue them out. Later it is in this cave that Tom and Huck find the treasure.

有一次，汤姆参加了为自己举行的葬礼。由于蓓琪和他怄气，他与好友乔·哈泼一起离家出走，和哈克贝利一起坐筏子到一个小岛上去当"海盗"。镇上的人不知道他们的去向，以为他们在河里淹死了，正在搜寻他们的尸体。汤姆晚上偷偷回到了姨妈家，发现波莉姨妈正在为他的"死"悲痛哭泣，他觉得十分内疚。在为他们举行葬礼的那天，他们三人却奇迹般地出现了。汤姆成了学校里的英雄，蓓琪也在不久之后与他重归于好。还有一次，汤姆又想出了一个主意：寻找宝藏。汤坶和哈克贝利偶然发现了印第安人乔赚了一大笔不义之财，但他们却不知道他把钱藏在哪里了。此时，汤姆和蓓琪在野餐时走进了一个山洞，因为洞穴太深，结构复杂，他们迷路了。村民费尽周折救出了他们。后来就是在这个洞里汤姆和哈克找到了那笔宝藏。

Comment: Through the adventures of the hero Tom Sawyer, the author aims to make satire and criticism on the vulgarity of American social customs, the hypocrisy of religious sermon, and the stereotype of school education. The vivid depiction of children's care-free state of mind and the humorous writing style make this book a masterpiece in children's literature. It is also a pastoral of the American"Golden Times".

作者通过主人公的冒险经历，对美国庸俗的社会习俗、伪善的宗教训诫和陈腐的学校教育进行了讽刺和批判。小说以欢快的笔调描写了少年儿童无忧无虑的心理状态，并以其幽默的写作风格成为一部儿童文学的杰作，也成为了一首美国"黄金时代"的田园牧歌。

第二十一篇　美国人的健康观

一、Octuplets and Evolutionary Sense（八胞胎与进化论）

Eight kids at once. It's great those octuplets are here and healthy, but really, humans aren't designed to have litters. It's basic energetics. Every individual has only so much energy. Some energy is spent staying alive that is, finding food and not being somebody else's food—and what's left over can be spent on reproduction. In other words, there are limits to reproduction.

　　一胎生八个孩子。八胞胎健康地来到人间是好事，但说实话，人类并非是一窝一窝生孩子的。这是基本的能量学原理。每个个体只有这么多能量。有的能量为生存而消耗——即寻找食物而不被沦为食物，余下的能量可用于生殖。换言之，用来生殖的能量是有限的。

Of course, the various slices of that reproductive energy pie also vary between males and female of all species. Males don't gestate or lactate so they pass on the most genes by flitting from female to female making as many babies as they can, and then walking away. The female reproductive pie is much more complex. There are costs to pregnancy, lactation for mammals, and then whatever else is needed to bring a kid up to sexual maturity so they can pass on genes as well.

　　当然，在所有物种中，雄性和雌性投入生殖的能量都不同。雄性不怀孕也不哺育。所以它们轻浮地同一个又一个雌性相交，尽可能多生后代，使尽可能多的基因得以传承，然后扬长而去。而雌性为生殖的付出要复杂得多。怀孕、哺乳都要付出代价，还得把孩子抚养到性成熟，使之有能力传承基因。

But there are all sorts of ways, from an evolutionary point of view, for females of a species to distribute that energy and bring up babies successfully. She might have as many babies as she can in one shot, litters that is, and have them as often as possible. For that kind of female, reproduction is an assembly line of cheap production per kid. Or a female might opt for the other end of the scale and make one baby at a time and wait for a very long time to see if that one investment pays off.

但是，从进化论的观点看，一个物种的雌性有各种方法来分配能量，成功地抚育幼儿。她可以一次生下尽可能多的幼崽，同时尽可能频繁地生育。对这种雌性而言，生殖就是一条流水线，每个幼崽的生产成本低。或者雌性可以选择另一个极端，一次生一个孩子，等很长时间再看这次投资是否值得。

Obviously, humans are on slow side of the baby production continuum.Evolution has selected for this path because there are features of our species that require great investment by mothers. Human infants might have big brains compared to other mammals, but they need to get even bigger once outside the womb. And so human infants are actually born neurologically unfinished. They can't cling, sit up, feed themselves, or run from predators. And so the very nature of what it takes to be an adult human puts constraints on how many children a mother can have at a time. A woman is designed to care for—two, at most. It doesn't seem right to have eight kids at once because it isn't right in the evolutionary sense.

显然，在繁衍这个连续体上人类在缓慢的这一端。进化选择了这条道路，因为人类的特点要求母亲做出巨大投资。同其他哺乳动物相比，人类婴儿的大脑也许大一些，但一旦出生它还要继续长大。人类婴儿实际上生来神经系统就发育不完善，它不能抓拿东西，不会坐，不会自己吃东西，也不会躲避要吃它的动物。所以，正是抚养成人所需的投入本身限制了母亲一次能生多少孩子。女人是为照料多少孩子而设计的——但最多两个。一次生八个小孩看来似乎不当，因为从进化论的观点来看这不对头。

二、Eat less, Live Longer（吃少与长寿）

Eating less really can lead to a longer life，scientists have said recently. The first human study on a calorie-controlled diet has resulted in a reduction in the signs of ageing. It found that just six months on the regime cut volunteers' chances of developing diseases associated with old age such as cancer.

科学家近日宣称，吃得少确实可以让人活得更长久。首次控制热量摄入的研究结果显示，若对人体热量摄入加以控制，人体老化的迹象就会减弱。该项研究还发现，仅仅 6 个月的养生试验，便降低了志愿者染上诸如癌症等与年老相关的疾病的几率。

The U.S.study supported previous research on monkeys which established a link between diet and longevity. Louisiana State University researchers monitored a group of 48 overweight men and women aged between 25 and 50 for a six-month period. A quarter were put on a diet of 25 percent less calories than they would be expected to eat for their age and weight. Another quarter had their calories intake cut by 12.5 percent and were also put on a strict exercise regime and a third group stuck to a very strict diet of 890 calories a day. The rest were placed on a regime designed to maintain their weight. Volunteers on the fewest calories lost an average 14 percent of body weight in the six months，while the other calorie-restricted dieters both lost 10 percent. All of those who cut down on their calories showed a fall in average body temperature and lower fasting insulin levels, both of which have been linked to living longer.

这项在美国进行的研究支持了早先一项在猴子身上进行的试验，该试验表明，饮食和寿命有关联。美国路易斯安那州立大学的研究人员对 48 位年龄在 25—50 岁的超过标准体重的男女进行了为期 6 个月的监控。其中 1/4 的人的热量摄入比按照他们的年龄和体重制定的摄入量减少 25%；另 1/4 的人的热量摄入减少 12.5%，并严格执行运动计划；第三组严格执行每天 890 卡热量的饮食计划。其余的人执行保持其体重的计划。结果是摄入最少热量的志愿者在 6 个月内平均减去了 14% 的体重，限制热量摄入的人减去了 10%。所有减少热量摄入的人均显示出平均体温下降和较低的空腹胰岛素水平，这两项指标都和长寿有关。

The rate at which their DNA decayed also slowed, cutting their chances of developing age-related mutations and degenerative diseases such as cancer. The study, in Journal of *The American Medical Association*，follows earlier research which found hearts of people on calorie-controlled diets appeared more elastic than others on the same age and gender.

这些人的 DNA 衰退过程也相应减慢，从而减少出现如癌症那样的与老年有关的突变和退化性的疾病。近日发表在《美国医学学会学报》上的一项研究，跟踪了早些时候的研究，发现在饮食上对热量进行限制的人，他们的心脏与同年龄和同性别的人相比更富有弹性。

After an average of six years on the regime, the Washington University experiment established that their hearts were able to relax between beats in a manner linked to much younger people. Dr Smith said the research was the first to show a significant fall in DNA damage from calorie restriction."The value of these studies is they suggest possible mechanisms of ageing in humans and points of intervention to modify the effects of aging."he said.

经过平均 6 年的养生试验，华盛顿大学发现参与者的心脏能在跳动间隔放松，这种现象只会在年轻很多的人身上发生。史密斯博士说，该项研究首次显示限制热量引起 DNA 损伤明显下降。他说：“这些研究的价值在于它们提出了人类老化可能的形成机制以及减轻老化作用的干预点。”

三、Brain is Still Evolving（大脑在进化）

Two genes involved in determining the size of the human brain have undergone substantial evolution in the last 60 000 years, researchers say, suggesting that the brain is still undergoing rapid evolution. The discovery adds further weight to the view that human evolution is still a work in progress, since previous instances of recent genetic change have come to light in genes that defend against disease and confer the ability to digest milk in adulthood.

研究人员说决定人类脑容量的两个基因在过去的 6 万年里经历了实质性的演化，不过他们认为人脑目前仍然处于急剧的进化过程中。此项发现进一步强调了这样的观点，即人类的进化过程仍然在继续。先前人类基因中抗病和赋予成年人牛奶消化力基因的出现就是关于近期人类基因改变的例子。

The new finding could raise controversy because of the genes' role in determining brain size. New versions of the genes, or alleles, as geneticists call them, appear to have spread because they enhanced the brain's function in some way, the report suggests, and they are more common in some populations than others.

由于基因在人类脑容量中所起的决定性作用，这种观点可能会引起争议。有报道认为基因的新变体或如一些基因学家称之的等位基因，似乎在扩散。这些基因在某些方面增强了大脑的功能，并且在有些人群中这种基因变体比其他的更常见。

But several experts strongly criticized this aspect of the finding, saying it was far from clear that the new alleles conferred any cognitive advantage or had spread for that reason. Many genes have more than one role in the body, and the new alleles could have been favored for some other reason, these experts said, such as if they increased resistance to disease.

但是有数位科学家强烈批评这方面的发现，他们说这种新的等位基因是否因上述原因赋予任何人类认知优势或已经扩散的情况极不明朗。这些专家们说，许多基因在人体中起的作用不止一种，而等位基因也许由于其他的原因受益，比如它们是否增强了人体的抗病能力还有待于证实。

Even if the new alleles should be shown to improve brain function, that would not necessarily mean that the populations where they are common have any brain-related advantage over those where they are rare. Different populations often take advantage of different alleles, which occur at random, to respond to the same evolutionary pressure, as has happened in the emergence of genetic defenses against malaria, which are somewhat different in Mediterranean and African populations.

即使这种新的等位基因确实显示出改善了人类大脑的功能，那也不一定意味着普遍具有这种基因的人群会比拥有极少量这种基因的人群具备更多任何与大脑相关的优势。不同的人群常常具备不同的等位基因优势，这些等位基因是对同等进化压力做出的反应而随机产生的，比如抗疟疾基因的出现，这些基因在地中海和非洲人群中稍有差异。

If the same is true of brain evolution, each population might have a different set of alleles for enhancing function, many of which remain to be discovered.

假如大脑的进化同理，那么每一人群都会有各自不同的增强脑功能的一组等位基因，而许多这些等位基因尚待发现。

The Chicago researchers began their study with two genes, known as microcephalin and ASPM, that came to light because they are disabled in a disease called microcephaly. People with the condition are born with a brain that is much smaller than usual, often with a substantial shrinkage of the cerebral cortex that seems a throwback to when the human brain was a fraction of present size.

芝加哥的研究人员开始着手对小脑症基因和 ASPM（异常纺锤形小脑畸形症）这两种基因进行研究，这两种基因是一种叫作小脑畸形症疾病致残因素。患有这种症状的人的大脑天生小于常人许多。他们的大脑皮质常常大幅萎缩，其脑容量似乎返回到了人类大脑只有现在人脑一小部分大的那个时代。

Last year a select group of researchers showed that a group of twenty brain associated genes, including microcephalin and ASPM, had evolved faster in the great ape lineage than in mice and rats. They concluded that these genes may have played important roles in the evolution of the human brain.

去年，一些精英研究人员展示了一组基因群，该基因群由 20 个与大脑相关的包括小脑症基因和 ASPM 在内的基因组成，该组基因群在大猩猩一族中的演变速度快于鼠类身上的同类基因。他们得出结论，也许此类基因在人脑的进化中起了重要的作用。

As part of this study, they noticed that microcephalin and ASPM had an unusual pattern of alleles. With each gene, one allele was much more common than all the others. They have now studied the worldwide distribution the alleles by decoding the DNA of the two genes in many different populations.

作为此项研究的一部分，他们注意到小脑症基因和 ASPM 有一个特异的等位基因结构。相比之下，其中有一个基因比其他所有的基因都常见得多。通过对存在于许多不同人群中的这两种基因进行 DNA 解码，他们现在研究了这种等位基因在全世界范围里的分布情况。

They report that with microcephalin, a new allele arose about 37 000 years ago, although it could have appeared as early as 60 000 or as late as 14 000 years ago. Some 70 percent or more of people in most European and East Asian populations carry this allele of the gene, as do 100 percent of those in three South American Indian populations, but the allele is much rarer in most sub-Saharan Africans.

他们报告说一种新等位基因大约在 37 000 年以前就随小脑症基因一起出现，虽然这种基因有可能早在 6 万年以前或迟在 14 000 年以前出现。大约 70% 或更多欧洲和东亚的人群中带有这种基因的等位基因，在 3 个南美印第安人群中，100% 的人带有这种等位基因，但是在大多数的撒哈拉边缘地区的非洲人中，这种基因颇为少见。

With the other gene, ASPM, a new allele emerged some time between 14 000 and 500 years ago, the researchers favoring a mid-way date of 5 800 years. The allele has attained a frequency of about 50 percent in populations of the Middle East and Europe, is less common n East Asia, and found at low frequency in some sub-Saharan Africa peoples.

随着另一种基因，ASPM，在 14 000 年前到 500 年前的某个时间里出现了一种新的等位基因，研究人员倾向于居中定位在 5 800 年这个时间段。这种等位基因在中东和欧洲的人群中有 50% 的显现率，东亚地区较少见，而在一些撒哈拉边缘地区的非洲人群中出现率很低。

The Chicago team suggests that the new microcephalin allele may have arisen in Eurasia or as the first modern humans emigrated from Africa some 50 000 years ago. They note that the ASPM allele emerged at about the same time as the spread of agriculture in the Middle East 10 000 years ago and the emergence of the civilizations of the Middle East some 5 000 years ago, but say any connection is not yet clear.

芝加哥的研究小组认为这种新的小脑症等位基因可能出现在欧亚地区或当第一批现代人在大约 5 万年前从非洲移居时出现的。他们注意到 ASPM 等位基因出现的时间大约与 1 万年以前农业在中东推广的时候以及大约 5 000 年以前文明在中东出现的时候相同。不过他们说任何有关这方面的关联尚不明了。

They said there may be a dozen or so genes that affect the size of the brain, each making a small difference yet one that can be acted on by natural selection. It's likely that different populations would have a different makeup of these genes, so it may all come out in the wash. In other words, East Asians and Africans probably have other brain enhancing alleles, not yet discovered, that have spread to high frequency in their populations.

他们说也许有 10 多个基因影响人类的脑容量。每一个基因都通过自然选择的方式作用于人脑从而产生出小小的差异。很可能这些基因在不同的人群中会有不同的组合，因此最终人们也许会搞清楚这一切。换句话说，东亚和非洲人很可能有其他尚待发现的人脑增强等位基因，这种基因在他们的群体中会有较高的显现率。

They expected more such allele differences between populations would come to light, as have differences in patterns of genetic disease. They do think this kind of study is a harbinger for what might become a rather controversial issue in human population research. But their data and other such findings do not necessarily lead to prejudice for or against any particular population.

他们期待更多这类不同人群之间的等位基因差异——如基因疾病的结构差异那样昭示出来。他们确实认为这种研究在该领域先行了一步，很可能在人类研究方面引起有相当争议的问题。但是他们的数据和其他的发现未必一定导致对任何特定人群的偏见或对立。

四、Job Woes, Health Blues（工作郁闷，健康忧心）

How gloomy economic news may be affecting us physically—and what you can do to make your health more recession-resistant.

令人沮丧的经济消息会影响我们的健康——你所能做的就是让你的身体有更强的抵御经济衰退的能力。

Being fired or laid off is undeniably one of life's biggest blows and can lead to clinical depression, violence and alcohol abuse, as well as strokes and heart attacks. Even the fear of losing a job produces more doctor visits and health worries. In short, the recent news about rising unemployment and job insecurity may be bad news for our health.

遭遇解雇或下岗毫无疑问是人生最大的打击之一，可能会导致临床忧郁症、暴力和酗酒，以及中风和心脏病。即使人们只是担心失业，也会增加看病的次数，愈加为健康担忧。总之，最近关于失业率不断攀升和就业不稳定的消息，也许是影响我们健康的最坏消息。

Layoffs create a sense of hopelessness. Stress-related complaints such as insomnia and headaches tend to follow, lingering even after victims find new jobs. Employees affected by a mass layoff at a plant were 15 percent more likely to die of any cause over the next two decades. Experts blame the cascade of misfortune that often ensues after a layoff, including the loss of health insurance.

下岗会令人失望。与压力有关的失眠和头痛症状，甚至在受害人找到新工作之后仍会持续很长时间。受过集体裁员影响的某工厂的员工们在未来 20 年中因此而死的可能性大于 15%。专家将其归咎于下岗后出现的一连串厄运，包括因健康保险的损失而带来的问题。

Your health can suffer simply from fear of losing your job, says a sociologist at the University of Michigan. Alter crunching data from two large national surveys, he concluded that chronic job insecurity over a two-year period rivals the anxiety of a-job loss or a major illness.

密歇根大学的一位社会学家说，即使只是担心失业，也可能会影响你的健康。在统计了两次大型国家级调研的数据之后，他认为，长达两年的工作不安定感要强过对失业或重大疾病的焦虑。

He adjusted his data for what psychologists call"neuroticism"and found that even people who aren't typically worriers report worse health when they believe their jobs are in danger. Fears of poor job prospects may have similar consequences. When Swedish researchers asked 21-year-olds about their health during a recession, they reported more problems than a comparison group during a boom.

他根据心理学家所称作的"神经紧张症"来调整其检测资料，结果发现，即使不是典型的杞人忧天者，人们的健康状况在他们认为工作处于危险状态时也会更差。担心工作前景渺茫会产生同样的后果。瑞典的研究人员在询问 21 岁年轻人萧条期的健康状况时，发现他们的问题比在经济繁荣期的同组人要多。

Economic stress may even show up in national public-health measures, although experts disagree about how to calculate those effects. Harvey Brenner, professor emeritus at Johns Hopkins's Bloomberg School of Public Health and a professor of public health at the University of North Texas, argues that the 1 percentage point increase in unemployment since a year ago could have serious health repercussions for the next two years.

虽然专家对如何计量这方面的结果意见不一，可经济压力也许在国家的公共健康措施中仍易凸显。约翰斯·霍普金斯大学布鲁姆博格公共卫生学院的名誉教授哈维·布瑞纳和北得克萨斯大学的一位公共卫生教授坚持认为，过去一年1%的失业增长率可能会给相关人员未来两年的健康状况造成严重影响。

According to Brenner's projections, there could be as many as 47 000 more deaths than would have otherwise occurred, including 1 200 more suicides, as well as nearly 26 000 more heart attacks. Should unemployment continue to rise, these numbers are likely to increase too, he says.

根据布瑞纳的估计推测，此类死亡案例可能比其他原因死亡的案例多47 000件，其中包括自杀案例1 200多件，还有多出近26 000例的心脏病突发事件。他说，如果失业率继续升高的话，这些数据有可能会继续上升。

If your stomach starts churning when you hear bad economic news, Susan Joyce, who now runs a job hunting Web site, has some tips. Start a discreet search as soon as you see danger signs in your current position. Prepare financially by cutting costs and building up adversity funds. Get help if you or a loved one can't shake the blues. Watch for signs of depression changes in eating and sleeping habits, significant changes in weight, loss of interest in sex or other pleasures. And, if possible, make health insurance a priority, as you may be more vulnerable to illness.

如果一听到坏的经济消息，你就开始胃痛，现在经营一家工作招聘网站的苏珊·乔伊斯有一些小窍门可以帮助你。一旦在现有职位上看到危险信号，就要仔细寻索探究，用消减成本和积累风险基金来未雨绸缪。如果你或你爱的人不能摆脱沮丧时，就要设法寻求帮助。警惕萧条带来的心情沮丧信号：饮食睡眠习惯改变、体重突变、性欲丧失或其他乐趣的消失。另外，若有可能，优先加入健康保险，因为你可能更易生病。

Gloomy forecasts aside, there can be health benefits during tough times. Ralph Catalano, a professor of public health at the University of California, Berkeley, points out that some people seek help for neglected medical problems and cut back on risky behaviors like problem drinking in order to stay employed or make themselves more employable. Call it personal recession-proofing.

在黯淡的前景之外，艰难时期也存在健康益处。加利福尼亚大学伯克利分校的公共健康教授拉尔夫·卡塔兰诺指出，有些人会为曾经忽略的健康医疗问题而寻求帮助，并且会为了能维持工作或更容易受雇佣而减少像酗酒之类的冒险行为。这也算得上是个人保护了。

五、An Empty Nest and Happier Parents（空巢，父母更幸福）

The empty nest may not be such an unhappy place after all. Since the 1970s, relationship experts have popularized the notion of empty nest syndrome, a time of depression and loss of purpose that plagues parents, especially mothers, when their children leave home. Dozens of web sites and books have been created to help parents weather the transition.

空巢也许根本不是令人伤心的地方。自 20 世纪 70 年代以来，研究夫妻关系的专家们已普及"空巢综合症征"这一说法，它是指当子女离家后，其父母，尤其是母亲们，感到抑郁、茫然的一段时间。为帮助父母们挺过这段过渡期，人们已创立了多家网站，各种书籍也相继问世。

But a growing body of research suggests that the phenomenon has been misunderstood. While most parents clearly miss children who have left home for college, jobs or marriage, they also enjoy the greater freedom and relaxed responsibility.

但越来越多的研究却表明，人们对这种现象存在误解。尽管多数父母对离家上大学、外出工作或结婚的子女表现出明显的思念之情，但他们也很享受子女离家后更自由、更轻松的生活。

And despite the common worry that long-married couples will find themselves with nothing in common, the new research, published in the journal *Psychological Science*, shows that marital satisfaction actually improves when the children finally take their exits.

尽管人们普遍担心，老夫老妻会发现彼此间已没有了共同语言，但《心理科学》杂志的最新研究却表明，当成年子女最终离家独立生活后，父母们对婚姻的满足感实际上有所提高。

 It's not like their lives were miserable, said Sara the researchers. Parents were happy with their kids. It's justthat their marriages got better when they left home.

研究人员指出，他们的生活并不糟糕。父母和孩子们在一起时很开心。当子女长大离家后，他们的婚姻生活则变得更加幸福。

While that may not be surprising to many parents, understanding why empty nesters have better relationships can offer important lessons on marital happiness for parents who are still years from having a child-free house.

尽管许多家长或许并不对此感到惊讶，但了解空巢夫妻关系更融洽的原因，能够给那些几年之后孩子才离家的父母们提供宝贵的经验，使其婚姻生活更加幸福。

Indeed, one of the more uncomfortable findings of the scientific study of marriage is the negative effect children can have on previously happy relationships. Despite the popular notion that children bring couples closer, several studies have shown that marital satisfaction and happiness typically plummet with the arrival of the first baby.

实际上，对婚姻所做的科学研究得出了多项令人更为不安的发现，其中之一即子女可能对父母以往融洽的情感产生负面影响。尽管人们普遍认为孩子会使夫妻关系更为亲密，但几项研究结果却均表明，婚姻的满足感和幸福感通常在第一个孩子出生后开始下降。

The Journal of *Advanced Nursing* reported on a study from the University of Columbia College of Nursing that looked at marital happiness in 200 men and women. Scores declined starting in pregnancy, and remained lower as the children reached 5 months and 24 months. Other studies show that couples with two children score even lower than couples with one child.

《高级护理杂志》报道了哥伦比亚大学护理学院对 200 名男女的婚姻幸福感所做的研究。结果显示，婚姻幸福感自女性怀孕起开始下降，在孩子 5—24 月的这段时间里，婚姻幸福感一直处在较低水平。其他研究表明，有两个孩子的夫妇比有一个孩子的夫妇幸福感还要低。

While having a child clearly makes parents happy, the financial and time constraints can add stress to a relationship. After the birth of a child, couples have only about one-third the time alone together as they had when they were childless.

显而易见，孩子能给父母带来幸福，但经济能力和时间方面的制约可能会使夫妻关系变得紧张。在孩子出生后，夫妻单独相处的时间仅是他们没有孩子时的 1/3。

The arrival of children also puts a disproportionate burden of household duties on women, a common source of marital conflict. After children, housework increases three times as much for women as for men.

孩子们的降生也大大加重了妇女的家务负担，这也是夫妇间产生矛盾的普遍原因。在孩子出生后，夫妻双方分担的家务均有所增加，但对妻子而言，增加的家务是丈夫的 3 倍之多。

But much of the research on children and marital happiness focuses on the early years. To understand the effects over time, researchers tracked marital happiness among one hundred women for fifty years.

但多数关于孩子对婚姻幸福影响的研究主要关注孩子出生的前几年。为了解孩子对婚姻幸福的长期影响，研究人员对 100 名女性婚姻幸福状况进行了长达 50 年之久的跟踪研究。

The study is important because it tracks the first generation of women to juggle traditional family responsibilities with jobs in the work force. In the empty-nest study, researchers compared the women's marital happiness in their 40s, when many still had children at home; in their early 50s, when some had older children who had left home; and in their 60s, when virtually all had empty nests.

这项研究之所以重要，是因为它跟踪研究了第一代设法兼顾传统家庭责任和社会工作的女性。在此项空巢研究中，研究人员比较了妇女在以下三个阶段的婚姻幸福状况：即 40 多岁，多数人家中都有子女；50 出头，一部分人大一些的子女已经离家；60 多岁，此时几乎所有女士都独守空巢。

At every point, the empty nesters scored higher on marital happiness than women with children still at home. The finding mirrors that of a report presented last year at the American Psychological Association, tracking fifty parents who were interviewed at the time of a child's high school graduation and ten years later. That small study also showed that a majority of parents scored higher on marital satisfaction after children had left home.

在任何一个年龄段，与家中仍有孩子的妇女相比，独守空巢者的婚姻幸福感都更为强烈。这一结果与美国心理协会去年提交的一份研究报告结果一致，该报告跟踪调查了 50 位家长，他们分别在孩子中学刚毕业及毕业 10 年后接受过采访。尽管这项调查规模并不大，却也表明了多数父母在子女离家后对婚姻的满足感有所提升。

While the researchers had hypothesized that the improvement in marital happiness came from couples' spending more time together, the women in the same study reported spending just as much time with their partners whether the children were living at home or had moved out. But they said the quality of that time was better.

尽管研究人员曾假设，婚姻幸福感的增加源于夫妻间有更多的时间相处，然而该研究中接受调查的妇女却报告说，无论子女是生活在家里还是已搬出去住，她们和伴侣相处的时间是一样多的，但她们称子女离家后与伴侣共度的时光质量更高。

The study notes that the lesson from the empty nest may be that parents need to work to carve out more stress-free time together. In the sample studied, it was only relationship satisfaction that improved when children left home.

研究认为，通过对空巢的了解，父母们或许应该意识到，他们需要努力挤出更多的时间，在一起轻松地度过。通过对样本的研究发现，在子女离家后仅夫妻关系的满足感有所提高。

六、Stem Cell Research: The Quest Resumes（干细胞研究）

Scientific inspiration can come from anywhere—a person, an event, even an experiment gone awry. But perhaps nothing can drive innovation more powerfully than the passion born of tragedy. Or, in Douglas Melton's case, near tragedy.

科学灵感可能源于任何地方——某个人、某个事件甚至某个实验失误都可能带来意外的发现。但是或许悲剧是最强有力的变革推动者，抑或对道格拉斯·梅尔顿来说，一场近乎演变为悲剧的事件会成为强有力的推手。

The director of the Harvard Stem Cell Institute（HSCI）is one of the leading figures in the search for cures for presently incurable diseases, and his breakthrough work is challenging many long-held beliefs about the ways biology and human development work. But it was a very personal experience that brought Melton to stem cells, one that seventeen years later he still finds difficult to discuss.

这位哈佛大学干细胞研究所的主任是当前一些不治之症研究治疗方面的领军人物。他的开创性工作向生物和人类生长发育等方面的传统观点发出了挑战。但使他走上干细胞研究之路的正是他的个人经历，一段即使是17年后的今天也不愿谈及的经历。

When his son Sam was six months old, he became ill with what his parents thought was a cold. He woke up with projectile vomiting and before long began taking short, shallow breaths. After several hours, he started to turn gray, and Melton and his wife Gail brought the baby to the emergency room. For the rest of that afternoon, doctors performed test after test, trying to figure out what was wrong. It was not until that evening that a nurse thought to dip a testing strip into Sam's urine and they finally got a diagnosis. The boy's body was flooded with sugar; he had Type 1 diabetes.

他儿子萨姆6个月大的时候，生了一场病，父母开始以为是感冒，后来起床后呕吐，且呕吐呈喷射状，然后呼吸也呈现短促无力的状态。几个小时后，他的脸色突然苍白，梅尔顿和妻子迅速将孩子送入医院的急诊室。整个那天下午，医生们做了多项检查，试图找出病因，但没有结果。直到后来一位护士将一片试纸在萨姆的尿液中浸了一下才真相大白。孩子的体内含糖量超标，他患有I型糖尿病。

Then, as now, the disease had no cure, and patients like Sam need to perform for themselves the duties their pancreas cannot—keeping track of how much glucose they consume and relying on an insulin pump to break down the sugars when their levels climb too high.

这种病至今没有治愈的方法，患者的胰腺无法正常行使功能，像萨姆的父母这样的家长就必须自己承担起这个责任——跟踪记录患者葡萄糖的消耗量，当血糖水平过高的时候就用胰岛素泵注入胰岛素来分解过多的葡萄糖。

The diagnosis changed not only Sam's life but the lives of his parents and older sister Emma as well. Throughout Sam's childhood, Gail would wake every few hours during the night to check his blood sugar and feed him sugar if his concentration fell too low or give him insulin if it was too high.

这一诊断结果不仅改变了萨姆的生活，而且也改变了他的父母和姐姐爱玛的生活。萨姆小的时候，盖尔晚上每隔几个小时就要起来一次，检查萨姆的血糖水平，如果血糖水平过低，就给他服一些葡萄糖，如果血糖水平过高，就给他注射胰岛素。

"I thought, this is no way to live,"says Melton."I decided I was not just going to sit around. I decided I was going to do something."Trained as a molecular biologist in amphibian development, Melton began the work he pursues today: trying to find a way to make insulin-producing cells by using stem cells."It was a courageous thing to do because he was at the pinnacle of his career,"says Gail."He brought home textbooks on the pancreas to figure it all out."Nearly two decades later, Melton is convinced that stem cells will be a critical part of new therapies that will treat and maybe cure not only diabetes but also other diseases for which there are no answers today.

梅尔顿说："我觉得人不能这样一个活法。我下定决心，绝对不能坐以待毙。一定要采取行动。"梅尔顿是两栖动物生长发育方面的分子生物学家，于是他开始从事现在所做的研究：利用干细胞制造出能够分泌胰岛素的细胞。盖尔说："这么做可是有些冒险，因为他当时已经处于他事业的巅峰了。他把关于胰腺的所有教材都搬回家，开始自学。"20年后的今天，梅尔顿确信：干细胞不但可以成为治疗甚至治愈糖尿病的方案中的关键一步，而且还有助于治疗其他至今尚无确切治疗方法的疾病。

Melton's confidence is testament to the extraordinary advances in stem-cell science, some of which have brought the promise of breakthrough therapies for conditions like diabetes, Parkinson's and heart disease closer than ever before. The cells filling Petri dishes in freezers and incubators in Melton's lab and others around the world are so vastly different—in provenance, programming and potential—from the stem cells of just two years ago that even the scientists leading this biological revolution marvel at the pace at which they are learning, and in some cases relearning, rules of development.

梅尔顿的信心证明了干细胞研究已经取得飞速进展，有些则预示着糖尿病、帕金森氏症和心脏病的治疗即将出现突破性的进展。梅尔顿实验室冰箱和恒温箱中皮氏培养皿中盛放的这些细胞，无论是在来源上，还是在基因的组合和潜在作用方面都与两年前的干细胞不可同日而语。生物进化的速度之快就连这些引领生物革命的顶尖学者也不禁为之赞叹，他们也在学习或者说重新学习生长发育的规则。

Until recently, the field has revolved around either embryonic stem cells—a remarkably plastic class of cells extracted from an embryo that could turn into any of the body's 200 tissue types—or their more restricted adult cousins, cells taken from mature organs or skin that were limited to becoming only specific types of tissue. On Jan. 23, 2009, after nearly a decade of preparation, the Food and Drug Administration approved the first trial of an embryonic stem-cell therapy for a handful of patients paralyzed by spinal-cord injuries.

直至最近，这一领域还一直对究竟是使用胚胎干细胞还是使用它的近亲——成人干细胞而争论不休。胚胎干细胞从胚胎中提取，具有良好的再生修复功能，而且可以产生人体 200 多种组织类型的细胞，而成人干细胞是从成人器官或者皮肤中提取出来的，仅能够分化为某些特定类型的组织。2009 年 1 月 23 日，经过近 10 年的准备，胚胎干细胞疗法临床试验获得美国食品药品管理局批准，用于治疗因脊髓受伤而瘫痪的几名患者。

But today the field encompasses far more than just embryonic and adult stem cells; it has expanded into the broader field of regenerative medicine, and Melton's lab at Harvard is at the vanguard, bringing the newest type of stem cells, which do not rely on embryos at all, closer to the clinic, where patients will actually benefit. Last summer, Melton stunned the scientific community with yet another twist, finding a way to generate new populations of cells by reprogramming one type of fully mature cell so it simply became another, bypassing stem cells altogether."If I were in high school, I can't imagine anything more interesting than stem cells,"says Melton."This is so cool. It's so amazing that cells in the body have this potential that we can now unlock by asking question after question."

但是现在，这一问题早已超越了胚胎干细胞和成人干细胞的争论，进一步拓展成为一个更为广阔的天地——修复性药物。梅尔顿在哈佛的实验室处于这一领域的前沿，正一步步将与胚胎干细胞无关的新型干细胞引入临床治疗，这最终将会使患者从中受益。去年夏天，梅尔顿再次震惊科学界，他发现了对其中一类完全成熟的细胞进行重组并产生全新细胞的方法，完全不涉及干细胞。"如果我现在是高中生，没有什么会比干细胞更让我感兴趣，"梅尔顿说，"这简直太酷了。人体细胞有这种潜力，简直令人称奇，这样我们就可以把问题一个个给攻破了。"

The fact is that the hidden power in each of us did not become obvious until 1963, when Canadian researchers Ernest McCulloch and James Till first proved the existence of stem cells, in the blood. These cells possess the ability to divide and create progeny—some of which will eventually expire, others that are self-renewing. The pair irradiated mice, destroying their immune cells. They then injected versatile bone-marrow cells into the animals' spleens and were surprised to see a ball of cells grow from each injection site. Each mass turned out to have emerged from a single stem cell, which in turn generated new blood cells.

实际上我们每个人都具有这种潜力，而这种潜力直到 1963 年，当厄内斯特·麦克库罗克和詹姆士·蒂尔首次证实血液中存在干细胞时才引起人们的注意。这些细胞具有分裂和产生后代的能力——有些最终会死亡，而有些具有自生能力。这两位研究人员首先用射线照射老鼠，破坏其免疫细胞，然后将各种骨髓细胞注入老鼠的脾脏。他们惊奇的发现每个注射点都生长出一团细胞，并转化成为新的红细胞。

That discovery led, 35 years later, to James Thomson's isolation of the first human embryonic stem cells, at the University of Wisconsin in 1998. And that milestone in turn inspired researchers to think about directing these cellular blank slates to eventually replace cells that had been damaged or were depleted by disease. The key lay in finding just the right recipe of growth factors and nutrients to induce a stem cell to become a heart cell, a neuron, an insulin-making cell or something else. It would take decades, the researchers all knew, but new therapies were sure to come. For scientists, that means "we can stop the silliness".

35 年后，这一发现使得威斯康星大学的詹姆士·汤姆逊成功地在 1998 年分离出人体胚胎干细胞。后来这一生物学上的里程碑又反过来启发研究人员对这些原细胞进行干预，并最终替代损坏或因疾病而损耗的细胞。关键在于能否找到生长因子和营养物质的正确配方，只有这样才能诱使干细胞转化为心脏细胞、神经细胞、造胰岛素细胞或其他需要的细胞。研究人员清楚，这一过程可能会耗费数年之久，但是肯定可以找到这一配方。对于科学家而言，这意味着"我们可以遏制疾病"。

Science in Steps: A Decade of Conflicts and Breakthroughs

科学进展：干细胞研究 10 年的冲突与突破

1998 James Thomson, University of Wisconsin, isolates human embryonic stem cells.

1998 年威斯康星大学的詹姆士·汤姆逊成功地分离出人体胚胎干细胞。

2001 President Bush restricts federal funding for research on human embryonic stem cells.

2001 年布什总统禁止将联邦资金用于人体胚胎干细胞研究。

2004 Douglas Melton of Harvard creates more than 70 embryonic-stem-cell lines using private funding and distributes free copies of the cells to researchers around the world.

2004 年哈佛大学的道格拉斯·梅尔顿利用私人资金成功研制出 70 多种新胚胎干细胞，并将这些细胞的副本分发给世界各地的研究人员使用。

2006 Shinya Yamanaka, Kyoto University, turns back the clock on mouse skin cells to create the first induced pluripotent stem（iPS）cells, or stem cells made without the use of embryos. He uses only four genes, which are inserted into a skin cell's genome using retrovirus vectors.

2006 年京都大学的山中伸弥逆转了这一过程——他仅将 4 种转录基因通过逆转录病毒载体注入老鼠皮肤细胞，从而首次创造出诱导多功能干细胞，即在不使用胚胎的情况下培养出的干细胞。

2007 Yamanaka and Thomson separately create the first human iPS cells.

2007 年山中伸弥和汤姆逊分别培养出了首例人类诱导多功能干细胞。

July, 2008 Kevin Eggan at Harvard generates the first patient-specific cells from iPS cells — motor neurons from two elderly women with ALS.

2008 年 7 月哈佛大学的凯文·埃格安首次利用诱导多功能干细胞制成针对特定患者的细胞——从两名患有肌肉萎缩性侧面硬化症的女性患者身上成功培育出运动神经细胞。

August, 2008 Melton bypasses stem cells altogether and transforms a type of mouse pancreatic cell that does not produce insulin into one that does.

2008 年 8 月梅尔顿绕过干细胞，成功地将一种不分泌胰岛素的老鼠细胞转化为分泌胰岛素的细胞。

September, 2008 Konrad Hochedlinger at Harvard creates iPS cells in mice using the common-cold virus rather than retrovirus vectors—an important step in making the technology safer for human use.

2008 年 9 月哈佛大学的康拉德·霍克德灵格利用常见的感冒病毒而不是逆转录酶病毒载体在老鼠身上培育出诱导多功能干细胞。这朝着在人类身上安全使用这一技术迈出了重要的一步。

October, 2008 Melton's team makes human iPS cells by replacing two of the four genes, known to cause cancer, with chemicals. All four must be swapped out before iPS-generated cells can be transplanted into people.

2008 年 10 月梅尔顿的研究小组用化学物质成功地替换了已知能够引发癌症的 4

种基因中的两个，并且培育出了人类诱导多功能干细胞。

七、Mentally Ill Patient and the Court（精神病打官司）

Last year, a mentally ill genius, incarcerated for making death threats, won the right to refuse antipsychotic drugs that he said would dull his mind and his passion for physics. In this case, the Supreme Court ruled, 6-3, that a medical review board had wrongly concluded the patient could be given medication against his will to curb a number of severe mental ailments. "The enforced injection of mind-altering drugs against the respondent's will is highly offensive to his dignity and autonomy and is to be avoided unless it is demonstrated that he lacked the capacity to make his own decision."the court said.

去年，一位精神有问题的天才因对他人发出死亡威胁而被监禁，他赢得了拒用抗精神病药物的权利。据他说这些药物会使他心智迟钝，减弱他对物理学的热爱。在这宗案件中，最高法院以 6：3 的多数裁定一个医学评估委员会判断失误，后者认为人们可以不顾病人本人的意愿强行用药物来遏制他身上的一系列严重精神症状。法院说："违背患者意愿强行注射影响精神的药物严重损害了患者的尊严和自主。此种情况应予避免，除非有证据表明患者已经丧失了自主决断的能力。"

Although the patient, 47, has no formal scientific training, he has authored papers on topics such as antigravity. His thinking was termed"10 years ahead of its time"by a professor at Stanford University in California.

这位 47 岁的患者没有接受过正规的科学训练，但却写出了一些有关反引力之类问题的论文。加利福尼亚州斯坦福大学的一位教授认为他的思想"比它的时代超前了十年"。

But since 1990 he has shown increasing signs of mental illness and delusion. In 1998 he was found not criminally responsible of uttering death threats and a court ordered he be detained in a maximum security mental institution. In various media interviews over the years he has claimed to be married to a U.S.comedienne and said that the Pope works for him.Doctors at the hospital wanted to treat him with mood stabilizers, anti-psychotic drugs, anti-anxiety drugs and medication to treat the symptoms of Parkinson's disease.

不过，从 1990 年开始，他身上的精神病和妄想症症状日益明显。1998 年，人们发现他以死亡威胁他人，但情节尚未构成犯罪。法院于是下令将他拘禁在一所戒备森严的精神病院里。多年以来，他在接受各种媒体采访时一直声称美国一喜剧女演员是他的老婆，而教皇在给他打工。精神病院的医生打算对他施行情绪稳定剂、抗精神病药物、抗焦虑药物以及治疗帕金森氏病的药物。

But he refused, saying his previous encounters with such medications have always been the most horrible experiences of his because they fogged his brain. He said normalizing medication would be worse than death for him because he has always considered normal to be a term so boring it would be like death as he told a hearing into his case.

但是他拒绝用药，并说他以前接受过的此类治疗一直是他生命中最可怕的经历，原因是这会让他思维混乱。他在一次案件听证会上说：对他来说，正常药物治疗比死还痛苦，因为他始终认为"正常"这个词让人厌烦透顶，跟死也没什么两样。

The case echoes that of a schizophrenic U.S.mathematician and Nobel Prize winner, who was forcibly given medication after suffering a breakdown. The review board ruled the patient could be forcibly given the drugs because he was incapable of making up his own mind. Two lower courts backed the patient's right to refuse but his doctors appealed all the way to the Supreme Court. The top court ruled that while the patient acknowledged he was mentally ill and knew medication could improve his condition, he was within his rights to refuse medication. "His choice, which he was entitled to make, was to remain as he was and to continue psychiatric therapy, in spite of his condition and the hope of others. I would dismiss the appeal."said the Chief Justice.

这宗案件与一位美国数学家、诺贝尔奖得主的遭遇颇有神似：他患有精神分裂症，并在精神崩溃之后接受了强制性药物治疗。评估委员会裁定可以对那个病人强制用药，因为他已经做不了自己的主了。两家下级法院支持患者拒绝用药的权利，但病人的医生们锲而不舍，一直上诉到了最高法院。最高法院认为，鉴于这个病人承认自己有精神病，也知道药物治疗可以改善症状，因此他有权拒绝药物治疗。大法官说："他有权进行选择，而他的选择是保持现状并继续接受心理治疗，不管自身状况怎样或是他人如何期望。据此我驳回上诉。"

八、Maintaining Biodiversity（保护生物多样性）

Diversity of life and living systems are a necessary condition for human development. Many question the importance of maintaining biodiversity in today's world, where conservation efforts prove costly and time consuming. The fact is that the preservation of all species is necessary for human survival. Species should be saved for aesthetic and moral justifications; the importance of wild species as providers of products and services essential to human welfare; the value of particular species as indicators of environmental health or as keystone species crucial to the functioning of ecosystems; and the scientific breakthroughs that have come from the study of wild organisms.

生命和生物系统的多样性是人类发展的必要条件。许多人对当今世界保持生物多样性提出质疑，这项保护工作确实代价很大，而且非一日之功。事实上，保护所有物种对人类生存很必要。保护物种不仅出于美学和道德的缘由，还因为野生物种为人类幸福生活提供必要的产品和服务。特殊物种是生态健康与否的指示器，是生态系统正常运行的标志，还是我们在野生植物方面研究的重要突破。

In other words, species serve as a source of art and entertainment, provide products such as medicine for human wellbeing, indicate the welfare of the overall environment and ecosystem, and provided research that resulted in scientific discoveries.

换句话说，丰富的物种是我们艺术和娱乐的来源，可以给人类的生活提供一些物品比如说药材，还能反映整个生态环境和生态系统的状况，是科学发现的重要研究成果。

An example of an"aesthetic justification"in conserving endangered species is that of the introduction of the gray wolf into Yellowstone National Park. The gray wolf has brought numerous amounts of tourists to the park and added to the biodiversity in the protected region.

有个保护濒危物种时考虑到美学因素的例子，就是将灰狼引进黄石国家公园。灰狼的到来吸引了大量游客，而且也使保护区内生物种类更加多样。

Another example, supporting the conservation of endangered species as providers of products for human wellbeing, is the scrub mint. It has been found that the scrub mint contains an antifungal agent and a natural insecticide. Also, the deterioration of the bald eagle and the peregrine falcon"alerted people to the potential health hazards associated with the widespread spraying of DDT and other persistent pesticides". This serves as an example of how certain fish can serve as identifiers of environmental health and protect human life as well as other species.

另外一个例子是矮薄荷树，也证明保护濒危物种确实为人类生活提供了些有用物品。人们发现薄荷树含有杀菌物质和天然的杀虫剂。而且，秃鹰和猎鹰的退化使人们面临潜在的健康危害，而这危机与广泛喷洒的 DDT 和其他顽固性杀虫剂有直接关系。这里提供了个例子，证明某些鱼是怎样检验环境健康状况，同时保护人类和其他物种的。

Finally, an example of species providing for scientific discoveries is the instance of the Pacific yew which became the source of taxol, one of the most potent anticancer compounds ever discovered.

最后，证明丰富的物种是科学发现的来源还有个例子，那就是太平洋紫杉。它是"分类学产生的源泉，也是迄今发现最有效的抗癌混合物"。

九、Girl and Power（女孩与耐力）

The sexes differ in utilizing fat as an energy source during exercise. The body composition of females is almost identical to males until around puberty, at which point the pituitary hormones trigger an increase in production of estrogen in females and testosterone in males. Generally, this results in an increase in body fat for females and a larger body frame and greater muscle mass for males. Some people may see this as a disadvantage for women, but research is beginning to show that it has some advantages for female endurance athletes.

由于性别差异，人在运动时将脂肪作为能源使用的情况不同。女性的身体构成在青春期之前与男性并无多大差异。到了青春期，垂体激素会使雌激素在女性体内增加，使睾丸素在男性体内增加。其结果通常是女性身上脂肪增多，男性则身体骨架增大，肌肉增多。有些人认为这对女性不利。但研究已开始显示，脂肪增加对于耐力型的女运动员有一定益处。

In men and women, fat is stored all over the body as well as within the muscle in fat cells. Even though we have little or no control over which of the fat cells to release their fat for energy during exercise, the latest research has found that women and men metabolize body fat differently during aerobic exercise.

无论男女，脂肪储存在全身各处以及肌肉内的脂肪细胞中。尽管我们无法控制让哪些脂肪细胞在运动时释放能量，但最新的研究发现男女在做有氧体操时身体脂肪的代谢各不相同。

A more recent study in the United States found that women metabolized more fat than men. They took 100 men and 100 women, all with similar fitness levels, and had them work out for 90 minutes a day at a moderate intensity level. Prior to this, they all ate the same controlled diet for eight days. The results revealed that the women on average had a 25 percent decrease in muscle fat, while the men's intramuscular fat levels were relatively unaffected from the training. The researcher's explanation was the additional fat metabolized by women came from fat located in the muscle and not from fat deposited beneath the skin.

美国一项最新的研究发现，女性消耗脂肪比男性多。他们用身体情况相近的男女各 100 名做试验，让他们每天以中等强度锻炼 90 分钟。在此之前，试验者均连续 8 天等量控制饮食。结果显示，女性肌肉脂肪平均减少 25％，而男性的肌肉内脂肪含量几乎未受影响。研究者的解释是：女性额外代谢的是肌肉内的脂肪，而不是沉积在皮下的脂肪。

The results demonstrate that women and men metabolize fat differently. For those women who are not particularly active, this may not be the greatest of news, especially if weight and fat loss is their goal. But for women who exercise or train in endurance events such as long distance running, cycling or swimming, this ability to utilize intramuscular fat stores is a great asset since fat burning is vital to success in this area.

研究显示，男性和女性脂肪代谢方式不同。对于不怎么运动的女性——尤其对以减轻体重和减少脂肪为目标的女性而言，这也许算不上什么喜讯。然而对参加运动或诸如长跑、自行车、游泳等耐力型项目训练的女性来说，利用肌肉内脂肪储存的这种能力却是一个很大的优势，因为脂肪转换为能量对于在此领域取得成功是至关重要的。

十、Poets and Life Span（诗人与寿命）

Poets die young—younger than novelists, playwrights and other writers, a U.S. researcher says. It could be because poets are tortured and prone to self-destruction, or it could be that poets become famous young, so their early deaths are noticed, said a professor of the Learning Research Institute at California State University. For the report, published in *The Journal of Death Studies*, he studied many dead writers from various centuries from the United States, China, Turkey and Eastern Europe.

一位美国的研究者说，诗人通常比较短命，他们的寿命比小说家、剧作家和其他类型的作家都要短。加利福尼亚州立大学学习研究所的一位教授认为，其原因可能是诗人承受着巨大的痛苦并有自我毁灭的倾向，也可能是诗人往往年少成名，他们的早夭容易引起人们的注意。他的报告发表在《死亡研究杂志》上，为了撰写报告，他对来自美国、中国、土耳其和东欧的多名不同时代的已故作家进行了研究。

He classified the writers as fiction writers, poets, playwrights, and non-fiction writers. He did not study the causes of death."Among American, Chinese and Turkish writers, poets died significantly younger than non-fiction writers,"he wrote in the report. "Among the entire sample, poets died younger than both fiction writers and non-fiction writers."Because he studied some writers who lived hundreds of years ago, it is impossible to compare their average age of death to that of the general population."On average, poets lived 62 years, playwrights 63 years, novelists 66 years and non-fiction writers lived 68years."he said.

他将作家们分为小说家、诗人、剧作家及非虚构作家等几个类别，但并没有分析其死亡原因。"就美国、中国和土耳其的作家而言，诗人比非虚构作家死得早得多，"他在报告中写道，"而就我研究的所有作家而言，诗人比小说家和非虚构作家都短命。"由于他研究的一些作家生活在数百年前，因此无法拿他们的平均死亡年龄与全体人口的平均死亡年龄来做比较。他说："平均下来，诗人的寿命是 62 年，剧作家是 63 年，小说家是 66 年，而非虚构作家则是 68 年。"

He has also studied poets and mental illness."What I found was pretty consistent with the death finding actually, female poets were much more likely to suffer from mental illness (e.g., be hospitalized, commit suicide, attempt suicide) than any other kind of writers and other eminent women."he said.

他也对诗人和精神疾病之间的关系进行了研究。他说："实际上，我在这方面的发现与死亡研究的结论相当一致。跟其他类型的作家和杰出女性相比，女诗人遭受精神疾病折磨（比如被送入精神病院、自杀或企图自杀）的可能性要大得多。"

There could also be a more benign explanation for poets' early demise."Poets produce twice as much of their lifetime output in their twenties as novelists do."he said. So when a budding novelist dies young, few people may notice."A great novelist or non-fiction writer who dies at 28 may not have yet produced her or his master piece."He said poets should not worry, but should perhaps look after their health."The fact that some poets may die young does not necessarily mean an Introduction to Poetry class should carry a warning that poems may be hazardous to one's health."he said.

诗人的早逝也可能有一个更为美好的解释。他说："诗人二十多岁时的著作在其毕生著作中所占的比例是小说家的两倍。"因此，没什么人能注意到渐露峥嵘的小说家过早离世的事情。"如果一位伟大的小说家或非虚构作家在二十八岁去世，那他或她可能还没有写出自己的代表作。"他说，诗人们用不着为此担心，不过也许该保重身体。"一些诗人可能英年早逝，但这并不等于我们应该在诗歌欣赏课上发出这样的警告：诗歌可能有害健康。"

十一、Swine Flu（猪流感 / 甲型 H1N1）

The presence of A/H1N1 flu in Mexico and the United States is"a serious situation" that could develop into a pandemic, the World Health Organization's director-general said Saturday.

世界卫生组织总干事周六说，目前在美国和墨西哥爆发的甲型 H1N1 疫情情况非常危险，有可能在全球大面积传播。

"This is an animal strain of the H1N1 virus and it has pandemic potential because it is infecting people." she said Saturday speaking to reporters by phone.

她在周六的电话采访中说：“这是一种动物病毒的变体，并且能够传染给人，所以有可能在全球大面积传播。”

In Mexico, 68 people have died from swine flu, according to a statement from the U.S.Embassy in Mexico. Eight people were confirmed to have swine flu in the United States; six in California and two in Texas, according to the U.S.Centers for Disease Control and Prevention. All eight have recovered, according to CDC's acting Director.

美国驻墨西哥大使馆发表声明说，目前墨西哥已经有 68 人死于猪流感。来自于美国疾病预防与控制中心的报告说，美国已经有 8 人感染此病毒，其中加利福尼亚州 6 人，德克萨斯州 2 人。该中心的执行主任说 8 名受感染者目前已经康复。

The Center has tested fourteen samples of the virus from Mexico and found seven were identical to the virus found in the U.S. cases. "This situation has been developing quickly," he said. "This is something we are worried about."

中心对来自墨西哥的 14 个样本进行了检测，结果发现有 7 个与美国发现的病毒一样。“目前的情况可能会进一步恶化，我们非常担心。”他说。

He said the World Health Organization was convening an emergency committee Saturday to advise the director-general on appropriate action.

他说，世界卫生组织于周六组建了应急委员会，目的是为总干事提供可行的解决方案。

Asked whether the committee would address raising the agency's alert concerning the virus to 6, a pandemic alert and the highest level on WHO's scale, he said:"Yes, indeed." The alert stands at 3, meaning"No or very limited human-to-human transmission". He said Saturday that WHO does not have indications of similar outbreaks elsewhere.

当问及世界卫生组织是否会公布此病毒为世界卫生组织确定的最高传染病预警级别——6 级，他说：“是的，毫无疑问。”预警级别为 3 级时，意味着“没有或较小范围的人与人传播”。他周六说，世界卫生组织目前还没有接到此疫情在世界其他范围传播的报告。

However, he said: "The situation is evolving quickly. A new disease is by definition poorly understood." Mexico City has closed all of its schools and universities until further notice because of the virus, and on Saturday, the country's National Health Council said all soccer games would be played Saturday without public audiences.

他说："情况正在迅速恶化,毕竟我们现在对此病毒的了解很少。"由于疫情的发生,墨西哥已经关闭了所有的学校甚至大学,等待进一步的通知。周六,国家卫生部发出通知所有的足球比赛将在周六进行,并不得有观众观看。

More than 1 000 people have been sickened in the country, and officials are trying to determine how many of those patients had swine flu, the country's health minister said.

墨西哥卫生部长说,墨西哥全国目前有 1 000 名病人,政府正在努力确诊这些人中到底有多少猪流感患者。

In the United States, New York health officials announced Friday they are testing about 75 students at a Queens school for swine flu after the students exhibited flu-like symptoms this week.

在美国纽约,卫生部门的负责人周五时宣布他们正在对皇后学校的 75 名有流感迹象的学生进行猪流感的检测。

A team of state health department doctors and staff went to the St. Francis Preparatory School in Queens on Thursday after the students reported cough, fever, sore throat, aches and pains.

一支由州卫生局的医生及工作人员组建的队伍已经赶赴皇后学院的圣弗朗西斯科预备学校,那里有不少学生被报告有咳嗽、发烧、咽喉红肿、疼痛等症状。

No cases of swine flu were confirmed there. The test results are expected as early as Saturday.

但并没有发现猪禽流感的病例。检测的结果最早将在周六出来。

None of the U.S.patients had direct contact with pigs, though a patient who lives in San Diego had traveled to Mexico.

在美国发现的 8 例病例中并没有直接与猪接触的历史,只有一位在圣地亚哥居住的病人曾去墨西哥旅游过。

He said officials had not found common exposure or behavior among the eight U.S.patients. "We have not seen any linkage at all between the cases in Texas and California." he said.

他说,在美国的 8 位患者中并没有发现有过相同的接触或活动。"在德克萨斯和加利福尼亚的病人中我们没有找到任何的共性。"他说。

The new virus has genes from North American swine influenza, avian influenza, human influenza and a form of swine influenza normally found in Asia and Europe, said an expert, chief of the CDC's Influenza Division.

疾病预防控制中心负责禽流感研究的一位专家说，新的病毒具有北美洲猪流感病毒、禽流感病毒、人流感病毒，以及一种经常在亚洲和欧洲发现的猪流感病毒的基因形式。

Swine flu is caused by a virus similar to a type of flu virus that infects people every year but is a strain typically found only in pigs—or in people who have direct contact with pigs. There have, however, been cases of person-to-person transmission of swine flu, the CDC said. Officials found evidence, for example, that a patient transmitted the disease to health care workers during a 1988 apparent swine flu infection among pigs in Wisconsin.

猪流感病毒由一种病毒引起，这种病毒和每年都爆发的人流感病毒一样，一般只在猪身上爆发，会传染给与猪有直接接触的人。防控中心说有人感染人的病例发生，并且已经找到了证据，例如，1988 年在威斯康辛州的猪中爆发的猪流感就发生了人传染给医务工作者的案例。

Experts think coughing, sneezing and contaminated surfaces spread the infection among people. The new strain of swine flu has resisted some antiviral drugs, officials said. The human influenza vaccine's ability to protect against the new swine flu strain is unknown, and studies are ongoing, said an expert, the CDC's interim deputy director for science and public health program. There is no danger of contracting the virus from eating pork products, she said.

专家认为，咳嗽、打喷嚏以及污染的表面都有可能传播病毒。新型的猪流感病毒对一些药物有抵抗性。防控中心负责科学和公共健康计划的一位专家说，人类流感疫苗对猪流感病毒的免疫能力还是未知的，研究还在继续进行。同时她还说，吃猪肉没有传播病毒的危险。

Canada is also testing samples from Mexico and has placed a travel alert for travel to Mexico, CDC spokesman told CNN by e-mail. The United States had not issued any travel alerts or advisories by late Friday, but some private companies issued their own warnings.

防控中心的发言人向 CNN 发邮件说，加拿大也在对墨西哥的病毒样本进行检测，同时对到墨西哥旅游发出了预警。美国在周五前还没有发布旅游预警，但一些私企公司则发出了警告。

China's General Administration of Quality Supervision, Inspection and Quarantine issued an emergency notice Saturday night requiring people to report flu-like symptoms at the point of entry when coming from the deadly swine flu affected places. This is China's latest move in response to the outbreaks of human infection of Swine Influenza A/H1N1 in Mexico and the United States.

中国质检管理局周六晚公布紧急通知，要求在各海关口岸报告来自猪流感爆发地区，并有类似感冒症状入境的旅客人数。这是中国对于墨西哥、美国爆发猪流感（A/H1N1）后的最新反应。

People who developed flu-like symptoms after returning from the disease affected regions within two weeks should also report to the local entry-exit inspection and quarantine authorities, the administration said.

中国质检局要求：两周内从猪流感传染地区返回，有疑似感冒的人也将报告给当地海关出入境检验机构。

These people reporting flu-like symptoms must be scrutinized and those who have been infected or are suspected to be infected by the virus should be isolated and treated. China's Ministries of Health and Agriculture said they are closely monitoring the development of the situation.

对于有流感症状的人必须认真检查，被传染猪流感或疑似被猪流感病毒传染的人必须隔离治疗。中国的卫生部和农业部说：他们正在密切注意形势的发展。

The Ministry of Health said it has organized experts to study prevention measures and would enhance contact with the World Health Organization（WHO）and the governments of Mexico and the U.S. to learn about the latest developments.

卫生部说，他们已经组织专家研究预防措施和加强与世界卫生组织及墨西哥、美国政府的联系，以了解最新疫情发展动态。

The new flu strain—a mixture of swine, human and avian flu viruses has killed more than 60 people among around 2 000 suspected cases in Mexico and infected several thousand in the United States.

新的传染病病菌是一种猪、人及鸟流感病毒的混合体，在墨西哥 2 000 多疑似病例中，已死亡 60 多人，在美国被传染的人大约为数千人。

十二、Internet Searching and Brain（网络搜索和大脑）

Searching the Internet may help middle-aged and older adults keep their memories sharp, U.S.researchers said.

美国研究人员表示，网络搜索可以帮助中老年人保持好的记忆力。

Researchers at the University of California Los Angeles studied people doing Web searches while their brain activity was recorded with functional magnetic resonance imaging scans.

加州大学洛杉矶分校的研究人员使用"功能磁共振成像"来记录网页搜索时被研究者的大脑活动情况。

"What we saw was people who had Internet experience used more of their brain during the search," Dr. Gary Small, a UCLA expert on aging, said in a telephone interview. "This suggests that just searching on the Internet may train the brain—that it may keep it active and healthy."

在电话访谈中，衰老问题研究专家加里·斯莫尔博士谈道："我们发现，有网络经验的人在进行网络搜索时大脑活动更为激烈。这就表明，网络搜索能锻炼大脑——从而使大脑保持健康，充满活力。"

Many studies have found that challenging mental activities such as puzzles can help preserve brain function, but few have looked at what role the Internet might play.

很多研究发现，一些挑战智力的活动，比如说猜谜等可以保持大脑的功能，但是究竟网络搜索发挥了怎样的作用，这个方面的研究还为数不多。

"This is the first time anyone has simulated an Internet search task while scanning the brain." Small said. His team studied 24 normal volunteers between the ages of 55 and 76. Half were experienced at searching the Internet and the other half had no Web experience. Otherwise, the groups were similar in age, gender and education.

斯莫尔称："这是第一次在网络搜索模拟的同时，进行大脑活动扫描。"他的研究小组对 24 位正常志愿者进行了研究，被研究者的年龄段为 55—76 岁。其中一半的人有较好的网络搜索经验，而另一半人则毫无经验。另外，两组被研究者在年龄、性别和受教育程度上都很接近。

Both groups were asked to do Internet searches and book reading tasks while their brain activity was monitored.

两组研究对象都被要求进行网络搜索和在线阅读，与此同时监控他们的大脑活动。

"We found that in reading the book task, the visual cortex—the part of the brain that controls reading and language—was activated," Small said."In doing the Internet search task, there was much greater activity, but only in the Internet-savvy group."

斯莫尔表示："我们发现，研究对象在读书时，控制阅读和语言部分的大脑的视觉皮层就被激活了。但在进行网络搜索时，只是有网络经验的研究对象的脑部区域活动大大增强了。"

He said it appears that people who are familiar with the Internet can engage in a much deeper level of brain activity."There is something about Internet searching where we can gauge it to a level that we find challenging."

他表示，这说明熟悉网络的人可以进行更深层次的大脑活动。"在网络搜索过程中涉及一些对我们的大脑具有挑战性的东西。"

In the aging brain, atrophy and reduced cell activity can take a toll on cognitive function. Activities that keep the brain engaged can preserve brain health and thinking ability.

在大脑老化过程中，脑萎缩和脑细胞减少会降低人的认知能力，而使大脑得到锻炼的活动则可以保持大脑的健康和思考能力。

Small thinks learning to do Internet searches may be one of those activities. "It tells us we probably can teach an old brain new Internet tricks." he said.

斯莫尔认为，学习网络搜索可能就是这些活动的其中之一。"这说明，我们可以教中老年人一些基本的网络搜索知识。"

十三、Chocolate and Health（巧克力与健康）

Craving chocolate? A preliminary research suggests a little bite might not be quite as sinful as its reputation. The study suggests chocolate seems to contain some heart-healthy compounds. But doesn't mean it's ok to become hooked on chocolate.

对巧克力上瘾？一项研究初步发现：也许适量吃一些巧克力不会像人们通常认为的那样"糟糕"。这项研究显示：巧克力中可能含有有益心脏健康的化合物。但这并不说明人们可以毫无节制地嗜食巧克力。

Plus, chocolate is fat-and calorie-laden. So even if the strange-sounding finding that it has some heart-healthy micro-nutrients pans out, it still won't help the waistline, dietitians note. However, early findings made public suggest dark chocolate contains some micro-nutrients called"flavonoids"that seem to give red wine a health boost. And they appeared to temporarily stimulate antioxidant and blood clot-inhibiting effects in the chocolate eater's blood.

当然，巧克力含有大量脂肪和热量。营养专家认为，即使现在先进的科技发现巧克力中含有益心脏健康的微量营养元素，大量摄入过多巧克力也无法保持苗条。然而，研究发现：黑巧克力中存在一种叫类黄酮的微量营养素。这种类黄酮好像能使红葡萄酒更有助于健康。在吃了巧克力的人的血液中，这些元素有抗氧化功能，对于控制血栓也有很好的功效。

"We're not saying eat a chocolate bar every day. "a lead researcher, nutrition chairman at the University of California, Davis, stressed in an interview. Instead, he says the studies suggest people shouldn't feel so guilty when they indulge."I certainly enjoy chocolate. I don't have it every day. I don't feel guilty about it."He said at a news conference unveiling the studies at an American Association of the Advancement of Science meeting.

接受采访时，该研究负责人、美国加利福尼亚大学戴维斯研究院营养学主任强调说："我们并不建议人们每天都吃一大块巧克力。"但是，他建议人们不必因为喜欢吃巧克力而过分自责。他在美国科学研究联合会召开的记者招待会上说："我非常喜欢吃巧克力。虽然我不是每天都吃，但我觉得每天吃也不是什么罪过。"

Ancient cultures in Mexico drank chocolate for medicinal purposes, such as to gain weight, calm agitation and improve digestion, said a UC Davis nutritionist who studies chocolate's history. Chocolate was considered only a drink until about 1830.

据加州大学戴维斯研究院从事可可历史研究的一位教授介绍，古代墨西哥人就将巧克力作为药物，巧克力能起到增加体重、稳定情绪和帮助消化的作用。在 1830 年以前，人们一直只把巧克力当作一种饮料。

The new research concerns flavonoids, substances that act as antioxidants, thought to offset some artery-damaging effects of oxygen. Fruits and vegetables are full of flavonoids, but the substances became trendy after scientists found them in red wine and concluded a glass a day could be heart-healthy.

这个新研究发现，类黄酮是一种抗氧化体，它能抵消过多的氧对动脉的损坏作用。蔬菜水果中含有丰富的类黄酮。但直到科学家们在红葡萄酒中提取到了类黄酮，并告知人们每天喝一杯红葡萄酒有益心脏健康后，食用含有类黄酮的食品才成为一种时尚。

Nutritionists at UC-Davis studied dark chocolate because it contains some of red wine's flavonoids. They gave 10 healthy adults a cup of hot chocolate made from special flavonoid-rich cocoa powder. After the drink, blood cells were temporarily less prone to clot, he said. The effect was similar to how aspirin affects blood, although aspirin is much stronger.

加州大学的学者研究黑巧克力正是因为它含有红葡萄酒中的类黄酮。他们要求 10 个健康的受测验者每天喝一杯用类黄酮含量很高的可可粉制的热巧克力。他说，经过测量，喝过这种巧克力后，人体中的血红细胞不易在血管中凝结。巧克力的功能和阿司匹林对血液的作用效果相似。当然，阿司匹林的效果更强。

The latest trend in food science is to hunt micro-nutrients that claim healthy effects, but that doesn't mean people should flock to those foods, said a spokeswoman for the American Dietetic Association.

目前，食品学中最前沿的研究是针对各种食物中有益健康的微量营养元素的。但美国饮食卫生组织发言人告诫道，这并不意味着人们都必须食用这些食物。

十四、Foodborne Disease（食源性疾病）

In modern times, rapid globalization of food production and trade has increased the potential likelihood of food contamination. Many outbreaks of foodborne diseases that were once contained within a small community may now take place on global dimensions. Food safety authorities all over the world have acknowledged that ensuring food safety must not only be tackled at the national level but also through closer linkages among food safety authorities at the international level. This is important for exchanging routine information on food safety issues and to have rapid access to information in case of food safety emergencies.

当今，食品生产和贸易的全球化也使食品污染的潜在可能性迅速上升。以前只在小社区内爆发的食源性疾病，现在却可能在全球爆发。各国的食品安全部门都承认，解决食品安全问题不能只停留在单个国家层面，还要通过各国食品安全部门在国际层面上紧密联系、共同应对。交流食品安全方针常规信息，及时了解食品安全信息，以防止食品安全紧急情况。

It is difficult to estimate the global incidence of foodborne disease, but it has been reported that last year about 2.1 million people died from diarrhoea diseases. Many of these cases have been attributed to contamination of food and drinking water. Additionally, diarrhoea is a major cause of malnutrition in infants and young children.

虽然估计全球食源性疾病事件比较困难，但是据报道在去年大约有 210 万人死于腹泻，其中很多病例都归咎于受过污染的食物和饮用水。此外，腹泻还是婴儿和儿童营养不良的主要原因。

Even in industrialized countries, up to 30% of the population has been reported to suffer from foodborne diseases every year. In the U.S., around 76 million cases of foodborne diseases, which resulted in 325 000hospitalizations and 5 000 deaths, are estimated to occur each year. Developing countries in particular, are worst affected by foodborne illnesses due to the presence of a wide range of diseases, including those caused by parasites. Foodborne illnesses can and did inflict serious and extensive harm on society. In 1994, an outbreak of salmonellosis due to contaminated ice cream occurred in the U.S., affecting an estimated 224 000 persons. In 1988, an outbreak of hepatitis A, resulting from the consumption of contaminated clams, affected some 300 000 individuals in China.

即使在工业化国家中，据报告每年高达 30% 的人口遭受着食源性疾病的困扰。据估计在美国每年有大约 760 万食源性疾病病例，其中造成 32.5 万人住院治疗，5 000 人死亡。发展中国家，由于各种疾病（包括那些寄生虫引发的疾病）层出不穷，食源性疾病影响最为严重。食源性疾病能够对社会造成严重且影响广泛的危害，过去确实也有过这样的案例。1994 年，由于冰激凌受到污染，沙门氏菌病在美国爆发，据估计大约 22.4 万人受到影响。1988 年，由于食用了污染过的蛤蚌，甲型肝炎在中国爆发，30 万人受到影响。

Food contamination creates an enormous social and economic strain on societies. In the U.S., diseases caused by the major pathogens alone are estimated to cost up to U.S.$35 billion annually in medical costs and lost productivity. The re-emergence of cholera in Peru in 1991 resulted in the loss of U.S.$500 million in fish and fishery product exports that year.

食品污染不仅造成社会危机，也会使经济上受到巨大损失。据估计，美国每年单就主要病原体造成的疾病就要花费 350 亿美元，这包括医疗花费及损失掉的生产力。1991 年霍乱在秘鲁重现，对当年渔业及渔业产品的出口造成了 5 亿美元的损失。

十五、Music in Workouts（音乐与健身）

A new study from Hampden-Sydney College in Virginia confirmed that listening to your favorite music will help you push harder in your workouts. Men who listened to music while going hard on an exercise bike for 10 minutes pedaled 11% farther than those who listened to silence or static for the same amount of time.

最近弗吉尼亚州的汉普敦悉尼学院开展的一项研究证实：在健身运动期间听听自己最喜欢的音乐有助于加大运动量。骑车进行大运动量锻炼的男子，如能在运动期间听 10 分钟音乐，骑车距离要比听不到音乐的男子长 11％。

Music makes the people come together—Science has backed up what anyone who has ever worked out with an iPod may have guessed: Listening to music makes exercise more fun, and that can help you stick to your routine. "Music inspires movement," says a sports psychologist at Brunel University in London. "Like smell, it can penetrate areas of the brain that language alone doesn't reach." In fact, research has shown that synchronizing the speed of music with exercise gets people to train harder.

人们因为音乐相聚在一起，这就是它的魅力所在——喜欢边运动边听音乐的人似乎都有一种感觉：边听音乐边运动会更有趣，从而有助于将运动进行到底，科学研究也证实了这一点。伦敦布鲁内尔大学一个运动心理学家说："音乐有激发运动的功效。就像气味一样，音乐可以触及到人脑的某些区域，而这些区域一般语言是触及不到的。"事实上，有研究表明，若能让音乐的节拍与动作节奏同步，就能让人加大运动量。

In his latest study, he compared participants' heart rates with the number of beats in music and found that matching the tempo to workout intensity mattered most for those who exercised the moststrenuously. But you don't have to be training for a marathon to tailor your playlist to your workout. Choose inspirational, upbeat songs such as *The Best* or *Spring* in *The Four Seasons* for your warm-up and fast tracks with driving rhythms for the main part of your workout; he likes Michael Jackson songs and *I Got You* (*I Feel Good*) by James Brown, whereas an Ethiopian runner has set world records by running while listening to John Larkin's *Scatman*.

他最近做了一项实验，对参加实验者的心率和音乐节拍之间的关系做了对比分析，结果发现：运动强度与音乐节拍比较协调的健身者，其健身运动往往都是最卖力的。不过，你也大可不必为了健身而刻意设计自己的播放清单，搞得像进行马拉松训练那么隆重。热身的时候，可选一些欢快一点的唤醒式音乐，如《精选专辑》或《四季》系列中的《春天》专辑；真正开始健身运动之后，大部分时间都可播放一些节奏快而有力的歌曲。他自己就比较喜欢迈克尔·杰克逊的歌和詹姆士·布朗的《有了你》，而埃塞俄比亚的长跑运动员在比赛期间一边跑一边听着约翰·拉金的《斯卡曼》，已经创造了好几项世界纪录。

In a 2004 study at the University of California at San Diego, researchers irritated people by giving them a difficult task then nudging them to go faster. Afterward, the subjects listened to classical music, jazz, pop, or total silence. Silence was least calming—their blood pressure spiked almost 11 points. Jazz and pop relieved stress a bit more. But the BP of the classical-music listeners rose only 2 points. We suggest this starter kit: Bach's six unaccompanied cello suites; Beethoven's Concerto for Violin in D; Brahms's Violin Concerto in D, op. 77; and Mozart's symphonies 35 through 41.

2004 年，圣叠戈加州大学科研人员做了一项实验，他们让受试者从事一些高难度的作业，并不断催促他们做快点，再快点，直到把受试者搞得心烦意乱大发脾气为止。然后把他们分成 4 组，分别听古典音乐、爵士乐、流行歌曲或者什么都不听。

实验结果是：安静的环境对于平静心情的作用最差——受试者的血压几乎升高 11 个百分点；爵士乐和流行歌曲的作用稍高一点；而听贝多芬古典音乐的受试者血压只升高了 2 个百分点。我们建议开始试用此法的音乐套装为：巴赫的无伴奏大提琴组曲 6 首；贝多芬 D 大调小提琴协奏曲；勃拉姆斯 D 大调小提琴协奏曲，作品 77 号；以及莫扎特第 35—41 号交响曲。

Soothe the savage back—Cranking your favorite music may help eliminate back pain. In a study of 65 people who'd been hospitalized for chronic lower-back pain, researchers found that men who relaxed and listened to music for 25 minutes a day slept better and had less pain than men who didn't listen to music.

腰酸背痛音乐治——播放最喜欢的音乐还有助于舒缓各种腰背疼痛症。在一项有 65 名因慢性下腰痛疾而需要接受住院治疗的病人参加的研究中，科研人员发现，那些能够放松下来每天听 25 分钟音乐的病人，其睡眠效果要比不听音乐的病人好一些，病痛也要轻一些。

Listen for calm—When you're anticipating a stressful situation—a performance review with the boss, a big presentation—listen to music while preparing. An Australian study found that music prevented stress-related reactions—spikes in heart rate, blood pressure, and cortisol levels—in people preparing for an oral presentation. Those who prepared in silence had significant increases in all measures.

平心静气音乐好——准备从事一些压力较大的工作之前，例如准备接受老板对你的业务考核或准备大型业务报告之前，可以边听音乐边准备。澳大利亚有一项研究发现，音乐对那些准备演讲的人具有防止出现各种与情绪压力有关的应激反应的作用，可缓解演讲者出现心率加快、血压升高、皮质醇水平升高等现象。那些演讲前不听音乐的人，上述指标均明显升高。

Beat it—A recent study found that when staffers in a high-burnout industry participated in drumming sessions, they experienced a 50 percent improvement in mood that continued for at least 6 weeks. The people in this study also reported a decrease in fatigue, anxiety, and depression. Pick up a pair of sticks at the music store, crank up *Live at Leeds*, and slam away the day's stress.

敲敲打打有好处——最近有人开展一项研究，办法是让高体力消耗行业的员工参加打击乐健身，结果有 50%（的人）情绪得到改善，且持续至少 6 周之久。参与研究的受试者也说疲劳感、焦虑感及压抑感都有所减缓。去乐器店买上一对节拍器，回家后播放《活力里兹》摇滚乐，然后尽情地敲打吧，把一天的压力尽数释放掉。

Head banger—Dartmouth College researchers scanned the brain activity of people listening to music recordings containing gaps of silence. When participants knew the song, the auditory cortex stayed active during the gaps, as though the music is playing in your head. To exercise a song, try listening to it, then playing it all the way through in your mind.

摇头晃脑也放松——达特茅斯学院的科研人员让受试者听音乐，音乐与音乐之间留出一段无音空间，然后对受试者的脑电波进行扫描，结果是：如果受试者听到的是熟悉的歌曲，那么在无音时段，他们的脑电波仍然保持活跃，感觉就像脑子里还在播放着刚刚听过的歌曲。如果你希望学唱某一首歌，你可以先试听一遍，然后在心里一直播放下去。

Rock-a-bye baby—Listening to soft music for 45 minutes before bedtime can slow breathing and heart rates, helping you drift off faster and slumber soundly according to a Case Western Reserve University study.

轻柔舒缓好睡觉——凯斯西储大学的一份研究报告表明：睡觉前，听一听柔和的催眠曲 45 分钟，有利于放慢心率和呼吸频率，这样有助于快点入睡，而且睡得也香甜。

十六、Night Shifts and Cancer Risk（夜班与癌症风险）

Shift work is hard on the body. It's a schedule that reprograms the biological clock every few days. Those adjustments can disturb sleep patterns, impair mental acuity, and foster irritability. In fact, it might be even worse than that. Two new studies find evidence that women who work the graveyard shift also increase their chance of developing breast cancer.

倒班工作对身体有害。在这种安排下，每隔几天就要重新编排生物钟，这些调整可能会干扰睡眠模式，致使精神不佳，增长烦躁情绪。事实上，情况可能会更糟，两项新研究发现的证据证明：上夜班的女性也会增加患乳腺癌的机会。

Both reports, published in *The Journal of the National Cancer Institute*, raise the prospect that the increased risk results from chronic suppression of melatonin. Concentrations of this brain hormone normally peak during darkness, usually around 1 a.m.. Previous studies have indicated that in animals, nighttime lightingwhich suppresses melatonin release—boosts the growth of cancers.

发表在《国家癌症学会杂志》的两篇报告表明增加癌症的风险来自于降黑素的长期抑制，这种大脑荷尔蒙的浓度在黑暗中达到峰值，通常是在凌晨一点钟。早先的研究指出：夜间的光亮能抑制动物体内降黑素的释放，这会促使癌症生长。

In the first of the new studies, the working hours of 800 Seattle-area women with newly diagnosed breast cancer were compared with those of an equal number of healthy women their age.

在第一项新研究中，对西雅图地区 800 个新诊断为乳腺癌的妇女的工作时间与同等数量同样年龄的健康妇女的工作时间做了对比。

Among the 1 600 women, only 11.4 percent reported that commonly they weren't asleep during the period around 1 a.m.. The researchers found that women with breast cancer were more likely to have been among those who sometimes slept at atypical times. Half of the woman who slept during odd hours periodically worked at night. Women who averaged at least 5.7 hours of night work each week faced double the risk of developing this cancer compared with women who didn't work nights. The study reported "clear evidence of a trend of increasing [cancer] risk with increasing years of graveyard shift work".

在 1 600 名妇女中，只有 11.4% 的妇女通常在凌晨一点还不睡觉。研究人员发现患乳腺癌的妇女更可能出现在那些有时在不正常休息时间睡觉的妇女中，而在不固定时间睡觉的妇女中有半数定期在夜间工作。平均每周夜间工作至少 5.7 个小时的妇女比起夜间不工作的妇女面临患癌症的风险加倍。这项研究报告说"有明确的证据证明随着夜间工作年限的增加，患癌风险也呈上升趋势"。

In the second study, the researchers analyzed data from 78 500 nurses taking part in a long-running health study. Some 2 400 developed breast cancer during the decade. The researchers compared the work history of these women with that of women who remained cancerfree. Overall, 60 percent of the nurses reported at least occasional shift work. Risk of breast cancer increased with the years of shift work. Those who worked some nights for at least 30 years faced a 36 percent higher risk of breast cancer than those who never worked at night.

在第二项研究中，研究人员分析了来自参加长期健康研究的 78 500 名护士的数据，约有 4 400 名在 10 年间患上乳腺癌。研究人员把这些妇女的工作史同那些未患癌症的妇女进行了比较。总的说来，据报告至少有 60% 的护士偶尔倒班，患乳腺癌的风险随着倒班工作年限的增多而增加。那些 30 多年一贯都要加些夜班的妇女同夜间从不加班的妇女相比，患乳腺的风险要高出 36%。

The two studies point out an urgent need to further explore links between light at night and cancer, argue the researchers of the Danish Cancer Society in Copenhagen. Indeed, they note in an accompanying editorial, these and apparently all other epidemiological studies published so far on different indirect measures of light at night and breast-cancer risk seem to relatively consistently point to an increased risk. Of occupational factors that have been at least tentatively linked to cancer, working at night is the most common.

哥本哈根丹麦癌症学会的研究人员说，这两项研究指出了进一步探索夜间的灯光与癌症关系的迫切需要。他们还在同期发表的社论中指出，显然上述研究和其他到目前为止发表的有关各种非直接测量夜间灯光与乳腺癌风险的关系的全部其他流行病学的研究似乎比较一致地表明这会提高患癌风险。至少在初步认为与癌症有关的职业因素中，夜间工作是最常见的因素。

第二十二篇　美国人的嗜好

一、Computer Games and Violence（电脑游戏与暴力行为）

Violent computer games have been strongly linked with aggression in teenage boys in a study that shows the machines are increasingly becoming substitutes for friendship. The research lends powerful support to the suspicion that virtual violence could be one of the factors behind the surge in crimes of aggression involving young people.

一项研究显示：电脑暴力游戏与青少年男孩的攻击行为联系密切，电脑正日益成为友谊的替代品。涉及青少年的暴力犯罪事件屡屡发生，虚拟暴力可能是这种现象背后的因素之一，此项研究证实了这一观点。

The researchers reported aggression in boys seemed to increase with the amount of exposure to such games. There is a growing body of evidence to suggest there is a link between playing computer games and aggression, they said.

科研人员称，接触这类游戏越多，男孩的攻击欲似乎越强。越来越多的证据显示，玩电脑游戏与攻击行为之间有联系。

Previous studies have shown only a correlation between such games and aggression. This conclusion was ambiguous because it could mean that children who played the games did so because they had a predisposition to violence.

之前的研究仅表明了这类游戏与攻击行为之间相互关联，其结论是模棱两可的，因为它可能仅仅意味着：玩电脑游戏的孩子之所以进行暴力犯罪，是因为他们本身就有暴力倾向。

The latest study shows, however, that there is a strong causal link, meaning that playing such games makes children more aggressive. They reached the conclusions after studying the behavior of 300 pupils aged 12-14 from a comprehensive school.

然而，最新研究表明，两者间有密切的因果联系，即玩这类游戏使孩子们更好寻衅。他们研究了一所综合学校的学生行为之后，得出了此结论。这些学生共计 300 名，年龄在 12—14 岁。

Children became markedly more aggressive the longer they had been playing violent games. They shouted, pushed and hit other children. Those who played in occasional bursts showed little discernible effect.

孩子们玩暴力游戏的时间越长，他们的攻击性就越强。这些孩子大吼大叫，推推搡搡，还会袭击别的孩子。偶尔玩几次暴力游戏的孩子所受影响甚微。

All the children spent many hours playing such games. Nearly 97% of boys and 88% of girls were regular users. Among the boys the heaviest computer users tended to have the fewest friends and reported seeing their machine as a substitute friend.

被调查的所有儿童都花费了大量时间玩这类游戏。将近 97％的男孩和 88％的女孩经常玩这类电脑游戏。男孩中，玩电脑暴力游戏最多的孩子几乎没有朋友，报告称他们会把电脑看成自己的朋友。

The recent work found that children aged between four and eight allowed to play mildly violent games showed a dramatically higher level of aggression. The games they used were not violent by adult standards because they could not experiment on children in that way. But even mild levels of aggression on screen would alter the way the children behaved afterwards.

最新的研究发现：让 4—8 岁的孩子玩稍有暴力的游戏，他们的主动攻击欲望会大大提高。他们所采用的游戏按成人的标准不算是暴力的，因为他们不能用暴力游戏在孩子身上做实验。但是，即使是程度轻微的电脑游戏也会改变孩子们以后的行为方式。

The studies tally with another carried out recently in America which showed that playing games with interactive violence raises aggression levels further and faster than watching violent television or films.

这些研究与最近在美国进行的另一项研究相吻合。这项研究表明，玩互动式暴力游戏比观看暴力电视或电影影响更大，能更快地增强人的攻击欲望。

The researchers at Iowa State University asked 300 students to play violent games such as *Wolfenstein* 3D, in which a human hero is shown in graphic detail killing Nazi guards; *Doom*, also very violent; or *Myst*, a non-violent, role-playing adventure game.

爱荷华州立大学的研究人员请300名学生玩诸如《伍尔芬斯坦》三维立体游戏、《厄运》、《神秘剧》等游戏。《伍尔芬斯坦》里面展示了一位英雄杀死纳粹卫兵的逼真细节；《厄运》暴力色彩也非常浓厚；《神秘剧》是非暴力的角色扮演冒险游戏。

All are sold in Britain. After 15 minutes, the students were switched to another game where they were told they could punish their opponent with a blast of noise. Those who played the violent game delivered longer blasts.

以上这些游戏盘在英国都有出售。玩上述游戏15分钟后，再让这些学生换玩另一个游戏。在这个游戏里，他们被告知可以用刺耳的尖叫声来惩罚自己的敌手。那些玩暴力游戏的孩子发出的尖叫声比其他的孩子要长。

In America such findings are taken seriously, largely because of a spate of killings by young people. Research has shown that people with aggressive tendencies can be detected by scans that show their brains have slightly different configurations. Some experts believe such people could be particularly influenced by computer games, and that this may have been a cause of the massacres on campuses

在美国，这样的研究结果颇受重视，这主要是由于年轻人制造的杀戮事件激增。研究表明，通过仪器扫描能够检测出是否有攻击倾向，扫描显示有攻击倾向的人的脑外形略有不同。一些专家相信，这样的人尤其会受电脑游戏的影响——这可能会造成校园惨案。

二、Bogus Papers（造假论文）

A bunch of computer-generated gibberish masquerading as an academic paper has been accepted at a scientific conference in a victory for pranksters at a university in U.S.. One of the"authors"said that he and two fellow graduate students of this university questioned the standards of some academic conferences, so they wrote a computer program to generate research papers complete with nonsensical text, charts and diagrams. The trio submitted two of the randomly assembled papers to the World Conference on Computer Information, scheduled to be held next month in another university.

美国一所大学的几个捣蛋鬼取得了胜利：他们拿计算机自动生成的一堆胡言乱语的东西来冒充学术论文，而这篇东西竟然为一个科学会议所接纳。其中一位"作者"说，他和另外两位该校的研究生怀疑一些学术会议的水准。于是就编了一个计算机程序来自动生成由无意义的文字、表格和图示组成的"研究论文"。这个三人帮把胡乱组合的两篇东西呈交给了将于下月在另外一所大学举行的世界计算机信息大会。

To their surprise, one of the papers was accepted for presentation. The prank recalled a hoax ten years ago in which a New York University physicist succeeded in getting an entire paper with a mix of truths, falsehoods, non sequiturs and otherwise meaningless mumbo-jumbo published in the journal *Social Text*. They said they only learned about the *Social Text* affair after submitting their paper.

出乎他们意料的是，大会竟然同意他们在会上宣读其中的一篇论文。这次恶作剧让人想起 10 年前的一个骗局，当时纽约大学的一个物理学家成功地在《社会文本》杂志上发表了一整篇"论文"，该"论文"融事实、谬误和不合逻辑的推论为一体，还有就是毫无意义的胡说八道。他们说，他们是在呈交"论文"之后才知道"《社会文本》事件"的。

The trio targeted the World Conference on Computer Information because it is notorious within the field of computer science for sending copious e-mails that solicit admissions to the conference."We were tired of the spam",they told reporters in a telephone interview, adding that the team wanted to challenge the standards of the conference's peer review process. A man named Smith, a conference organizer, said the paper was one of a small number accepted on a"non-reviewed"basis—meaning that reviewers had not yet given their feedback by the acceptance deadline."We thought that it might be unfair to refuse a paper that was not refused by any of its three selected reviewers,"he wrote in an e-mail."The author of a non-reviewed paper has complete responsibility of the content of their paper."

他们三人选择世界计算机信息大会的原因是这个会总是大量发送电子邮件邀人参会，故而在计算机科学圈内臭名远播。"我们已经对这样的垃圾邮件忍无可忍"，他们在电话采访中对记者说，并补充说他们三人团队打算对这个会议的同行评审程序提出质疑。作为会议组织者之一的斯密思说，这篇"论文"是少数在"未评审"状态下获得接纳的论文之一，"未评审"的意思是评审者没有在论文征集截止期内给出评审意见。"我们认为拒绝这样一篇论文是不公平的，因为我们为它挑选的三位评审者都没有表示反对，"斯密思在一封电子邮件中写道，"未评审论文的作者应该对其论文的内容负全责。"

However, Smith said conference organizers were reviewing their acceptance procedures in light of the hoax. Asked whether he would disinvite the three students, he replied:"Bogus papers should not be included in the conference program."However,these three students said conference organizers had not yet formally cancelled their invitation to present the paper. The students were soliciting cash donations so they could attend the conference and give what they billed as a"randomly generated talk". So far, they have raised more than $2 000 over the Internet.

　　不过，斯密思也表示会议组织者会以此次骗局为鉴，重新审核大会的论文通过程序。在被问及是否会取消那三个学生参会资格的时候，他回答道："假造论文不应该进入大会议程。"但这三个学生却说，会议组织者还没有正式取消邀请他们宣读论文的决定。这几个学生正在募集现金捐助，以便参会并发表他们所称的"随机生成的演讲"。迄今为止，他们已经从网上筹到了 2 000 多美元。

三、Americans with Guns（美国人的恋枪情节）

　　More people in the U.S.can buy a gun and more people die by the gun than in any other country in the world. This is what appeared in an American newspaper in December 1980, after the murder in New York of John Lennon, the British pop star. His murder shocked the Americans. Most Americans today admit that they may possibly be mugged some time during their lives. At the root of this violence is the gun which Americans can buy and keep in their homes as easily as if it was a toy weapon.

　　世界上没有哪个国家会像在美国那样有那么多人购买枪支和死于枪击。这是1980 年当英国流行歌手约翰·伦农在纽约被谋杀之后出现在美国一家报纸上的话。这一谋杀案震惊了整个美国。今天，很多美国人不得不承认，他们一生中不定哪个时候也许就会遭到被抢劫的噩运。美国人买枪和拥有枪支的容易程度就像是在玩一个玩具武器。

　　There are gun stores pretty well everywhere. And you can get a license easily. You don't even have to say what you want it for. You could even buy guns by mail order. Why are Americans so eager to own a gun?

　　几乎在美国的任何地方都能看到出售枪支的商店，而且人们还能很容易搞到许可证。你甚至不用说明你买枪的目的是什么，你还可以通过邮购方式来购买枪支。为什么美国人对拥有枪支如此着迷？

　　Self-defense might be one reason. Actually Americans seem to have a long history of owning guns. Their forefathers of frontiersmen had once used guns against outlaws, and cattle rustlers. Today people want to use guns to protect them against gangsters, muggers and burglars. Another reason is that hunting is popular there.

　　自卫也许是一个原因。实际上，美国人拥有枪支的历史似乎已是源远流长——那些开拓边疆的祖先们就曾用手里的枪打退不法之徒和偷牛贼。但今天，人们用枪主要是为了对付歹徒、抢劫犯和窃贼。还有一个原因就是，打猎在美国很流行。

　　Now many Americans want a new law to control the ownership of guns. But it doesn't help. There is the National Rifle Association. There are several million members, and they have friends with influence in Congress. They also have strong support from the gun manufactures. And many Americans themselves wouldn't like to give up their guns. They think it's their right as free men to own a gun. It was written into the Constitution in 1790.

现在，许多美国人希望政府能对枪支的拥有权制定出新的法规。但这种愿望却无法实现。因为有国家枪支协会的存在，它拥有几百万个会员，他们在国会里有很有影响的朋友。而且，他们的身后还有枪支制造商强有力的支持。再说，许多美国人本身也不愿放弃枪支的拥有权，他们认为那是自己作为自由人应该具有的权利，这一权利曾于 1790 年被写进了美国宪章。

So the result is violence and murder. New York is a wonderful city, but male New Yorkers between the age of 21 and 44 are more likely to be murdered than to die of any other cause. And murders take place mainly in poor districts—in Harlem, and parts of the Bronx, and on the West Side of Manhattan. Most of the murders are gangsters killing gangsters. Sometimes people even get mugged in the centre of Manhattan, in their own fiats. Maybe this is why people have chains and peepholes on their doors, and sometimes a locked turnstile and an armed security guard downstairs.

这样一来，枪支泛滥的结果便是暴力和谋杀。纽约是一个迷人的城市，但对于21—44 岁的纽约男性来说，被谋杀而死在各种死亡因素中占第一位。谋杀事件多发生在贫民区内，如哈雷姆、布朗克斯区的某些地方和曼哈顿西区。大多数凶杀案发生在歹徒们之间的自相残杀。有时，人们就是在曼哈顿的市中心，在其家里都会遭到抢劫。也许，这就是为什么人们不仅要在自己家的门上装上锁链和猫眼，有时还在楼下装上旋转栅门和配上带枪的门卫。

四、Mixed-gender Roommates（男女混居舍友）

In the 1970s, the advent of coed dorms caused a stir, with *Life* magazine proclaiming the development"an intimate revolution on campus". Coed floors came along over the next three decades, giving college students immediate proximity to each other. The next step, coed suites and bathrooms, brought the sexes even closer together.

20 世纪 70 年代，男女混住一栋宿舍引起了轰动，《生活》杂志称其为"校园里的亲密革命"。在随后 30 年中，男女混住一层楼，使大学生能互相直接接触。接下来男女共住一个套间、共用卫生间使男女更亲密起来。

Now, some colleges are crossing the final threshold, allowing men and women to share rooms. At the urging of student activists, more than 30 campuses across the country have adopted what colleges call gender-neutral rooming assignments.Once limited to such socially liberal bastions as Hampshire College, Wesleyan University, and Oberlin College, mixed-gender housing has edged into the mainstream, although only a small fraction of students have taken advantage of the new policies.

现在一些大学正在跨越最后的门槛，允许男女学生混居一室。在学生积极分子的推动下，美国现有 30 多所大学已不分性别安排房间。这种社交自由堡垒曾经只限于汉普郡学院、卫斯理安大学和奥博林学院，虽然迄今只有小部分学生利用这种新政策，可男女混居一室已渐成主流。

So far. Clark and Dartmouth universities introduced mixed-gender rooms last fall, and Brown and Brandeis announced plans recently to follow suit.

去年秋天克拉克大学和达特茅斯大学采用了男女混居的方法。最近布朗大学和布兰戴斯大学也宣布实行男女混居。

The University of Pennsylvania, Skidmore and Ithaca colleges, and Oregon State University also allow roommates of different genders.Students at New York, Harvard, and Stanford universities, among many others, are calling for gender-blind dormitory rooms.

宾夕法尼亚大学、斯基摩尔学院和伊厦卡学院，以及俄勒冈州立大学也允许男女生混居一室。同许多其他大学一样，纽约大学、哈佛大学和斯坦福大学的学生也正在要求男女混居。

"It's definitely a growing movement on campuses across the country,"said the dean of students at Clark, where about 30 students are living in mixed-gender rooms."It's a new world, and gender has taken on all kinds of new definitions. It's about being more inclusive, and it's about keeping pace with the times."While the trend predictably prompts prurient thoughts, most coed roommates are just friends, students and college officials say.

"这无疑是全国大学校园正在发展的运动，这是一个崭新的世界，性呈现出各种各样新的定义。要有更大的包容性，要跟上时代步伐。"克拉克大学主管学生的负责人说。该大学现有约 30 名学生混居。可以预见，这种趋势自然会引起人们对性的联想，但学生和校方都说，大多数混居者仅为朋友而已。

Most colleges discourage students who are romantically involved from living together, but a few schools freely admit that some roommates are in sexual relationships, which they say is none of their business. Supporters hail the trend as a key advance for homosexual and transgender students that eliminates a gender divide they see as outdated, particularly for a generation that has grown up with many friends of the opposite sex.Traditional rooming policies, they say, infringe upon students' rights and perpetuate gender segregation.

大多数学校劝阻学生不要因恋情而混居，有些学校也大胆承认一些室友之间有性关系，但对外宣称此事与校方无关。支持者为这一趋势而欢呼，认为这对同性恋和变性恋学生是重大进步，消除了他们认为过时的性别界限，对成长过程中有许多异性朋友的一代人尤其如此。传统的宿舍规定侵害了学生的权利，会使性别隔离持续下去。

But some observers say the policies promote promiscuity. And most colleges do not believe coed rooms are wise and see no reason for them. The dean of student affairs at Tufts University, where students have unsuccessfully pushed for gender-neutral housing in the past, said the university is willing to allow coed suites, but believes coed bedrooms raise practical and moral concerns."We're not ready to provide coed bedrooms,"he said."That's a position we don't see changing in the near future."Allowing coed living situations would create unnecessary distractions and problematic romantic entanglements, he added.

但一些观察者说这种做法鼓励了异性之间乱交。大多数学校认为混居并不明智。塔福特大学的学生过去曾强烈要求宿舍安排不分男女，但未成功。该校主管学生事务的负责人说，学校愿意让男女生合用套间，但认为混居一室会引发对实际问题和道德问题的担忧。他说："我们不愿提供混居卧室，这种立场在不久的将来也不会改变。"他还说，允许混居会引起不必要的分心，引发消极的恋情纠葛。

五、Asexuality（无性恋）

Sex is what life is all about. Every high street is dominated by shops selling clothes to make you sexier, beauty products to make you more attractive, cars to make you stand out, books promising you wit at the turn of a page. If you really look at life with a cynical eye, it's all about being better than the next person, top of the heap, the alpha male/female, the most sexually appealing. So, if you really don't want sex, is the world just not your sort of place? Not straight, bisexual or gay. Time takes you to have a look at the fourth option.

性是生命的所有意义。主宰着每条繁华街道的店家，总是在向你推销着让你更性感的衣服，让你更吸引人的化妆品，让你更出位的香车，保证让你立马变聪明的书籍。如果你用愤世嫉俗的眼光来看待生活，其意义全在于超越身边的人，出类拔萃，成为人中龙凤，最具性感魅力的人。所以，当你真的不想要性，是否这世界不是适合你的地方呢？不是异性恋，也不是双性恋或者同性恋。时代带你领略"第四种选择"的世界。

Being asexual is not being celibate. The difference between celibacy and asexuality is simply the desire. If you are celibate, you are making the effort not to do something that you really want to do.

无性恋者并不等于独身主义者。独身主义和无性恋的区别只是在于欲望。如果你是独身主义者，你只是努力不去做自己很想做的事。

Asexuality is a fast growing sexual preference. In a world that is screaming out that sex should be everybody's raison d'etre, a large number of males, females, gays, bisexuals and heterosexuals are deciding that for them, sex just isn't that big a deal. Figures prove that more people are becoming asexual, even if they don't realize what it is! In surveys on sexual orientation, the number of people who ticked the"not interested in either gender"box has risen from 1% from ten years ago to 3% today. At that rate of growth, it won't be long before there are as many asexual people in the world as there are homosexual.

无性恋是一种正在快速增长的性倾向。在一个无时无刻不在向人们宣称性是人生的终极意义的世界里，一部分为数甚众的男男女女，同性恋、双性恋或异性恋开始觉得性对他们来说不再是什么了不起的事。数据证明越来越多的人正在成为无性恋者，甚至在完全不了解这个概念的情况下！在关于性倾向的调查中，勾选"对任何性别都不感兴趣"的人数从 10 年前的 1% 增加至现在的 3%。以此增速，不久之后，世界就会有跟同性恋数目同样众多的无性恋者。

There is a correlation between the emergence of this new fourth sexuality and that of the gay movement some sixty years earlier. Whilst not on the same level as the suffering of the early gay rights advocates, prejudice is still very much a part of an asexual's life.

这股新崛起的第四性潮流跟 60 多年前的同性恋运动有关。虽不至于遭受早期同志权利提倡者的磨难，但是偏见仍然是无性恋者生活中的一部分。

Some religious leaders have also spoken out against fourth sexuality. A U.S.Christian organization recently stated that"sexuality is a gift from God thus a fundamental part of human existence".The remarks came in the annual magazine of the National Religious Vocation Conference and even suggested that an asexual was simply"not a person".

一些宗教领袖也公开表示反对第四性。一个美国基督教组织最近开始宣称"性是上帝赐予的礼物，是人类存在的基本要素"。一篇发表于全国宗教职业会年刊的文章甚至说无性恋者根本就"不是人"。

Scientifically, asexuality has mostly been discussed in relation to plants, worms and other creatures that don't need to have sex to replicate themselves. While the academic community are obsessed with who finds who sexually attractive and why, the concept of not finding anybody attractive seems to have passed most scientists by. But there are a few studies about asexuality out there. A decade ago a study of sheep showed that about 10% of rams weren't interested in ewes at all. Any dairy farmer will also note the rather unimpressed reaction of cows when a bull is introduced to the herd! In the animal kingdom, asexuality definitely exists.

科学意义上讲，无性通常涉及的是一些植物、蠕虫以及其他不需要性来实现繁殖的生物。当学术团体沉迷于"谁觉得谁有性吸引力和为什么"，大部分科学家都忽视了"不觉得任何人有性吸引力"这个概念。但也确实有一些发表了的关于无性恋的研究。10年前，一份调查表显示有大概10%的公羊对母羊完全不感兴趣。任何职业牧民也会注意到当公牛被引入牛群时，母牛那种相当漠视的反应。在动物王国中，无性恋绝对存在。

But aren't asexuals setting themselves up for a very lonely life? Someone disagrees."There is no reason why I can't have a girlfriend and even get married. If I wanted to, I'm sure I could have kids. It would only mean doing it once or twice, which isn't too much of a stress! To be honest, what I want from life is a close companion, like the sort older widows and widowers have, somebody to share your life with, comfort and respect but not necessarily sleep with. Whether it is a man or a woman doesn't really matter either. When I find somebody who feels like the other half of me, then I will stick by them and be committed, whoever they are. It's actually not restrictive at all if you think about it. Any person of any age or any sex could be the person I spend the rest of my life with!"

但是难道无性恋者们不会打算终身孤独吗？有人并不同意，"完全没有理由否定我将会找一个女朋友甚至结婚。如果我愿意的话，我相信我一定会有小孩。但那意味着性只是偶尔为之，而不会形成压力。说实话，我真正想要的生活是有一个亲密的伴侣，有点像那些老鳏夫和寡妇之间的关系。与之共享此生，彼此安慰、尊重，但不一定要上床，是男是女也并不重要。当找到了我的另一半，我会寸步不离的陪伴着他/她，并忠贞不贰，不管他/她是谁。如果你想想看的话，这完全没有限制。任何年龄的任何人都可能成为我愿意共度余生的另一半！"

To those whose lives do not have to include sex, the new asexual movement has opened up a whole new community.

对于那些生活中不想有性的人来说，这种新的无性恋运动为他们打开了一个全新的圈子。

AVEN（the Asexual Visibility and Education Network）is a web forum devoted specifically to asexuals and is one of the first"community" based organizations. On their site, other asexuals can discuss their condition and celebrate who they are, again mirroring the valuable outlet for the gay community that the worldwide web provides. In one such forum, a group in the U.S. has even speculated about the idea of setting up an "asexual bar" where like minded people can mix freely and meet other people just like themselves.

AVEN（无性恋曝光度和教育网）是一个专门面向无性恋的网络论坛，并且是第一个基于"（无性恋）圈子"的组织之一。在其站点上，无性恋者可以交换彼此的感受，并为自己引以为豪，同时也反衬出同志群体在世界范围网络上极高的曝光度。一个来自美国的团体其至考虑要建立一个"无性恋酒吧"，在那里想法一致的人们可以自由交往并且遇到跟自己相同的人。

Everyone should have the right to shout what they are from the rooftops, let the world know that they exist and demand tolerance. Sexuality is no longer about whom you sleep with, but also who you don't!

每个人都有站在楼顶大声喊出自己是谁的权力，让世界知道他们的存在，并宽容以待。性倾向不再是只关于你跟谁上床，也同样关于跟谁你也不上床！

六、Americans and Drug-Addict（美国人与毒瘾）

A U.S. presidential commission said last week that illegal drug trafficking，business that nets $ 110 billion a year，has become America's number one crime problem.There was time when the Americans were shocked to learn that a popular movie star or a professional baseball player was wasting his time and talents on drugs.Today Americans are learning that such things happen to ordinary people like themselves and their children. Illegal drugs have invaded the work place, that few U.S.industries are immune. Drug use among teenagers is reaching epidemic levels. By official estimates 20 million Americans smoke marijuana on a regular basis. Between 5 to 6 million regularly use cocaine and some 500 thousand are addictive to heroin.

一个由美国总统授权的委员会上星期报道说，非法贩卖毒品的交易，每年净赚 1 100 亿美元，已经成为美国头号犯罪问题。以前美国人听说某位著名影星或某位职业棒球手把时间和才气浪费在了吸毒上，都会倍感吃惊。如今美国人了解到，像他们那样的普通人或者他们的孩子也吸毒。非法吸毒已侵入工作场所，没有几个行业能够幸免。青少年吸毒已经到了泛滥的地步。据官方统计，有 2 000 万美国人经常吸食大麻；500 万—600 万人常服用可卡因；约 50 万人吸海洛因成瘾。

Of greatest concern is the sudden rise in the number of workers and students who now admit to trying cocaine, a dangerous addictive and very costly drug. Recent surveys show that this drug has spread from the entertainment world to small town high schools where many seniors say they tried cocaine. Because there is little agreement about the causes of this surge in drug abuse, there is even less agreement about what should be done to solve it. While schools and parents have formed a network of counseling services, some experts say young Americans will continue to try drugs long as older Americans do the same.

人们最担忧的是在工人和学生中承认吸用可卡因的人数剧增。可卡因是一种极其危险、容易上瘾而且昂贵的毒品。最近调查表明，这种毒品已经从娱乐圈蔓延到小城镇的中学里。很多中学高年级学生承认自己试着吸食过可卡因。因为对吸毒泛滥的原因没有达成一致的看法，所以在应该采取什么措施来解决方面，更没有统一的意见。尽管学校和家长成立了咨询服务网来解决这一问题，但一些专家说，只要年长的人还在吸毒，年轻人就会吸毒。

The fact that the sale of all drugs and the possession of most drugs is illegal has yet to persuade drugs users to abandon their habits. A growing number of American employers are now waiting for workers to give up what for many is a newly found habit. Companies worried about falling production rates and rising absenteeism are fighting drug problems. The problems have crept into clerical offices and factories alike and, surveys say, cost U.S.economy $60 billion a year. Some firms have come to rely on urinalysis and even hidden cameras to locate drug users while others provide rehabilitation clinics or workers who choose their jobs over drugs.

贩卖任何毒品和拥有大多数毒品都是违法的，可是这并未能够使吸毒者放弃吸毒恶习。越来越多的美国资方迫不及待地希望工人们放弃这个对许多人来说是新近养成的恶习。担心生产下降和缺勤增多的公司与吸毒展开了斗争。调查表明，这一问题在工人和职员中都存在，使美国的经济每年损失 600 亿元。一些公司采用尿检或隐藏的照相机来发现吸毒者。另外一些公司在设立康复诊所，为那些愿意放弃吸毒而选择工作的人们提供治疗。

Strong remedies even for the most serious problems provoke equally reactions from Americans. When the presidential commission called drug trafficking a national menace and urged drug tests for all U.S.government workers and private workers under federal contract, the cries of protests were as loud as they were predictable. Civil Libertarians, public employee unions, and members of Congress condemned what one outraged group called an attempted war against innocent American citizens.Fewer Americans are ready to accept testing or other real or perceived threats to their privacy or individual rights. But the drug threat is too big to dismiss. And as more and stronger drugs make their way into the nation's classroom and factories，more Americans realize they can no longer treat the problem as some body else's. At this stage most people are still casting about for answers.

即使是为了解决吸毒这一严峻问题而采取的强硬手段也引起了美国人的强烈反应。当政府授权的调查组把贩毒称为国家的威胁，坚持对公务员和与国家签有合同的私企工人进行尿检时，抗议的呼声之高果然不出他们所料。那些坚持保护公民自主权不受侵犯的人、公职职员协会和国会议员谴责尿检。一些愤怒的人称尿检是一场试图侵犯无辜美国公民的战争。几乎没有人愿意接受检查或是其他任何可能对其隐私权或个人权利带来威胁的举动。可是吸毒问题太严重，不能置之不理。当数量更多、毒性更强的毒品进入教室和工厂时，越来越多的美国人意识到再也不能将其视为与己无关。目前，许多美国人仍然在寻找解决的办法。

七、Addicted Gamers Get into Trouble（上瘾玩家深受其害）

About one in ten videogame players show signs of addictive behavior that could have negative effects on their family, friends and school work, according to a new study.

一项新研究显示，约1/10的电子游戏爱好者打游戏都上瘾，这会对他们的家庭、朋友和学习带来负面影响。

Researchers at Iowa State University (ISU) and the National Institute on Media and the Family found that some gamers show at least six symptoms of gambling addiction such as lying to family and friends about how much they play games, using the games to escape their problems and becoming restless or irritable when they stop playing.

艾奥瓦州立大学和美国媒体和家庭研究所的研究人员发现，一些游戏玩家表现出了至少6种赌瘾症状，比如就打多少游戏向家人和朋友说谎，通过玩游戏逃避问题并且不玩游戏时变得坐立不安或容易发怒。

They may also skip homework to play videogames or spend too much time playing the games and do poorly in school.

他们还可能为了打游戏不做家庭作业，或者将大量的时间浪费在玩游戏上，在校成绩很差。

"While the medical community currently does not recognize video game addiction as a mental disorder, hopefully this study will be one of many that allow us to have an educated conversation on the positive and negative effects of video games."An assistant professor of psychology at ISU, said in a statement.

艾奥瓦州立大学心理学助理教授在一项声明中表示："目前医学界还没有将电子游戏瘾认定为心理紊乱，希望这项研究能在电子游戏的积极和消极影响问题上给我们提供一个谈话的根据。"

Dr David Walsh, the president of the National Institute on Media and the Family which strives to minimize the harm of media on the health and development of children and families, said the findings are a wake-up call for families.

美国全国媒体和家庭协会研究致力将媒介对于儿童和家庭健康和发展的危害降低到最小，会长大卫·沃尔什博士说，研究结果为爱玩电子游戏者的家长敲响了警钟。

"This study gives everyone a better idea of the scope of the problem."he explained.

他解释说："此项研究使每个人对这个问题有了更深的了解。"

The researchers, who studied 1 178 American children and teenagers, aged 8 to 18, found some displayed at least six of 11 symptoms of pathological gambling as defined by the American Psychiatric Association.

研究者共对美国 1 178 名年龄在 8—18 岁的儿童和青少年进行了研究，发现在美国精神病学会所定义的 11 种病态赌瘾症状中，有些人表现出了 6 种。

Addicted gamers played videogames 24 hours a week, twice as much as casual gamers. Some addicted gamers even steal to support their habit, according to the findings that will be published in the journal *Psychological Science*.

玩电子游戏成瘾的玩家每周打游戏的时间长达 24 个小时，是那些偶尔玩玩游戏人的两倍。据将在《心理科学》期刊上发表的研究结果称，有的上瘾的玩家甚至通过偷窃来为打游戏筹集资金。

"While video games can be fun and entertaining, some kids are getting into trouble. I continue to hear from families who are concerned about their child's gaming habits. Not only do we need to focus on identifying the problem, but we need to find ways to help families prevent and treat it."said Walsh.

沃尔什表示："电子游戏确实很好玩，很有趣，但却让一些孩子深受其害。我经常收到一些家长的来信，担心孩子玩游戏上瘾。我们不仅要尽力查明问题，而且要找到帮助家长预防和解决孩子打游戏成瘾的途径。"

八、Salt Addiction and Drug Addiction（盐瘾等于毒瘾）

Scientists suggest we may add extra salt to our food because it boosts our mood, even though we know too much is bad.

科学家认为，尽管我们知道摄入过多的盐对身体有害，不过我们可以往食物中稍稍多添加点盐，因为盐有助于改善我们的情绪。

The researchers with a university in America writing in *Psychology and Behavior* say salt may act as a natural antidepressant. Tests on rats found those with a salt deficiency shied away from activities they normally enjoyed—a sign of depression. But experts warn eating too much salt is linked to high blood pressure.

美国一所大学的研究人员在《心理与行为》杂志上发文指出：盐可作为一种天然抗抑郁药。研究人员通过鼠类试验发现，那些盐摄取不足的老鼠对平时喜欢的活动失去了兴趣，这正是抑郁症的体征。但专家们警告说，盐分摄入过多会引发高血压。

The body needs sodium—which along with chloride makes up salt—to function, but having too much and raising blood pressure is linked to an increased risk of stroke and heart attack. The UK's Food Standards Agency says the average adult should eat no more than 6g of salt a day.

盐由钠和氯两种元素构成。人体需要钠以维持正常功能，但盐分摄入过量以致血压上升会增加患中风和心脏病的风险。英国食品标准署建议，一般成年人每日盐分摄入量不应超过 6 克。

Salt intake is falling, but last year the average was 8. 6g. Around three quarters of the salt we eat comes in pre-prepared foods. The findings are published as the FSA renewed its advice for people to eat more healthily. It backed an independent panel of experts warning that celebrity chefs were promoting high-fat recipes, and contributing to the obesity crisis.

盐分摄入量近年一直在下降，但去年却达到了人均每日 8.6 克。我们摄入的盐分约有 3/4 来自预先做好的食物。英国食品标准署再次建议人们要注意健康饮食，并随之公布了上述研究结果。此前，一个独立专家组警告说，一些名厨正在推广高脂肪食谱，加重肥胖危机。英国食品标准署此举有力声援了该专家组。

The tests carried out by U.S.researchers found that when rats were deficient in salt, they shy away from activities they normally enjoy, like drinking a sugary substance or pressing a bar that stimulates a pleasant sensation in their brains.

美国的研究人员进行了一系列的试验，发现当老鼠体内缺乏盐分时，它们会避免参加平时热衷的活动，如饮用含糖物质或按动小棒等。这些活动能刺激它们的大脑，从而令其愉悦。

A famous psychologist, who led the research, said:"Things that normally would be pleasurable for rats didn't elicit the same degree of relish, which leads us to believe that a salt deficit and the craving associated with it can induce one of the key symptoms associated with depression."

该研究的带头人——一位著名心理学家说：“通常情况下会令老鼠感到愉快的事物未能激发起同等程度的兴趣，这一点使我们相信，盐分摄入量不足和对盐分摄入的渴望是能诱发抑郁症的一项主要症状。”

He said that a loss of pleasure in normally pleasing activities is one of the most important features of psychological depression. And he said there were signs salt could be addictive.

他指出，对昔日热衷的活动失去兴趣是心理抑郁症最重要的特征之一。他还谈道，有迹象显示，盐可使食用者上瘾。

One sign of addiction is using a substance even when it is known to be harmful—and even though people know they should cut their salt intake, they like the taste and find low-salt foods bland so continue to eat it.

上瘾迹象之一即明知一种物质有害，却仍使用该物质——尽管人们知道该减少盐摄入量，但因为喜欢盐的味道，感觉低盐食品食之无味，因此仍继续大量摄入盐分。

Another strong aspect of addiction is the development of cravings if something is withheld. The researchers say tests they carried out showed similar changes in brain activity whether rats are exposed to drugs or salt deficiency. This suggests that salt need and cravings may be linked to the same brain pathways as those related to drug addiction and abuse.

上瘾的另一个典型迹象是，越是对某一物质加以抑制，人们就越发渴望能得到该物质。研究人员说，他们的实验显示，老鼠在缺乏盐与缺乏毒品时的脑部活动相似。这意味着当老鼠渴望摄入盐分时，其大脑的活动方式可能与其染上毒瘾和滥用毒品时相同。

But a spokesman for Consensus Action on Salt and Health (CASH), which campaigns to raise awareness about the health risks of eating too much salt, said:"Our bodies need a very small amount of salt to function, but nothing like the quantities that most of us eat."

但是一位“食盐与健康共识行动”（CASH）组织的发言人发起活动，期望人们能对盐分摄入过多带来的健康隐患加深认识。他说：“我们的身体只需要很少量的盐就能维持正常功能，远不是我们大多数人所摄入盐分的量。”

"This research may help us to understand why some people still eat too much salt, even though they know it's bad for them. I personally have never felt depressed by not eating too much salt: I think it would be far more depressing to have a heart attack or stroke that could have been avoided by not eating so much salt."

　　"这项研究可以帮助我们理解，为何有些人即使知道食盐过量有害健康却还是吃太多的盐。我个人从未因为吃盐不够多而感到沮丧：我认为心脏病发作或患中风才是更令人堪忧的现象，因为这本来是少吃点盐就可以避免的。"

第二十三篇　美国的名胜

一、Bryce Canyon National Park（布赖斯峡谷国家公园）

As December storms paint Bryce Canyon National Park with fresh snow, you won't find a more beautiful winter landscape anywhere in the world. But for some of us, catching this park in South-central Utah on the perfect winter morning is an annual and urgent quest.

当 12 月的初雪覆盖了布赖斯峡谷国家公园时，我十分确信，它就变成了世界上最美的景点。但是对我们当中的一些人来说，要在美丽的冬天的早晨一睹犹他州中南部美丽的公园景色却是一年一度的急切愿望。

You will look for those days when the snow still hangs heavy on the ponderosa pines, when a new layer of white intensifies the canyon's red-orange turrets and towers. Some guys search for big waves. Some are searching for Bryce on ice. Not that it's always easy.

当厚厚的雪还悬挂在美国黄松林上，当大峡谷橙红色的角楼和塔上新添一层白雪时，你就会开始期待那些令人激动的日子。有的人渴望汹涌的海浪，而有的人向往雪中的布赖斯峡谷国家公园，因为看到它很不容易。

Bryce typically receives about 7 feet of snow each year; in a normal winter, the park, which tops out at 9 115 feet, gets its first big hit in late fall. But so far this season, the winter storms have lacked oomph.

一般说来，布赖斯峡谷国家公园每年都会有 7 英尺（1 英尺＝ 0.3048 米）左右的积雪。在平常的冬天，这个高达 9 115 英尺（1 英尺＝ 0.3048 米）的公园，在晚秋之际会迎来第一次大雪的降临，但是到这个季节为止，冬天的暴风雪缺少了一些魅力。

Chasing winter—What is it about a good winter storm? Nothing is happening yet, but the chill in the air has an extra heft, and people can practically taste the coming snow: dry, with lingering hints of Alaska.

追逐冬天——对于冬天的暴风雪有什么好的东西出现吗？其实什么也没有出现，但是空气中的寒气格外重，人们甚至可以尝到即将到来的雪的味道：有些干燥，还带着留在阿拉斯加的一些味道。

Higher up in the park, the snow swirls in wispy cyclones across the road. A mule deer and her fawns move through the forest, apparently attempting to reach lower elevations as the storm crashes into the Paunsaugunt Plateau. Sitting atop the Natural Bridge turnout sign, a pair of ravens appears uninitiated by the weather. Catching flakes of snow, their coal black feathers ruffle in the wind, and as people pass, the ravens grudgingly shuffle a few inches sideways along the sign, as welcoming as grumpy old dudes making room for new arrivals on a park bench.

在公园的高处，雪在路上呈小束的气旋旋转着，一只长耳鹿和她的孩子慢慢地穿过森林，显然是试图在暴风雪到达沙岗特高原之前到达更低的海拔。坐在自然桥上，一对乌鸦不顾天气的恐吓在飞翔。由于沾上了雪花，它们黑亮的羽毛在风中显得有些乱。当人们经过的时候，乌鸦不情愿地向那个标志的边上挪了几步，就像古时候脾气不好的花花公子给新来的人在公园的长椅上让了一点空间以示欢迎似的。

Beyond the ravens, people can get their first real taste of Bryce in winter. With a crenellated top that gives it the appearance of a giant rock, Natural Bridge seems to shiver under its frosting of snow. Snowflakes whirl up through the arched opening like ocean spray through a blowhole, obscuring the forest in the canyon below.

在观察完乌鸦之后，人们才真正体验到了布赖斯峡谷国家公园在冬天的美景。有雉堞的顶使得布赖斯峡谷国家公园像一块大岩石，在雪的覆盖下，自然桥似乎有些颤抖，雪花沿着拱形的缺口盘旋上升。

Trying to get beneath the weather, some people usually head down toward Mossy Cave, a hidden spot that many Bryce visitors miss.

为了可以沉浸在这种天气里，人们常常向苔藓穴前进，这是一个许多来布斯赖斯峡谷国家公园的游客经常会忽略的比较隐蔽的景点。

二、Golden Gate Park（金门公园）

What's larger than New York's Central Park, once consisted of sand dunes, is now covered with more than one million trees and is bison-friendly.

哪一个公园比纽约的中央公园还大，而且有沙丘，有 100 万林木覆盖，属于环境宜人型的公园？

Golden Gate Park—the ultimate haven away from urban chaos—was deeded to the people in 1870 out of the prescient notion that San Franciscan would one day feel overcrowded. This foresight proved invaluable, as 75 000 people now visit the park on an average weekend. Finding the land was the easy part. Someone still had to make grass and trees grow out of sand dunes blasted by harsh Oceanside winds. The person to do it was John McLaren, a brazen Scotsman and ardent nature lover. He arrived in San Francisco in the 1870s, and by 1890 he had established grass, trees and numerous plants in an environment most thought too barren for lush foliage.

金门公园——这一远离城市喧嚣的终极天堂的建成，要感谢人们在 1870 年预言旧金山有一天会过于拥挤。这一远见日后被证实还是非常有价值的，今天每周末都有 75 000 人游览该公园。找到能够建立金门公园的土地倒是很容易，难点是人们不得不在这片被海风袭扫的沙丘上植树种草。约翰·麦克莱恩就是从事这项工作的人。他是一位声音洪亮的苏格兰人，一位热心的自然热爱者。他于 19 世纪 70 年代来到旧金山，到 1890 年他在公认的不毛之地种植了草、树和各种植物。

The first buildings came with the Midwinter Fair, a sprawling expo and carnival meant to boost the economy and increase tourism. S.F. wanted to prove that it had culture—so a fine-arts museum was built. To prove that outdoor activities could be pursued, horse stables and vast greens were preserved. And to showcase the exotic and quirky atmosphere of the city, several theme areas were developed, including Cairo Street, Japanese Village and an Eskimo habitat.

此地第一座建筑是应冬季博览会而建，那是一场无计划占用山林建造厂房的博览会和狂欢节，旨在刺激经济和旅游业的增长。旧金山想证明它有文化氛围，因此建成了这个相当不错的艺术博物馆。为了证明游客在该地能从事户外活动，此地还保留了马厩和大量的植被。为了彰显城市的奇特氛围，这里开发了几个主题中心地带，包括开罗街、日本村和爱斯基摩栖息地。

The fair succeeded at what it set out to do. Millions of people visited San Francisco, business boomed and locals found renewed pride in their formerly sand-covered park. Today, the only remnants of that enormous events are the Memorial Museum、the Japanese Tea Garden、and the Music Concourse esplanade.

博览会成功达到了其既定目标。有几百万的人来到旧金山，促进了商业繁荣，使得当地人重新对他们先前被沙覆盖的公园感到骄傲不已。如今，当年大量活动后遗留在当地的还有纪念博物馆、日本的茶场和熠熠生辉的音乐大厅。

What remains today is a testament to the will of the City to preserve a place to play, relax and grow culturally.

金门公园所保留下的，是城市意识的一笔财富，它为人们娱乐、消遣和文化发展保留了一席之地。

三、Alaska Aurora Borealis（阿拉斯加北极光）

As an ultimate natural wonder, it lights up the night sky in both the far northern and southern hemispheres... Imagine the night sky suddenly filled with tall, long rays of light. It's an incredible sight.

作为世界奇观，它能够照亮遥远的南极与北极的夜空……想象一下，夜空突然充斥着高阔绵延的光线，那景象真是令人难以置信。

Alaska is known for its dark cold winters and long daylight summers. People venture there for its beautiful scenery, majestic vistas and to witness its spectacular light show virtually every night of the year.

阿拉斯加以其黑暗寒冷的冬季与夏季的长时间光照而著名，人们冒险到那里是为了欣赏它的奇丽风景和一年中每晚都会出现的极光景观。

Jan Curtis says that observing the northern lights is just like looking into the God's eye. That's the way he looks at it. In the south they call it aurora australis, in the north, call it aurora borealis or northern lights. Jan Curtis is a scientist and photographer who's not only looked into God's eye but taken his picture.

简·柯蒂斯说，观看北极光如同看到了上帝的眼睛，他是这么感觉的。在南半球它被称为南极光，在北半球称为北极光或北极风神光。简·柯蒂斯是一名摄影师兼科学家，他不仅看到了上帝的眼睛，还拍了一些照片。

Photographing the northern lights is a unique challenge because in the wintertime when the lights are most prevalent it's extremely cold. Temperatures can get 40 or 50 below zero and the camera can't be left outside more than just a couple of minutes because it will freeze up. Jan braves the cold in order to capture images like these. Because film is not as sensitive as the human eye; special time lapse techniques are used. Some people when they see Jan's work just can't believe that it's real.

拍摄北极光是一种独特的挑战，因为冬季北极光盛行时天气非常寒冷，温度会在零下40—50℃，照相机放在外面的时间只能有几分钟，不然就会被冻住。简不畏寒冷，只是为了拍这样的照片，因为胶片不会像人眼那样敏感；他采用了特别的慢速拍摄技术。当有些人看到他的作品时，简直不相信那是真的。

In ancient times, mythological gods were credited with this creation. But these mysterious lights get their powerful glow from the same awesome force that gives our planet life. The sun is the source of energy for everything on planet earth, all life, all weather, and all activity that we know. Explosions and solar storms on the surface of the sun send charged particles known as solar winds hurtling towards earth. When they reach the earth's magnetic field the energy is transformed into visual light toward the earth's Polar Regions. The earth has magnetic field lines that loop out into space from the northern hemisphere to the southern hemisphere, arching away from the earth and it is those magnetic field lines that organize the solar storms that cause it to create auroras. In the far north and far south the earth's magnetic charges are the strongest.

在古代，人们认为传说中的神仙创造了这种景象，但实际上这种神秘的光线来自于给予地球生命的同一种强大力量。太阳是地球上一切事物的能量来源，包括我们知道的所有生命、所有天气以及所有活动。太阳表面的爆炸与太阳风暴高速喷射出带电粒子吹向地球，这就是太阳风暴。当它们进入地球磁场后，能量在地球极区附近转化为可视的光线。地球有从北极向南极之间的空间循环的磁力线，在地球上呈空拱形存在，正是磁力线对于太阳风暴的作用形成了极光。地球的最北端和最南端磁场作用最强。

Witnessing the northern lights is spectacular. It's awe inspiring because you can't really explain what they are and why they are there.

观看北极光令人印象深刻。北极光令人惊叹，这是因为你不能解释它们是什么以及它们为什么会在这里。

While scientists know the cause of the aurora, exactly how it affects earth is still in question. Though infrared cameras have captured solar storms like this one, the aurora remains a mystery.

虽然科学家已经知道极光如何形成，但它到底如何影响地球则仍然是一个正被讨论的问题，虽然红外线照相机能够拍出这样的太阳风暴，但极光仍然是一个谜。

There are so few things in nature that's so unique, that's so mystical that sets it apart from almost anything that anybody could ever experience. For creating the planet's greatest nighttime lightshow, the aurora makes people feel surprise.

自然中很少有东西如此独特、如此神秘，那几乎不是人们能经历到的事物。因为它是地球上最伟大的夜间光线表演，极光确实让人感到惊奇。

四、Cleveland（克利夫兰）

Cleveland grabbed headlines in the 1970s as a financially strapped town. Today it boasts not only a very clean Cuyahoga River, but a stunning, revitalized downtown area as well. The city is home to the Rock and Roll Hall of Fame and Museum (a million facility designed by famed architect I.M. Pei) and the Great Lakes Science Center.

克利夫兰曾因其财政危机成为 20 世纪 70 年代被头条报道的城镇。今天它不仅以其清澈的凯霍加河而著称，而且以其令人称奇的复兴的市中心而自豪。该城是摇滚乐名人堂（由著名建筑师贝聿铭设计的 1 000 000 个设施）和五大湖自然中心的所在地。

For a taste of culture, spend some time in University Circle, the nation's largest concentration of cultural institutions within one square mile. Here you'll find first-class museums like the Cleveland Museum of Art, the Cleveland Museum of Natural History, the Center for Contemporary Art, and the Western Reserve Historical Society (which also houses the Crawford Auto-Aviation Museum).

要体味该地的文化，你可以在附近的美国最大的教育机构，大学圈度过一段时间。在这儿，你可以找到一流的博物馆，比如，克利夫兰艺术博物馆、克利夫兰自然历史博物馆、当代艺术中心、西部保留地历史社会（也是克劳福德汽车航空博物馆的所在地）。

Noteworthy historic exhibits include Hale Farm and Village in the town of Bath, with authentic Western Reserve buildings dating back to the 1820s, and Dunham Tavern, once a stagecoach stop on the Buffalo-Detroit road.

重要的历史展览包括巴斯镇的哈里农庄，那里有可以追溯到 19 世纪 20 年代的真正的西部保留地建筑，还有布法罗到底特律通道上的驿站、敦汉姆旅店。

The world-famous Cleveland Orchestra performs at Severance Hall in the winter and at Ohio's Music Festival at Blossom Music Center, where you can attend concerts, ballet, and popular music programs in a woodland setting in the summer. Playhouse Square, a complex of four restored 1920s movie palaces, is the second largest performing arts center in the country and houses the city's opera, ballet, and theater festival. It also hosts touring Broadway shows. Karamu House African American Theater is an international center for the performing arts.

世界上著名的克利夫兰管弦乐队冬季时在西俄兰斯礼堂演出，夏季时在布鲁斯姆音乐中心举办俄亥俄音乐节，在那里你可以参加设在林地的音乐会、芭蕾舞会以及流行音乐节目。剧院广场由 4 个 20 世纪 20 年代保留的电影院组成，它是美国第二大艺术表演中心，也是该城的歌剧、芭蕾舞以及戏剧节的演出地。它也举办百老汇巡演。卡拉姆美国黑人剧院是国际表演艺术中心。

For a magnificent view of downtown Cleveland and the Lake Erie shoreline, head to the top of Terminal Tower, which provides a bird's-eye view from over 700 feet up.

如果要饱览克利夫兰市中心以及伊利湖畔的风光，请登上终点塔顶，您能从 700 英尺的高处俯瞰全貌。

Take a walk on the wild side with a visit to the Cleveland Metro parks Zoo and its Rain Forest, an indoor tropical ecosystem featuring more than 600 animals and thousands of plants, a 25-foot waterfall, and simulated rainstorms. Enjoy year-round outdoor activities in Cleveland's Metro park reservations, which span approximately 19 000 acres.

去克里夫兰市动物园和热带雨林走一走，那里有一个室内的热带生态系统，有 600 多种动物和几千种植物，一个高 25 英尺的瀑布和人工暴风雨。在克利夫兰铁路公园保留地，可以全年享受户外活动，这里面积达 19 000 英亩。

There's no shortage of fun for kids in the Cleveland area. Visit the Children's Museum or take a tour of the NASA Lewis Research Center. Sea World of Ohio in Aurora, an 80-acre marine-life park, features live shows and new exhibits like Dolphin, Eagle, and Shark. For thrill rides and amusements, visit Geauga Lake Park, or the larger Cedar Point in Sandusky.

在克利夫兰，孩子们的乐趣不会少。参观儿童博物馆或者美国宇航局李维斯研究中心。参观奥罗拉的俄亥俄海洋世界，那里有 80 英亩的海洋生物公园，有现场表演以及海豚、雄鹰和鲨鱼的新表演。如果你想寻求刺激，就去吉尔戈湖公园或者更大的桑迪思琪的雪松中心。

五、Camp David （戴维营）

Located seventy miles from the White House in the Catoctin Mountains of Maryland, Camp David was established in 1942 as a place for the President to relax and entertain.

戴维营——美国总统休闲娱乐的地方——建于 1942 年，位于马里兰州凯托克廷山上，距白宫 70 英里（1 英里≈1609 米）。

The Camp is operated by Navy personnel, and troops from the Marine Barracks in Washington, D.C., provide permanent security. Marine One carries the President from Nation's capital. Guests at Camp David can enjoy a pool, putting green, driving range, tennis courts, gymnasium, and the many guest cabins—Dogwood, Maple, Holly, Birch, and

Rosebud, etc.. The presidential cabin is called Aspen Lodge.

戴维营由海军人员管理，驻华盛顿海军舰队负责日常安全工作。海军第一舰队负责将总统从首都华盛顿用直升飞机送往戴维营。客人们可以在戴维营里游泳、打高尔夫球、赛马、打网球、做体操，同时还可以享受很多小屋别墅，例如椋木屋、枫木屋、冬青屋、白桦屋、蔷薇花蕾屋等。总统别墅叫白杨小屋。

Camp David has been the site of many historic international meetings. It was there, during World War Ⅱ, that President Franklin Roosevelt and British Prime Minister Churchill planned the Allies' invasion of Europe. Many historical events have occurred at the Presidential Retreat; the planning of the Normandy invasion, Eisenhower-Khrushchev meetings, discussions of the Bay of Pigs, Vietnam War discussions, and many other meetings with foreign dignitaries and guests. President Jimmy Carter chose the site for the meeting of Middle East leaders that led to the Camp David Accords between Israel and Egypt.

戴维营见证了很多历史性国际会议。在第二次世界大战期间，罗斯福总统和英国首相丘吉尔就是在这里策划了欧洲同盟国进攻欧洲。总统修养所里发生了很多历史性事件，例如，诺曼底登陆计划、艾森豪威尔—赫鲁晓夫会晤、猪湾会谈、越南战争会谈，总统还在这里会晤过很多其他国外高官贵宾。卡特总统就选择了戴维营会晤了中东领导人，最终达成了以色列—埃及戴维营协定。

Camp David continues to serve as the Presidential Retreat. It is a private, secluded place for recreation, contemplation, rest, and relaxation. The Presidential Retreat still remains within park boundaries but is not open to the public. It is a place where presidents can relax, unwind, contemplate, entertain distinguished guests in an informal setting, and cope with the pressures of modern day society.

如今，戴维营仍然作为总统的修养所，它是一个安静隐蔽的消遣、研究、休息、放松的胜地。总统的修养所仍然处于公园境内，但是不对外开放。这里是总统休息、放松、研究、非正式地接见贵宾以及消除现代社会压力的胜地。

The Presidential retreat is not open or accessible to the public, but the eastern hardwood forest of Catoctin Mountain Park has many other attractions for visitors: camping, picnicking, fishing, hiking trails, scenic mountain vistas, all await exploration.

总统修养所不对外开放，公众不能接近，但是凯托克廷山公园的东面的阔叶树林很多迷人的地方可以对游客开放：露营、野餐、钓鱼、徒步旅行、观山望景，所有这一切都在等待游人们的光临。

六、Empire State Building （帝国大厦）

Although New York's Empire State Building has now been dwarfed by several other buildings in the Big Apple, when it was completed in 1931 it was over 61m taller than its nearest rival, the Chrysler Building, and at 381 m remained the tallest building in the world for 41 year. The story of the Empire State Building begins with two men's race to build the highest man-made structure in the world.

纽约的帝国大厦尽管现在和"大苹果城"——纽约市中几幢高楼相比它显得矮小，但在 1931 年完工时，它比排名第二的克莱斯勒大厦高出 61 米，并以 381 米的高度在世界上保持了 41 年的最高建筑的纪录。帝国大厦的兴建源自于两人的竞争，他们都要建立世界上最高的人造建筑。

In 1889 the central feature of the World's Fair in Paris was Eiffel's massive tower, constructed with wrought iron and standing 300 m high. Architects in the United States viewed this as something of a challenge, and by the early 20th century the race was on to erect taller buildings than ever before. Soon skyscrapers were springing up along the New York skyline. In 1928 the founder of the Chrysler corporation, Walter Chrysler, announced the building of a huge new skyscraper, taller than anything so far constructed in New York.

1889 年巴黎世博会的中心标志为巨大的埃菲尔铁塔，它是用熟铁建造的，高达 300 米。美国的建筑师将其视为一种挑战。所以在 20 世纪初开始了建造世界最高建筑的竞赛。不久摩天大楼不断地涌现在纽约的天际。1928 年，克莱斯勒汽车制造公司的创始人——沃尔特·克莱斯勒宣布要建立一座新的巨型摩天大楼，比当时纽约所有的高楼大厦都高。

It soon became clear that the new building was part of Chrysler's aim to rival the motoring giant General Motors. So John Jakob Raskob, of General Motors, decided to race Chrysler to the top. The final height of Chrysler's building was kept secret until it was complete, so Raskob instructed his architects to construct the highest tower they could. Their architectural plans had to be modified as the Chrysler Building grew ever higher, but when it topped out at seventy-seven stories the Empire State team knew that they could beat it.

不久人们都清楚了这座新大楼是克莱斯勒与汽车界巨头通用汽车公司竞争的一部分。因此通用汽车公司的经理约翰·雅各布·拉斯格伯决定要同克莱斯勒决一雌雄。克莱斯勒大厦的最终高度直到它建完之后才予以公开。于是拉斯格伯命令他的建筑师要倾其所能来建设一座最高的楼宇。由于克莱斯勒大厦逐渐变得越来越高，他们的建筑计划也不得不修改，但是当克莱斯勒大厦在 77 层封顶时，帝国大厦的设计者们就清楚他们可以打破这个纪录。

No building project has yet surpassed the Empire State Building's record for speed of construction. Nobody lives in the Empire State Building, but it has many floors of offices and shops. As you might imagine, it is a very popular tourist attraction, visited by 3.8 million people every year. It boasts incredible views from its two observation platforms, on the 86th and 102nd floors. It is a popular spot for proposals and for marriages: there is a group wedding ceremony each year on St. Valentine's Day.

迄今为止，还没有任何建筑工程的建设速度超过帝国大厦。没有人居住在帝国大厦中，但它却有很多层是办公室和商店。正如你可能想象的那样，它也是很受欢迎的观光点，每年有 380 万人前来参观。人们在 86 层和 102 层两个观光平台，可看到奇妙的景色。这是一个非常受欢迎的求婚和结婚的地方：每年情人节都有人在这里举行集体婚礼。

The Empire State Building takes its name from a phrase coined by George Washington, who remarked that the Hudson River was"the key to the new Empire". Thus New York State became known as the"Empire State", and hence the building's name.

帝国大厦的名字源于乔治·华盛顿杜撰的一个警语，他说哈得逊河是"新帝国的钥匙"。这样纽约州也就成了"帝国州"，从而就有了"帝国大厦"这个名称。

七、National Gallery of Art（国家艺术馆）

Though the visually stunning National Gallery of Art, the nearest of the Mall museums to the Capitol, is not in fact a government institution, it fully deserves its name.

尽管令人叹为观止的国家艺术馆是距离国会大厦最近的博物馆，但它事实上并不是一个政府机构。

It owes its prominence to the efforts of industrialist Andrew Mellon, who bought the building and donated most of the paintings (many were purchased from the cash-poor post-revolutionary government of the USSR, where they had previously hung in the Hermitage). His family has continued as benefactors, raising countless millions to build I M Pei's modernistic East Building in 1978.

它的声望得益于实业家安德鲁·梅隆的努力。他买了这个大楼而且捐赠了很多油画（大多数的油画都是从革命后贫穷的前苏联政府买来的，那些画以前都是在前苏联的修道院里悬挂着的）。梅隆的家人至今还在继续捐助，1987 年筹资上百万元建造贝聿铭现代派东方大厦。

The original neoclassical gallery, designed by John Russell Pope in 1941, is now called the West Building and holds the bulk of the permanent collection.

原来的新古典美术馆是 1941 年由约翰·拉塞尔·蒲柏设计的，现在叫作西楼，收藏了许多固定的藏品。

From the domed central rotunda, where you can pick up a floor plan and gallery guide, a vaulted corridor runs the length of the building. If you only have limited time, latch onto one of the informative daily free tours—ask for a schedule at the information desk.

在圆形大厅的中间，你可以拿到整个建筑的平面图和艺术馆的导游词，一条拱形的走廊横穿整个建筑。如果你时间有限，就参加一个免费的一日游，在信息台要一份时间安排表。

Galleries to the west on the main floor display major works by Renaissance masters, arranged by nationality: half a dozen Rembrandts fill the Dutch gallery, Van Eyck and Rubens dominate the Flemish, and El Greco and Velázquez face off in the Spanish, near eight progressively darker Goyas. There's also the only Leonardo in the U.S., Ginevra de' Benci，the 1474 Ginevra de' Benci, painted in oil on wood, plus works by Botticelli, Crivelli and Raphael—including the latter's celebrated Alba Madonna (1520)，one of Mellon's purchases from the Hermitage.

主层西面的画廊中展示着文艺复兴时期大师的一些杰作，是按照其国别分类的，六幅伦布兰特的画摆满了荷兰的画廊，凡·艾克和鲁宾斯的画占据着弗兰德画廊，格雷克和委拉兹开斯的画摆在西班牙画廊，靠近八幅戈雅黑暗的画。还有，在美国画廊里有唯一的利奥纳多 1474 年所画的画，当时是在木板上用油画的。再加上波提切利、克瑞威罗和拉斐尔的一些作品，包括拉斐尔创作的圣母玛利亚画像，那是梅隆从修道院买来的藏品之一。

The other half of the West Building holds an exceptional collection of nineteenth-century French paintings—Gauguin from Pont-Aven to Tahiti, a couple of Van Gogh, some Monet studies of Rouen Cathedral and water lilies.

西楼的另一半是对 19 世纪法国油画的一些独特的收藏，从高更的阿旺桥到塔希提岛，还有梵高的一些作品，莫奈的有关鲁昂大教堂和荷花的一些作品。

At either end of the building, the skylights, fountain-filled Garden Courts make an ideal place to rest weary feet, while Salvador Dali's Last Supper guards the escalators down to the cafe. The triangular East Building houses twentieth-century paintings and sculpture. As in the Guggenheim in New York, the attention-grabbing spatial choreography of the architecture all but overpowers the works of art.

在艺术馆的两边，都有天窗，带喷泉的花园庭院，为您疲倦的双脚提供理想的休息场所。三角形的东楼收藏着 20 世纪的一些油画和雕塑。就像纽约格瓦拉的追随者一样，整个建筑吸引人眼球的三维空间设计使它压倒了艺术品。

八、Miami（迈阿密）

Miami is the most populated city in Florida. It sits at the southeastern tip of the Florida, the most southeastern state of the United States, bordered by the Atlantic Ocean to the east, the Gulf of Mexico to the west and the neighboring states of Alabama and Georgia to the north. The Greater Miami Area, which includes Miami and Miami Beach as well as distinctive neighborhoods like Little Havana and Little Haiti, is a melting pot that America's founding fathers would be proud of. Half of Miami's population is Hispanic.

迈阿密是佛罗里达州人口最多的城市。它位于美国最东南部的佛罗里达州的东南端，东部与大西洋相邻，西部与墨西哥湾比邻，北部与阿拉巴马州和佐治亚州接壤。大迈阿密地区，包括迈阿密和迈阿密海滩，如同与它相邻的小哈瓦那和小海地一样别具特色，是美国开国元勋们引以自豪的一个大熔炉。迈阿密的一半人口是西班牙裔美国人。

Little Havana: the section of town to which Cuban exiles had been gravitating for years blossomed into a distinctly Cuban neighborhood, now known as Little Havana. Spanish is the predominant language here, and you'll run into plenty of people who speak no English. The heart of Little Havana is Calle Ocho and the entire length of Calle Ocho is lined with Cuban shops, cafes, record stores, pharmacies, and clothing and bridal shops.

小哈瓦那——这个地区过去好多年曾经是放逐古巴流放犯的城区，已经发展成了古巴人居住的社区，现在以小哈瓦那而闻名。西班牙语是这儿的主要语言，你会碰到很多不会讲英语的人。小哈瓦那的中心是卡勒奥乔。在卡勒奥乔的整条街上，古巴人开的商店、咖啡馆、音像店、药房、服装店和婚纱店鳞次栉比。

Key Biscayne: south of downtown Miami, along Biscayne Bay's shore, lie a number of the city's best attractions. The Miami Museum of Science & Space Transit Planetarium share a building at Miami's southern city limit, near the entrance to the Rickenbacker Causeway, the bridge that connects Miami with Key Biscayne. The Science Museum has excellent displays on the Everglades and Florida's coral reef.

基比斯坎湾——在迈阿密市区的南部，沿着基比斯坎湾海岸，有许多最吸引人的景点。迈阿密自然科学博物馆和太空经纬仪天文馆都在迈阿密南部城市边界的一座建筑内，在通往里肯巴克堤道入口附近，是连接迈阿密和基比斯坎湾的桥梁。自然科学博物馆有极好的佛罗里达的大沼泽地和珊瑚礁展览。

Florida Keys & Key West: the strings of islands to the south of Miami were once underwater coral reefs. Linked to Miami by a precarious island-hopping 135-mile highway, the string of islands ends at Key West, the legendary land of Hemingway.

佛罗里达群岛与基韦斯特岛——迈阿密南部的一系列岛屿曾经是水下的珊瑚礁。与迈阿密相连接的是一条长135英里崎岖的越岛公路，这一系列岛屿的末端是基韦斯特岛，这里是传说中的海明威的故居。

Key West's reputation as a tropical paradise with gorgeous sunsets and sultry nightlife is well earned. It's been overrun by tourists, but if you look carefully you'll find fleeting images of the Key West of the past: walking through the narrow side streets away from the action, you'll see lovely Keys architecture.

基韦斯特岛由于有着灿烂的夕阳和狂热的夜生活，因而赢得了热带天堂的美誉。虽然来此旅游的人一直过多，但是如果你仔细观察，你就会在脑海中形成对过去的基韦斯特岛的印象：步行穿过远离最热闹的地方的狭窄的街道，你就会看到岛上美丽的建筑。

These days, you can carouse at dozens of clubs, pubs and beach nightspots, as long as you dress respectably and behave yourself. And for those visitors who insist on getting out in the daylight, Fort Lauderdale has a surprising number of cultural and historical sites for a beach town.

现在，只要你穿着体面，行为得体，你就可以到许多俱乐部、酒馆和海滩夜总会狂欢作乐。对那些坚持要在白天出去玩的游客，劳德代尔堡作为一个海滨小镇有着令人吃惊的、大量的文化和历史遗址。

九、The White House（白宫）

The White House—An American Treasure.
白宫——美国的财富。

For almost two hundred years, the White House has stood as a symbol of the Presidency, the United States government, and the American people.
200年以来，白宫一直以总统职位、美国政府和全美国人民的象征矗立着。

Its history, and the history of the nation's capital, began when President George

Washington signed an Act of Congress in December of 1790 declaring that the federal government would reside in a district"not exceeding ten miles square…on the river Potomac".President Washington, together with city planner Pierre L'Enfant, chose the site for the new residence, which is now 1 600 Pennsylvania Avenue. As preparations began for the new federal city, a competition was held to find a builder of the"President's House". Nine proposals were submitted, and Irish-born architect James Hoban won a gold medal for his practical and handsome design.

　　它的历史，整个美国首府的历史是从 1790 年 12 月乔治 · 华盛顿总统签署国会法案开始的，宣告联邦政府在波拖马克河上不超过 10 平方米区域建立。华盛顿总统和城市规划者皮埃尔为新的政府驻地选择了地点，就是现在的 1 600 宾夕法尼亚大街，当新的联邦政府城市开始筹划时，为了选择白宫的建筑者，一场竞争开始了，一共递交的提议有 9 份，最后爱尔兰裔的詹姆斯·豪邦因其实用且壮观的设计获得了金牌。

Construction began when the first cornerstone was laid in October of 1792. Although President Washington oversaw the construction of the house, he never lived in it. It was not until 1800, when the White House was nearly completed, that it's first residents, President John Adams and his wife, Abigail, moved in. Since that time, each President has made his own changes and additions. The White House is, not private home. It is also the only private residence of a head of state that is open to the public, free of charge.

　　1792 年，当第一块奠基石铺上之后，整个建筑开始了。尽管华盛顿总统一直在监督着白宫的建设，他却从未在里面住过。直到 1800 年，当白宫基本竣工的时候，约翰·亚当斯和他的妻子阿比盖尔搬入，成为第一批居住者。从那时开始，每一个总统都做了自己的变化和一些添加。白宫不是一个私人的家，但它是国家首脑的唯一住所，免费对公众开放。

The White House has a unique and fascinating history. It survived a fire at the hands of the British in 1814 (during the war of 1812) and another fire in the West Wing in 1929, while Herbert Hoover was President. Throughout much of Harry S.Truman's presidency, the interior of the house, with the exception of the third floor, was completely gutted and renovated while the Truman lived at Blair House, right across Pennsylvania Avenue. Nonetheless, the exterior stone walls are those first put in place when the White House was constructed two centuries ago.

　　白宫有独一无二，吸引人的历史。其在两场大火中存活下来了，一场是在 1814 年英国人的手中（1812 年战争时期），另一场是在 1929 年，赫伯特·胡佛任总统期间的白宫风云。在哈里·杜鲁门任职期间，除了第三层之外，白宫的全部内部环境一概翻新，当时杜鲁门住在布莱尔宫，正好在宾夕法尼亚大街的对面。尽管如此，白宫外部的石墙在两个世纪之前就一直在合适的位置上。

Presidents can express their individual style in how they decorate some parts of the house and in how they receive the public during their stay. Thomas Jefferson held the first Inaugural open house in 1805. Many of those who attended the swearing-in ceremony at the U.S. Capitol simply followed him home, where he greeted them in the Blue Room. President Jefferson also opened the house for public tours, and it has remained open, except during wartime, ever since. In addition, he welcomed visitors to annual receptions on New Year's Day and on the Fourth of July.

总统可以通过他们如何装饰白宫的一些部分和在任职期间如何接待公众来反映他的个人风格。托马斯·杰弗逊在 1805 年召开了第一次总统就职招待会，许多来美国首都参加总统宣誓就职仪式的人仅仅只是跟着他到白宫，在蓝房子里问候他们。杰弗逊总统也为公众参观开放了白宫，除了战时，它一直是开放的。除此之外，他还欢迎在新年和 7 月 4 日来参加年度招待会的参观者。

In 1829, a horde of 20 000 Inaugural callers forced President Andrew Jackson to flee to the safety of a hotel while, on the lawn, aides filled washtubs with orange juice and whiskey to lure the mob out of the mud-tracked White House. After Abraham Lincoln's presidency, Inaugural crowds became far too large for the White House to accommodate them comfortably. However, not until Grover Cleveland's first presidency did this unsafe practice change.

1829 年，2 000 多名就职来访者使安德鲁·杰克逊总统逃到了一个安全的宾馆里，在草坪上，副官们用橘子汁和威士忌酒装满了洗衣盆以引诱白宫里的暴民出来。在亚伯拉罕·林肯总统结束任职以后，参加就职仪式的人越来越多，白宫已经不能容纳下这么多的人。然而，直到格罗弗·克利夫兰第一次总统任职时这一不安全的形式才得以改观。

十、Hollywood（好莱坞）

If a single place-name encapsulates, the LA dream of glamour, money and overnight success, it's Hollywood.

如果一个地方可以形容为寄托着洛杉矶魅力、财富和一夜成名的梦想，它非好莱坞莫属。

Millions of tourists arrive on pilgrimages; millions more flock here in pursuit of riches and glory. Hollywood is a weird combination of insatiable optimism and total despair. It really does blur the edges of fact and fiction, simply because so much seems possible—and yet so little, for most people, actually is.

数以千计的游客来此朝拜，更多的人来此追求财富和荣耀。好莱坞是无尽的乐观和完全的绝望奇怪的结合体。好莱坞模糊了现实与虚拟的边界，只是因为貌似太多的可能而实际上对于大多数人而言又那么渺茫。

Natural place to begin exploring Hollywood Boulevard is the junction of Hollywood and Vine—the classic location for budding stars to be"spotted"by big-shot directors and whisked off to fame and fortune.

探寻好莱坞大道自然要从与洛杉矶餐馆交接处开始，这是崭露头角的新星们让大牌导演发现而获得名利的经典之所。

Hollywood is a district in Los Angeles, California, United States, situated west-northwest of Downtown Los Angeles. Due to its fame and cultural identity as the historical center of movie studios and movie stars, the word "Hollywood" is often used as a metonym of cinema of the United States. The nickname Tinseltown refers to the glittering, superficial nature of Hollywood and the movie industry.

好莱坞是美国加利福尼亚州洛杉矶的一个区，它位于洛杉矶市区西北方向。作为电影制作和电影明星诞生地的历史中心，由于具有高知名度和文化底蕴，"好莱坞"一词往往被看作美国电影的同义词。好莱坞的昵称是 Tinseltown，意为闪闪发光，也暗指好莱坞电影业的根基浅薄。

Many historic Hollywood theaters are used as concert stages to premiere major theatrical releases and host the Academy Awards. It is a popular destination for nightlife and tourism and home to the Hollywood Walk of Fame. In this site, you'll get closer to Hollywood's"biggest star"than you ever dreamed possible.

许多具有历史意义的好莱坞影院现在都被用作音乐会首演舞台或用于举办奥斯卡金像奖颁奖典礼。这里是追求夜生活和旅游活动的热门选择，也是好莱坞星光大道的始归地。在这里，你能比在世界其他地方更接近你梦想中的好莱坞的"最大牌明星"。

The myths, magic, fable and fantasy splattered throughout the few short blocks of Central Hollywood would put a medieval fairytale to shame. A rich sense of nostalgia pervades the area, giving it an appeal no measure of tourists or souvenir postcard stands can diminish.

神话、魔力、语言和幻象弥漫在好莱坞中心仅有的几个短小街道上，这使中世纪的童话黯然失色。怀旧之感四溢，游客和纪念卡终究无法降低其吸引力。

Griffith Park—The gentle greenery and rugged mountain slopes that make up vast Griffith Park northeast of Hollywood are a welcome escape from the mind-numbing hubbub of the city. The landmark Observatory here has been seen in innumerable Hollywood films, most famously *Rebel Without a Cause*, and the surrounding acres add up to the largest municipal park in the country, one of the few places where LA's multitude of racial and social groups at least go through the motions of mixing together.

里菲斯公园——得益于葱翠的草木和崎岖的山路，好莱坞东北方的里菲斯公园成为人们逃避极度拥挤的城市生活的好地方。地标性建筑天文台见于无数的好莱坞电影，最著名的是《无因的反叛》，总占地面积为国内最大的市政公园。洛杉矶各个民族各个社会团体至少会在此接踵比肩，洛杉矶仅存几处而已。

十一、Honolulu（火奴鲁鲁 / "檀香山"）

Diamond Head, a volcanic peak, offers sweeping views of Oahu. Honolulu is a harbor city at the southern end of Oahu, the most visited island of the Hawaiian archipelago. The city lies 2 550 miles (4 100km) southwest of Los Angles; 3 860 miles (6 220km) southeast of Tokyo; 5 060 miles (8 150km) northeast of Sydney; and 1 470 miles (2 370km) north of the equator. Not surprisingly, it's a major hub for trans-Pacific air travel.

钻石山是瓦胡岛上的一个火山口，在这里能看到瓦胡岛的全景。坐落于瓦胡岛南端的港口城市火奴鲁鲁是夏威夷群岛中最受旅客欢迎的地方。火奴鲁鲁位于落基山西南 2 550 英里（4 100 千米）处，东京东南 3 860 英里（6 220 千米）处，悉尼东北 5 060 英里（8 150 千米）处，北距赤道 1 470 英里（2 370 千米）。毋庸置疑，火奴鲁鲁是跨太平洋飞行途中一个主要的中枢。

Downtown Honolulu contains all Oahu's state and federal government buildings, including the state capitol and Iolani Palace, once home to Hawaii's last few monarchs and still the only royal palace in the U.S.. Chinatown is a few blocks northwest of the palace; the Aloha Tower and cruise ship terminals are a few blocks west.

州和联邦政府位于火奴鲁鲁市中心，其中州议会大厦和伊奥拉尼王宫是夏威夷王朝最后下榻过的地方，现在依旧是美国国内仅有的王宫。唐人街在王宫西北的几街区外，火山塔和巡游船的终点站西距王宫只有几个街区。

Southeast of downtown, Waikiki is the epicenter of all things touristy: All the big resorts and much of the city's nightlife are found here. Just southeast of Waikiki, 760ft (230m) Diamond Head rises up as the city's favorite geological landmark. All of these sites are within the boundaries of greater Honolulu.

市中心的东南是威基基海滩，旅游的中心地带，这里有着最大的度假胜地以及活力四射的夜生活。760 英尺（230 米）的钻石山耸立于海滩的东南，成为这个城市人们最喜爱的地标。所有这些景点都包括在大火奴鲁鲁中。

H-1, the main south shore freeway, passes east-west through Honolulu, connecting it to the airport and all other freeways on the island. Honolulu International (HNL) is a 9 mile (15km), 25 minute drive northwest of downtown via Ala Moana Blvd/Hwy 92 (Nimitz Hwy) or the H-1.

H-1 是南部海岸主要的高速公路，自西向东贯穿整个火奴鲁鲁，连接着飞机场和其他岛上所有的高速公路。火奴鲁鲁国际机场离市中心西北 9 英里（15 千米），车行 25 分钟，途径 Ala Moana Blvd/Hwy 92 (Nimitz Hwy) 或者 H-1 高速公路。

The Ala Moana Center, on Ala Moana Blvd just northwest of Waikiki, is the central transfer point for The Bus, the island's public bus network. Its routes branch across the island, with each line's destination written above the bus' windshield. The Ala Moana Center is the central transfer point. Overall, the buses are in excellent condition-clean and air-conditioned - though buses on popular routes tend to be packed and their pace is always dawdling.

位于威基基海滩西北的阿拉莫阿那大道上的阿拉莫阿那购物中心是公交换乘的枢纽，也是全岛公交网络的中心。公交支线遍布全岛，挡风玻璃上都写着每条线路的终点站。阿拉莫阿是转车的中心。虽然受欢迎的线路上的公交车上往往挤满了人，车速也总是缓慢的，但是整体上，公交环境值得称赞：干净、凉爽。

The Waikiki Trolley is an expensive, tourist-laden open-air bus geared primarily for sightseeing shopaholics.

露天威基基无轨电车价格昂贵，挤满了游客，主要为购物成癖的人观光游览而设计。

The attraction-lined route between Waikiki's Royal Hawaiian Shopping Center and downtown Honolulu is narrated.

位于皇家夏威夷购物中心和火奴鲁鲁市中心的引人入胜的观光线是人们喜爱的线路。

Oahu is not a big island, and few places are more than an hour's drive from Honolulu. If you plan on spending all your time in the resorts of Waikiki, forget about renting, but if you plan to get beyond the city limits, a car is the easiest way to do it. The minimum age to drive in Hawaii is 15 years, and most car rental agencies hike that limit to 25. Gasoline is about 25% more expensive on the island than on the U.S.mainland. Driving is on the right.

瓦胡岛不大，有些景点从火奴鲁鲁出发仅仅一个小时而已。如果你打算一直都待在威基基度假胜地，就不用租车了；但是要想去更多地方的话，乘小汽车最方便了。在夏威夷开车最小也得 15 岁，大部分租赁机构要求最小 25 岁。岛上汽油价格比在美国大陆上要贵 25%，但要靠右行驶。

Taxis wait at most major downtown hotels and at the airport. Otherwise, you'll need to phone for a cab. Bikes are available for rent in Honolulu and Waikiki, and most bike shops provide maps, helmets and locks. The city is poorly suited for cycling, though, and most riders prefer to use their bikes for longer jaunts around Oahu.

计程车大多都在市中心主要的宾馆和机场等候。要不然就得电话预定出租车。火奴鲁鲁和威基基可以租自行车，大部分还提供地图、头盔和锁。虽然火奴鲁鲁地势不利于自行车行驶，但是大部分人都更喜欢骑自行车环游瓦胡岛。

十二、Hawaii Volcanoes National Park（夏威夷火山国家公园）

Hawaii Volcanoes National Park displays the results of 70 million years of volcanism, migration, and evolution—processes that thrust a bare land from the sea and clothed it with complex and unique ecosystems and a distinct human culture. The world's most active volcano offers scientists insights on the birth of the Hawaiian Islands and visitors views of dramatic volcanic landscapes.

夏威夷火山国家公园展示了 7 000 万年间的火山作用、移民活动以及进化所带来的结果，正是这些过程使海洋中伸展出一块光秃秃的陆地，并且赋予这块地复杂独特的生态环境和别具特色的人类文明。世界上最活跃的火山为科学家们提供了有关夏威夷岛起源的观察点，并且展示着生动的火山地貌风景。

Volcanoes are monuments to earth's origin, evidence that its primordial forces are still at work. During a volcanic eruption, we are reminded that our planet is an ever changing environment whose basic processes are beyond human control. As much as we have altered the face of the earth to suit our needs, we can only stand in awe before the power of an eruption.

火山是地球起源的纪念碑，也是地球原始力量仍在发挥作用的证据。在一座火山爆发期间，它提醒我们：我们的星球是一个不断变化的环境，它的基本过程不受人类的控制。尽管我们实际上已经改变了地球容貌来迎合我们的需要，但是在火山爆发的威力面前，我们只能感到敬畏。

Why are there volcanoes in Hawaii, which is located in the middle of the Pacific plate? Plumes of magma rise from a"hot spot"deep within the mantle. This fluid charged with gas, melts and pushes its way to the surface, erupting on the ocean floor to create a seamount. After several hundred thousand years and countless eruptions, the volcano rises above sea level to form an island. The volcano continues to grow until movement of Pacific plate carries the island off the hot spot. Kilauea Volcano in Hawaii Volcanoes National Park continues today as the longest-lived rift activity in Hawaiian volcano history.

为什么火山会出现在处于太平洋板块中心的夏威夷呢？岩浆的热柱从地幔深处的一个"热点"升起。这种充斥着气体熔化并且向表面推进，在海底爆发形成海山。在经过了几十万年和无数次的爆发之后，火山升出海平面形成了一个岛。火山继续增高直到太平洋板块的运动使岛屿漂离热点。在夏威夷的火山历史上，夏威夷国家公园里的几劳亚火山的爆发作为最长久的断裂活动延续至今。

According to early Hawaiian traditions, there was a time in the mysterious past when the air was surrounded with spiritual beings, and a thin veil divided the living from the dead, the natural from the supernatural. During that time Pele, goddess of the volcano, came to Hawaii. Pele is volcanism in all its forms. When her molten body moves, the land trembles and the sky is afire with a crimson glow. Many Hawaiian legends speak of the relationships between Pele and other gods and human.

根据夏威夷早期传说，在神秘的过去有一段时间，空气中充满了灵魂，一层薄薄的幕帐把生与死、自然与超自然分隔开来。在那段时间里，火山女神培雷来到了夏威夷。培雷是火山活动所有形式的体现。当她熔化的身体移动时，大地在颤抖，天空中燃烧着深红色的火焰。许多夏威夷传说讲的都是培雷与其他诸神以及人类之间的关系。

第二十四篇　结　　论

　　美国社会文化的研究可以从很多方面入手，而要真正了解美国社会文化，又不得不从美国的历史说起。从某种程度上说，美国英语真实的记录下了美国发展的历程，一部美国英语的发展史又是一部美国历史的真实写照。美国英语不是一门独立的语言，它来源于英国英语。从历史的渊源说，如今的美国是从不列颠北美殖民地衍生、发展而来的。Planter（英殖民主义者），proprietor（英王特许独占某块殖民地的"领主"），Yankee（英格兰移民）等美语就是美国曾作为英殖民地的历史见证。用现代语言学的术语来说，美国英语是英语的一种变体，是近400年来英语使用于北美这个特殊的地理环境，受美国社会文化影响而形成的一种变体。美国历史虽然短暂，但它却成为了全球综合实力最强的国家，同时因为美国的主导地位而使得英语魅力无穷，美国英语扩展到美利坚合众国的各个角落，成为记载美国社会各领域重大历史事件的百科全书。

　　美国的国民来自世界上不同的民族和种族，他们操持着不同的语言，有着迥异的文化背景，代表不同的肤色和宗教信仰。移民的多源性构成了美利坚民族的多元性，而美国社会的多元性又构成了美国文化的多样性。各国各地区的移民，尤其是亚裔美国人，喜欢与同民族的人聚居在美国某些城市或城中的某一区域，由此形成了众多的国中之"国"，他们在自己的民族聚居区中保持着母族的生活方式、信仰、习俗和语言。美国英语是"合族国"人们用于社会交往、思想沟通和信息传递的工具。为了表达美利坚民族独具一格的特征，美国英语独创和发展了大量极富美利坚民族文化内容的词语。它们是人们了解美利坚的族裔构成、族裔渊源和族裔文化不可缺少的史料。

　　对于来自世界各国的移民来说，他们没有共同的祖先和传统，于是拓荒、冒险和个体主义至上的精神深入人心。在英语中，individualism 被定义为"主张个人正直与经济上的独立，强调个人主动性、行为与兴趣的理论，以及由这种理论指导的实践活动"。美国特有的历史文化造就了美国人特有的个人主义情结，个人主义极大地影响着美国的政治、经济和文化，并在不同的历史时期赋予个人主义不同的文化内涵，发挥着积极和消极的作用。它无时无刻不在影响和左右着美国社会发展的轨迹，特别是今日，个人主义已深入到了美国社会的方方面面。通过美国个人主义这面镜子，我们能够更准确理解和把握美国英语语言背后的实质。

美国地名作为美国历史文化的"化石"，从一个具体的侧面再现出美国的自然景观，揭示出美国历史上重大政治变革、经济发展、社会变迁，反映出美利坚民族的文化传统、历史背景、思维方式、宗教信仰，以及美国社会独有的多元文化特色。对于美国地名，学习英语者常会遇到意想不到的困惑。即使是英语达到较高水平的人，有时也会对一些美国地名感到费解。对这样一些美国地名，要搞清其渊源及其文化含义有时还真不容易。但一旦搞清楚了，我们就可以更多地了解美国的历史和文化背景。美国地名的由来有着丰富而广泛的文化背景，它与美国的民族传统、自然景观、社会变革、意识形态等诸多因素密切相关。它不仅渗透着美国民族文化的特质，也维系着这个民族的情感与精神。深入细致地研究与探讨美国地名的始源会有助于我们对美国英语语言所负载的文化意蕴的理解，从而使我们能更详尽地领悟到美国自身所特有的民族风味、文化风貌，以及美国文化发展史。

数不清的美国习语、俚语记载着北美大陆由殖民地到超级大国崛起的历程，它们成为美国历史文化的重要组成部分。英语习语受美国文化的影响，渐渐形成了具有独特魅力的美国英语习语。众所周知，美国是一个非常爱好体育运动的国家，这从他们的语言中可窥见一斑。美国英语中充斥着大量来自体育运动，尤其是拳击和球类运动的词汇。拳击和球类是世界性的体育运动，也是奥林匹克运动会的主要项目，对英语习语起到了重大的影响作用。了解美国英语习语和体育运动项目之间的联系，我们就可以更好地理解美国英语习语，也就能更好地使它们达到语言和文化的最佳结合点。

谈到美国文化就必然要谈到印第安人，印第安人是美国本土上最早的居民，他们世世代代在这里生活劳动、休养生息，是美国真正的主人。和世界各国、各地区的人民一样，土著印第安人为人类的历史发展做出过重大贡献。印第安人是美国历史上不少重大事件的涉及对象和直接参与者。北美印第安人对美国英语与文化的形成功不可没。他们对早期的美洲移民给予了很大的帮助，曾教他们种植农作物、开发森林、捕捉猎物、发展生产等。北美印第安人在帮助欧洲移民渡过最初难关的同时，也将自己的土著词汇传授给了他们。美洲的诸多地名以印第安语命名充分折射出当时的印第安文明对当时社会生活的影响，也反映出当时自然和社会环境的关系，使人们在看到这些名字的同时也能够回想起灿烂的印第安文明，同时对语言的发展也起了一定的作用。美国的自然州名中，有 34 个取自印第安人的名字，有 1 000 多条河流，200 多个湖泊和数不清的城镇、山丘、河谷、森林、公园等名称取自印第安语。印第安人创造了最灿烂的美洲文明，在多元文化的美国，印第安文化是最浓重的色彩之一，无论是美国语言，还是美国文化方面，处处体现着印第安人的印记。在当代美语中，约有 17 000 个词语来自印第安语。印第安语极大地丰富和充实了美国语言与文化，为美国英语与文化的形成注入了土著民族的元素。

黑人文化是构筑美国多元文化的重要部分。半个世纪以来，黑人英语在美国社会及世界上已有很大的影响。黑人英语不同于普通美国英语，是美国英语许多变体中的一种，作为黑人文化载体反映了黑人特有的文化特征。从语言学的角度看，在引起语言变异的过程中，民族因素往往与地域和职业等多种因素交织在一起，不同民族背景的人在用英语表达自己思想感情的时候都不可避免地带上了本族语言特点，这在受教育程度低下的人群中间尤为明显。美国黑人所遭受的种族压迫和种族隔离是促使语言变异的根本原因。黑人的方言在与英语的长期交往中形成了自己独特的风格，为坚持自己的文化传统极力保留带有民族特色的词汇，为美国标准英语的词汇赋予不同的意义，它既为英语输入了丰富的营养，同时又从英语中吸取新鲜血液，是美国英语的一部分。毫无疑问，独具特色的美国黑人英语使电影中的黑人形象更加栩栩如生。它与主流英语格格不入的句法规则，风格各异的独特词汇和非洲裔美国黑人奔放的舞蹈、激情的音乐一同构成了其文化的根基。随着黑人电影、音乐、小说、戏剧等不断地融入美国主流社会，黑人教育水平的提高以及黑人英语对美国社会各领域影响力的进一步增强，美国黑人在美国社会的发言权和话语权也越来越大。美国黑人英语作为一种成熟的英语变体，将更加广泛地活跃于荧屏之上，其语言的独创性也将成为展示美国丰富的多元文化的重要途径。

美国政治是导致美国成功的重要机制之一。美国能在很短的时间内成为强国，其国家体制起到了特别重要的作用。北美独立战争结束，依据 1781 年《邦联条例》美国实行邦联制。各州保持其主权、自由、独立。邦联仅仅是州之间的联合体，不是现代意义上的国家。1787 年，美国制定了一部新宪法——联邦宪法，开始从邦联制转变为联邦制。这次转变把美国变成为一个拥有统一的中央政权的联邦制国家。联邦制的确立，改变了早期政治关系无序的状态，使国家权力的运作步入正轨。美国是世界近代史上最早实行联邦制的国家。联邦制不仅是美国立国的基本制度，也是它治理国家的重要政治原则。联邦制的确立，为美国社会历史的发展奠定了政治基础。因此，正确理解和区分联邦制和邦联制，有助于我们理解今天美国的社会政治文化。

在美国政治中，总统扮演着最重要的核心角色，他集内政、外交、行政、立法、司法、军事大权于一身，是国家元首、政府首脑与三军统帅。作为美国政坛的核心人物，美国总统对美利坚合众国所起的举足轻重的影响体现在社会、政治、经济等诸多方面。历史学家和政治学家们一致认为，罗斯福、华盛顿和林肯是美国最伟大的三位总统。他们几乎用自己毕生的精力为美国的发展寻求最好的途径。也正是因为他们如此的付出，美国才发展到今天这个高度。总统日就是为了纪念华盛顿和林肯两位总统设立的美国联邦节日。一个国家的兴盛与否有很多因素的制约，但作为国家领导人，美国总统对国家的发展起着不可小觑的作用。这一点也可以从美国英语中与美国总统有关的词语中得到验证。美国总统就职演说具有鲜明的政治性和思想性，既是美国历史的缩影，也体现了美国的文化价值观。现任美国总统奥巴马，作为争议颇多的第一个黑人总统，在其就职演说中将自己的理想、面对的挑战及公众的希望融为一体。他的就职演讲中使用频率最高的词汇，包括"国家"、"美国"、"新"、"人民"及"每个人"等。奥巴马成为众人瞩目的焦点的同时，应运而生的奥巴马词汇也迅速地进入了美国英语词汇。

语言中的词汇对于各种变化最为敏感，容易受到政治、经济、社会文化等各方面的影响。新词汇是对社会变化最直接的反映，是社会发展的"晴雨表"。新词的产生、旧词的消亡，以及一系列词语替换，词义扩大、转移或者缩小，都是客观世界变化的直接反映。在美国英语中，gate 已经由原来的简单意义"门"演变出一个组合形式，被用来婉指丑闻（scandal）。新闻英语中用 -gate（门）来形容重大的政治丑闻。1975 年轰动美国内外的水门事件发生后，Watergate 一词可用来指任何类似的政治事件或大的丑闻。之后，多起牵涉与在任总统有关的 -gate（丑闻）不断被揭露出来。身居世界上唯一超级大国的第一把交椅的美国总统的一言一行都是全世界共同关注的对象。他们的软肋和私生活成为媒体和大众的关注焦点。美国总统大选过程成为一个丑闻大拆台的过程。

美国文学的历史不长，它几乎是和美国自由资本主义同时出现，较少受到封建贵族文化的束缚。美国人民富于民主自由精神，个人主义、个性解放的观念较为强烈，这在文学作品中有突出的反映。美国又是一个多民族的国家，移民不断涌入，各自带来了本民族的文化，这决定了美国文学风格的多样性和庞杂性。美国文学发展的过程就是不断吸取、融化各民族文学特点的过程。许多美国作家来自社会下层，这使得美国文学生活气息和平民色彩都比较浓厚，总的特点是开郎、豪放。内容庞杂与色彩鲜明是美国文学的另一个特点。个性自由与自我克制、反叛和顺从、高雅与庸俗、深刻与肤浅、积极进取与玩世不恭、对人类命运的思考和探索、对性爱的病态追求等倾向，不仅可以同时并存，而且形成强烈的对照。从来没有一种潮流或倾向能够在一个时期内一统美国文学的天下。美国作家永远处在探索和试验的过程之中。20世纪以来，许多文学潮流起源于美国，给世界文学同时带来积极的与消极的影响。

美国丰富的自然资源和多样的民族文化使它成为极具吸引力的旅游国家。它拥有神奇的自然景观、厚重的历史文化和充满艺术的现代气息。白宫，在美国人的心目中是有着十分重要的地位的，它不仅仅代表着权威，也是一个国家的象征，是美国文化的浓缩，来到这里的人们会深深地感受到美国的独特魅力。正因为美国的自然资源得天独厚，美国成为世界上第一个创立国家公园的国家。比较有名的有黄石公园、大峡谷等。在北部靠加拿大边界附近，有著名的五大湖游览区，其中最壮观的景点是尼亚加拉大瀑布，此外还有适于冒险者的科罗拉多大峡谷。位于美国西面太平洋上的夏威夷群岛也是全球闻名的度假胜地，是多数人梦想中的天堂。夏威夷也是多种文化汇集交融的大熔炉，历经了200多年的变迁，它已经变成当今美国种族最为多样、人口最为复杂的社会。岛上最原始的语言是夏威夷语，和其他波利尼西亚语关系密切。现在，英语是夏威夷群岛的通用语言，几乎所有的人都说英语。一些夏威夷语的词汇也悄然进入了日常用语中。

我们要研究词义，就不能不研究词源。在美国英语中有好多普通名词（还有少数动词、形容词）来源于人名名称，每个词都含有不同的社会文化、历史背景和文化典故。社会创造了语言，这些词义的转换是在漫长的语言发展历史过程中自然形成的，它使得美国英语词汇更加形象生动。这种词义的转换仍在继续。美国英语是在英国对北美进行殖民开拓的过程中逐渐形成的一种区域性的英语变体。美国英语所使用的词汇的意义与通用英语大多数是一致的，但是也有一些词汇在词义上存在着较大的区别，往往同一事物使用不同的单词来表示。或者，同一单词在通用英语和美国英语中表示不同的意义。随着美国历史的发展，美语中一部分词汇的意义变得"狭窄"。跟词义变"窄"相反，有一部分词汇随着美国历史的发展，出现了由本义引申出来的独特意义。换句话说，这些词的词义"扩大"了，产生了新的意思。词的本义可以是有理据的（motivated），也可以是无理据的，但词的转义总是有理据的。美国英语词语的转义受制于美国历史的诸多因素。美语词的转义无论是变"窄"或是变"宽"都是对美国历史现实的客观反映。

一个国家的社会与文化，在人民生活的点点滴滴中显露出这个国家的文化底蕴和这个民族的气度，国人的习性更是其历史的体现。通过对美国英语在衣食住行、文化产业、政治生活等独特之处展开深度透视与详细剖析，我们从中感受到美国这个年轻的世界发达国家的文化，更深入地看到这个国家成长的历史及文化底蕴；了解美国文化的多样性；了解美国人性格中充满了挑战与乐观、务实与自立的精神。从而我们以一个全新的视角来看待美国，汲取美国文化中积极的部分，来发展繁荣我们自己的文化。

附录一 美国各大景点简介

一、纽 约 州

（一）自由女神像（Statue of Liberty）

自由女神像，又称自由照耀世界（Liberty Enlightening the World），是法国在
1876 年赠送给美国的独立 100 周年的礼物。美国的自由女神像位于美国纽约州纽约
市哈德逊河口附近，是雕像所在的美国自由岛的重要观光景点。美国的自由女神像
以法国巴黎卢森堡公园的自由女神像作蓝本，法国著名雕塑家巴托尔迪历时 10 年艰
辛完成了雕像的雕塑工作，女神的外貌设计来源于雕塑家的母亲，而女神高举火炬
的右手则是以雕塑家妻子的手臂为蓝本。自由女神穿着古希腊风格的服装，所戴头
冠有象征世界七大洲及五大洋的七道光芒。

（二）布鲁克林桥（Broolyn Bridge）

纽约的布鲁克林大桥横跨纽约东河，连接着布鲁克林区和曼哈顿岛，1883 年 5
月 24 日正式交付使用。大桥全长 1 834 米，桥身由上万根钢索吊离水面 41 米，是当
年世界上最长的悬索桥，也是世界上首次以钢材建造的大桥，落成时被认为是继世
界古代七大奇迹之后的第八大奇迹，被誉为工业革命时代全世界 7 个划时代的建筑
工程奇迹之一。在这座大桥庆祝百年华诞时，美国曾发行 1 枚 20 美分面值的邮票来
纪念，展现了大桥的雄姿和风采。美国近代诗人哈特·克雷恩还专门为它写过一首
长诗，诗名就叫《桥》。

（三）帝国大厦（Empire State Building）

帝国大厦是位于美国纽约市的一栋著名的摩天大楼，共有 102 层，由 Shreeve, Lamband Harmon 建筑公司设计，1930 年动工，1931 年落成，只用了 410 天。它的名字来源于纽约州的别称帝国州（Empire State），所以英文本义实际上是 "纽约州大厦"，而 "帝国州大厦" 是以英文字面意思直接翻译之译法，但因此帝国大厦的译法已广泛流传，故沿用至今。帝国大厦位于曼哈顿第五大道 350 号，是纽约市著名的旅游景点之一。它的顶部的泛光灯的颜色会因时间或重大事件而改变，比如说在 9·11 事件后就亮了 3 个月的蓝色灯，以示哀悼。建筑历史学家威里斯说，今天的帝国大厦一方面象征美国工商业文化，另一方面也是纽约，甚至是全美国的永远地标。

（四）时报广场（Times Square）

纽约时报广场，是美国纽约市曼哈顿的一块街区，以一年一度的 "降球" 活动而闻名。纽约时报广场，原名 "朗埃克广场"（Longacre Square），又称为 "世界的十字路口"，常误被译为 "时代广场"。时报广场得名于《纽约时报》早期在此设立的总部大楼，中心位于西 42 街与百老汇大道交会处，构成曼哈顿中城商业区的西部。这是纽约剧院最密集的区域，1920 年开始时报广场五光十色的年代，以时报广场大厦为中心，附近聚集了近 40 家商场和剧院，是繁盛的娱乐及购物中心。

（五）华尔街（Wall Street）

华尔街是纽约市曼哈顿区南部从百老汇路延伸到东河的一条大街道的名字，全长仅 1/3 英里，宽仅 11 米，是英文 "墙街" 的音译。街道狭窄而短，从百老汇到东河仅有 7 个街段，却以 "美国的金融中心" 闻名于世。美国摩根财阀、洛克菲勒石油大王和杜邦财团等开设的银行、保险、航运、铁路等公司的经理处集中于此。著名的纽约证券交易所也在这里，至今仍是几个主要交易所的总部：如纳斯达克、美国证券交易所、纽约期货交易所等。"华尔街" 一词现已超越这条街道本身，成为附近区域的代称，亦可指对整个美国经济具有影响力的金融市场和金融机构。

（六）洛克菲勒中心（Rockefeller Center）

洛克菲勒中心是一个由 19 栋商业大楼组成的建筑群，占地 22 英亩（acre），在曼哈顿的中城，东西向，从 48 街到 51 街，占了三个街区；南北向，从第五大道到第七大道，更占了三个纵向街区。这个建筑群是由洛克菲勒家族投资兴建的。这个建筑在 1987 年被美国政府定为 "国家历史地标"（National Historic Landmark），这是全世界最大的私人拥有的建筑群，也是标志着现代主义建筑、资本主义的地标物，其意义的重大，早就超过建筑本身了。

（七）尼亚加拉大瀑布（Niagara Falls）

尼亚加拉大瀑布是美国最知名的风景之一，位于纽约州水牛城附近的美国与加拿大边境。上游的水流到了悬崖，一泻千里，超过 185 英尺的高度再加上洪流的巨大冲力，冲刷出 7 000 米长的峡谷，澎湃的气势，犹似千军万马，在峡谷回荡不已，令岸边的游客无不像着魔了一般，目瞪口呆，深深被尼亚加拉瀑布的爆发力震撼。尼亚加拉瀑布实际由两部分组成："新娘的婚纱"瀑布（Veil of the Bride Falls）及马蹄型瀑布（Horseshoe Falls）。事实上，在美国境内，人们看到的只是尼亚加拉瀑布的侧面，而在加拿大可以一览全貌。

（八）百老汇大街（Broadway）

百老汇，本义为"宽阔的街"，指纽约市中以巴特里公园为起点，由南向北纵贯曼哈顿岛，全长 25 千米的一条长街。百老汇大街两旁分布着几十家剧院，在百老汇大街 44 街至 53 街的剧院称为内百老汇，而百老汇大街 41 街和 56 街上的剧院则称为外百老汇。内百老汇上演的是经典的、热门的、商业化的剧目，外百老汇演出的是一些实验性的、还没有名气的、低成本的剧目，但这种区分越来越淡化，于是又出现了"外外百老汇"，其观点当然也就更新颖更先锋了。

（九）大都会博物馆（Metropolitan Museum of Art）

大都会博物馆是美国最大的艺术博物馆，也是世界著名的博物馆。位于美国纽约 5 号大道上的 82 号大街，与著名的美国自然历史博物馆遥遥相对。占地 13 万平方米，它是与英国伦敦的大英博物馆、法国巴黎的卢浮宫、俄罗斯圣彼得堡的列宁格勒美术馆（也称冬宫，音译艾尔米塔什博物馆）齐名的世界四大美术馆之一，共收藏有 300 万件展品。现在是世界上首屈一指的大型博物馆。

二、宾夕法尼亚州

（一）伊利湖（Erie Lake）

伊利湖是北美洲五大湖最东和最小的一个，略呈东西延伸，大致成椭圆形，主轴线东西长约 311 千米，南北最宽 85 千米。湖面海拔 75 米，比伊利湖低 99 米。著名的尼亚加拉大瀑布上接伊利湖，下灌安大略湖，两湖落差 99 米。平均水深 85 米。湖岸线较平直，仅东北端较曲折。北岸为平原，南岸为尼亚加拉崖壁。全年通航期 8

个月，上游 4 大湖湖水经尼亚加拉河流入，流域面积 7 万平方千米（不包括湖面积），湖水向东经圣劳伦斯河注入大西洋，与周围湖、河有运河相通，如西南经韦兰运河与伊利湖相连，西北经特伦特运河与休伦湖的乔治亚湾相连，东北经里多运河与渥太华河相连。

（二）落水山庄（Falling Water）

落水山庄，也称流水别墅，是坐落于宾夕法尼亚州西南部乡村、匹兹堡东南方 50 英里处的住宅，1934 年由美国建筑师弗兰克·劳埃德·赖特所设计。房舍建于费耶特县史都华镇、阿利根尼山脉的月桂高地，横跨在熊奔溪的瀑布之上。在茂密的丛林掩映下，在清清的溪流和嶙峋石块间，这座别墅从中心向各个方向伸展着、交错着，白色的巨大阳台凌空于水面之上，流水叮咚地从房子底下蜿蜒淌过，从平台下奔泻而出。这是 20 世纪的房屋设计中最著名、最具影响力的一个。

三、华盛顿哥伦比亚特区

（一）白宫（The White House）

白宫是美国总统府，坐落在华盛顿市中心的宾夕法尼亚大街，与高耸的华盛顿纪念碑相望，是一座白色的三层楼房，因其外墙为白色砂岩石，故而名为白宫。白宫坐南朝北，共占地 7.3 万多平方米，分为主楼和东西两翼，东翼供游客参观（每周二至周六开放），西翼是办公区域，总统的椭圆形办公室位于西翼内侧。主楼底层有外交接待大厅，厅外是南草坪，来访国宾的欢迎仪式一般在这里举行。主楼的二层是总统家庭居住的地方。主楼中还有图书室，地图室，金、银、瓷器陈列室，里面藏品颇丰。此外，白宫的东侧有"肯尼迪夫人花园"，西侧有"玫瑰园"。从正门进入的国家楼层（State Floor）共有五个主要房间，由西至东依序是：国宴室、红室、蓝室、绿室和东室，东室是白宫最大的一个房间可容纳 300 位宾客，主要用作大型招待会、舞会和各种纪念性仪式的庆典。

（二）美国航空航天博物馆（National Air and Space Museum）

1976 年 7 月开馆的美国国家航空航天博物馆，是史密森氏学会创建的众多博物馆之一，也是全世界首屈一指的有关飞行的专题博物馆。它坐落在美国首都华盛顿特区的东南方，每月接待观众达 10 万之多，第一年的参观人数超过 1 000 万人次，创美国各博物馆最高纪录。它是目前世界上最大的飞行博物馆，是由玻璃、大理石和钢材构成的现代化建筑。博物馆的 24 个展厅共有 18 000 平方米的展览面积。各展厅陈列飞行史上具有重要意义的各类飞机、火箭、导弹、宇宙飞船，及著名飞行员、宇航员用过的器物。除体积过于庞大的采用模型外，展品绝大多数都是珍贵的原物或备用的实物。

（三）华盛顿国家大教堂（Cathedral Church of St. Peter and St. Paul）

圣彼得和圣保罗大教堂又称华盛顿大教堂，俗称华盛顿国家大教堂是巴洛克建筑的杰作。它建于 1408 年，是长方形的哥特式大教堂。立陶宛著名的主教、诗人瓦兰袤斯葬于教堂内。后来不断改建，直到 1655 年俄瑞战争开始才告结束，200 年间，教堂的外形和构造逐渐吸收了文艺复兴时期及巴洛克建筑特色。教堂塔楼高 41.9 米，内设有 9 个祭坛。1895 年升格成为主教堂。威尔逊总统、第二次世界大战时的国务卿贺尔及盲人女作家海伦·凯勒的遗骨均葬于此堂；艾森豪威尔总统的葬礼、里根和布什总统的就职礼拜仪式也在此举行。

（四）国会大厦（United States Capitol）

国会大厦位于华盛顿 25 米高的国会山上，是美国的心脏建筑。国会大厦建于 1793—1800 年，与华盛顿的多栋重要建筑一样，亦未幸免于 1814 年英美战争的损毁。战后重建之后，百年以来，国会大厦又进行了包括 1851—1867 年的浩大重建工程在内的多次扩建，最终形成了今日的格局。国会大厦是一幢全长 233 米的 3 层建筑，以白色大理石为主料，中央顶楼上建有出镜率极高的 3 层大圆顶，圆顶之上立有一尊 6 米高的自由女神青铜雕像。大圆顶两侧的南北翼楼，分别为众议院和参议院办公地。众议院的会议厅就是美国总统宣读年度国情咨文的地方。它仿照巴黎万神庙，极力表现雄伟，强调纪念性，是古典复兴风格建筑的代表作。美国人把国会大厦称为 Capitol，把它看作是民有、民治、民享政权的最高象征。

（五）华盛顿纪念碑（Washington Monument）

华盛顿纪念碑是为纪念美国首任总统乔治·华盛顿而建造的，它位于华盛顿市中心，在国会大厦、林肯纪念堂的轴线上，是一座大理石方尖碑，呈正方形、底部宽 22.4 米、高 169 米，纪念碑内有 50 层铁梯，也有 70 秒到顶端的高速电梯，游人登顶后通过小窗可以眺望华盛顿全城、弗吉尼亚州、马里兰州和波托马克河。纪念碑内墙镶嵌着 188 块由私人、团体及全球各地捐赠的纪念石，其中一块刻有中文的纪念石是清政府赠送的。纪念碑的四周是碧草如茵的大草坪，这里经常会举行集会和游行。

（六）五角大楼（The Pentagon）

五角大楼（The Pentagon），又称五角大厦，位于美国华盛顿特区西南方的西南部波托马克河畔的阿灵顿区，因五角形建筑外观而定其名，建于第二次世界大战期间，以全世界最大的办公大楼而闻名于世，可容纳 25 000 个职员。五角大楼是美国最高军事指挥机关所在地，美国"海、陆、空"三军总部，美国国防部办公地。由于其特殊的职能，"五角大楼"一词不仅仅代表该建筑物本身，也常常用作美国国防部的代名词。

（七）林肯纪念堂（Lincoln Memorial）

林肯纪念堂是为纪念美国总统林肯而设立的纪念堂，位于华盛顿的国家大草坪西端，碧波如染的波托马克河东岸上，与东端的国会大厦遥遥相望，是一座用通体洁白的花岗岩和大理石建造的古希腊神殿式纪念堂。林肯雕像放置在纪念馆正中央，雕像上方是题词——"林肯将永垂不朽，永存人民心里"。林肯纪念馆不仅是对这位已故总统的称颂，同时也是对整个国家人民的称颂。林肯的葛底斯堡演说和他第二次就职演讲词也刻在大理石墙上。馆内 36 根圆柱代表林肯总统逝世时美国所划分的 36 个州。沿着纪念馆的阶梯往上走，绕过林肯雕像背面，你所能看到的就是美国国会大厦和华盛顿纪念塔的壮观景色，在池中还隐约透着华盛顿纪念塔的倒影。林肯纪念堂由美国国家园林局（National Park Service）管理，常年免费对外开放。

（八）美国国会图书馆（The Library of Congress）

美国国会图书馆建于 1800 年，是美国的四个官方国家图书馆之一，也是全球最重要的图书馆之一。美国国会图书馆是在美国国会的支持下，通过公众基金、美国国会的适当资助、私营企业的捐助及致力于图书馆工作的全体职员共同努力建成的，它是美国历史上最悠久的联邦文化机构，已经成为世界上最大的知识宝库，是美国知识与民主的重要象征。目前，该图书馆以 1 亿 2 800 万册的馆藏量成为图书馆历史上的巨无霸。图书馆书架的总长超过 800 千米。据美国国会图书馆网站最新介绍，目前藏品总数 1.3 亿，其中 0.29 亿书籍、0.12 亿照片、0.58 亿件手稿。读者只有使用借阅证才能进入读者阅览室和读书借阅。图书馆为读者提供美国国会的史料、会议记录、宪法等重要资料，供读者查阅。

（九）肯尼迪艺术中心（John F. Kennedy Arts Center）

肯尼迪艺术中心是 1966 年开始建造的，1971 年 9 月 8 日落成正式开幕。位于美国首都华盛顿特区西北边，旁边是水门大厦，另一面临水，景观十分秀丽。这幢白色的方形建筑物，对美国而言，具有双重意义：首先，它是国家文化中心，自艾森豪威尔总统开始，即计划要建立这样一个国家文化中心。其次，它是以美国总统肯尼迪之名命名，以纪念这位年轻遇刺的总统。多年来，肯尼迪艺术中心在美国文化界已占有举足轻重的地位。肯尼迪艺术中心共分四个厅。庞大的音乐厅"肯尼迪音乐厅"，座位多达 2 759 个，舞台可容纳 200 人的乐团，观众席分为三层，每层各有一间总统包厢，古意盎然、美轮美奂。音乐厅拥有一个全世界最大的休息室，长度是两个足球场再加十码，屋顶上装饰着水晶灯及许多国家致送的装饰物，闪闪发亮、眩人耳目。

四、怀俄明州

（一）魔鬼塔自然保护区（Devil's Tower National Monument）

怀俄明州东北角的克鲁克县，一片几乎平坦的土地上，不寻常地矗立一块巨石，傲视着周围的大地。它是大地的王者，印第安人的圣地，美国第一个国家纪念地（National Monument）——魔鬼塔。魔鬼塔的高度有 264 米，1906 年由西奥多·罗斯福总统签署法案成为第一个国家纪念地。它是玄武岩结构的火山颈地形，早期是一座火山，后来周围的山壁被侵蚀掉了，只留下坚硬的玄武岩火山颈。魔鬼塔的周围有一条环塔步道，一圈走下来大约 45 分钟，可以 360 度观看魔鬼塔及周遭的景色，感受魔鬼塔傲视大地的气魄。

（二）化石丘自然保护区（Fossil Butte National Monument）

化石丘国家保护区就在大提顿国家公园往南到科罗拉多的路上。化石丘这个地方是因为它岩层里丰富的化石而被列为保护区，并不是因为风景或地质特别。游客中心里展览不少这里挖出来的化石，其中最巨大的是有两三公尺长的鳄鱼化石，非常完整，而且保存状况很好。化石丘自然保护区保存了大量完整的淡水鱼类化石。这里的化石大多是 5 000 万年前生长在这个湖里的动植物。它完整地保存了生长在同一年代同一生态系的各种生物，有很大的研究价值。它们能拼出一个环境，说出一个完整的故事。不像博物馆里展览的恐龙或其他动物的化石，虽然看起来像是同种的动物，但是生长的年代可能相差几百万年以上。

（三）麋鹿保护区（National Elk Refuge）

在怀俄明州境内、黄石国家公园南面几十英里的地方，有一个麋鹿保护区。在每年冬季，成千上万的野生麋鹿会成群结队地游荡来此处过冬，因为这里有人类给它们提供的饲料。在这个离大提顿国家公园很近的保护区内，你会看到麋鹿在开阔地带悠闲地吃草。11月到次年4月间，您可以步行或乘车穿过保护区公路，或者付费骑马来此观赏麋鹿。

五、内华达州

（一）塔霍湖（Tahoe Lake）

塔霍湖是加利福尼亚州和内华达州交界处的湖泊，位于内华达山区，海拔1 897米。2/3在加利福尼亚境内。南北长35千米，最宽20千米，面积502平方千米，最深490米。冬季水温保持0℃以上。湖水注入特拉基河。附近国立塔霍森林是1960年冬季奥林匹克运动会的比赛场地。

（二）拉斯维加斯大道（The Strip）

拉斯维加斯大道是拉斯维加斯最繁荣的街道。这里汇集了最豪华的酒店、赌场、餐馆与购物场所，是拉斯维加斯的灵魂与象征。这里灯光璀璨，赌场中众生相尽收眼底。沿着大道而建的酒店都是可以免费进去参观游玩的，几乎所有酒店的一楼都是CASINO（娱乐场，供表演跳舞、赌博的地方），每到晚上就有很多客人进去玩老虎机。步行穿过大道，要观赏贝拉焦喷泉（Bellagio Fountain），MIRAGE门口有人造火山，每隔15分钟喷一次，据说每次要花费1 500多美金，都由MIRAGE酒店承担。另外，凯撒酒店的音乐喷泉也很壮观，吸引大量的游客驻足观看。

（三）胡佛大坝（Hoover Dam）

胡佛大坝在世界水利工程行列中占有重要的地位。胡佛大坝的建造耗费了大量资金，动员了大批人力，于1936年竣工并交付使用。它是一座拱门式重力人造混凝土水坝。坝高220米，底宽200米，顶宽14米，堤长377米。这样巨大的水坝在世界上是不多见的，它宛如一条巨龙盘卧在大地上，显得十分威武。坝下的科罗拉多河原本是美国最深、水流最湍急的河流，如今缓缓而行，就像一头驯服的野兽。

（四）拉斯维加斯金字塔酒店（Luxor Hotel）

金字塔酒店Luxor也许是世界上最宏伟和神秘的酒店。酒店内一座楼高30层的黑色玻璃金字塔和两座有阶梯的金字塔楼是古埃及艺术和现代科技的结晶，是拉斯维加斯最具创造力和想象力的建筑艺术杰作，该酒店在拉斯维加斯无与伦比。酒店金字塔的内部为中空的设计，建有主题游乐园，称之为金字塔的秘密，分为"过去"、

"现在"、"未来"三个主题。"过去"是飞行模拟器，"现在"是观看 3D 的立体电影，"未来"则是以一个 7 层楼高的银幕来欣赏超大银幕动感电影。

六、加利福尼亚州

（一）水晶大教堂（The Crystal Cathedral）

水晶大教堂位于美国加利福尼亚州洛杉矶市南面的橙县（Orange County）境内，一个叫"庭院树丛"（Garden Grove）的地方。1968 年开始兴建，1980 年竣工，历时 12 年，耗资 2 000 多万美元。这座建筑由美国著名的建筑师、金牌优胜者菲利普·约翰逊与他的伙伴约翰·布尔吉设计。教堂长 122m，宽 61m，高 36m，体量超过著名的巴黎圣母院。外壳全部为银色玻璃，晶莹透亮，由此得名。

（二）彻斯特神秘屋（Winchester Mystery House）

在加利福尼亚州圣何塞市附近有一座古色古香、规模庞大的建筑，造型怪得令人不可思议。原来这座耗资巨大的古怪房子，竟是一名美国"步枪之父"的妻子莎拉为了"赎罪"，造给死在丈夫发明的枪支下的"鬼魂"住的！温彻斯特神秘屋，是一座非常庞大的建筑，很多荒诞怪异的传说都在这里产生。温彻斯特神秘屋始建于 1884 年，直到莎拉去世后才停止建造，前后共历时 38 年。为了适于冤魂居住，神秘屋在设计上非常怪异和神秘。38 年时间中，莎拉不停地建造温彻斯特神秘屋，房子一间间不断增加，倒塌、又不断重建，直到莎拉 1922 年去世后，温彻斯特神秘屋才停止建造，直到如今仍保持着当时的规模。

（三）金门大桥（Golden Gate Bridge）

金门大桥是世界著名大桥之一，被誉为近代桥梁工程的一项奇迹，也被认为是旧金山的象征。金门大桥的设计者是工程师史特劳斯，人们把他的铜像安放在桥畔，用以纪念他对美国做出的贡献。大桥雄峙于美国加利福尼亚宽 1 900 多米的金门海峡之上。金门海峡为旧金山海湾入口处，两岸陡峻，航道水深，为 1579 年英国探险家弗朗西斯·德雷克发现，并由他命名。

（四）好莱坞环球影城（Universal Studios Hollywood）

好莱坞环球影城位于洛杉矶北郊的好莱坞。20 世纪初，电影制片商在此发现理想的拍片自然环境，便陆续集中到此，使这一块土地逐渐成为世界闻名的影城。环球影城是好莱坞最吸引人的去处，这里你可以参观电影的制作过程，回顾经典影片片断。影城由三个部分组成，分别是影城之旅（全程 50 分钟的电影之旅，有专门的讲解员）、上园区与下园区。你可以在电影拍摄现场亲身体验电影的拍摄过程。影城出入口旁还有一个风格时尚的购物区——环球城市大道。

（五）迪士尼乐园（Disneyland）

迪士尼乐园是一个位于加州安纳罕市（Anaheim）的主题乐园。由华特·迪士尼一手创办的迪士尼乐园是由华特迪士尼公司（The Walt Disney Company）所创立与营运的一系列主题乐园与度假区中的第一个，离洛杉矶市中心大约有 20 分钟的车程（高速公路）。加州迪斯尼乐园自 1955 年 7 月 17 日开幕以来就成为世界最受欢迎的主题乐园之一，被人们誉为地球上最快乐的地方（The Happiest Place on Earth）。以米老鼠为首的迪斯尼家族，每年都有新成员加入，加上迪斯尼乐园的软硬件不断推陈出新，使得这儿成为观光客前往洛杉矶，绝对不会错过的重要景点。迄今游览过加州迪斯尼乐园的游客已经超过 6 亿，这其中包括国家总统、皇室、世界顶级明星等等。

（六）格里菲斯天文台（Griffith Observatory）

它位于美国洛杉矶城中心西北方向的山上，与好莱坞 Hollywood Hills 遥遥相对。它是洛杉矶的标志性建筑，曾经是电影《霹雳娇娃 2》和《黄金眼》的外景地。天文台 1933 年建成，1935 年对公众开放，2002 年翻新装修，把天文台用钢筋水泥整体提升，在原有一层的下面加了一层，耗资 9 500 万美元，历时 4 年，到 2006 年重新对公众开放。它是世界上著名的天文台之一，对公众免费开放，包括各个展室及一个电影放映室。

（七）圣地亚哥海洋世界（Sea World Adventure Park San Diego）

圣地亚哥海洋世界位于风景优美的美国米慎湾。公园占地约 189.5 英亩，是世界最大的海洋主题公园。自 1964 年开业以来，已经招待了超过 1 亿 3 000 万名游客。海洋世界有 4 个主要的海洋动物秀及 20 个展出项目，其中最有名的秀莫过于杀人鲸招牌秀。在这里还有游客与动物亲密互动的机会。比弗利山庄海洋世界的母公司为美国啤酒百威的制造厂商 Anheuser-Busch，故游客可在公园内免费上啤酒酿造课。

（八）九曲花街（Lombard Street）

九曲花街，美国官方正式名称为伦巴底街，是一条美国加州旧金山东西方向贯穿 Presidio 区及 Cow Hollow 区的街道，其部分路段（从 Broderick 街到 Van Ness 大道）更是美国 101 高速公路的干线，该街道一直向东伸展，经过俄罗斯山、电报山后，尽头是旧金山海旁的 Embarcadero 区域。这段坡度非常陡的街道原本是直线通行的，但考虑到行车安全，1923 年这路段被改成目前所见的弯曲迂回情况，利用长度换取空间减缓沿线的坡度大小，并且用砖块铺成路面增加摩擦力。它是全美国最弯曲的一条街道，短短一段路上一共有八个急弯。街道上遍植花木：春天的花球、夏天的玫瑰和秋天的菊花，把它点缀得花团锦簇。在花街高处还可远眺海湾大桥和科伊特塔，如不开车，可顺着花街两旁的人行步道，欣赏美丽景色。

（九）斯坦普斯（Staples Center）

斯坦普斯中心，昵称订书机中心，是美国加利福尼亚州洛杉矶中心城区的多功能体育中心，位于洛杉矶会议中心附近。斯坦普斯中心是 NBA 洛杉矶湖人队（L.A. Lakers）的主场。距离球馆还有 3 千米时，就能看见远处并排的三幢大楼上有着湖人三位历史中锋张伯伦、贾巴尔和奥尼尔的巨幅画像，直观地向人们宣扬了湖人最骄傲的中锋传统。球场顶部悬挂的超大电视屏幕有六面，比赛中每个精彩画面都能及时慢镜头重放。整个球馆被分为 400 多区块，有近 200 条通道出入。

七、亚利桑那州

（一）科罗拉多大峡谷（The Grand Canyon）

大峡谷是科罗拉多河的杰作。这条河发源于科罗拉多州的落基山，洪流奔泻，经犹他州、亚利桑那州，由加利福尼亚州的加利福尼亚湾入海，全长 2 320 千米。"科罗拉多"，在西班牙语中，意为"红河"，这是由于河中夹带大量泥沙，河水常显红色，故有此名。科罗拉多大峡谷是一处举世闻名的自然奇观，它是联合国教科文组织选为受保护的天然遗产之一。

（二）羚羊峡谷（Antelope Canyon）

羚羊峡谷是世界上著名的狭缝型峡谷之一，也是知名的摄影景点，位于美国亚利桑纳州北方，最靠近的城市为佩吉市（Page），属于纳瓦荷原住民保护区。羚羊峡谷在地形上分为两个独立的部分，称为上羚羊峡谷（Upper Antelope Canyon）与下羚羊峡谷（Lower Antelope Canyon）。羚羊峡谷的出口只有一人多宽，山洪从这里以惊人的力量喷涌而出。而这里的光线也千变万化，只有正午很短的一段时间阳光才能透过几处间隙照到谷底。羚羊峡谷是北美最美丽的峡谷，它幽深、距离不长，但沿着山势深切地下。这里的地质构造是著名的红砂岩，谷内岩石被山洪冲刷得如梦幻世界。

（三）波浪谷（Paria）

波浪谷指美国亚利桑那州北部朱红悬崖的帕利亚峡谷，其砂岩上的纹路像波浪一样，所以这片地方叫作"The Wave"，即波浪，是一个由五彩缤纷的奇石组成的风景区。波浪谷展示的是由数百万年的风、水和时间雕琢砂岩而成的奇妙世界。波浪谷岩石的复杂层面，是由巨大的沙丘组成。在侏罗纪时期，这里的地貌好像撒哈拉沙漠一样，沙丘不断地被一层层浸渍了地下水的红沙所覆盖，天长日久，水中的矿物质把沙凝结成了砂岩，形成了层叠状的结构。目前前往这片荒原观看这个自然奇观的入口每天仅限 20 人通过。

八、犹他州

（一）圣殿广场（Temple Square）

圣殿广场是犹他州盐湖城市中心一组属于耶稣基督后期圣徒教会（摩门教）总部的建筑群，包括盐湖城圣殿、盐湖城大礼拜堂、盐湖城聚会堂、海鸥纪念碑和两个游客中心，占地 10 英亩，周围有围墙环绕。盐湖城圣殿是世界上最大的摩门教圣殿。圣殿广场是犹他州最热门的旅游景点，每年吸引游客 300 万—500 万，超过大峡谷和黄石公园。

（二）犹他湖（Utah Lake）

犹他湖是美国犹他州中北部的湖泊。面积 390 平方千米，为淡水湖，湖水经约旦河排入西北方的大盐湖。为史前邦纳维尔湖（Lake Bonneville）的残存部分。当地设有州立犹他湖公园及辟有水禽和鸟类保护区。在 21 世纪初，沿岸有超过 25 万人口。

（三）纪念碑山谷（Monument Valley）

纪念碑山谷是在科罗拉多高原一个由砂岩形成的巨型孤峰群区域，其中最大的孤峰高于谷底约 300 米。该区域位于亚利桑那州北方州界和犹他州南方州界的附近。纪念碑谷在纳瓦霍族保留地之内，可经由美国 163 号公路到达。在纪念碑谷公园范围内或整个纪念碑谷区域，游客也可以从各游客服务单位骑马游历，价格依照距离而定。骑马的时间可能从一小时到隔夜宿营不等。此外，每年 5 月 1 日到 10 月 31 日可以搭乘热气球，有时可搭乘小型飞机。

九、科罗拉多州

（一）卡纳维拉尔角（Cape Canaveral）

卡纳维拉尔角所在地是众人皆知的航空海岸，附近有肯尼迪航天中心和卡纳维拉尔空军基地，美国的航天飞机都是从这两个地方发射升空的，所以卡纳维拉尔角成了它们的代名词。这里还有一座灯塔和卡纳维拉尔港，城区在卡纳维拉尔角南面几英里远的地方。此外本地还有一个蚊子泻湖（Mosquito Lagoon）、印第安河、梅里特岛、国家野生动物保护区和卡纳维拉尔国家海岸。

（二）丹佛公共图书馆（Denver Public Library）

1990 年，丹佛市民共同投票通过了一个 9 100 万美元的合同——决定建造一个全新的丹佛公共图书馆。丹佛公共图书馆在 1995 年完工，拥有 54 万平方英尺的超大面积。在图书馆完工之前，其建筑师格雷夫斯预测该设计是其最好的一个作品。但是工程完工以后，却遭到了建筑界的一致批评。很多建筑师认为该图书馆内的设计和装饰要远远胜于其外貌。

（三）范尔滑雪场（Vail Ski Resort）

范尔滑雪场位于美国科罗拉多州，是美国最大的、也是最受欢迎的滑雪场，长期被评为顶级滑雪胜地，并享有全美最佳和最大单板滑雪胜地的世界美誉。这里有世界上最高落差的山顶滑雪道，这里的设计已经成为美国旅游胜地设计最成功的范例。范尔滑雪场有超过 120 个指定滑道，滑雪高手可以在这里尝试各种极具挑战性的地形。范尔滑雪场的垂直落差达 1 000 多米，滑雪者可随意选定一个地方，俯冲而下，体验垂直落差带来的刺激与快感。范尔滑雪场拥有 7 个充满传奇色彩山坳的滑雪场，在前山拥有绵长而令人心跳的雪道和几个不同的地形公园，是初学者的天堂；而后山，则不断拉伸，有着辽阔的林海雪原，最高处超过 3 500 米，是中级滑雪者和高级滑雪者的挑战胜地。

十、佛罗里达州

（一）佛罗里达环球影城（Universal Studios Florida）

佛罗里达环球影城是一座位于美国佛罗里达州奥兰多的主题乐园，在 1990 年 6 月 7 日开幕，乐园内的设施主题围绕在娱乐产业，特别是电影和电视作品。佛罗里达环球影城是奥兰多环球影城度假村的两座乐园之一，有两个主题公园：一个是具有大量影视资料的环球影城，一个是可以给游客带来惊险刺激体验的冒险岛。同时，影城推出的 4D 电影也吸引了不少游客。

（二）奥兰多迪士尼乐园（Walt Disney World Resort）

奥兰多迪士尼乐园是全世界最大的迪士尼主题乐园，总面积达 124 平方千米，约等于 1/5 的新加坡面积。自 1971 年 10 月开放以来，每年接待游客约 1 200 万人。这里设有 5 座 18 洞的国际标准高尔夫球场和综合运动园区，市中心还有迪士尼购物中心——结合购物、娱乐和餐饮设施，里面有夜间游乐区、杂技团、酒吧、各式商店和超过 250 家的餐厅。奥兰多迪士尼乐园拥有 4 座超大型主题乐园，分别是迪斯尼—未来世界、迪斯尼—动物王国、迪斯尼—好莱坞影城、迪斯尼—魔法王国，还有 2 座水上乐园（暴风雪海滩、台风湖）、32 家度假饭店（其中有 22 家由迪斯尼世界经营）以及 784 个露营地。

（三）奥兰多海底世界（Sea World Orlando）

这个占地超过 200 英亩的主题公园用独特的动物展览和海洋主题为众多游客和家庭带来了无尽的欢乐。与食人鲨和大白鲸面对面，和可爱的海豚一起游泳，细数鲨鱼的牙齿或给海豹和海狮喂食都是奥兰多海洋世界的"冒险"度假体验。Aquatica 是奥兰多海洋世界创建的独一无二的水上公园，于 2008 年 3 月 1 日正式对外开放。这座活力四射的水上乐园坐落在一片宛如南海岛屿的郁郁葱葱的景观之中，融合了沙滩、动物近距离体验以及从悠闲轻松的活动到刺激高速的水上骑乘项目。

（四）肯尼迪航天中心（Kennedy Space Center）

肯尼迪航天中心位于美国东部佛罗里达州东海岸的梅里特岛，成立于 1962 年 7 月，是美国国家航空航天局进行载人与不载人航天器测试、准备和实施发射的最重要场所，其名称是为了纪念已故美国总统约翰·肯尼迪（John F. Kennedy）。整个场地长达 55 千米，宽 10 千米，面积达到了 567 平方千米，大约有 17 000 人在这里工作。场地上还有一个参观者中心，参观者也可以随导游参观。肯尼迪航天中心是佛罗里达州的一个重要的旅游点。同时由于肯尼迪航天中心大部分地区不开放，它也是一个美国国家野生动物保护区。

（五）迈阿密海滩（Miami Beach）

迈阿密海滩是美国著名的海水浴场，也是全世界名列前茅的观光胜地，它位于迈阿密的海滩市，与迈阿密隔着比斯坎海湾相望，有几座跨海大桥与之相连。这个海滩海水浅，浪小涌平、沙细沙白、平坦广阔，延绵数千米，像一条长长的宽大白色玉带镶在海边，一眼望不到头。蓝天、碧海、白沙，加上群群海鸥时而在海上戏水，时而到沙滩觅食，时而又翱翔天空，组成了一幅十分美妙的立体图画。每年有数百万人来这里享受沙滩、阳光和海水带来的舒畅。

十一、其他奇景名胜

（一）大西洋城（Atlantic City）

大西洋城是美国新泽西州东南部海滨旅游胜地和疗养城市。濒大西洋沿岸，位于长约 16 千米、宽约 1.2 千米、地面低平和多沙滩的阿布西肯岛洲之上，东北距纽约约 160 千米，西北距费城约 96 千米。因接近纽约、费城高尔夫娱乐城，从 19 世纪末便成为旅游、疗养地。有巨大的市属会议厅，能容纳 4.1 万人，常为国内、国际召开会议的场所。100 多年前只有两户渔民居住，他们的茅屋至今仍保留完好。附近还有一块拥有 200 多年历史的阿布西肯灯塔古迹保留地、独立战争时期的战场史密斯村和一个天然动物园。

（二）布鲁克菲尔德动物园（Brookfield Zoo）

布鲁克菲尔德动物园正式名称为芝加哥动物园（Chicago Zoological Park）。园址位于芝加哥市南郊的布鲁克菲尔德（Brookfield），占地面积达 874 124 平方米，拥有约 450 种动物。该动物园以其大规模的开放式场地而闻名。它是全美国第一个展出大熊猫的动物园，其中一只名叫苏林的熊猫在死亡后被制成标本，如今被放在芝加哥菲尔德自然历史博物馆（Chicago's Field Museum of Natural History）中展示。20 世纪 80 年代建设了热带世界（Tropic World）——第一个全室内雨林模拟场景展室，随后又建设了世界最大的室内动物园展室。

（三）圣路易斯拱门（Gateway）

圣路易斯拱门是美国向西开发的一个象征。这座雄伟壮观的不锈钢抛物线形的建筑物，高达 192 米，是 1964 年动工后仅用两年时间建成的。拱门底部有电梯可以直达顶层。圣路易斯拱门为圣路易斯市的地标，高 630 英尺，比华盛顿纪念碑、自由女神像或是欧洲的比萨斜塔都还要高。

（四）66 号公路（Route 66）

呈对角线的 66 号公路，从芝加哥一路横贯到加州圣塔蒙尼卡。66 号公路，被美国人亲切地唤作"母亲之路"。66 号公路全长 2448 英里（约 3939 千米）。通车使用：1926 年 11 月 11 日——1985 年 6 月 27 日。研究 66 号公路 60 多年的学者迈克尔·华利斯说："66 号公路之于美利坚民族，好比一面明镜；它象征着伟大的美国人民一路走来的艰辛历程。"66 号公路是母亲之路，是飞翔之路。66 号公路见证了一个民族的苦难，却也见证了美国人自由、勇敢与进取的精神。

（五）麦金莱山（Mt. Mckinley）

麦金莱山原名迪纳利峰。这是当地印第安人的称呼，迪纳利在印第安语中的含义是"太阳之家"。后来，此山以美国第 25 届总统威廉·麦金莱的姓氏命名为麦金莱山。麦金莱山系有南北二峰，南峰即海拔 6 193 米的北美洲最高峰，北峰高 5 934 米。山上终年积雪，雪线高度为 1 830 米。南坡降水量较多，冰川规模较大，有卡希尔特纳和鲁斯等主要冰川。麦金莱山区由于受到温暖的太平洋暖流影响，气候比较温和，到夏季时也是青绿一片，海拔 762 米以下，发育了森林，以杉一桦树林为主。绿色的森林、雪白的山峰、广阔的冰川，在阳光下相互辉映、风光优美，令人耳目一新。1917 年，麦金莱山被辟为国家公园。

（六）恐龙湾自然保护区（Hanauma Bay Nature Park）

恐龙湾自然保护区是位于欧胡岛东南部的一个海湾，曾经是个火山口，因此风景非常美丽，特别是蓝天碧海，澄碧的海水，清澈见底，大片鲜活的珊瑚丛随着海水流动摇曳生姿，美丽多彩的热带鱼游弋其中，让人不禁怀疑这是某个时代遗失的天堂。恐龙湾还是一个重要的恐龙化石遗址。如今，这座被海浪不断侵蚀的火山口，已成为重要的自然保护区和岛上最受欢迎的浮潜目的地。在这里可以到海底珊瑚世界探索。

（七）威基基黄金海岸（Waikiki Beach）

威基基黄金海岸线是夏威夷州的象征。这里的海水像碧玉一样清纯，会水的和不识水性的都能在这里找到自己理想的下水的地方。金黄的海滩上，婆娑的椰子树下，老老少少、不同国界、不同肤色的人们，在恒温的夏威夷气候的轻拂下，感觉到自己生活得离上帝创世纪不远、世界还很纯净的时候。在威基基生活区，除了去威基基海滩游泳，还可以去卡皮哦拉妮公园（Kapiolani Park）走走。卡皮哦拉妮公园在威基基的东端，占地面积是 170 英亩，里面有火奴鲁鲁动物园（Honolulu Zoo）、威基基水族馆（Waikiki Aquarium）和威基基露天音乐厅（Waikiki Shell）。

（八）河滨步道（River Walk）

河滨步道指的是位于德克萨斯州的圣安东尼奥河的河滨步道。圣安东尼奥河的河滨步道号称是德克萨斯州第一娱乐胜地，这条绿荫大道吸引来了来自世界各地的游客。河道两旁聚集了餐馆、商店等众多娱乐场所。游客们游走在河滨步道上，沐浴着河面的微风，更能感受到一股浓浓的诗意。现在河滨步道约有两公里长，以30多座楼梯与上方的道路相连，有多家国际性大饭店进驻，商业林立，并有水上游船、公园等设施。如今它已成为最热门的观光据点了，每年有数百万游客到圣安东尼奥市来观光，有1 000多个大型会议在这里举行，而河滨步道是大家的必游之地。

（九）科德角海岸（Cape Cod）

在美国麻萨诸塞州的东南部，有一个弯弯的半岛，细细长长的伸向大西洋。那就是科德角，也叫鳕鱼角。高耸的灯塔、迷人的酸果蔓池塘，还有沙丘和森林，这些无与伦比的景色让科德角海峡熠熠生辉。在这个44 600英亩的保护区里，环境优美，细沙绵绵，游客们不仅可以感受大海的气息，还可以徒步旅行，欣赏沿途风光。

（十）休斯顿太空中心（Houston Space Center）

休斯顿太空中心是一个为游客设计的旅游服务设施。它是休斯顿地区最吸引游客的景点。它里面有很多珍贵的实物展品（如返回舱、月球岩石），有关登月球的介绍、高科技演示等。在这里游客可以用手触摸月球上采集回来的岩石块，可以看宇航、登月及星际旅行的电影（三场电影总共95分钟），看登月的火箭。全部游览下来要4—6个小时。如果您时间短，只要在大火箭旁照张相，就不必去花20美元去太空中心，直接进宇航中心的火箭公园即可，不要钱。从火箭公园再往里面走不远就是当年登月后召开新闻发布会的地方。

附录二　美国著名国家公园

一、大烟山国家公园（Great Smoky Mountains National Park）

大烟山国家公园，也称大雾山，位于田纳西洲与北卡罗林那州交界处，每年有大约 1 000 万游客，是美国游人最多的国家公园。从大雾山国家公园可以沿着山岭上长达 300 多英里的蓝岭公路（Blue Ridge Parkway）一直开到弗吉尼亚州的山那都国家公园。大烟山国家公园是业务最繁忙的公园，它每年大约吸引超过 900 万的游客前来，是美国其他任意一个国家公园游客人数的两倍。

二、大峡谷国家公园（Grand Canyon National Park）

大峡谷国家公园位于美国西部亚利桑那州西北部的科罗拉多高原上，全长 443 千米，是世界奇景之一。峡谷由于受到科罗拉多河的强烈下切作用而形成，所以又称科罗拉多大峡谷。1869 年，美军炮兵少校鲍威尔率领一支远征队，乘船航行，从科罗拉多河上游一直到大峡谷谷底。他将自己所目睹的峡谷风光、经历的惊险，写成游记，广为宣传，引起了全国的注意。1911 年建立了科罗拉多国家保护区。1919 年美国国会通过法案，将大峡谷最深最壮观的一段长约 170 千米划为大峡谷国家公园。该公园现已被联合国教科文组织列入世界自然遗产之一。

三、约塞米蒂国家公园（Yosemite National Park）

约塞米蒂国家公园为中国大陆的译名，台湾地区译作"优胜美地国家公园"，其他译名还有优山美地国家公园、约瑟米提国家公园等。约塞米蒂国家公园是美国西部最美丽、参观人数最多的国家公园之一，与大峡谷国家公园、黄石国家公园齐名，位于加利福尼亚州东部内华达山脉（Sierra Nevada，西班牙语：下雪的山）上。隐藏于公园深处的春之瀑有317英尺之高，此外约塞米蒂国家公园还拥有引以为傲的深谷、古杉和种类繁多的动物。身为"业务繁忙"第三名的优胜美地国家公园也是联合国教科文组织世界遗产之一。

四、黄石国家公园（Yellowstone National Park）

黄石国家公园是世界第一座国家公园，成立于1872年。黄石国家公园位于美国中西部怀俄明州的西北角，并向西北方向延伸到爱达荷州和蒙大拿州，面积达8 956平方千米。这片地区原本是印第安人的圣地，但因美国探险家路易斯与克拉克的发掘，而成为世界上最早的国家公园。它在1978年被列为世界自然遗产。园内森林茂密，是世界上最成功的野生动物保护区。园内设有历史古迹博物馆，还有数以千计的温泉，这些温泉碧波荡漾、水雾缭绕，上百个间歇泉喷射着沸腾的水柱。黄石公园大棱镜泉，被誉为"地球上最美丽的表面"。

五、落基山国家公园（Rocky Mountain National Park）

纵贯北美大陆的落基山脉在丹佛附近达到海拔最高点，巍峨壮观的落基山国家公园也就坐落于这个位置。公园于1915年成立，至今已有百余年历史。落基山国家公园以众多的高峰和高山公路闻名，其中朗茨峰（Longs Peak）海拔4 345米，是公园里的最高峰。落基山国家公园的特色在于园内有78座海拔超过3 658米的山峰，其中有20座山峰海拔超过了3 962米。与这种起伏的地形相映衬，在春天和夏天，野花从冻土中钻出来，大地充满了生机。在这里，人们能接触到高山地貌、矗立的山峰、高山冰斗湖和冰川冰碛。

六、奥林匹克国家公园（Olympic National Park）

奥林匹克国家公园坐落于华盛顿州的西北角，位于美国本土西北角华盛顿州（Washington State）的奥林匹克半岛（Olympic Peninsula）上。此国家公园的著名在于整个区域内结合了海岸、群山及雨林三种截然不同的生态环境形塑了奥林匹克国家公园，一个国家公园之内结合了极端的地面景观，堪称为美国西北最值得一游的国家公园。奥林波斯山（2 428米高）雄踞其中，公园因此而得名。公园内景色多变，生态系统多种多样，岩石垒垒的海边生长着许多海洋生物，美洲鹿徜徉其间的山谷中长着巨大的针叶树森林，崎岖的山巅覆盖着约60处活动冰川。联合国教科文组织将其列为国际生物圈保护区及世界遗产的名录。

七、大提顿国家公园（Grand Teton National Park）

大提顿国家公园位于美国怀俄明州西北部壮观的冰川山区，1929 年建立，占地 1 256 平方千米。公园内最高的山峰是大提顿峰，海拔 4 198 米，有存留至今的冰川。分布在该地的冰湖以珍尼湖为最著名。斯内克河上用水坝拦堵形成的杰克森湖为当地最大的水域。高耸入云的山巅，覆盖着千年的冰河，山连山、峰连峰，宛如进入人间仙境。公园内有成群的美洲野牛、麋鹿和羚羊，还有其他许多种哺乳动物。

八、锡安山国家公园（Zion National Park）

锡安山位于美国犹他州西南部，以色彩艳丽的峡谷著称于世。1919 年建成，面积为 6.07 万公顷。公园中风景集中地锡安山峡谷，约有 24 千米长，宽不到 1 千米甚至不到 1 米。谷内有些地方，两人并肩站立可触及两侧谷壁。峡谷深达 2 000—3 000 米，谷壁陡直，几乎可与地面成垂直状态，险象环生，难以攀援，让人望而生畏。锡安山峡谷最著名的是称为"大白皇座"的孤峰，此峰高达 427 米，从峡谷谷底平地而起，巍然耸立，其岩石色彩颇有层次，底部为红色，向上逐渐变为淡红、白色。孤峰顶上，绿树葱茏，十分俏立，仿佛一根华美的玉柱，立于五彩缤纷的峡谷之中。锡安山过去曾是摩门教拓荒者们的圣地，锡安山的意思即"上帝的天城"。

九、阿卡迪亚国家公园（Acadia National Park）

阿卡迪亚国家公园在美国缅因州大西洋沿岸，弗伦奇曼（Frenchman）湾两侧，面积 168 平方千米（65 平方英里）。1916 年初建，1919 年成为拉斐特（Lafayette）国家公园，1929 年改为现名。主要部分为芒特迪瑟特岛（Mount Desert Island）森林地带，以凯迪拉克山（Cadillac Mountain）为主体，有阿内蒙洞（Anemone Cave）和西厄尔德芒茨泉（Sieur de Monts Spring）；其他地区还包括峭壁耸立的半个欧岛（Isle au Haut）和斯库迪克（Schoodic）半岛。该园处在北方和温带交接处，寒冷的浅水海湾中栖息着大量海生动物。嶙峋的礁石、苍郁的森林、蜿蜒曲折的海岸线、高耸的山峰、深邃的峡湾、明镜般的湖泊、壮丽的潮汐，再加上一望无际的蓝得没有一丝杂色的大海，这一幅幅如诗如画的美景便勾勒出了阿卡迪亚国家公园的概貌。

十、死亡谷国家公园（Death Valley National Park）

死亡谷国家公园主要位于美国加利福尼亚州东南部，一小角延伸入内华达州境内。地理学上，公园位于北美的盆地与山脉区，这段地区地壳活动频繁，东面的地壳向东伸展、西面的地壳向西伸展，这里的地壳便呈条状下沉，分解成大致为南北走向的山脉和盆地。公园里有盐碱地、沙丘、火山口、峡谷、雪山等，有丰富的地质地貌，游客不难找到地壳里各式各样的断层，峡谷往荒漠注入时形成大大小小的冲积扇平原等。因地震而形成的死亡谷乃大自然的奇怪之作。放眼望去，尽是沙坪、锯齿状的峡谷，湖泊干涸留下的闪闪发光的晶体，一片荒芜的景象。这里酷热高温（夏天高达49℃），干旱少雨。死亡谷的沙丘也非常特别：周围的岩石受到侵蚀后，纷纷落下精细的石英颗粒。它们一堆堆地四处漂泊，最后形成了沙丘。但这里生长了1 000多种植物，其中50种是本地特有的。

十一、红杉树国家公园（Redwood National Park）

红杉树国家公园，位于美国西部加利福尼亚州西北的太平洋沿岸，1980年联合国教科文组织将红杉树国家公园作为自然遗产，列入《世界遗产名录》。近海处是大面积的海岸红杉，向内陆延伸后则以山脉红杉为主。公园南北绵延近600千米。成熟的红杉树树干高大，可达70—120米，树龄800—3 000年。红杉树生命力特强，生长神速，成活率高，甚至把它的树根切成碎片也能长出新树来，所以被认为是世界上最有价值的树种。红杉树国家公园是世界上罕见的植物景观。此外公园内还有多种珍稀的动植物。绵亘400多英里的狭长地带，拥有明媚的海滨、幽静的河谷，特别是那片片挺拔壮观的红杉树林，一座座红杉公园，使这个地区名播全球。

十二、化石林国家公园（Petrified Forest National Park）

化石林国家公园位于美国亚利桑那州北部阿达马那镇附近。这里是世界上最大、最绚丽的化石林集中地。数以千计的树干化石倒卧在地面上，直径平均在1米左右，长度在15—25米，最长达40米。在完整的树干化石周围，还有许多破碎零散的化石木块。这些石化的树木年轮清晰、纹理明显，宛如碧玉玛瑙夹杂着片片碎琼乱玉，在阳光之下熠熠发光，使人眼花缭乱，叹为观止。在石化林国家公园南部的末端有一间玛瑙屋（Agate House），这是一间由硅化木所构成的美国土著建筑，曾经在20世纪30年代被重建。化石林国家公园于1906年12月8日经由当时任总统的罗斯福（Theodore Roosevelt）宣布成立为美国国家保护区（National Monument），这在当时是美国第二个国家保护区。美国国会在1962年12月9日通过投票，决定将其升格为国家公园。

十三、布赖斯峡谷国家公园（Bryce Canyon National Park）

布莱斯峡谷国家公园位于美国犹他州西南部，其名字虽有峡谷一词，但其并非真正的峡谷，而是沿着庞沙冈特高原东面，由侵蚀而成的巨大自然露天剧场。其独特的地理结构称为岩柱（hoodoos），由风、河流里的水与冰侵蚀和湖床的沉积岩组成。位于其内的红色、橙色与白色的岩石形成了奇特的自然景观，因此其被誉为天然石俑的殿堂。其最高点为彩虹点，高 9 105 英尺（2 775 米），为该风景走廊的尽处。在该点，宝瓶星座高原（Aquarius Plateau）、布莱斯露天剧场、亨利山脉、赤岩断崖、白岩断崖皆可看到。

十四、峡谷地国家公园（Canyonlands National Park）

峡谷地国家公园位于犹他州东南格林河和科罗拉多河汇合处，系多年河流冲刷和风霜雨雪侵蚀而成的砂岩塔、峡谷等，成为世界上最著名的侵蚀区域之一，以峰峦险恶、怪石嶙峋著称。1964 年正式建为公园，占地面积 1 366 平方千米。该公园被分为三部分，最北面，入口靠近 Moab 小镇的叫作空中岛屿区，最南面叫作针尖景区，最西面叫作迷宫景区。峡谷地国家公园幅员辽阔，是一片规模巨大、大开大合的荒野风光。园内有依其形状、颜色及各种特征取名的台地、峡谷等景观，如黄金梯、大象峡、魔鬼蓬、天仙岛、娃娃石、挂毯石、马蹄谷，还有壮观台、石阵等。动物有鹿、狐和郊狼等。这里没有公路，只有越野车才能通行的小道，被认为最难以进入的地区之一。

十五、梅萨维德国家公园（Mesa Verde National Park）

梅萨维德国家公园是美国一个专为保护人造建筑而设立的国家公园，位于美国科罗拉多州西南部蒙特苏马山谷和曼科斯山谷之间，这里有 4 000 多处遗迹，主要景点包括绝壁宫殿、云杉树屋、悬崖宫殿等。梅萨维德，西班牙语意为绿色台地，为 18 世纪西班牙探险家起的名字。梅萨维德国家公园拥有保存完好的悬崖住所、陡峭的峡谷、崎岖狭窄的山路和美丽的沙漠。这样的一个地方，有历史在支撑、有灵魂在徜徉，自然有它的精神，让人为之动容。园内古迹是美洲大陆高度发展的印第安人文明的象征，对于了解哥伦布发现美洲大陆前的北美印第安人生活极有价值，同时也是一处历史文化旅游景观。联合国教科文组织已把它列为世界 12 大名胜古迹之一。

十六、甘尼逊黑峡谷国家公园（Black Canyon of The Gunnison National Park）

甘尼逊黑峡谷国家公园位于科罗拉多州西部，由美国国家公园管理局（National Park Service）负责管理。甘尼逊黑峡谷国家公园以其峡谷景观而闻名。根据黑峡谷的岩石构成可以推得其形成时间应该在 17 亿年前，前寒武纪片麻岩和片岩是其主要构成物质。最深的峡谷有 800 多公尺深，宽度约 2 千米。甘尼逊黑峡谷国家公园的峡谷景色气势磅礴，其壮观之处便是由于其峡谷的窄，很多狭谷壁近似于垂直，从而显得在谷底流经的甘尼生河（Gunnison River）格外湍急。峡谷岩石的色泽深暗且微泛蓝光，直上直下，棱角分外分明。

十七、大沼泽地公园（Everglades National Park）

大沼泽地国家公园建于 1974 年，现在已经覆盖 140 万英亩。它位于佛罗里达州南部尖角位置，6 英寸深、50 英里宽的淡水河缓缓流过广袤的平原，因而造就了这种独特的大沼泽地环境。辽阔的沼泽地、壮观的松树林和星罗棋布的红树林为无数野生动物提供了安居之地。这里是美国本土上最大的亚热带野生动物保护地。每年的 12 月到来年的 4 月是旅游的旺季，5—11 月是旅游的淡季。无论是步行、乘坐独木舟、坐船还是乘坐缆车，都可以很好地观察野生动物，其中包括美洲鳄和许多温顺而讨人喜欢的鸟类。

十八、猛犸洞穴国家公园（Mammoth Cave National Park）

猛犸洞穴国家公园（又译为马默斯洞穴国家公园），是美国肯塔基州西南部的一个国家公园，占地 207.83 平方千米，1926 年批准通过，1941 年建立，1981 年 10 月 27 日被联合国教科文组织认定为世界遗产，1990 年 9 月 26 日又被列入世界生物圈保护区名单。这里的洞穴网是世界上最大的石灰岩地下洞穴网。猛犸洞是现在世界上已知的溶洞系统中最大的一个，截至 2006 年已探明洞穴总长度达 350 英里（近600 千米），这个数字每年都会增加，究竟有多长，至今仍在探索。洞里宽的地方像广场，窄的地方像长廊，高的地方有 30 米高，整个洞平面上迂回曲折，垂向上可分出三层，洞中有 77 个地下大厅，最高的一座称为"酋长殿"，可容纳数千人，另有三条暗河、七道瀑布，还有多处地湖，有著名的柯林斯水晶洞，总延伸长度近 250 千米。

十九、卡尔斯巴德洞穴国家公园（Highway Carlsbad National Park）

卡尔斯巴德洞穴国家公园，面积为 189 平方千米。它是一处神奇的洞穴世界，迄今探查到的最深的洞穴位于地表以下 305 米，溶洞中最大的一处比 14 个足球场面积的总和还大，整个洞窟群长达近百千米，是世界上最长的山洞群之一。它的拱形洞口直通地下，漆黑一片，深不可测，其规模和气势令人悚然。它的形状和颜色令人惊叹，体积又如此庞大，以至于美国滑稽演员 Will Rogers 称这个地下奇景为 "带屋顶的大峡谷"。

二十、拱门国家公园（Arches National Park）

拱门国家公园位于犹他州东方，占地 76 519 英亩（309.7 平方千米），保存了包括世界知名的精致拱门在内的超过 2 000 座天然岩石拱门。园内最高处象峰海拔 1 753 米。最初于 1929 年 4 月 12 日成为国家历史遗迹，1971 年 11 月 12 日成为国家公园。自 1970 年，已有 42 座拱门因侵蚀作用而倒塌。拱门国家公园每年约有 85 万访客。有些人来此地是为了研究地质学，或者是对大自然的演变感到兴趣；当然更多的人是为了想一睹闻名遐迩的拱门，然后向别人描述经验。

二十一、大盆地国家公园（Great Basin National Park）

大盆地国家公园坐落于内华达州的中东部，成立于 1986 年，为内华达州唯一的国家公园，名字源于园内的大盆地沙漠，也是为了保护这一沙漠景观而建立的国家公园。因为地处偏僻，而且附近没有其他容易抵达的风景名胜，因此大盆地国家公园是游客造访最少的国家公园之一。虽然大盆地国家公园内气候干燥，但是生态依然具有多样性，有 11 种针叶树、超过 800 多种植物、61 种哺乳动物、18 种爬行动物、238 种鸟类、8 种鱼类以及 2 种两栖动物。为了方便游客更好的游览，园中建造了 12 条旅游小径，长度从 0.48—21.1 千米，游客可根据自己的爱好选择。园内的另一大看点就是神奇的洞穴，其中最知名的莫过于利曼岩洞（Lehman Caves），这个溶洞巧夺天工，洞内的石笋、石钟乳等惟妙惟肖，蟋蟀、蜘蛛、拟蝎、螨虫、弹尾虫等在此安居乐业，终其一生。

二十二、大仙人掌国家公园（Saguaro National Park）

大仙人掌国家公园位于亚利桑那州（Arizona）。公园因为长满了巨人柱这种巨柱仙人掌，被称为"大仙人掌国家公园"。公园被分为两个部分，分别位于亚利桑那州图森城（City of Tucson）中心以东近 32 千米，以及图森城以西 24 千米处。在2002 年时，其总面积为 370 平方千米，其中有 289 平方千米的地区属荒地。在公园的两个部分都有游客中心，而且从任意一个游客中心都可以驾车前往图森城，不过公园内没有公共交通设施。仙人掌国家公园是一个以欣赏仙人掌和沙漠风光为特色的国家公园。这个国家公园就是为了保护仙人掌所设。园中有多达 1 000 种来自世界各地不一的仙人掌。这里的树形仙人掌形体巨大，平均高度为 4—6 公尺高，满山遍野地矗立着，整片的仙人掌看起来就像是一群人站在山上。公园最初建立于 1933 年3 月 1 日，当时是仙人掌国家名胜保护区（Saguaro National Monument），在 1994 年10 月 14 日升级为国家公园。

二十三、大沙丘国家公园（Great Sand Dunes National Park and Preserve）

大沙丘国家公园位于科罗拉多州萨沃奇县和阿拉莫萨县的最西边，于 2004 年 9月 13 日被美国国会列入国家公园，总计面积约为 85 000 英亩（340 平方千米）。这里有一条通向美达诺山隘的原始道路，游客可乘坐全地形车沿这条路游览，但是探游沙丘最好的方式还是步行。大沙丘国家公园拥有超过 7 770 公顷的沙丘，还有高山湖泊、高山苔原、沙漠山谷、桑格累得克里斯托山脉、古老的云杉和松树林、草原及沼泽地。这里据说还是 UFO 经常出没的地方。关于在公园及其附近地带看见 UFO的报道已有 60 多起，在 20 世纪 70 年代还屡次上了美国报刊的头版头条。

二十四、比斯坎湾国家公园（Biscayne National Park）

比斯坎湾国家公园位于佛罗里达州（Florida）东南部的比斯坎湾。该国家公园内的珊瑚礁是北美洲最北部的珊瑚礁，同时也是美国大陆唯一的珊瑚礁。翡翠般的海岛上生存着天然的珊瑚礁——这些都使得比斯坎湾国家公园散发出无尽的魅力。该国家公园的典型景观还包括沿海岸线生长的漫长的红树林带和 1 万年的人类历史景观。1968 年 10 月 18 日命名为国家纪念地（National Monument），1980 年 6 月 28 日成为国家公园。对于游人而言，这个奇妙的国家公园是他们划船、航海、捕鱼、潜水和露营的绝佳场所。

二十五、夏威夷火山国家公园（Hawaii Volcanoes National Park）

美国夏威夷火山国家公园坐落在美国夏威夷岛东南沿岸的火山区上。该地区年降水量大约有 2 500 毫米，生长有热带蕨类树林。1961 年被辟为国家公园，1980 年成为联合国教科文组织生物圈保护区，1987 年被列入世界遗产名录。该公园中最著名的活火山是冒纳罗亚和基拉韦厄，它们溢出的奔腾汹涌的橘红色火山熔岩，是夏威夷火山国家公园最独特的景色。这里的火山不是猛烈爆发，气体是缓缓释放的，但经常能看见大地上渗出的缓慢移动的红色熔岩，有时候甚至会出现在公园的道路上；有的熔岩通过地下通道在几千米之外流出。过去 20 年间，基拉维亚火山的喷发将价值约 1 亿美元财产毁于一旦。

二十六、中央公园（Central Park）

中央公园是世界上最大的人造自然景观之一，也是全世界大都市中最美的城市公园。它南起纽约第 59 街，北抵第 110 街（南北距约 2.5 英里），东西两侧被著名的第五大道和中央公园西大道所围合（约 0.5 英里），公园占地约 843 英亩，长跨 51 个街区，宽跨 3 个街区。宏大面积使她与自由女神、帝国大厦等同为纽约乃至美国的象征。中央公园实行免费游览。公园每年游览人数达到 2 500 多万，在夏季每天达到近 30 万人次，冬季每天大约 3 万人次。中央公园四季皆美，春天嫣红嫩绿、夏天阳光璀璨、秋天枫红似火、冬天银白萧索。

二十七、布希公园（Busch Gardens）

布希公园位于弗洛里达州坦帕湾（Tampa Bay）。园区的自然环境野性十足，让人仿佛置身非洲大陆。跟随园区向导，你就可以徒步走进河马、土狼、秃鹰、鳄鱼、狒狒等野生动物的栖息地；而穿过瀑布和笼罩在原始森林上的迷雾，你甚至可以看到藏身于茂密丛林深处的灵长类动物，如大猩猩、黑猩猩等。园区内分为不同的主题，游客们不仅可以和野生动物亲密接触，而且还能欣赏到非洲传统的民族风情。

二十八、好时公园（Hershey's Park）

好时公园是美国巧克力巨头好时集团于 1903 年在宾夕法尼亚州建成的好时镇。这里号称是世界上最甜美的地方：公园的地图被制成好时 kisses 的样子，所有的路灯是"含苞未放"的巧克力形状。从门口穿过热带可可林后，映入眼帘的就是巧克力加工厂。在这里，你既能了解巧克力生产的全部秘密，又能随身带走一块刻有你自己信息的巧克力纪念品；玩累了，你还可以泡在可可中，洗一个舒服的可可浴。

二十九、费城国家独立历史公园（Independence National Historical Park）

1948 年经美国国会决定，将费城的独立大厅以及周围的所有历史性建筑物辟为国家独立历史公园。公园内保存有当年进行独立革命活动的场所、文物，独立后第一任总统和美国联邦议会厅，最早的哲学馆、图书馆、教堂等。坐落在独立广场北侧的独立大厅，是一栋用红砖建造的乔治王朝式二层楼房，建于 1732—1756 年，曾为宾夕法尼亚州的议会厅；1774 年、1775 年第一次、第二次美洲大陆会议在此召开；1776 年 7 月 4 日，杰斐逊执笔的《独立宣言》也在此通过。当华盛顿签署《独立宣言》时，挂在独立厅钟楼上的大钟响彻全城。此外，在公园里还有华盛顿总统 1793—1798 年的寓所，富兰克林任职美洲大陆会议和制宪会议主席及宾夕法尼亚州州长时期的住宅，埋葬富兰克林及华盛顿等名人的基督教教堂、国会议事厅、旧市政府和在独立战争中牺牲的无名英雄墓等胜迹。

三十、水果和香料公园（Fruit and Spice Park）

坐落于弗罗里达州迈阿密的水果和香料公园占地 35 英亩。在这个热带植物园里有来自全世界各地的水果和香料。游客可以乘坐电瓶车游览植物园，了解水果的历史和起源。这里有 70 种香蕉，125 种不同的芒果：橙色、绿色、紫色还有黄色的。公园有两条有意思的规则：你可以吃落在地上的任何东西；水果必须存进你的胃。所以来这里游玩，就不必担心自己的用餐问题，这里有丰富的水果等你品尝。

三十一、波托马克公园（Potomac Park）

波托马克公园是一个狭长的半岛，河水环绕，长约 4 英里的俄亥俄路绕岛而筑。岛的尽头是著名的"觉醒者"雕塑。一个金属雕成的巨大人形，仿佛在土里挣扎起身，只露出手脚和头脸，俗称"大手大脚"。雕塑的凸出部分被游人摸得溜光，被认为是最富戏剧性的公园景观。波托马克公园是休闲运动的乐园，公园内有高尔夫球场、单车径、行人专用道、泳池、网球场等。在春夏周末的午后，车辆禁行，让这里成为慢跑、散步与骑单车人士的天堂。

后　记

　　本书作者对语言与文化、词汇与文化、翻译与文化有比较广泛和深入的研究，先后在国内多种学术期刊、多家大学学报上发表相关论文 100 多篇（包括合著）。出版语言与文化研究专著（合著）10 部；主编英语词汇书十几部。

　　本书所研究的课题曾以学术论文的形式先后发表于《中国科技翻译》、《外语与翻译》、《语言与翻译》、《外语学刊》、《四川外国语学院学报》、《天津外国语学院学报》、《北京第二外国语学院学报》、《英语研究》、《外语论坛》、《外语与外语教学》、《山东外语教学》、《山东师大外国语学院学报》、《外语艺术教育研究》、《外语教育》、《大学英语教学》、《英语世界》、《江苏外语教学研究》、《大学外语教学研究》、《研究生英语教学与研究》、《湖南大学学报》、《大连理工大学学报》、《华中科技大学学报》、《辽宁大学学报》、《兰州学刊》、《广西社会科学》、《中山大学学报论丛》、《吉林师范大学学报》、《西南农业大学学报》、《长春理工大学学报》、《长春工业大学学报》、《华北电力大学学报》等学术刊物。以下论文发表于外语语言类期刊上。

　　[1] 戴卫平 . 语言学同一术语多种译法：成因与对策 [J]. 语言与翻译，2011（2）.

　　[2] 戴卫平，高丽佳 . 当代汉语准 X 词族探微 [J]. 语言与翻译，2007（4）.

　　[3] 戴卫平，高丽佳 . 现代汉语英文字母词刍议 [J]. 语言与翻译，2005（3）.

　　[4] 高娜娜，戴卫平 . 点绛唇与武陵春及物性对比分析 [J]. 外语与翻译，2011（3）.

　　[5] 戴卫平，于红 . "头 /head" 的隐喻研究 [J]. 外语与翻译，2009（2）.

　　[6] 戴卫平 . 上下与 Up Down 空间隐喻对比研究 [J]. 外语与翻译，2004（4）.

　　[7] 戴卫平 . 英语词语与岛国文化 [J]. 外语与翻译，2000（1）.

　　[8] 戴卫平，高维佳 . 美国英语与美国文化 [J]. 四川外语学院学报，2001（2）.

　　[9] 戴卫平，高维佳 . 英语词语与不列颠文化 [J]. 四川外语学院学报，2001（5）.

[10] 戴卫平 . 英国人姓名与英国文化 [J]. 四川外语学院学报，2000（2）.

[11] 戴卫平 .Zion • Hebrew • Jew • Israel——成因解读 [J]. 英语研究，2012（3）.

[12] 戴卫平 . 英语"eye"隐喻研究 [J]. 英语研究，2009（4）.

[13] 戴卫平 . 汉英词汇与歧视女性 [J]. 英语研究，2009（2）.

[14] 戴卫平 . 英汉视觉词的思维义 [J]. 英语研究，2008（4）.

[15] 戴卫平 . 英语爵词——成因解读 [J]. 英语研究，2011（4）.

[16] 戴卫平，张燕 . 生成语法术语翻译：思考与对策 [J]. 英语研究，2010（3）.

[17] 戴卫平 ."Dead"喻义研究 [J]. 英语研究，2014（2）.

[18] 戴卫平，田平 . 岛国生境与英语鱼 / 船文化解读 [J]. 中国科技翻译，2010（3）.

[19] 戴卫平 . 当代英语流行结构 Zero X 探析 [J]. 中国科技翻译，2007（1）.

[20] 戴卫平 . 美国总统与美国总统词 [J]. 中国科技翻译，2006（1）.

[21] 戴卫平，赵秀凤 . 美语选举词汇知多少 [J]. 中国科技翻译，2004（1）.

[22] 戴卫平 ."构式中心论"之优及对教学的启示 [J]. 英语教师，2011（6）.

[23] 于红，戴卫平 . 认知语法基于使用模式及对外语教学的启示 [J]. 英语教师，
2011（6）.

[24] 于红，戴卫平 ."味觉"词的"思维"义研究 [J]. 外语艺术教育研究》，2012（2）.

[25] 戴卫平，杨东 .Zero X 词族与 Zero 翻译 [J].《外语艺术教育研究，2011（1）.

[26] 戴卫平 . 关于"Chinese"一词的思考 [J]. 外语艺术教育研究，2012（4）.

[27] 戴馨洋，戴卫平 ."XX 帝"构式的转喻认知机制分析 [J]. 外语艺术教育研究，
2013（3）.

[28] 戴卫平 . 福克纳与沈从文的地域文化观刍议 [J]. 外语艺术教育研究，2014（2）.

[29] 焦莹，戴卫平 . 刍议英汉诗歌中"死亡"隐喻 [J]. 外语艺术教育研究，2014（4）.

[30] 袁晓红，戴卫平 . 乔姆斯基"语法"解读 [J]. 外语学刊，2009（4）.

[31] 戴卫平，徐方赋 . 词汇与民族 [J]. 外语学刊，2001（5）.

[32] 戴卫平 . 美国词汇与美国历史 [J]. 外语学刊，2000（5）.

[33] 于红，戴卫平 .Big ＋ N 与 Small ＋ N 不对称性原因分析 [J]. 外语教育，2010.

[34] 高娜娜，戴卫平 . 点绛唇与武陵春及物性对比分析 [J]. 外语教育，2012.

[35] 戴卫平 . 机构名称"委员会"的英译刍议 [J]. 外语教育，2008.

[36] 戴卫平，张丽丽 . 构式观与语言习得 [J]. 江苏外语教学研究，2011（1）.

[37] 戴卫平，连洁 . 刍议语块与二语教学 [J]. 江苏外语教学研究，2013（1）.

[38] 张学忠，戴卫平 . 现代美国文化与现代美语词汇嬗变 [J]. 外语与外语教学，
2001（9）.

[39] 戴卫平，张学忠 . 美语与美式选举政治 [J]. 北京第二外国语学院学报，2002（5）.

[40] 戴卫平．词汇与文化 [J]．山东外语教学，1999（2）．

[41] 戴卫平．美国文化与美国词汇 [J]．山东师大外院学报，2000（1）．

[42] 戴卫平，张燕．认知语言学语义中心观对英语教学启示 [J]．大学英语教学，2010（5）．

[43] 戴卫平，于红．澳洲英语—澳洲民族—澳洲文化 [J]．外语论坛，2008（2）．

[44] 戴卫平．美国语与美利坚民族 [J]．外语论坛，2007（1）．

[45] 戴卫平．美国的反恐与美国英语 [J]．外语论坛，2006（2）．

[46] 戴卫平．汉英死亡代用语文化解读 [J]．外语论坛，2005（1）．

[47] 戴卫平．现代汉语英文字母词刍议 [J]．外语论坛，2004（2）．

[48] 戴卫平．新词新语与民族文化心理 [J]．外语论坛，2003（4）．

[49] 戴卫平，赵秀凤．英语词与英语史 [J]．外语论坛，2003（1）．

[50] 戴卫平．论美国英语词汇拓展的基础 [J]．外语论坛，2002（1）．

[51] 张丽丽，戴卫平．美国 X Generation/Generation X[J]．英语世界，2012（8）．

[52] 戴卫平，张志勇．美语词汇的文化意蕴 [J]．天津外国语学院学报，2002（4）．